D0993035

SPORTS

A Social Perspective

Timothy J. Curry
Robert M. Jiobu
The Ohio State University

PRENTICE-HALL, INC., Englewood Cliffs, New Jersey 07632

Library of Congress Cataloging in Publication Data
Curry, Timothy J.
   Sports: a social perspective.
   Includes bibliographical references and index.
   1. Sports—Social aspects—United States.   2. Sports—
Social aspects.   I. Jiobu, Robert M.   II. Title.
GV706.5.C87   1984   796′.0973   83-13750
ISBN 0-13-837823-1

Editorial/production supervision and interior design: Elizabeth H.
   Athorn
Manufacturing buyer: Harry Baisley
Cover design by Diane Saxe
Cover illustration of lacrosse game by Henry K. Brown, c. 1850,
   courtesy of the Library of Congress
Cover photograph of women's basketball game by Doug Martin

Printed in the United States of America
10   9   8   7   6   5   4   3   2   1

ISBN 0-13-837823-1

Prentice-Hall International, Inc., *London*
Prentice-Hall of Australia Pty. Limited, *Sydney*
Editora Prentice-Hall do Brasil, Ltda., *Rio De Janeiro*
Prentice-Hall Canada, Inc., *Toronto*
Prentice-Hall of India Private Limited, *New Delhi*
Prentice-Hall of Japan, Inc., *Tokyo*
Prentice-Hall of Southeast Asia Pte. Ltd., *Singapore*
Whitehall Books Limited, *Wellington, New Zealand*

Dedicated to

Pamela, Christine, Denise, and Brian
Karen and Eric

CONTENTS

PREFACE

We had two goals in mind for this book: (a) explaining sport from the sociologist's point of view; and (b) capturing the passions—the grins, tears, whoops, and groans—that lie behind the sociology. To achieve the first goal, we follow the contours of the research and allow it to dictate the length, scope, and subtopics of each chapter. This, we feel, is preferable to cutting and stretching materials to fit preconceived ideas of chapter length. At the same time, we strive for balance between such differing schools of sociology as conflict versus functionalism, quantitative versus qualitative analysis, and grand versus middle range theory.

The first eight chapters of the book cover the fundamentals of sport and sociology. As yet no orthodoxy exists in the sociology of sport, so these chapters provide a blend of basic sociology and application of basic sociology to sport. Chapters 9 through 13 discuss specific social issues in sport: The basic material presented in the earlier chapters is applied to issues such as violence, politics, deviance, and sexism in sport. Some new material will be introduced and some old material will be expanded to accommodate the specific issue under discussion. Of course, treating some of these topics as issues rather than as fundamentals is arbitrary, reflecting our society's fluctuating concern over certain topics and minority groups. Nonetheless, it seems to us that the issues section presents topics that have not been resolved and are viewed as problems to many people.

When professional sociologists write for an audience of other professionals, they often use jargon, abstraction, and complicated statistics and tables. Consequently, the nonprofessional reader sometimes finds sociology tough going. In order to make the going less tough, we use a prose style combining serious journalism and academic "sociologese." We include biographies, quotes, and vignettes. We often work inductively—presenting the vignette or biography first, and then moving up the ladder of abstraction to the general sociological point. Hopefully, the reader will want to turn the page to see what comes next.

Following academic custom, our names appear in alphabetical order to indicate the collaborative nature of the work. Practicality did, however, dictate a division of labor. The first author selected the photographs, charts, and tables, gathered much of the raw material for the text, and did editing; special trips to the Library of Congress were required of him. The second author, on the other hand, took no trips; he stayed home, hunched over a word processor, and wrote the text. At this time, the second author begs an indulgence from the reader. All his life he has been asked, "How do you pronounce your name?" He would like now to say publicly, "Pronounce it 'Joe-Boo.' "

Both authors take pleasure in acknowledging the assistance of several people:

Angelo Alonzo, Bob Kaplan, Katherine Meyer, Barbara Nelson, and several anonymous reviewers, for their critiques of various portions of the manuscript; Pamela Park-Curry, who proofread the manuscript and helped with the literature review for the chapter on the sportswoman; Bob Thoresen, Doris Michaels, and Ray O'Connell of Prentice-Hall for their encouragement and support; Cindy Brown and David Eeles, who typed the bulk of the manuscript; and especially Ed McGillavry, who helped with the library research and editorial work and took care of hundreds of administrative details. Finally, we must also mention the members of the Ohio State wrestling team, who allowed themselves to be observed and studied as part of this project.

Robert M. Jiobu
Timothy J. Curry
The Ohio State University

1

PROLOGUE
AND BASIC CONCEPTS

One reason sport is all around us is the massive amount of coverage sport receives from television, much of it made possible by mobile television studios brought to sports arenas. A record 207.5 hours of live coverage were programmed for the 1984 Summer Olympics. Photos © 1980 American Broadcasting Companies, Inc.

"Who's going to win?" A man calls out to pedestrians passing a hotel in downtown Manhattan, "Who's going to win?" The man is an imposing figure—six feet eight inches tall and 260 pounds—wearing a beard and dressed in a dark suit and tie. It is drizzling, and people do not stop to discuss the question. This takes place during the strident campaign for mayor between a famous incumbent (Lindsay) and a serious challenger (Proccacino).

All in all, the man asks 150 pedestrians: 27 call back something irrelevant or mention a third name; the same number say the incumbent will win; 6 say the challenger will win; and 103 say the Mets will win!

The Mets? . . . A baseball team? Now wait a minute, you ask, what does a baseball team have to do with a mayoral election of national importance?

The noted sports sociologist Harry Edwards took this poll. He was deliberately informal and deliberately used a vaguely worded question so people could fill in the blank—"Who's going to win *what*?"—with whatever was uppermost on their minds at the moment. Edwards's little poll does not prove anything, but it does illustrate something sociologically important: "The average person on the street in New York City," he says, "was much more keenly attuned to the possible impending fate of the Mets baseball team . . . than to the possible [political] fate to New York City itself."[1]

But, you say, this doesn't make sense. Something must be wrong. Surely politics is (or should be!) more important than sport!

Perhaps—but nevertheless Edwards's results make perfect sense if you consider them as reflecting a broader feature of American society, namely, that sport saturates American culture and that we can't escape it. And so when asked "Who's going to win?" Americans tend to think first of sports.

Sport in Society

Traces of sport can be found everywhere, especially in our mass media and popular culture. Here are some examples.

The motion picture was at one time the most popular dramatic medium. Of all the film genres—detective story, musical, romance, etc.—the sports film exceeds even the western in longevity. Several have become pop classics dealing with themes that vary from maudlin biography (*The Babe Ruth Story*), to falling from grace (*Bang the Drum Slowly*), to religious fulfillment (*Chariots of Fire*), to the striving for and the meaning of success (*Rocky I, II, and III*). Sport is a durable and flexible theme, and sports films are continually produced.

Nowadays television rivals cinema in popularity. Over 95 percent of all United States households have sets.[2] For the truly addicted sports spectator, some cable stations

---

[1] Harry Edwards, *Sociology of Sport* (Homewood, Illinois: The Dorsey Press, 1973), p. 4; and personal letter.

[2] U.S. Bureau of the Census, *Statistical Abstract of the United States: 1971* (Washington, D.C.: U.S. Government Printing Office, 1971), p. 487.

carry nothing but sports twenty-four hours a day. Even without cable, the spectator doesn't lack for viewing opportunities. Most daytime TV on weekends consists of sports programs; football and baseball take up many Monday nights; and sports specials— pennant games, World Series, NCAA and NBA basketball championships, and championship boxing matches, to cite a few—often fill the tube on other nights. Viewing audiences can be immense. One-fourth of all the people on earth watch some part of the World Cup soccer matches on TV.[3] Only such events as the first walk on the moon can compare.

It's not just on screens that sports images appear. Look closely at the next magazine or newspaper you pick up and note how many advertisements incorporate sports images. Using sports to sell products is nothing new. In 1905 a Coca-Cola ad featured "a young man with golf clubs and a girl with a tennis racket."[4] Current examples abound—Bausch and Lomb sunglasses with skiers, *Time* and *Newsweek* with boxers, Canon cameras with tennis players, Paramount vodka with hang gliders, and so on—page after page of sports images used to tout the good life and the products that go with it.

Of course you must buy products to have the good life. Participation sport has developed into an industry. Not only do conventional sporting goods stores exist; so do specialized stores that sell nothing but running gear, for example, or tennis equipment, or ski equipment. Sport dress has become fashionable, quite apart from function. We suspect that more running shoes and warm-up suits are bought for walking than for running. Men and women wear puffy down ski clothing for warmth and for fashion rather than for skiing; they are now de rigueur. As much as 70 percent of the over four billion dollars spent on sports clothing may be for nonsports use.

Now even the nonathlete seeks the athletic body. At one time in history corpulence denoted status; when most people starved only the affluent could afford to be fat. But no more. Now thin is in. Advertisements for commercial gyms show pencil-thin models in Danskin tights radiating health: "Let us help you stay slim!" says one; "I lost forty-one pounds and fifty-two inches," says another; "When you look good you feel good," says yet another. Over two million Americans have bought the message and signed up.

There's more to sport than body images. A participation boom is underway. People no longer sit back and watch others engage in sport; they now want to participate themselves. About 40 percent of the adult population in this country engages in some kind of organized sport, about 50 percent in regular exercise. For example, twenty million joggers fill the streets, parks, and trails everywhere.[5] Try getting a tennis court during the weekend! Some courts require reservations two weeks in advance.

Not too long ago, the medical profession held exercise in low esteem. Athlete's heart was something to avoid, not seek; rest was the preferred treatment. But now all that has changed. Modern medicine holds that exercise is healthy and you can't escape the

---

[3]*Columbus Citizen-Journal*, June 2, 1978, p. 22.

[4]Robert H. Boyle, *Sport—Mirror of American Life* (Boston: Little, Brown & Company, 1963), p. 24.

[5]Data from Tony Velocci, "The Games People Play—and Pay to Watch," *Nations Business*, March 1979, pp. 28–35; U.S. Department of Health, Education, and Welfare, "Exercise Participation in Sports among Persons 20 Years of Age and Over: United States, 1975," *Advancedata*, March 15, 1978; George Vecsey, "Sports of the Times," *New York Times*, March 16, 1983, sec. Y, p. 25.

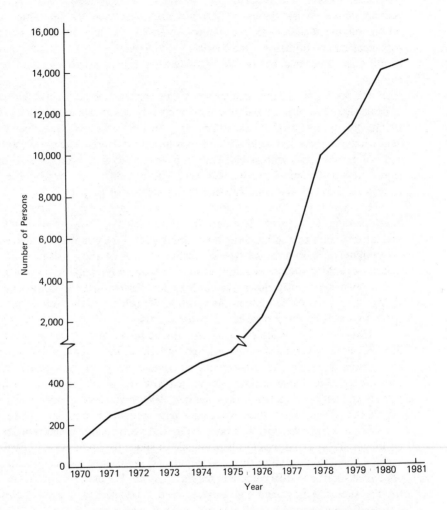

Figure 1.1. Number of Persons Starting the New York City Marathon, 1970–1981

Another way to document the growing interest in sports is to note the increasing participation in marathon racing. In 1970 the New York City Road Runners Club held its first New York City Marathon, with 126 starters. Eleven years later, 14,496 persons started the race!
SOURCE: New York City Road Runners Club, 1981.

message. Riding a jet transport at 35,000 feet, we picked up the airline magazine only to be told again that "You Have to Be in Shape to Climb the Corporate Ladder." It's hard to get to the top and stay there with a coronary condition. As a result, some 50 percent of American corporations now sponsor recreation-exercise-sport programs for their employees, and more and more of the upper echelons are participating. Not only is it good health, it's good economics. American businesses lose about twenty-seven billion dollars each year because of unfit and ill employees.[6]

Sport also leads to social and mental fitness. Many articles and books have been published describing the mental benefits of sport. "Running highs," "going through trances," "the inner game," "Zen and the art of ____" (you fill in the blank) are becoming part of everyday vocabulary. Sport is touted as a way to cope with the tensions and turmoils of modern society, and some psychiatrists now use it as part of their therapy programs.

Sport has also become a part of our literary heritage. The classic *Tom Brown's School Days* praised sport as builder of sound body and forthright character. Frank Merriwell, the hero of several nineteenth-century sports books, set the pattern of the success story of the young intrepid athlete. Homer, Shakespeare, Twain, Hemingway, Faulkner, Fitzgerald, Updike, Malamud—all have used sports motifs in their work. From the lowest lowbrow literary work to the highest highbrow, the sports hero and the sports image have been used to symbolize such aspects of human existence as success and failure through striving, and the fulfillment and emptiness of winning. In *Voices of a Summer Day*, Irwin Shaw uses a sports metaphor to carry us back to our youth and denote the continuity of life:

> The generations circle the bases, the dust rose for forty years as runners slid from third, dead boys hit doubles, famous men made errors at shortstop, and forgotten friends tapped the clay from the spikes with their bats as they stepped into the batter's box. Coaches' voices warned, across the decades, "Tag up, tag up!" on fly balls. The distant mortal innings of boyhood and youth. . . .[7]

These examples should be sufficient to demonstrate the basic point. *Sport is all around us*. That much is clear. Unfortunately the sociological implications of that fact are not at all clear; nor will it be easy to ferret out the implications. Sociologists have just recently begun to pay formal attention to sport. We examined twenty textbooks on introductory sociology and found that although several briefly mentioned sport when discussing leisure and recreation, only one had a separate chapter on sport as a social institution. To judge from these books, which try to be compendiums of the field, sport hardly deserves mention.

---

[6]Grant Pick, "You Have to Be in Shape to Climb the Corporate Ladder," *TWA Ambassador*, June 1980, pp. 60–64.

[7]Irwin Shaw, *Voices of a Summer Day* (New York: Delacorte Press, 1965), p. 12. See also: Christian Messenger, "Sport in the Dime Novel," *Journal of American Culture*, 1 (Fall 1978), 495–506; Robert J. Higgs and Neil D. Isaacs, eds., *The Sporting Spirit: Athletes in Literature and Life* (New York: Harcourt Brace Jovanovich, Inc., 1977).

The reasons for the neglect of sport cannot be precisely documented, but they undoubtedly have something to do with the academic nature of sociology and the nature of academia.

Athletes in Academe: Cool Reception

Most sociologists see themselves as academics, and academics glorify the intellect. While this is perfectly natural because their jobs involve intellectual tasks, glorifying the intellect can all too easily lead to dismissing the physical. This attitude goes back to ancient Greek times. Contemporary philosopher Paul Weiss writes, "As befits the well-placed in a slave society, Aristotle and other Greek thinkers dealt mainly with what concerned the well-born," that is, what was genteel and intellectual.[8] (That disdain is somewhat paradoxical since much of the Western sports tradition originated in ancient Greece.)

Criticizing athletes from a different angle, Thorstein Veblen, a cynical and iconoclastic but perceptive social thinker, wrote in 1899: "Addiction to athletic sports, not only in the way of direct participation, but also in the way of sentiment and moral support, is . . . a trait which the leisure class shares with the lower-class delinquents, and with such atavistic elements throughout the body of the community as are endowed with a dominant predacious trend."[9] Veblen agreed with the ancient Greeks.

More recently, the well-known sociologist Herbert Gans has summarized the criticism leveled against popular culture (which includes sports). He claims that devotees of high culture dislike popular culture because it is supposedly mass produced for profit and quick, cheap gratification; because it debases high culture; and because the content of popular culture reduces the quality of civilization and opens the way to totalitarianism. Gans then goes on to argue that none of these criticisms have much validity. All culture has importance, but different groups have learned to like different kinds.[10] (Less charitably, another sociologist labels the views expressed by some critics as plain snobbery.)[11]

Sport has detractors, there's no question about that. However, we should not conclude that hostile academics limit the sociology of sport or prevent its development. The sociology of sport is now growing. Even if coverage in introductory textbooks is still limited, there are increasing numbers of research articles, specialized texts, and college courses dealing with the sociology of sport. Sport is simply too big and too important an institution to ignore. The noted educator Jacques Barzun makes the point this way: "Whoever wants to know the heart and mind of America had better learn baseball, the rules and realities of the game—and do it by watching first some high school or small town teams."[12]

---

[8]Paul Weiss, *Sport: A Philosophic Inquiry* (Carbondale and Edwardsville, Illinois: Southern Illinois University Press, 1969), p. 6.

[9]Thorstein Veblen, *The Theory of the Leisure Class: An Economic Study of Institutions* (1899; reprint, New York: Mentor Books, 1953), p. 180.

[10]Herbert J. Gans, *Popular Culture and High Culture: An Analysis and Evaluation of Taste* (New York: Basic Books, Inc., 1974).

[11]Thomas M. Kando, *Leisure and Popular Culture in Transition* (St. Louis: The C. V. Mosby Company, 1975), p. 57.

[12]Jacques Barzun, *God's Country and Mine* (Boston: Little, Brown & Company, 1954).

BASIC CONCEPTS: CLEARING THE UNDERBRUSH

Philosophers give three rules for clear communication: first, define your terms; second, define your terms; and third, define your terms. Good rules—simple, clear, and often, unfortunately, overlooked. How many times have you been in a heated debate only to find that what you mean by a term isn't what the other person means, and that once you've straightened that out, there is nothing to dispute? Poor semantics prevented you from realizing you were in agreement. Such disputes, however silly and avoidable they seem, take place all the time.

These disputes take place in intellectual discourse too, and preventing them is the reason scholars carefully, even tediously if need be, define terms. This is especially true in the social sciences where everyday words denote formal concepts. Concepts are groups of specific ideas. *Race* is an everyday word and a formal concept; so is *sport*; so is *sociology*. As formal concepts these everyday words are the hubs around which theories spin and their exact meaning becomes critical to analyzing the theories.

Under these circumstances—with everyday words used as formal concepts—you can see why poor semantics can easily lead to confusion. We should therefore take whatever time is necessary to settle semantic matters before confusion arises.

What Is Sport?

When sociologists ask people what activities the word *sport* brings to mind, over 75 percent say football, basketball, and baseball; over 50 percent also mention swimming, tennis, track, ice hockey, and volleyball.[13]

This list of sports seems fairly straightforward. You're probably not surprised by them. The point is this: When you ask people, they don't have to pause and wonder what *is* sport? They know, and they agree. And the reason is that all of us unconsciously learn which activities our culture defines as sport, just as we learn which activities our culture defines as art or as work. For most everyday purposes—informal talk and convivial interactions—we can take it for granted that people know these definitions and agree on them.

Unfortunately just getting a list of activities commonly called sport does not satisfy the requirements of a formal analysis. Many a discussion has been devoted to the semantics of sport, work, play, games, contests, recreation, and athletics. One author even argues that sport can't be defined to begin with because it lacks inherent essence of meaning or behavior.[14]

Formal Definition.   Since this book is not a treatise on semantics, for our purposes stipulating a working definition will do; one which demarcates the general area of

---

[13]Wilbert Marcellus Leonard, II, *A Sociological Perspective on Sport* (Minneapolis, Minnesota: Burgess Publishing Co., 1980), p. 8.

[14]Howard S. Slusher, *Men, Sport and Existence: A Critical Analysis* (Philadelphia; Lea and Febiger, 1967), p. 141.

our inquiry without intending to be a definition suitable for all other inquiries. Here is our definition:

> *Sport* is a physical activity that is fair, competitive, nondeviant, and that is guided by rules, organization, and/or tradition.

We encounter cases that meet this definition all the time. On a typical May Sunday the sports page of the *New York Times* ran, among others, the following headlines:

> EXPOS STOP METS, 5 to 3
>
> LAKERS BEAT 76ers, 111–101
>
> OLD AND YOUNG BLEND TO HELP FLYERS WIN
>
> MCENROE, GERULAITTIS REACH TENNIS FINALS
>
> POTTER OF WHITE PLAINS 1,600 METER VICTOR

Sports fans will read thousands of headlines like these over their lifetimes. They call attention to activities which are clear-cut examples of what we mean by sport: professional baseball, basketball, hockey, tennis, and amateur track.

To consider one specific case, examine baseball. It is obviously a physical competition (which is not to say that intellect isn't required); it is fair (or tries to be); it is nondeviant (in fact, it's often idealized); it is regulated by rules, it is organized (into leagues with a high commissioner); and it has a long tradition. Unambiguously, baseball is a sport, and so are all the other activities mentioned in those headlines.

Fairness.   Clear-cut cases present no particular problem for the definition of sport. The difficulty occurs with marginal cases. An incident we are personally familiar with exemplifies this.

> **"It's not fair!"**   On a hot summer day at the bullring in Mexico City, an American tourist couple were overheard, loudly telling their Mexican guide that they didn't think much of bullfighting. As the man watched the fight in progress, he kept saying, "It's not fair. Give him a fair chance, a fair chance." By "him" the man meant the bull.
>
> The guide always answered something like, "Well, do you want to see the matador get killed?"
>
> As it turned out, the couple and their guide left early and that bit of conversation was all that was heard.

We, as objective sociologists, conclude that the tourist erred. He took "fair" from sport and used it to judge bullfighting—a clear misapplication. What he should have said was that he didn't like bullfighting because he found it morally repugnant or aesthetically repulsive. Those descriptions would be accurate. Furthermore his statement was out-and-out incorrect if you take "fair" to mean "following the rules"—one legitimate meaning of the term. In that sense the bullfight was fair—the rules were being followed.

The guide was on the correct line of reasoning. As he implied, the purpose of a bullfight is not to see if the bull can kill the matador—it's just the reverse—to see how gracefully the matador can control and kill the bull according to prescribed rituals and rules. In that sense the matador always "wins," and *fairness* has nothing to do with it. Bullfighting is simply not a sports competition. Although bullfights are usually reported in the sports section of U.S. newspapers, Spanish newspapers have a separate section for bullfight reports (more akin to reviews), which are done by special critics rather than sports reporters.

As this vignette shows, then, for an activity to be a sport, it must be fair. All contestants must be given a reasonable chance to win.

We observe this, usually without thinking about it, in all sports. For example, the requirement for fairness has led to separating college football into divisions, and to having weight classes in boxing, judo, weight lifting, and wrestling. Match a 190-pound wrestler against one weighing 110 pounds and the lighter wrestler has virtually no chance, regardless of skill and motivation. He is simply outweighed from the very start. In the words of the man at the bullfight, "Give him a fair chance!"

A small college team will sometimes play and occasionally upset a major football school. But in the long run small college teams serve mainly as a warm-up or breathing spell for major teams, which often start easy and work their way into the season. If the teams are grossly mismatched, the game actually becomes more like a bullfight than a sport in that the issue of who will win is a foregone conclusion. The real objectives of these mismatches are to try new tactics, to get a look at new players, to avoid key injuries, and to see by what margin and with what style victory will be achieved.

Of course, mismatches occur, sometimes unavoidably and other times with the underdog's cooperation. However if mismatches became the rule rather than the exception, the activity would eventually lose its status as sport. It would have to be defined as something else—perhaps as an exhibition, as when a major league baseball team plays one of its farm clubs. But whatever the designation, it would not be sport.

Tradition and Culture. Our definition of sport includes tradition, which is part of culture as a whole. Over eighty years ago the famous sociologist-anthropologist Emile Durkheim showed that the laws and implicit rules of contract make sense only to people sharing a common cultural understanding of whatever is being agreed upon.[15] Formal rules rest upon unstated but very real cultural agreements and understandings. The point also applies to sport. To illustrate:

Differing Interpretations. Imagine you live in another universe and had never heard of football. One day the rule book of the National Football League mysteriously falls into your hands. You study it and then gather a group of friends on an empty lot and start playing. After a few years of trial and error, you end up with a sport you are comfortable with.

If a group of fans from the United States then came to watch you play, would they recognize your game? Probably not, although they would undoubtedly come away with some sense of déjà vu about what they saw. They would feel they had even seen something vaguely like it somewhere, sometime before.

[15]Emile Durkheim, *The Division of Labor in Society*, trans. George Simpson (New York: Macmillan, Inc., 1933), chap. 7.

This scenario is not as fanciful as you might think. In actuality American college athletes found themselves in a similar situation during the nineteenth century. They were playing British rugby, or trying to. They had the rule book of the British Rugby Union to consult, but little cultural understanding of what the sport was all about. One study quotes Walter Camp, a founder of American football: "The American players found in this code [English Rugby Rules] many uncertain and knotty points which caused much trouble in their games, especially as they had no *traditions*, or *older* more *experienced* players, to whom they could turn for the necessary explanations."[16]

Take what was known as the "heel-out." When the ball heeled out (popped out) from the scrum to someone behind the scrum, he could run with the ball, provided the heel-out was unintentional. The rules clearly stated that. However the British Rugby Union just assumed that everyone knew what constituted an unintentional heel-out. The Union further assumed, apparently, that a knowledgeable audience would be present and would help officiate, and that players would accept these audience-referees. As a result of these unstated assumptions, the rules made sense only in the environment of the British school. Since these assumptions didn't hold true at American colleges, the original rules proved unworkable in the United States and rugby soon evolved into American football.[17] The problem of recognizing the unintentional heel-out, for example, was solved by always having an intentional heel-out, which became the center snap we now see.

These anecdotes illustrate Durkheim's argument that rules presuppose cultural agreement and further presuppose an understanding of the culture in which rules will be applied. Sociologists Peter Berger and Thomas Luckmann described these cultural agreements and understandings as the "taken-for-granteds of everyday life."[18] They could never be set down in a rule book because too many exist and, more fundamentally, because we are largely unaware of them.

Tradition and culture also certify or stamp an activity as being a "true" sport. You may recall the "Celebrity Challenge of the Sexes," once a popular television program. As the name implies, male celebrities competed against female celebrities in events such as footracing and swimming. The events were organized, guided by rules, and fair; and therefore by some definitions, the "Celebrity Challenge of the Sexes" was a sport.[19]

Yet somehow . . . it never *seemed* like a sport.

True, if you analyzed it point by point, the "Celebrity Challenge of the Sexes" might meet the definition. Physical? Yes. Competitive? Yes. Rules? Yes. And so on. But, overall, when you paused and reconsidered it, it did not have the ring of a sport.

Why?

We suggest lack of tradition, lack of cultural certification. The "Celebrity Chal-

---

[16]David Riesman with Reul Denney, "Football in America: A Study in Cultural Diffusion," in David Riesman, *Individualism Reconsidered and Other Essays* (Glencoe, Illinois: The Free Press, 1954), p. 246. Italics added.

[17]Ibid.; William J. Baker, *Sports in the Western World* (Totowa, New Jersey: Rowan and Littlefield, 1982), chap. 9.

[18]Excerpt from *The Social Construction of Reality* by Peter L. Berger and Thomas Luckmann. Copyright © 1966 by Peter L. Berger and Thomas Luckmann. Reprinted by permission of Doubleday & Company, Inc.

[19]For example, see D. Stanley Eitzen and George H. Sage, *Sociology of American Sport* (Dubuque, Iowa: William C. Brown Co., Publishers, 1978), pp. 17–18.

lenge of the Sexes'' and other similar contests have never been culturally stamped as true sport, and hence our reluctance to accept them as such. The sports media certainly do not accept them. The media deride them as ''trash sports,'' and describe them as vulgar, cheap, contrived. This category also applies to roller derby, commercial wrestling, demolition derby, and other sportlike activities designed more to entertain spectators than to allow contestants to compete against each other. Unlike some marginal sports, these probably will never become true sports.

We do not need to become involved in that argument. Most of the time our focus can remain fixed on those activities which tradition unambiguously certifies as true sport. Possibly the biggest exception to the focus will occur when we trace the historical development of sport in the next chapter.

Nondeviance.   Our definition further stipulates nondeviant physical activity. By that we mean activity conforming to the commonly accepted norms and values of society. At the same time, however, we must remember that what is deviant in one culture, subculture, or historical epoch, might be sport in another. Consider these examples: At one time gladiators killed each other, fairly, for the viewing pleasure of Roman audiences, and, less fairly, fought with wild animals; at other times knights on war horses charged each other in tournaments with long, blunt lances and left piles of mangled opponents in their wake (at certain times in history more knights were killed in the sport of jousting than in medium-sized battles); and at still other times boxing was considered so indecent as to be declared illegal. Today many people still feel that way about boxing, yet it is recognized as a sport. Clearly deviance is relative to specific times, places, and peoples.

Given this relativity, no competitive physical activity could possibly be nondeviant in all of the thousands of cultures and subcultures existing in the world, let alone across the epochs of history. But then our definition does not require that. Our definition only requires an activity to be nondeviant by the general standards of modern American culture. Consider the following contrast.

Many people condemn boxing on moral grounds, yet it still falls within the acceptable bounds of our overall culture. Boxing is a sport. In contrast, topless female boxing, which has been and still might be practiced, could meet every other requirement of a sport but still be deviant by American cultural standards. Accordingly our definition rejects it as a sport.

In general, deviant activity does not fit our cultural ideas about what sport is or should be. Sport has moral overtones about it. It's supposed to represent the ideals and high goals of our society, something deviance does not do. We therefore find it advisable to keep deviance separate from sport. (To be sure, we recognize that deviance exists within the institution of sport; but that is different from saying the activity itself is deviant. Chapter 12 goes into this in some detail.)

Physical Exertion.   This is a tricky phrase to define: Upon close examination, the idea of physical exertion turns out to consist of several elements. Physical exertion could be strength, such as lifting a certain amount of weight; it could be stamina, such as lifting that weight a certain number of times in succession, or swimming or running a certain distance in a given time. Physical exertion could be effort relative to one's present capacity; or it could be something else. Just what physical exertion is, is not at all clear.

And further, even if you knew precisely what it is, how do you measure it? Through specific activities? Oxygen consumed? Calories burned? Lactic acid accumulated? A scale of subjective feelings? Other ways? Though research goes on, measurement problems have not been solved.

Complicating things even more, you can easily observe that some activities which require very little physical exertion are called sport and reported on the sports news. Is dart throwing a sport? Shooting pool? Horseshoes? How about tiddlywinks? Shuffleboard? Bowling on the green?

Along with several other students of sport, we readily admit to not knowing the answers to all these issues; but we can justifiably sidestep them. Some activities called "sport" actually fall into a gray area somewhere between sport and purely intellectual contests such as chess or bridge (which many sports publications also report). The precise relation between such activities and sport needs to be decided only as the situation demands.

Competition and Organization.   Our definition mentions competition and organization as two key elements of sport. However, competition involves so much complexity that a separate chapter is required to dissect it.[20] At this point we only note that competition can be against another person, another team, a physical barrier such as a mountain, or an abstraction such as a world record.[21]

For the same reasons of complexity, we also postpone dissecting the concept of organization as it applies to sport. It is enough now to say that organizations govern and supervise, and that they can be either formal or informal.

What Sport Is Not.   Thus far we've asked what *is* sport and then answered by listing key requirements (fair, competitive, nondeviant, physical, rules, tradition, organization). Anything that meets those requirements is a sport. An equally valid approach asks what sport is *not*. The two approaches complement each other. Oftentimes understanding a complicated concept is helped along by considering both sides of the definition: what it is, and what it is not.

The issue of what sport is not was greatly influenced by Johan Huizinga's classic monograph on play. He described play as free, voluntary, outside of real life; not serious but nevertheless intensely absorbing. He further said play is "connected with no material interest, and no profit can be gained from it," and that play "proceeds within its own proper boundaries of time and space according to fixed rules and in an orderly manner." By its very nature, he argued, play is escapist and nonutilitarian. "Into an imperfect world and into the confusion of life [play] brings a temporary, a limited perfection."[22]

---

[20]See Allen Guttmann, *From Ritual to Record: The Nature of Modern Sports* (New York: Columbia University Press, 1978); Jay J. Coakley, *Sport in Society: Issues and Controversies* (St. Louis: The C. V. Mosby Company, 1978).

[21]Eitzen and Sage. *Sociology of American Sport*, p. 18.

[22]Johan Huizinga, *Homo Ludens: A Study of the Play Element in Culture* (Boston: Beacon Press, 1950), p. 13, p. 10.

Both Roger Caillois and Allen Guttmann, two sports scholars, consider play to be purely autotelic and games to be rule-bound play. Caillois divides games into four kinds: games of competition (such as soccer), games of chance (such as dice), games of mimicry (such as playing doctor), and games of vertigo (such as skydiving).[23] Guttmann goes on from games to define contests as competitive games, and sport as physical contests.[24]

When watching athletes engage in sport, you might observe their different states or attitudes toward their sport. Sometimes athletes engage in the activity for the pure joy of the movements regardless of outcome or rules ("autotelic" play). At other times the activity becomes what Huizinga calls "rule-bound" play—fun so long as everyone follows the rules, both written and unwritten. And then at other times the activity can be "work"—done primarily for material rewards. As the activity goes on, athletes' feelings about their actions can change from autotelic play to rule-bound play to work and back again. It is possible for some athletes to be "playing" at the same time others are "working."

A former college basketball player, now a sociologist, illustrates these states: "It was a lot of fun when I was a freshman [rule-bound play] . . . but after a while, after I got injured, things didn't go so well. Most of it I did just because I wanted to get through college [work]." This person still plays though: "After I've had a couple of beers and watched the game on TV, I love to go out and shoot around and dunk. Am I good then! [autotelic play]."[25]

The existence of these different states, and the ability of athletes to shift from one to another, lead us to conclude that play, whether autotelic or rule-bound, exists in sport and that sport can also be work. This means that a little looseness remains in the definition of sport, but this is tolerable. As long as we recognize the elements of play and work when they appear, they should not cause confusion. On the contrary, the looseness in the definition could be to our advantage. We have more freedom to pursue sport in more directions, and as we shall see in the next chapter, sport historically grew out of play and recreation to become what it is today.

What Is Sociology?

All of us, whether trained as social scientists or not, have a view of our social environment, a way of looking at it and structuring it. That is, we all have a frame. Without this frame our social environment would resemble a confused kaleidoscope of events flashing by, fading in and out, isolated and unrelated to each other.

But ordinarily that does not happen. Most of the time the world makes sense (not necessarily a lot of sense) and that is because we have our frame—our scheme for organizing seemingly senseless, unrelated events into a comprehensive, structured picture. Sociologists use a sociological frame, obviously. That frame gets more complicated later in the book, but the basic part is quite simple. According to a popular text, *"human behavior is largely shaped by the groups to which people belong and the social interaction*

---

[23]Roger Caillois, *Man, Play and Games* (New York: The Free Press, 1961).

[24]Guttmann, *From Ritual to Record.*

[25]Communication from a colleague.

that takes place within those groups. We are what we are and we behave the way we do because we happen to live in particular societies at particular points in space and time.''[26] The human is, by far, the most social creature on earth.

Historical Roots.   Expanding this idea, sociologist Peter Berger said,

> To ask sociological questions, then, supposes that one is interested in looking some distance beyond the commonly accepted or officially defined goals of human actions. It presupposes a certain awareness that human events have different levels of meaning, some of which are hidden from the consciousness of everyday life. It may even presuppose a measure of suspicion about the way in which human events are officially interpreted by authorities. . . . [It presupposes] an openness to the world, to other ways of thinking.[27]

This orientation, this suspicion, is an outgrowth of the way sociology began. As a formal discipline, sociology originated in the early nineteenth century when the old European order was disintegrating under pressures from industrial technology and quasi-democratic, experimental forms of government. During that century, the French social philosopher Auguste Comte published a series of treatises in which he proposed a new "science of society," and which he named "sociology." Subsequent developments have outmoded Comte's specific ideas; but his belief in sociology as a science, and his basic view of the field, have been pretty consistently followed over the more than 150 years between his time and ours.

Comte expected sociology eventually to become the most general of the sciences: the study of why societies are orderly and why they change. He described the subject matter as follows: "order consists . . . in a permanent harmony among the conditions of social existence; and progress consists in social development; and the conditions in the one case; and the law of movement in the other, constitute the statics and dynamics of social physics [i.e., sociology]."[28] (Comte modeled sociology on physics, and originally referred to sociology as "social physics.")

The first sociology text, published in 1921, offers the same essential view of sociology but in different words: "sociology, speaking strictly, is a point of view and a method for investigating the process by which individuals are inducted into and induced to cooperate [dynamics] in some sort of permanent corporate existence [order] we call society."[29]

The "standard" text of the 1950s through 1970s described sociology as being

---

[26]Ian Robertson, *Sociology*, 2nd ed. (New York: Worth Publishers, Inc., 1981), p. 4.

[27]Excerpt from *Invitation to Sociology* by Peter L. Berger, p. 29. Copyright © 1963 by Peter L. Berger. Reprinted by permission of Doubleday & Company, Inc.

[28]Auguste Comte, *The Positive Philosophy of Auguste Comte*, freely translated and condensed by Harriet Martineau (London: Trubner and Co., 1875) II, 62.

[29]Reprinted from *Introduction to the Science of Sociology*, 3rd ed., revised, p. 42, by Robert E. Park and Ernest W. Burgess by permission of University of Chicago Press. Copyright © 1921 by the University of Chicago.

"mainly concerned with interactions [dynamics] that attain stability, that is, those that are recurrent and patterned [order]."[30]

Today there is no single standard text, but most give some variation of these descriptions (though changing a word or two, and shifting the emphasis a little, to suit their particular approach). As a colleague of ours said, "Comte got it right the first time."

Structure and Process. In current sociological jargon, Comte's "statics" and "dynamics" have been superseded by "structure" and "process." These are abstract, general concepts which can be used to analyze the workings of an entire society or two people talking to each other.

You have undoubtedly seen a basketball coach get into an argument with a referee. The give-and-take of the argument illustrates social process: the interaction between social actors.

Coach will stomp and rage at Referee over some injustice, real or imaginary (it often makes no difference). When Coach screams, Referee listens and then explains, cooly and rationally. Then Coach screams again, Referee explains again, and so on—each interpreting and taking into account the other person's responses. This *taking into account* is the heart of the relationship, the feature that makes it interactive and social.

If you just watch the arm-waving and listen to the shouting, you might get the impression that disorder and chaos prevail. However if you watch carefully, you soon perceive that the dispute has structure and stable patterns of interaction.

Coach isn't screaming and hopping around at random, or if he were we would say he was losing his cool; and if Coach lost his cool permanently, we would probably say he had lost his mind.

If Coach disregards the social structure by continually interrupting Referee's explanations, for example, Coach might end up getting a technical foul; not necessarily for what Coach said but because of inappropriate behavior—ignoring the stable patterns (structure) everyone unconsciously assumes should govern social interactions. In other words, he was being rude and/or unpredictable.

Structure and process also describe entire societies. To illustrate, American society is organized into stable social classes. A relatively small number of people own most of the nation's wealth and can easily afford exclusive country clubs. (In the United States, the top fifth of the population owns about 75 percent of all the nation's wealth; the bottom fifth owns less than 1 percent.[31]) Others own almost nothing and have never been on a golf course except possibly as workers or caddies. And most people lie somewhere in between: if they play golf, they go to the public links. Sociologists often debate the processes that lead to the structure of American classes, and what the future might hold for them. Here we only emphasize that structure and process can apply to entire societies as well as to basketball coaches and referees.

---

[30]Leonard Broom and Philip Selznick, *Sociology: A Text with Adapted Readings*, 4th ed. (New York: Harper & Row, Publishers, Inc., 1968), p. 18.

[31]Metta Spencer, *Foundations of Modern Sociology* (Englewood Cliffs, New Jersey: Prentice-Hall, Inc., 1976), p. 246.

Sociology and Science.   Comte also believed that sociology would some day become a science much like physics or chemistry. He would be surprised at the controversy this idea now generates. The controversy concerns whether or not sociology can, or should, be "nomothetic" or "romantic."

Nomothetic means being based on scientific laws. Most sociologists hold to a nomothetic goal and try to be as scientific as possible. They therefore use scientific procedures and logic to obtain clues, concepts, insights, perspectives, facts. Yet all the while they recognize that sociological knowledge doesn't come close to the rigor and accuracy of the hard sciences; that sociology has yet to reach the nomothetic stage of development. If pressed, most sociologists will claim to be in a scientific discipline rather than in a Science with a capital "S". In the same way, a person could be in an artistic field but not in an Art.

But as you might have guessed, some sociologists take an entirely different tack. They argue that while sociology provides understanding, it is not the same kind as found in the hard sciences. Unlike physical things or lower animals, humans have volition; they make choices and endow their choices with meaning. So it will never be possible to explain human behavior in the same way a physicist might explain the acceleration of a falling ball. These sociologists conclude that their discipline should strive for understanding of human behavior rather than for scientific laws. This view is sometimes called "romantic," "humanistic," or "idiographic."

A resolution to this controversy does not exist at present, but we can briefly suggest an attempt at resolution, one which governs our exploration into sport. Our view is this: Right now sociology is not a purely nomothetic discipline and it might never be. Some romantic elements may always be a part of it; sociologists explain humans, not things. And in any event, the two views are not mutually antagonistic. Peter Berger states it this way: "The botanist looking at a daffodil has no reason to dispute the right of the poet to look at the same object in a very different manner. There are many ways of playing. The point is not that one denies other people's games but that one is clear about the rules of one's own."[32] One can be nomothetic or romantic, as the situation or personal preference dictates. The injunction we stress is not to confuse the two approaches unwittingly. While that sounds simple, there are many instances when the injunction is difficult to obey.

Formal Definition.   We started this section by asking What is sociology? Up to this point, we have managed to talk all around the question without giving a direct answer. We think we now have provided enough background and will end this section with a one-sentence definition:

Sociology is the scientific study of social structure and social process.

---

[32]Excerpt from *Invitation to Sociology* by Peter L. Berger, p. 52. Copyright © 1963 by Peter L. Berger. Reprinted by permission of Doubleday & Company, Inc. See also Fred N. Kerlinger, *Behavioral Research: A Conceptual Approach* (New York: Holt, Rinehart & Winston, 1979), chap. 15; and Robert M. Pirsig, *Zen and the Art of Motorcycle Maintenance* (New York: Bantam Books, Inc., 1974), part I.

Sociology and Sport

Having spent some time defining and discussing sport and sociology separately, it is now appropriate to consider what the one has to do with the other. At the beginning of this chapter we casually addressed this issue. Now we formally examine the relation between sport and sociology.

Sport Is Sociological.   Perhaps the most basic relation comes about because sport *is* sociological. All sports involve humans interacting with other humans in a structured way. Even marathon swimming, a lonely activity, takes place within a social setting. Swimming the English Channel is fairly common these days, but you can't just dive in the surf at Dover and climb out on the beach at Calais. The swim requires sponsors, coaches, trainers, boats, pilots, official permissions, and official observers. All of that bespeaks the sociological.

On a more abstract level, sociology is, to use the old but still serviceable phrase, the "science of society," and society is a series of social institutions—law, family, sport, and so on. These institutions do not exist in isolation from each other. For example: In school sport becomes part of the required curriculum via physical education classes, and of course, sports are major extracurricular activities. The institution of sport thus mixes with the institution of education, and so influences all of us whether we want to be influenced or not. Other illustrations might be given but at the moment our only point is this: For good or bad, like it or not, sport significantly affects our society. That warrants sociological attention.

Sport Mirrors Society.   Many social processes and structures which exist in broader society are reflected in sport. To use two common metaphors: sport is a mirror of society; sport is a microcosm of society.

Think about current events. Even if you only follow the news cursorily, you know that social problems permeate American society: drugs, violence, crime, cheating, sexism, racism, corruption, inflation, recession . . . the list goes on and on. And because sport reflects society, you can read about these problems either on the front page of your newspaper or in the sports section.

Sport is a natural laboratory for studying these problems and other basic structures and processes. Sports events take place at known times and places and follow known rules and customs. Formal organizations govern sport and maintain extensive records. The news media cover popular sports and thus provides researchers with narrative accounts of what happened. Few activities both reflect American society as accurately and provide such research advantages. Even researchers not interested in sport per se still find it a valuable laboratory in which to conduct studies.

Sociology of Sport as a Subarea.   Had we been writing this book several years ago, a longish defense of the sociology of sport would have been necessary at this point. But the defense of the sociology of sport took place largely during the late sixties and the seventies. Now it's basically over. Even by the middle seventies, a prominent sports sociologist concluded that "the sociology of sports is shedding its lumpen [disreputable] heritage and is gaining respectability. Sociologists in general can look forward to some interesting contributions from this fledgling subfield in the years to come."[33] Those "years to come" are now here. A wide variety of respected journals in sociology and related disciplines now routinely carry articles discussing sport. Some of the journals we used in writing this text are presented in Table 1.1.

Muckraking Versus Value-Free Science

As the work of researching sport goes on, knowledge accumulates. Indeed, a substantial amount already exists. While the amount is not huge, it is large enough to raise an age-old philosophical issue, namely, What is the purpose or reason for doing all the research? What is the goal?

The issue hinges on two responses that you might reasonably give: knowledge for knowledge's sake, or knowledge for some other end.

If forced to choose between responses, we'd guess most sociologists would choose, "some other end." Sociologists have been, and still are, notoriously suspicious of society. Says one: "the first wisdom of sociology is this—things are not what they seem."[34] Consequently sociologists often go peeking into society's closets and peering behind the curtain. Many spend a lot of time debunking and demythologizing what most people take for granted.

As applied to the sociology of sport, the phrases, "things are not what they seem" and "debunking and demythologizing" can be condensed into the single term, *muckraking*. Muckraking and sociological criticism go hand in hand, the former being an intensification of the latter. According to one author, "the sport sociologist who engaged in muckraking research would be primarily interested in searching out and publicly exposing misconduct on the part of prominent individuals as well as discovering scandal and incriminating evidence."[35]

Muckraking.   The role of muckraker has been adopted by most sports sociologists. A favorably received text on the sociology of sport says its goal "is to combine a scientific stance with the muckraking role. The latter is important because it forces us to examine such social problems . . . as the perversion of the original goals of sport."[36]

---

[33]Eldon E. Snyder and Elmer Spreitzer, "Sociology of Sport: An Overview," in *Sport Sociology: Contemporary Themes*, ed. Andrew Yiannakis and others (Dubuque, Iowa: Kendall/Hunt Publishing Company, 1976), p. 9.

[34]Excerpt from *Invitation to Sociology* by Peter L. Berger, p. 23. Copyright © 1963 by Peter L. Berger. Reprinted by permission of Doubleday & Company, Inc.

[35]Merrill J. Melnick, "A Critical Look at the Sociology of Sport," in *Sport in Contemporary Society: An Anthology*, ed. D. Stanley Eitzen (New York: St. Martin's Press, 1979), p. 30.

[36]Eitzen and Sage. *Sociology of American Sport*, pp. 13–14.

Table 1.1.   Some of the Journals Used in Researching this Text.

Academe
Administrative Science Quarterly
American Anthropologist
American Behavioral Scientist
American Economist
The American Journal of Economics and Sociology
American Sociological Review
Annals of the Academy of Political and Social Science
British Journal of Sociology
Canadian Journal of History of Sport and Physical Education
The Canadian Review of Sociology and Anthropology
Criminal Law Quarterly
Educational Record
Human Relations
The International Journal of Sport Psychology
International Review of Sport Sociology
Journal of Abnormal and Social Psychology
Journal of American Culture
Journal of the American Medical Association
Journal of Conflict Resolution
Journal of Drug Issues
Journal of Physical Education and Recreation
Journal of Sport and Social Issues
Journal of Sport Behavior
Journal of Sport History
Law and Contemporary Problems
New England Journal of Medicine
Pacific Sociological Review
Psychology Today
The Quarterly Journal of Economics
Quest
Research Quarterly
Research Quarterly for Exercise and Sport
Science
Signs
Social Psychology Quarterly
Social Science Information
Social Science Quarterly
Society
Sociological Focus
Sociological Methods and Research
Sociological Symposium
Sociology of Education
Sociometry
Sport Sociology Bulletin (now called *Review of Sport and Leisure*)

Another text says "we do not attempt to maintain a scientific detachment from the material in order to avoid value judgments. On the contrary, we feel free in our analysis to implicitly and explicitly express values, sentiments, opinions, and recommendations."[37]

Muckraking presupposes an intense concern for the subject matter under study. (If you're not concerned, why bother to stir up the muck?) And we suspect the popularity of muckraking might be traced to the typical sports sociologist's "love of sport." This sentiment obviously runs through the field. Listen to what several sports sociologists say.

A recent book: "The final beauty of writing this text resides in the fact that one of my lifelong *loves* and interests—sport . . ."[38]

A popular book concerning sport used in some college courses: "This book was written by a man who loves sport."[39] That is the very first sentence of the book.

An article in a professional journal: "It is clear that most researchers in the sociology of sport have a strong intrinsic interest and existential involvement in the subject matter of the subfield that is not characteristic of most other specialities within sociology."[40] (Translation: They love and participate in sport.)

Love of subject matter, laudable as it is, can be both a strength and a weakness when combined with scientific research. Many sports sociologists love sport; therefore they muckrake; and therefore they must eschew being quietly dispassionate, disinterested, neutral, or *value free*.

Value-Free Sociology.   Eschewing value-free inquiry follows quite naturally from a muckraking stance. Muckrakers contend that everyone has values, commitments, morals, and an ethical obligation to help achieve a better world. This includes sociologists. Even if researchers don't personally feel that way, they are not completely value free if only because values determine the discipline they go into and, within the discipline, the specific problem they study.

Unfortunately, by eschewing a value-free stance muckrakers open themselves to attack from the opposite side. Being value free, other sociologists contend, is the only way to ensure objectivity; the only way to guard against conscious and unconscious bias; the only way to convince people to believe the research findings. And finally they contend that without it you don't have science—value free is what science is, in the first place.

The way we have just stated the issue, it seems like an either-or debate. If the muckraking sociologists are right, the value-free sociologist must be wrong, and conversely so. That implication misleads a little. In practice, we think a compromise of sorts can be achieved. And based on our philosophical values, we advocate compromise and a balanced approach.

---

[37]Eldon E. Snyder and Elmer Spreitzer, *Social Aspects of Sport* (Englewood Cliffs, New Jersey: Prentice-Hall, Inc. © 1978), p. x.

[38]Leonard, *Sociological Perspective*, p. vi. Italics added.

[39]James A. Michener, *Sports in America* (New York: Random House, Inc., 1976), p. 9.

[40]Snyder and Spreitzer, "Sociology of Sport," p. 9.

Balanced Approach.   First, a qualification: We sympathize with some muckraking philosophy. Undeniably when you stir the muck, ugly things come floating to the surface: crimes, exploitations, injustices, suffering. Perceiving them, though unpleasant, has value. Muckraking might not lead to immediate political action, but it raises the level of public consciousness about social problems in sport. It helps counter the blind and sometimes mindless defense of sports found in the mass media. The media typically treat sports with all the awe and reverence reserved for sacred institutions—"sport can do no wrong without just cause." Muckraking demonstrates the absurdity of that logic. The sociology of sport should not be the sociology of apology.

But there is a flip side too. We believe that the moral commitments of muckraking, though sincere and noble, bias one's conclusions about objective situations. And it seems manifestly obvious that biased conclusions cannot, in the long run, enlighten policy or alleviate social suffering. If anything, that kind of "knowledge" will surely make matters worse. Thus, while sympathizing with the muckrakers' concern for sport, we still strongly believe that sociologists should *try* to be value free.

The key is *trying* to be value free in accumulating evidence and explanations. In so trying we know that we will not totally succeed; we may fail because humans are fallible. But we must try, for the very act of trying will help us consciously and forcefully expunge bias from our research. To recognize human fallibility, we argue, is not the same as giving in to it.

While we know that solutions to social problems will not come about without concern, sometimes in our concern we slough over the fact that problems require correct solutions. "It is not enough to do good; one must do it in the right way."[41] The issue gets down to this: Would you rather have a heartfelt wrong answer, or a coldblooded right answer? We opt for the right answer.[42]

SUMMARY

1. Having a thorough understanding of key concepts is critical in scholarly analysis. This is especially true when everyday words are used to denote formal concepts.
2. Sport is defined as a physical activity that is fair, competitive, nondeviant, an activity that is guided by rules, organization, and tradition.
   a. Fair competition means that all contestants have a reasonable opportunity to achieve victory. The primary purpose of rules is to make competition fair.
   b. Tradition is necessary to the definition of sport because sport presupposes cultural agreements and understandings of what is being regulated and tradition certifies activities as "true" sport.

---

[41] John Morely, quoted in Everett K. Wilson, *Sociology: Rules, Roles, and Relationships* (Homewood, Illinois: The Dorsey Press, 1971), p. 536.

[42] Compare with Gerald S. Kenyon, "A Sociology of Sport: On Becoming a Subdiscipline," in *New Perspectives on Man In Action*, ed. Roscoe C. Brown, Jr., and Bryant J. Crotty (Englewood Cliffs, New Jersey: Prentice-Hall, Inc., 1969), pp. 163–79. A statement not about but indirectly applicable to sociology can be found in Herman Kahn, *Thinking About the Unthinkable* (New York: Avon Books, 1962), chap. 1.

   c. According to our definition, only nondeviant activities can be sport.
   d. Precisely what constitutes physical exertion is unclear but it is suggested that physically undemanding activities are not sport; rather, they are some form of recreation, game, or play.
   e. Sport can include small elements of work and play.
3. The sociological frame or perspective emphasizes the social nature of human existence.
4. Sociology studies social structure and social process as applied to individuals as well as to entire societies.
   a. Process involves interacting in such a way that others are taken into account.
   b. Structure is stable interaction.
5. The majority of sociologists hold that sociology should be as scientific as possible, but a substantial minority maintain that sociology should strive for romantic rather than nomothetic understanding of social structures and processes.
6. The sociology of sport is the study of sport from the sociological perspective. It is argued that sport is sociological, that it mirrors society, and that it provides a natural laboratory in which many social phenomenon can be studied.
7. Sport can be studied sociologically either from the viewpoint of muckraking sociology, which stresses exposing social issues, or from the viewpoint of value-free sociology, which stresses detached, uninvolved analysis. The popularity of muckraking derives from the sport sociologists' love of sport. We argue for the value-free position but do recognize the importance of muckraking.

2

HISTORY AND SPORT
The Rise of An American Institution

This reproduction of a watercolor, circa 1897, by Wm. T. Smedley, illustrates the post–Civil War boom in sports. Golf became associated with the upper class when it became a country club sport. Golf was also one of the few sports then considered proper for females. But by 1930 there were 300 municipal golf courses in the country, and golf was on its way to becoming a popular upper middle class sport. Courtesy of the Library of Congress.

In all studies of social custom, the crux of the matter is that the behavior under consideration must pass through the needle's eye of social acceptance, and only history in its widest sense can give an account of these social acceptances and rejections.[1]

Ruth Benedict, Anthropologist

EXPLAINING THE RISE OF SPORTS

As Ruth Benedict says, history shows how social changes become permanent parts of culture, how changes become socially accepted. In an article on American history in *Time* magazine, Lance Morrow amplifies:

> The past constantly achieves renewals and transmogrifications as political symbol and polemical weapon. The present and past are always in an almost constant state of argument and consultation. . . . Many of the new social views of history amount to cultural anthropology [which is essentially identical to sociology,] and . . . new quantitative methods . . . demonstrate ways in which computers can define trends and correct the errors of historical preconception.[2]

"Except for the fact that the subject of inquiry is located in the past," claims a history professor, "the new political historian is indistinguishable from the political scientist, social scientist or political sociologist."[3]

That history and sociology can go hand in hand is now well accepted; but we should not overemphasize the point. Sociology is not history. In this chapter we will use history to find out how sport became integral to American culture. We will ask why there is sport, and then search through the work of historians to try to piece together a sociological answer. The history of sport is the history of how new behaviors and new norms associated with the institution of sport become fused with those of other major institutions.

Unfortunately, as you probably guessed, no single simple answer exists to the question of why there is sport. Sociologists of different intellectual schools will examine the same historical record and come up with entirely different explanations.

A Marxian Explanation

One large school of sociological thought consists of Karl Marx's intellectual heirs. (We use the term *Marxian* as a catchall for various branches of Marxist thought. We also

---

[1]From *Patterns of Culture* by Ruth Benedict, p. 232. Copyright 1934 by Ruth Benedict. Copyright renewed © 1962 by Ruth Valentine. Reprinted by permission of Houghton Mifflin Company.

[2]Lance Morrow, "Rediscovering America," *Time*, July 7, 1980, pp. 22–23. Copyright 1980 Time Inc. All rights reserved. Reprinted by permission from *Time*.

[3]Gertrude Himmelfarb, "The New History," *New York Times Book Review*, August 17, 1980, p. 3. © 1980 by The New York Times Company. Reprinted by permission. A technical discussion of these points is found in Barbara Laslett, "Beyond Methodology," *American Sociological Review*, 45 (April 1980), 214–28. Also Wilhelm Dilthey, *Pattern and Meaning in History* (New York: Harper Torchbook, 1962).

recognize that this is a vast oversimplification.) Marxian sociologists contend that the people who control the wealth of a society—the rich and whomever they favor—ultimately control the society. The "masses," meaning almost everyone else, are nothing more than pawns who have been duped or forced into blindly following the bidding of the ruling class. One popular Marxian-oriented writer calls sport the "child of monopoly capital." He claims, "In general, the rules of the game depend on what is profitable to the bosses. On a deeper level, the incidence of modern sport was something created by the material conditions of modern monopoly capitalist society." And later: "Participation in sports for the elite was gradually readapted into spectator-consumption for what was to become the 'masses': a sort of opium for the people"[4] —something to drug them, to keep them quiet and uninterested in such radical ideas as upsetting the class system.

Why, then, is there sport? Marxians respond: because sport is profitable; because the "masses" can be duped into liking it; because sport diverts the "masses" from thinking about their plight.

Not everyone agrees with this.

A Functional Explanation

Functionalism provides a much different explanation. Sport exists because it satisfies a biological or cultural need to play or disport. Talking about the negative Victorian attitudes towards recreation, one social historian writes, "For the recreational scene to broaden . . . as it eventually did, was proof of an underlying *need*. . . . It was the expression of an *unconscious determination* in the pursuit of pleasure.[5]

Why, then, is there sport? Functionalists respond: because humans have an urge or need for recreation. Sport helps satisfy that need and therefore sport comes into existence.

Both the Marxian and functionalist arguments make some sense. (That they also have shortcomings need not concern us right now.) Since competitive games have been found in all known societies, a universal cultural need for them presumptively exists. The functionalists have a point there. At the same time, the Marxians have a point; for who could deny the influence of wealth and social class, or that sport takes time and effort that might be devoted to other issues?

An Alternative Explanation

However sensible Marxian and functionalist perspectives might be at certain times, we still doubt that a single perspective can totally explain the rise of a major institution over a long historical period. Social reality has too many complications for that. We prefer being

---

[4]Excerpt from *Rip Off the Big Game* by Paul Hoch, p. 38. Copyright © 1972 by Paul Hoch. Reprinted by permission of Doubleday & Company, Inc.

[5]Foster Rhea Dulles, *A History of Recreation: America Learns to Play*, 2nd ed. (Englewood Cliffs, New Jersey: Prentice-Hall, Inc. © 1965), p. 86. Italics added. An excellent but difficult discussion of both Functionalism and Marxism is: Jonathan H. Turner, *The Structure of Sociological Theory*, rev. ed. (Homewood, Illinois: The Dorsey Press, 1978). As applied to sport, see Allen Guttman, *From Ritual to Record: The Nature of Modern Sports* (New York: Columbia University Press, 1978).

more eclectic and less dogmatic, and opt for what we call a "mostly structural" perspective. The basic premises are quite simple: Many structural and nonstructural forces influence the growth of an institution. These forces do not necessarily act in concert (sometimes they actually work against each other), nor do they always act at the same time. The social world is a complicated place.

Before we get into history proper, though, one more bit of underbrush needs to be cleared out. There are two basic ways to write history: by topic or by chronology. We use chronology most of the time. This has the advantage of flowing with history rather than artificially slicing it up. But it also scatters pieces of the mostly structural perspective over a long period. To alleviate any resulting confusion, we will gather the pieces together at the end of the chapter.

EARLY SPORT IN AMERICA

Native Americans

Reports of early explorers indicate that the North American Indians participated in several sports, complete with large crowds, wagering, and sometimes combined with religious festivals and feasts. Among the Algonquins, for instance, lacrosse was popular—a game in which each player held a stick with a leather pouch attached to one end. The object was to catch a wooden ball in the pouched racket and pass it through the opponent's goal posts. Teams could consist of several hundred players. An early traveler describes one game:

> More than two thousand persons assembled in a great plain, each with his racket; and a wooden ball was thrown into the air. Then all that could be seen was the flourishes and motions through the air of all those rackets. . . . Games of this sort are usually followed by broken heads, arms and legs; and often persons are killed.[6]

A sport roughly resembling football was also played. It is interesting that men competed against women. The men were not allowed to use their hands. An explorer's account:

> The contending parties arranged themselves in the center of the lawn—the men on one side and the women on the other. . . . The side which succeeded in driving the ball through the stakes, at the goal of their adversaries, were proclaimed victors, and received the purse, to be divided among them.
> The contest . . . was finally decided in favor of the women by the herculean strength of a mammoth woman, who got the ball and held it, in spite of the efforts of

---

[6]Emma Helen Blair, ed. and trans., *The Indian Tribes of the Upper Mississippi Valley and Region of the Great Lakes as Described by Nicolas Perrot* (Cleveland, Ohio: The Arthur H. Clark Company, 1911), I, 345.

the men to shake it from the grasp of her uplifted hand, till she approached the goal, near enough to throw it through the stakes.[7]

While a few Indian sports eventually found their way into European and thence into American life (for example, North American Indians invented lacrosse and French settlers adopted it), such cultural remainders are few. The settlement of the continent resulted in the almost total destruction of Native American culture, and thus European influences predominate in this country's sports history.

Puritan Opposition

The first Europeans to settle along the northeastern coast of the American wilderness were the Puritans. They emigrated largely for religious reasons. The Puritans especially detested the British custom of playing games on the Sabbath. James I had gone so far as to proclaim a royal decree, published as the *Book of Sports*, giving his subjects the legal right, after Divine service, to engage in "lawful Recreation; such as dancing, . . . archeries for men, leaping, vaulting and other harmless Recreations . . . and other sports therewith used."[8] When the Puritans briefly assumed power in England, they ordered the state executioner to publicly burn the *Book of Sports*.

In America, the Puritans dispassionately implemented their beliefs and practices. Their peculiar coldness has been remarked upon many times. In 1850 Nathaniel Hawthorne wrote:

> They were a people amongst whom religion and the law were almost identical, and in whose character both were so thoroughly interfused, that the mildest and severest acts of public discipline were alike made venerable and awful. Meagre, indeed, and cold, was the sympathy that transgressors might look for.[9]

This passage hints at the Puritan world view (or *Weltanschauung*). To them religion was everything and they did away with anything that interfered with it. The Puritans thus forbad dancing, drama, and fiction, as well as recreation-sport. (We use the term *recreation-sport* to refer to activities with sportlike elements and overtones, because during this period there were probably no American activities that had developed sufficiently to meet the modern definition of sport laid down in Chapter 1.)

To a certain extent, their detestation fitted the harsh demands of wilderness life.

---

[7]Jacob Burnet, *Notes on the Early Settlement of the Northwestern Territory* (Cincinnati, Ohio: Derby, Bradley and Company, 1847), pp. 68–69. Also see Jerry Jaye Wright, "History of Sport, Games, and Amusements Among Pioneer Cultures in Indiana, 1670–1820" (unpublished Ph.D. dissertation, Department of Health, Physical Education, and Recreation, The Ohio State University, 1980). Also, Steward Culin, *Games of the North American Indians* (New York: Dover Publications, Inc., 1975).

[8]Quoted in Dulles, *A History of Recreation*, p. 10.

[9]Nathaniel Hawthorne, *The Scarlet Letter* (1850; reprint, Boston: Houghton Mifflin Company, 1960), p. 51–52. See also Kai T. Erikson, *Wayward Puritans: A Study in the Sociology of Deviance* (New York: John Wiley & Sons, Inc., 1966).

There simply wasn't much opportunity for recreation. Some functionalist scholars claim that this is the major reason the Puritans disdained recreation. However, while living in England the Puritans could have participated in recreation if they had so desired; but they did not. From this we can infer that their detestation originated from something other than lack of opportunity.

Colonial Recreation-Sport

As long as Puritanism remained the dominant religion in America, neither sport nor recreation could thrive. But as time went on, the Puritan influence over New England declined. New settlers with different religious beliefs arrived and pioneers pushed west. The need for relentless toil diminished, and some small amount of time could be set aside for recreation.

The wealthy upper classes had more time for recreation than most people. Among the wealthy, raising and racing horses became almost a mania. They could also afford to hunt foxes from horseback and race yachts. (The ships were not yachts as we think of them but working vessels temporarily diverted to racing).[10] Among the less wealthy who lived in the settled parts of the country, early forms of bowling (skittles and ten pins), golf, and ice-skating began to develop. Recreation also took place as part of holiday festivals: "Great and Thursday Meetings" (a kind of religious gathering), militia training days, and quilting and corn-husking bees.

Oftentimes colonial gatherings were held on large open fields. Though colonial games might strike us as historical oddities, the colonist viewed them as legitimate recreation-sports. For instance, colonists might enjoy "clubbing the cat"—a game in which a live cat was shut inside a loosely staved barrel that was suspended from a rope stretched between two posts. For a small fee, contestants would hurl wooden clubs at the barrel. The object was to be the first person to break the barrel and dump the now terrorized and crazed cat on the ground. The cat would then tear madly around and whoever could grab it would win a bottle of wine. "Pulling the goose" consisted of hanging a live goose upside down between high poles. Galloping riders on horseback would then try to jerk the goose down by grabbing its head, a task made more difficult by smearing grease over the goose.

Hunting contests of all kinds naturally developed from colonial life. A "turkey shoot" is actually a misnomer. Barnyard fowls were tied to stakes on an open field while marksmen tried to shoot them. The successful marksman got to keep the bird as a prize. In thinly populated areas mass hunts took place. Wolves might be driven into a pen and shot by hunters standing on the pen fences. "Fowling" with what amounted to a small cannon mounted on the prow of a punt, served both to stock larders and as recreation-sport. Almost an entire flock of ducks or geese could be killed with a single blast.

Cockfights were common. So were rat baits. Several dozen rats would be thrown into a low ring and a small ratting dog set loose among them. Spectators bet on how many rats the dog could kill in a fixed amount of time. The world record presumably still stands

---

[10]This section depends heavily on John Allen Krout, *Annals of American Sport*, The Pageant of America Series (New Haven, Connecticut: Yale University Press, 1929).

at 500 rats killed in ninety minutes.[11] In other instances, large dogs were turned loose on a chained bear, or a dog pitted against another dog.

Human contestants participated in "eye-gouging," a no-holds-barred wrestling match which allowed gouging the opponent's eyes. An early traveler describes a bout between a man from Virginia and a man from Kentucky: "The Virginian . . . pitched himself into the bosom of his opponent. . . . The shock received by the Kentuckian, and the want of breath brought him instantly to the ground. The Virginian never lost his hold; fixing his claws in his hair and his thumbs on his eyes, gave them an instantaneous start from their sockets. The sufferer roared aloud, but uttered no complaint."[12]

In colonial times taverns often served as centers of fun and sociability for the surrounding countryside. On occasion they became a primitive kind of recreation center featuring animal baitings, eye gouging, or turkey shoots. Along with these diversions went much drinking, gambling, and rowdy behavior. In fact, most of the fun seems to have come from the gambling and drinking.

Rudimentary Sports

Even though we might go on describing these colonial recreation-sports, it's worthwhile to pause and ask what these examples tell us. Are they anything more than oddities? Obviously, since we described them, we have a sociological point in mind. Pulling the goose and clubbing the cat probably impress the modern person as inhumane, a little abnormal, or both. But then what is intrinsically normal about modern sport? About chasing calves from horseback, lassoing their necks, and tying their legs? Or about dressing in plastic football armor and hurling your body at another person dressed in plastic armor? Or about diving from a forty-foot tower into a concrete pool filled with chlorinated water? In the last chapter we maintained that sport should be defined relative to the norms and values of its culture and historical epoch. As sociologist William Graham Sumner wrote long ago, "the mores can make anything right."[13] The examples of colonial recreation-sport affirm that point for American sport.

And just as important, the colonial examples show the genesis of the institution of sport. Looking beyond their peculiarities, we discern sportlike elements. The activities were obviously physical, nondeviant by the standards of the day, and competitive. We might also note that colonial recreation-sport developed out of what was available— horses, bears, cats, rats, and strong drink and quick fists.

At this time, recreation-sport had not yet developed into modern sport as we defined it in Chapter 1. That could not take place until American society developed further, as would happen in the next century—a century characterized by great technological upheaval and sweeping social changes.

---

[11]*Guinness Book of World Records* (New York: Bantam Books, Inc., 1979). This record was set in Liverpool, England.

[12]From J. A. Krout, *Annals of American Sport*, vol. 15 in The Pageant of America Series, copyrighted by U.S. Publishers Assn., Inc., p. 28.

[13]William Graham Sumner, *Folkways* (New York: Mentor Books, 1960), p. 468. Originally published in 1906 by Ginn and Company, Lexington, Massachusetts.

NINETEENTH CENTURY: GROWTH

During the early part of the nineteenth century, recreation-sport grew rather slowly. The Puritan disapproval of idleness regained popularity. Pulpit, press, and politician once again attacked recreation-sport while promoting work and discipline. "All young countries," states a New Hampshire law of the period, "have much more occasion to encourage a spirit of industry and application to business, than to countenance schemes of pleasure and amusement."[14]

The lyceum was about the only organized recreation given widespread approval. It was a kind of public lecture intended to be as much an educational experience as a recreational one. People would, somewhat ironically, spend their free time listening to a lyceum speaker exhort them to work harder and longer and thus to have less free time to attend lyceums.

Industrial Revolution

This did not last long. Within a short period (from about 1750 to 1850 in Europe), a sequence of technological inventions interacted with social and economic forces to change Western society forever: The Industrial Revolution occurred. Though not revolutionary as measured by time—it went on for about 100 years—it was revolutionary in magnitude and scope. One authoritative book on social demography states that the economic changes of the Industrial Revolution constituted "the first fundamental advance since the establishment of preindustrial cities several millenia before."[15]

Even though the United States lagged behind Europe and did not get fully caught up in the Industrial Revolution until the middle of the nineteenth century, technological stirrings were taking place before that. By the 1830s steamboats could be seen on American rivers. In *Life on the Mississippi* Mark Twain describes a steamboat race:

> In the "flush times" of steamboating, a race between two notoriously fleet steamers was an event of vast importance. . . . People, people everywhere; the shores, the housetops, the steamboats, the ships are packed with them, and you knew that the borders of the broad Mississippi are going to be fringed with humanity thence northward twelve hundred miles, to welcome these racers. . . . Bands bray "Hail Columbia," huzza after huzza thunders from the shores, and the stately creatures go whistling by like the wind.[16]

But regardless of the excitement and publicity, races did not make much economic sense. Why risk an exploded boiler or running aground? Much more sensible were the profits from transporting race horses, and especially fans, to the matches that could then be staged at distant places. For instance, in 1856 a major race brought thousands of fans

---

[14]Quoted in Dulles, *A History of Recreation*, pp. 85–86.

[15]Excerpt from *Population*, 3rd ed., by William Petersen, p. 42. Copyright © 1975 by William Petersen. Used by permission of Macmillan Publishing Company, Inc.

[16]Mark Twain, *Life on the Mississippi* (New York: Harper & Row Publishers, Inc., 1923), pp. 145–47.

and several stables to New Orleans. A newspaper of the time recorded: ''We have already mentioned that arrival of Messrs. Lecomte & Co's stable, and now we have the pleasure of announcing that the steamboat Natchez has arrived this morning, bringing Col. Binga-man's and Cap. Minor's stable in good order and well conditioned.''[17] Horse racing was the first mass spectator sport (or recreation, if you prefer that terminology) to flourish in the United States.

Not everyone lived near a major river, of course, but in 1830 the first passenger train, the Baltimore and Ohio, went into service and soon steam-powered trains connected cities and towns. Like steamboat lines, railroad companies quickly discovered the profit to be made from sport. Owners began shipping their horses by rail and fans increasingly relied on trains to get them to the track. In 1842, when the Long Island Railroad over-booked its cars to the Union Course, angry fans rioted, overturning and smashing the coaches. In 1852 the Boston, Concord, and Montreal line encouraged the first rowing match between Harvard and Yale by giving the athletes free passage to Lake Win-nipesaukee, New Hampshire, the site of the race. The railroad's profits came from running special excursion trains to the match.

Later in the century both rail and steamboat companies encouraged prizefighting even though it was blatantly illegal. (Most often the police obligingly looked the other way). Not knowing where the fight was to be held, fans purchased special excursion tickets with the implicit understanding that the train or boat would take them to the fight. As with horse races and rowing, many thousands turned out for important matches.

All during the nineteenth century and especially after the Civil War ended, technol-ogy rapidly became a routine part of American culture. Writes one historian: ''Between the Civil War and 1900 steam and electricity replaced human muscle, iron replaced wood, and steel iron. . . . Machines could now drive steel tools. . . . The telephone, the type-writer, and adding machine speeded up the work of business.''[18]

Inventions of all kinds diffused into daily life and changed the world of sports. The telegraph and later the wireless radio were both used to flash sports news across the nation and from Europe. The lithograph, the high-speed printing press, and the halftone print made the modern newspaper possible. (William Randolph Hearst developed the sports section to hype sales.) The still camera and the motion picture appeared. (One of the first films ever made was of a prize fight.) The percussion cap and smokeless powder improved firearms and thereby made hunting more efficient. Stop watches were invented, then ball bearings (for wheels and gears), artificial ice (for all-weather skating rinks), and sewing machines (for mass-produced uniforms and leather-stitched goods).

Mass production meant standardized products, including sporting goods: bats, gloves, uniforms, golf clubs, bicycles, balls. Before that, craftsmen had produced sports equipment, much of it by hand, and their output was slow, expensive, and nonstandard.

New technology opened the night. Coal-gas lighting appeared in the early

---

[17]Quoted in John Rickards Betts, *America's Sporting Heritage: 1850–1950* (Reading, Massachusetts: Addison-Wesley Publishing Co., Inc., 1974) p. 27. Betts's work is the most authoritative work linking technol-ogy to the rise of American sport. This section heavily relies on it.

[18]Howard Zinn, *A People's History of the United States* (New York: Harper & Row, Publishers, Inc., 1980), p. 247.

nineteenth century and some seventy years later, with the coming of mass electrification, Thomas Edison's light bulb proved even more effective. In an age which considered the twelve-hour workday short, nighttime was about the only time available for entertainment. Artificial light greatly stimulated theatres, music halls, restaurants, and many sports events. In 1881 a tennis rally took place under electric light in a New York City armory.

Sponsors preferred indoor events because outdoor events, such as road races, bicycling, and rowing, were difficult to supervise and hard for audiences to see. Perhaps more important, at outdoor events sponsors needed an "army of scouts to ward off freeloaders."[19]

Though many sports proved to be natural indoor events—boxing and hockey for instance—it was not until well into the twentieth century that night baseball and football became routine. Outdoor fields required banks of floodlights for night games, which purists opposed on the grounds that the artificial light changed the games too much.

In the latter part of the nineteenth century a bicycling rage swept the country. Enthusiasts touted bikes as fun, healthy, and daring, and predicted that they would make the horse obsolete. The New York Police Department even experimented with bicycle-mounted cops.[20] (The Cincinnati Police tried the same thing in 1980; again showing that the "more things change, the more they stay the same.")[21] The early bicycles with large front wheel and tiny rear wheel were called "bone crushers" because riders frequently broke an arm, skull, or clavicle if thrown over the front wheel. They were not popular with "proper Victorian ladies" nor with timid boys. But when the "safety" bicycle (the kind we see now) replaced the bone crushers, everyone could ride. Bicycle rinks, bicycle paths, and studios that taught riding became common.

The safety bicycle was more than a passing fad; it had far reaching social consequences. It helped free women from the restrictive whalebone and hoops of Victorian dress. As women took up bicycling and athletics in general, "sports clothes, which eventually came to include the modern bathing suit together with shorts and slacks, symbolized the new status of women. . . . The athletic era also brought an end to the chaperone. The older women couldn't be persuaded to ride bicycles, and the younger ones couldn't be kept off!"[22] (See Chapter 9.)

At about this time inventors and tinkers were developing another device that would, unlike the bicycle, really replace the horse—the automobile. In 1895 the *Chicago Times-Herald* sponsored an automobile race. This race had an enormous indirect impact on the history of industrialization. It so fascinated Henry Ford, then a wishful auto entrepreneur, that he decided to make his mark on the racing track. Accordingly Ford built the racing car 999 and hired Barney Oldfield to drive it. Oldfield raced the 999 to a new

[19]Excerpt from *The Great American Sports Book* by George Gipe, p. 186. Copyright © 1978 by George Gipe. Reprinted by permission of Doubleday & Company, Inc.

[20]Edmund Morris, *The Rise of Theodore Roosevelt* (New York: Coward, McCann & Geoghegan, Inc., 1979), p. 533.

[21]*Columbus Citizen-Journal*, July 24, 1980, p. 1.

[22]Frederick W. Cozens and Florence Scovil Stumpf, *Sports in American Life* (Chicago: The University of Chicago Press, 1953), p. 29.

speed record and Henry Ford found financial backing. He writes, "A week after the race I formed the Ford Motor Company."[23]

Henry Ford wasn't the only one to build a huge economic complex. Economic competition in the nineteenth century might be described as unbridled, fierce, and cutthroat. Free enterprise—laissez faire—was the dominant economic philosophy and quite compatible with the developing doctrine of social Darwinism. Highly publicized among intellectual circles of the day, social Darwinism maintained that social competition results in the survival of the socially fittest and, by implication, the morally worthiest.

Sometimes historians call the nineteenth century, especially the period after the Civil War, the "Age of the Robber Barons," a phrase that reflects the *Zeitgeist*[24] of the period and that directly refers to the vast business baronies established by magnates such as John D. Rockefeller (oil), Andrew Carnegie (steel), Philip Armour (meat packing), and J. P. Morgan (finance). Although they were hated—at one time Rockefeller had the distinction of being the most despised man in America—robber barons did help organize society. Even critical historians concede that. Says one such historian of J. P. Morgan: "While making his fortune, Morgan brought rationality and organization to the national economy. He kept the system stable."[25]

Bureaucratic Social Organization

Stability is always a critical concern, especially when society is being thrown into flux. The Industrial Revolution was now spinning off one subrevolution after another. Old traditions, customs, and rituals, as well as the folk groups of family and friends, were being replaced with such radically different social inventions as standardization, centralization, division of labor, impersonal authority, and rational planning. Bureaucracy and formal organization were proving to be effective ways to organize the emerging social order. This included recreation-sport.[26]

Horse racing led the way. Even though a few racing organizations predate the Industrial Revolution—the South Carolina Jockey Club and the Jockey Club of Lexington were both founded in the 1700s—the major growth occurred in the nineteenth century. The National Course of Washington, D.C. opened in 1801 and patrons included congressmen, government officials, and presidents. Andrew Jackson, an intense horse-racing fan, sometimes entered his own horses and usually lost heavily betting on them. Three race tracks soon opened in the greater New York area, and one, the Long Island Union Course, hosted the most famous race of the day: Eclipse, a northern thoroughbred, beat a southern horse, Sir Henry, in a series of match races watched by thousands of fans. Reports historian John Betts in his highly regarded book, *America's Sporting Heritage*:

---

[23]Quoted in Betts, America's Sporting Heritage, p. 82.

[24]*Zeitgeist* means the spirit of the times, or dominant thesis or prevailing collective attitude. The names of epochs often describe the Zeitgeist: Roaring Twenties, Age of Conformity (1950s), the Turbulent Sixties.

[25]Zinn, *A People's History*, p. 250.

[26]This section is heavily based on Krout, *Annals of American Sport*.

"Meetings increased from 56 in 1830 to 130 in 1839; although there were less than 40 tracks in 1830, ten years later there were nearly twice the number."[27]

Around this time professional gamblers had control of many tracks and stables. Some fans gave up on the track altogether because of its crookedness. Wealthy horse lovers formed Matinee Driving Clubs in order to race informally and to appreciate horse flesh without the influence of gambling.

Boat racing also achieved popularity. The sport "extended from Virginia to Texas and the Northeast and the heyday of its existence was from the 1830's to the Civil War."[28] This period witnessed the founding of the numerous boating organizations. The New York Garden Amateur Boat Club sponsored competition among smaller craft. Similar clubs existed in Philadelphia, Mobile, Savannah, New Orleans, Detroit, and other places. The New York Yacht Club supervised competition among ocean-going vessels. In 1851, they sponsored the *America*, which beat eighteen other yachts in a race around the Isle of Wight and won a trophy now called the America's Cup—one of the most prestigious prizes in racing.

Rowing developed into the first big-time college sport. Races attracted multitudes of people who stood along the shores to watch and cheer. Harvard, Yale, the University of Pennsylvania, and other schools organized rowing clubs. Just before the Civil War broke out, several eastern colleges joined together to create an umbrella organization, the College Union Regatta Association. This move presaged trends in sports organization. Professional rowing also achieved some popularity but then disappeared from the sports scene, as did professional long-distance running, which at one time drew large crowds. The "ultimate" goal was to run ten miles in sixty minutes (a goal that also illustrates how much performances have improved—any number of today's runners can do that).

Although cricket was played quite extensively and was organized by the Young American Cricket Club in 1855, the American public cherished baseball more than any other bat-and-ball sport (perhaps more than any sport of any kind). American baseball evolved from the English game of cricket, rounders, one-old-cat, and four-old-cat. In 1845 the New York Knickerbocker Club was established to promote baseball. In fact, the club served as an upper-class social organization. Members tended to be "more expert with knife and fork at post-game banquets than with bat and ball on the diamond," reports one commentator.[29]

Regardless of their culinary skills, the Knickerbockers did help develop the sport we recognize as modern baseball. By the time the Civil War broke out, baseball clubs regularly competed against each other all over the northeast and in Chicago, Detroit, St. Louis, and San Francisco.

The Civil War interrupted the development of sports organizations, but afterwards the trend continued apace. Some 200 clubs were founded between 1865 and 1867—nearly two per week!—and the National Association had a membership of 237 amateur baseball

---

[27]Betts, *America's Sporting Heritage*, p. 12.

[28]Ibid., p. 37.

[29]Quoted in Robert H. Boyle, *Sport-Mirror of American Life* (Boston: Little, Brown & Company, 1963), p. 16.

clubs. In 1869 the Cincinnati Red Stockings went on tour as a professional team and drew large enthusiastic crowds. Professional baseball quickly followed.

Baseball (like horse racing) had its bureaucratic beginning amid controversy and gambling. Fixing, point shaving, bribery, and rigged odds took place routinely. Indeed the motivation to organize the National League came from the inability of the former organization, the National Association, to handle these problems.

Corruption, however, was not by any means unique to sport. Much of American society was corrupt, though not always defined as such. Rather, people frequently shrugged it off as an evil that was necessary to make the wheels of business and government spin smoothly—ostensibly for everyone's benefit. (Remember that during this historical period the robber barons ruled the economic order and the party bosses controlled politics.)

Within the robber baron Zeitgeist, sport could easily be a business enterprise. Certain sports, such as baseball, horse racing, footracing, and boxing generated large revenues, especially gambling revenues. Horse racing provides an illustration.

Fans bet on horses. Betting involves money and money involves business. Horse racing is thus both a business and a sporting enterprise. Even though the wealthy entrepreneurs who founded race tracks might love horses, their love could not change the laws of economics, nor did they want it to. Within this Zeitgeist, the notion of competition in sport fits with the notion of competition in business. Both could be interpreted as tests of the spirit, tests of will, and work. Why shouldn't sport and business go together?

The same general point was (and still is) valid for other professional sports. In the long run, love of the game cannot override the enterpreneurial essentials of paying players, attracting fans, and showing a profit. Sport mirrored the young capitalist society within which it arose. Eventually the United States would commercialize sport to a greater extent than any other society.

Nationalism

When the Civil War broke out, Robert E. Lee fought for the Confederacy because he considered himself a Virginian first and an American second. After the war regional identification weakened. Better communications, better roads, and more sophisticated and widespread technology, along with interregional and international economic and social ties, acted as bonds drawing the country closer together. A single *nation* began emerging from a loose affiliation of regions or states. And again, sport mirrored the trend of American society. Teams could now go on extended tours via rail or boat. The news of their victories and defeats could be spread by telegraph and newspaper. Fans could come from miles around. Regional boundaries no longer acted as fences.

As national competition increased, so did the need for some kind of broader sports organization with a national scope. Soon local clubs were affiliating with umbrella associations in order to regulate competition between teams from all parts of the country. The words "National," "America(n)," or "United States" began appearing in the names of organizations like the following: United States Golf Association, United States Lawn Tennis Association, United States Skating Association; National Association of Archers,

National Croquet Association, National League, National Rifle Association, National Rod and Reel Association; American Amateur Bowling Union, American Association for the Advancement of Physical Education, American Jockey Club, American Trotter Association, American Yacht Club, Rowing Association of American Colleges.

We can reasonably infer from the scope of these organizations that parochialism in sport was dying out. Sport had reached large-scale national significance, and in the not-too-distant future international competition would become important. The Olympic movement was not far off (but that's a separate development, which we will cover in Chapters 10 and 11).

Urbanization and Reform

The Industrial Revolution had another consequence. The first Federal Census shows that in 1790 scarcely five Americans out of a hundred lived in urban areas. The nation was overwhelmingly rural. Today it's just the opposite: more than seventy out of a hundred Americans live in urban areas.[30] Between that time and this, the United States turned into an urban society.

This occurred because centralized manufacturing and the activities that go with it attracted thousands upon thousands of immigrant workers from abroad and from the American hinterland. No one planned this move to the city; it just happened. And it caused problems. Vice flourished and living conditions were vile. People jammed into rickety tenements that were cold in winter, hot in summer, with neither water nor privacy. Corruption was rampant and the government was indifferent or ineffectual. In the nineteenth-century city, most people did not live nicely.

This situation indirectly affected the development of sport. Nowadays we take for granted certain features of the urban environment which hardly existed before this century. These features include public parks, playgrounds, tennis courts, swimming pools, and supervised beaches. Those facilities that did exist in the past might have been unusable. For instance, the stench and offal from the raw garbage dumped close offshore made Coney Island beaches unfit for bathing.[31] The city of New York had only one park, Central Park, and it was mainly for the benefit of the social elite such as the Astors and Roosevelts, who drove their buggies around the park on afternoon outings.[32] The poor couldn't get to Central Park because they lived too far away. "The most astounding feature of the land of plenty," notes an archivist about the nineteenth century city, "is the absolute indifference of the rich toward the poor."[33]

Such indifference did not go unchallenged, however. New ideas began fermenting. Religious and secular leaders started preaching the new "social gospel," an ideology

---

[30]U.S. Bureau of the Census. *Historical Statistics of the United States, Colonial Times to 1970*, Part I (Washington, D.C.: U.S. Government Printing Office, 1975), Table A, 57–72.

[31]Otto L. Bettman, *The Good Old Days—They Were Terrible!* (New York: Random House, Inc., 1974), p. 196.

[32]Morris, *The Rise of Theodore Roosevelt*, p. 141.

[33]Bettman, *The Good Old Days*, p. 43.

asserting that people are neither intrinsically good nor intrinsically bad but are products of the environment, and that they can be improved by improving the environment. The Establishment perceived this social gospel as radical—as radical as other reform movements aimed at ending seventy-hour work weeks, sweat shops, child labor, and political corruption. The quest for social justice and reform became part of the Zeitgeist.[34]

As part of this reform Zeitgeist, a parks and playground movement developed, led by such stalwarts as Jacob Riis. In a letter to Riis, Theodore Roosevelt, who was a member of the social elite but a reformer nonetheless, supported the movement: "It is a good deal more important, if you look at the matter with a proper perspective, to have ample playgrounds in the poorer quarters of the city, and to *take the children off the streets so as to prevent them growing up toughs*."[35] To this day, the ideas expressed in Roosevelt's letter are major justifications for supporting recreational facilities out of public revenues.

This movement began inauspiciously enough. In 1895 Boston donated three sand lots for children to use. While the movement did succeed, its full impact would not be felt until later in the twentieth century. (Table 2.1 shows this pattern of development.)

Table 2.1. Municipal and County Parks and Recreation Areas, 1910–1960

YEAR	PLAY- GROUNDS UNDER LEADERSHIP	SWIMMING POOLS	BATHING BEACHES	GOLF COURSES (9 AND 18 HOLE)	TENNIS COURTS	BASEBALL DIAMONDS (90-FOOT)	SOFTBALL DIAMONDS (60-FOOT)
1960	20,100	2,800	1,000	600	15,700	7,000	14,800
1950	14,700	1,600	800	500	13,100	5,500	12,300
1940	9,900	1,200	600	400	12,100	4,000	10,000
1930	7,700	1,000	500	300	8,400	4,300	(NA)
1920	4,300	400	300	—	—	—	—
1910	1,200	—	—	—	—	—	—

NA: Not available.
Facilities reported by cities of 20,000 and over population. All figures rounded to nearest hundred.
SOURCE: U.S. Bureau of the Census, *Historical Statistics of the United States, Colonial Times to 1970, Bicentennial Edition*, Part 2 (Washington, D.C., 1975), Series H 849–61.

Business Support

Oddly, the electric trolley car brought about many recreational facilities. The more passengers trolleys carried, the more money the company made. So, like the steamboat and train companies before them, trolley companies encouraged people to attend events held at faraway places. In doing this, the companies were hardly subtle. Trolley lines often ended and started back by circling a baseball stadium, race course, or amusement park in the

---

[34]Howard P. Chudacoff, *The Evolution of American Urban Society* (Englewood Cliffs, New Jersey: Prentice-Hall, Inc., 1975).

[35]Quoted in Cozens and Stumpf, *Sports in American Life*, p. 25–26. Italics added.

outskirts of the city—a service to the fans and a moneymaker for the company. Trolley companies also financed parks and playgrounds located where else but at the line's end.

Private industry got involved in other ways. As labor gained power and the workday shortened, employers and unions began providing facilities and equipment for company or union teams. In the early days of bowling, softball, and basketball, industrial competition was the best to be found. Companies carried their employee-athletes mainly as players rather than as workers. (In Europe and Asia industrial leagues are still the top rung of competition in many sports, for example, basketball in Europe and baseball and volleyball in Japan.) Today private industry spends more money on sports equipment than any other single institution, including secondary schools and colleges combined. (While speaking of sports equipment, we should mention Albert G. Spalding. He could appropriately be called the "Robber Baron of Sports Manufacturing." By the late 1890s he had a virtual monopoly on producing and jobbing sporting goods in this country. The company which bears his family name is still a major one).

Club Support

During this period another bureaucratic development took form: athletic clubs. The New York Athletic Club was organized in 1868 and soon Chicago, New Orleans, and San Francisco had their athletic clubs. By the late 1880s, an observer on the scene claimed, "scarcely a city can be found having a population of 30,000 inhabitants, in which there is not at least one club in this class. In the large cities, there are from five to twenty-five; sometimes more."[36] Historian John Betts says that, "No single agency gave a greater impulse to sport than the formalized athletic club of the metropolis."[37] We question the degree but concur with the general thrust of Betts's statement.

A different type of sports club also proved important. German immigrants had brought the *Turnverein* to the United States before the Civil War. The Turnverein were gymnastics clubs dedicated to both physical culture and political ends. By the time the Civil War erupted, about seventy turner clubs existed, and they overwhelmingly supported the Union cause. After the war, the turners continued to grow and were instrumental in getting over fifty school systems to adopt physical training as a regular part of the curriculum.

Religious Support

Religion remained one of the few major institutions opposing recreation-sport. Harking back to the old Puritan philosophy, one minister told his congregation, "You can not

---

[36]Quoted in Betts, *America's Sporting Heritage: 1850–1950*, © 1974 by Addison-Wesley, Reading, Massachusetts, pp. 98–108. Reprinted with permission. President Theodore Roosevelt also caused changes in intercollegiate football and indirectly caused the development of the NCAA. See James V. Koch and Wilbert M. Leonard, II, "The NCAA: A Socioeconomic Analysis: The Development of the College Sports Cartel from Social Movement of Formal Organization," *The American Journal of Economics and Sociology*, 37 (July 1978), 225–39.

[37]Betts, *America's Sporting Heritage*, p. 98.

serve God skylarking on a bicycle.''[38] Had he added, "especially on Sunday," his pronouncement would have neatly summarized the predominant religious view. Few things infuriated the church quite as much as sport and games on the Sabbath.

Nevertheless, along with all the other changes wrought by the Industrial Revolution, religious views changed too. The church now confronted a new social order. The frontier disappeared—the federal government officially declared it closed in 1890. The old farm was rapidly vanishing. The factory system had been established. Electric lines criss-crossed the countryside. Cities grew larger. Depending on which historian's view you accept, the quality of life may or may not have improved, but it certainly had changed.

One difference concerned the church's hold on free time. European immigrants maintained their tradition of recreation on Sunday afternoon. They enjoyed picnics and baseball, and the bicycling mentioned in the minister's pronouncement. Saloons were popular too. (The police usually ignored Sunday dry laws—for the proper "fee.")

Faced with this competition, the church began turning to "muscular Christianity." Advocates of the muscular approach argued that if it took recreation-sport to get converts then that's what the church should provide. Far better that than having people drink away Sunday afternoon in a saloon. The Young Men's Christian Association (YMCA) adopted the muscular approach fairly early. By 1869 YMCAs with gyms, baths, and bowling alleys served New York, Washington, D.C., and San Francisco. By the late 1880s, approximately one hundred seventy such YMCAs existed. Their purpose was to "safeguard young men against the allurement of objectionable places of resort," one leader stated.[39] A separate organization with similar name and function, the Young Women's Christian Association, also started to provide athletic facilities for women. As the century came to a close, all facets of American society were starting to accept sport and adopt it in all realms of life.

By the end of the nineteenth century, sport was fairly well established as a social institution. However the beginning and end of historical developments seldom neatly coincide with the beginning and the end of centuries. The chronology of the rise of sport continues into the first part of the twentieth century.

TWENTIETH CENTURY: PERMANENCE

Sport and the Military

The United States entered World War I in 1916. About one-third of the men called to military service could not pass the physical examination. This statistic shocked the nation. It was disgraceful. What had happened to the *robust* Americans who had just finished conquering the frontier? A cry went out, as it would go out during World War II and again during the cold war of the 1950s, to improve the fitness of the American populace. Quite

---

[38]Quoted in Dulles, *A History of Recreation*, p. 206.

[39]Quoted in Betts, *America's Sporting Heritage: 1850–1950*, © 1974 Addison-Wesley, Reading, Massachusetts, p. 108. Reprinted with permission.

naturally, sport and exercise were singled out as ways to achieve the goal. On a larger scale than ever before, the military used sport to develop physical fitness and, since soldiers always spend a lot of time waiting around, to keep the troops busy. Many men first became acquainted with sport while in the service. (Later, the war experience became an important factor in pressuring state governments to adopt compulsory physical education in the school.)

World War I had a widespread effect on sport. According to two historians, "there is no question about the effect which various aspects of World War I had on sports; . . . it led to pressures in American culture to set the stage for the great boom in sports participation and interest which developed in the nineteen-twenties."[40]

The Golden Age of Sport

The Roaring Twenties followed World War I, then came the Great Depression and then World War II. Despite the depression, sports historians sometimes call the period between the two wars the "Golden Age of Sport." Though we cannot precisely measure such things, the adulation, interest, and naive wild enthusiasm for sport probably reached a peak at that time. The golden age is the age of sports heroes: Babe Ruth (baseball), Bobby Jones (golf), Bill Tilden (tennis), Gertrude Ederele (swimming), Babe Didrikson (track and field, golf), Wilbur Shaw (auto racing), Red Grange (football), Jesse Owens (track), and, above all heroes, sports or otherwise, Charles Lindberg (aviator).

Radio became the dominant medium of mass communication, as revolutionary as television would be some twenty years later. For the first time people could follow distant events as they actually took place. By 1924, radio regularly carried college football and by 1927 so much radiocasting was going on that a federal regulatory agency had to be established. In the same year radiocasts of the World Series began, and an unknown number of millions listened as Jack Dempsey tried to regain his heavyweight championship from Gene Tunney. Dempsey failed in the famous "long count fight,"[41] but the morning headline of the *New York Times* ignored *that* fact. Rather, it said, "Millions Listen on Radio." By the next year over ten million radio sets were in use.[42] Today so many sets exist that no one can count them.

Football became *the* sport and stadiums began to appear on campuses everywhere, including high schools. Sportswriter Grantland Rice, in his writing about Notre Dame's backfield, the "Four Horsemen," gave them a kind of sport immortality. The Gipper, another of ND's many stars, died of pneumonia and was reborn into legend when coach Knute Rockne asked his players to "win one for the Gipper."

The Roaring Twenties ended with the stock market crash of 1929, though in ac-

---

[40]Cozens and Stumpf, *Sports in American Life*, p. 81–82.

[41]This is one of the most famous boxing matches of all time. Dempsey solidly floored Tunney in the seventh round but forgot about the new rule requiring him to retreat to a neutral corner. The ensuing delay allowed Tunney almost seventeen seconds—the "long count"—in which to recover. Could Tunney have recovered in ten seconds? We'll never know. (Wells Twombley, *200 Years of Sports in America*, New York: McGraw-Hill Book Company, 1976, p. 160.)

[42]Betts, *America's Sporting Heritage*, p. 272.

tuality the economy had been weakening for several years. The Great Depression dates roughly from the crash to the start of World War II in 1941. During the depression there were times when one-third of the people willing and able to work couldn't find a job; when soup lines wound around the block two or three times over; when drought and dust storms laid bare the farms of the Midwest. In order to dramatize their petition for government assistance, twenty-five thousand military veterans and their families established a shantytown of tents and packing crates in Washington, D.C., and Army troops routed them and burned their dwellings. Seven thousand banks closed.

Sport suffered too. Financial difficulties forced many schools to completely abandon varsity athletics. Baseball, then the major professional sport, lost money, and big stars meekly accepted pay cuts. Even the Commissioner of Baseball, Judge Kenesaw Mountain Landis, took a symbolic cut from $65,000 to $50,000 per year.

Yet, despite all the upheavals and turmoil, people continued to believe in the norms and values of sport. By the middle of the depression, professional baseball began picking up attendance and colleges resumed competition as before. The government also played a part. In order to increase employment, the federal government financed programs and facilities for sport, recreation, and wilderness conservation. According to one study, this stimulus advanced the whole area of recreation by twenty-five years.[43] All in all, considering the depth of the economic downturn and the social upheavals, sport weathered the depression remarkably well.

The institution of sport had become a permanent part of American society by the end of the depression. The superstructure was in place and subsequent events would not tear it down. Quite the contrary, they usually reinforced it, as in the case of television, affluence, and leisure time, and the participation boom. These topics, however, are better addressed in other chapters. Insofar as this chapter is concerned, the goal has just about been reached.

CAUSAL FACTORS

We originally set out to interpret the rise of American sport from a mostly structural perspective. We did that, interspersing the perspective throughout the three-hundred-year chronology of sport. Now, considering that three hundred years is a long time, it would be useful to collect together the pieces of the perspective in order to highlight them. The major pieces, or causal factors, are as follows:

- *Technology.* Sociologists occasionally talk about *necessary* and *sufficient* conditions. For sport to have taken the form it did, technology was necessary (we can't imagine modern society without technology). Yet technology alone was not enough. Other developments had to occur before sport could become a major societal institution.
- *Social class.* Example 1: Originally the colonial aristocracy supported horse

---

[43]Reported in Cozens and Stumpf, *Sports in American Life*, p. 173.

racing and yachting for the obvious reason that only they could afford such expensive activities. Example 2: Football, now identified as a middle-class sport, developed on college campuses which in the nineteenth century were attended by upper-class males. Example 3: Clubs of wealthy men (the Knicker-bockers, for example) first organized and popularized baseball, which is now our national pastime. To sociologists there is nothing exceptional about these examples. The pattern of development fits a widely accepted principle: Cultural items flow from higher socioeconomic groups into popular culture. This also tends to be true for fashion, art, political opinion, and technical inventions. (This is not to say that the upper strata invented all sports, but only that social class affects the way sport flows and spreads throughout society.)

- *Bureaucracy.* Recall the number of sport clubs, leagues, and associations (bureaucracies) that were founded, especially after the Civil War. Bureaucracies are characterized by long life. They seldom die. This means that once the norms and values of sport become part and parcel of bureaucratic structures, they attained a sort of social immortality; that is, they attained permanence or fixity.

- *Institutional support.* We discussed how other segments or institutions of American society used sport: how the military used sport to develop physical fitness, how the church used sport to attract new members, how business used sport to make money. Because sport was useful to many institutions, they supported it, and thus diffused it throughout American culture and helped it become a permanent part of society.

- *Ideological compatability.* The presence of a favorable ideological climate greatly encouraged the rise of sport. Social Darwinism emphasized winning and struggle. The social gospel stressed the changing nature of human character. These factors were favorable to the norms and values of sport, or at least didn't hurt. Puritanism is an exception, but even the Puritan emphasis on hard work and discipline fitted the ideology of sport. Sport could flow with prevailing ideological currents rather than having to fight them, and could influence the direction of the currents to some degree.

- *Sport as recreation.* For most people, sport was (and is) recreation: colonists playing pull-the-goose, college students cheering their teams on, weekend bicyclists, and sedentary gamblers. Such people enjoyed the *play* part of sport. Play was what Puritanism objected to, and play is what leads certain social scientists to say that sport is an innate human need. While we would not go that far, it does seem reasonable to argue that the enjoyment of sport contributed to its rise and eventually fixity.

The causal factors, then, are technology, social class, bureaucracy, institutional support, ideological compatibility, and sport as recreation. The last two factors are not structures, as sociologists use the term. They are doctrine and emotional release, and since we include them, our perspective is *mostly* rather than *totally* structural.

SUMMARY

1. The main question posed is, How did sport develop into a permanent American social institution? The answer to this question varies according to your perspective and purpose. It turns out that for our purposes, the two major perspectives, Marxism and functionalism, are too narrow. We therefore opt for a mostly structural perspective which looks for various causal factors and which incorporates some Marxism and some functionalism.

2. Native Americans participated in sport, but the destruction of their culture meant that few Indian sports influences remain in modern American culture. Lacrosse is an exception.

3. The Puritans eschewed recreation-sport for religious reasons. Later, colonists developed many sportlike games such as clubbing the cat and turkey shooting.

4. During the early part of the nineteenth century, sport developed slowly. Puritanism temporarily reasserted itself, but an entertainment boom, which included sport, took place nevertheless. Throughout its development, sport usually flowed downward from higher socioeconomic groups into the general culture and became a widespread recreation.

5. The Industrial Revolution vastly changed American society, technologically, socially, economically, and spatially. The Industrial Revolution had manifold effects on sport. Improved transportation and communication made interregional competition possible. Mass production standardized sports equipment. Indoor lighting allowed events to be held at night. After the Civil War, sport was intensively bureaucratized while other societal institutions actively encouraged sport. At the same time, ideologies such as social Darwinism and the social gospel were compatible with sport.

6. By the end of the nineteenth century sport was fairly well established as an institution. World War I and the Roaring Twenties established it even more firmly. Sport survived the Great Depression rather well.

7. The main causal factors in our mostly structural explanation were technology, social class, bureaucracy, institutional support, ideological compatibility, and sport as recreation. At present, this broader perspective is required to understand the rise of sport.

3

COMPETITION AND SOCIALIZATION
Why Athletes Appear

This elementary school football player—Bubba—is blessed with above average athletic skills; sports come easy to him, and he receives a lot of encouragement from his family, friends, and coaches to continue on in sports. Many less lucky young players are screened out of sports by the time they reach high school. Photo by Timothy J. Curry.

Here is a fact we often ignore: Virtually all athletes must fail. This is true because sports competition is zero sum: What one party loses the other wins and vice versa. This isn't unique to modern American culture by any means. Consider pok-tat-pok as played by the ancient Aztecs, Mayans, and Incas. It illustrates a zero-sum contest. Pok-tat-pok also illustrates competing for high stakes.

Losing Is Dying. In some parts of Mesoamerica before the Spanish conquest, pok-tat-pok was a major sport. The specifics of the game varied from place to place but the outlines were similar.

Teams of eight to ten players representing various municipalities competed with each other. Each team tried to drive a large, hard rubber ball through a vertical hoop placed several feet above the ground at the end of a large outdoor playing field. The ball had to be propelled with the body (hands and feet were not allowed). Since this task was extremely difficult, the game often took several days and ended with victory going to the team that scored the first goal.

Important matches were played in stadiums built specifically for pok-tat-pok, and before large partisan audiences, many of whom wagered substantial sums on the outcome.

After an important match, the losers became the chattel of the winners; and the captain of the losing team was executed.[1]

ZERO-SUM COMPETITION

We mention pok-tat-pok for both its historical interest and because it has implications for modern sport. Today athletes and coaches are not enslaved or executed for losing, but the tenor of the pok-tat-pok remains with us: Losing is hardly rewarding. Objective defeat—defeat on the scoreboard—means disappointment, frustration, and even disgrace, not to mention loss of job or career. Losing is punishing and, because competition is zero sum, one party must end up being punished. Most sports ensure that only one clearly defined, objective victor emerges by the use of overtime periods, extra innings, sudden deaths, and so on. And sports ideology supports this. Ties are denigrated, and boos and hisses go to coaches who play for ties when they could go for wins. The media will surely condemn them the following day.

Zero-sum competition demands—indeed is defined by—wins and losses, and in most societies the winners get the lion's share of the rewards: fame, money, praise, and ego gratification. With perhaps a few exceptions, it is much better to win than to lose.

We should not give the impression that zero-sum competition must be totally grim and severe. Benign effects can come about. Zero-sum competition can produce what one sports sociologist calls the "associational response."[2] Competing does not necessarily mean you wish your opponents ill. Athletes have been known to help their competitors train, to give each other advice during a competition, to recognize outstanding performances. Friendship and comradeship develop. And on a formal basis, organizations come about. Associations are formed.

Zero-sum competition thus has dual consequences. On one side it promotes divisiveness and conflict, and on the other it promotes cooperation and organization.

[1]Celso Engriquez, *Sports in Pre-Hispanic America* (Mexico City: Litographia Machado, S.A., 1968).

[2]Gunther Luschen, "Cooperation, Association, and Contest," *Journal of Conflict Resolution*, 14 (1970), 34.

CULTURE, COMPETITION, CREED, AND SPORT

Culture

Culture is all the social learning passed on from one generation to the next. This social learning includes symbols, such as words and signs; physical objects, such as tools and computers; customs, such as manners and decorum; institutional arrangements, such as family and sport; and so very much more we couldn't possibly enumerate it all.

Most behavior is governed by rules which are not written down but which nevertheless are standard, well known throughout society, and binding; that is, norms that determine behavior. Comparing Japanese to American baseball illustrates this point. The two versions are played under virtually identical written rules and avidly followed by millions of fans.

> **How You Harmonize.**   In 1873 an American professor introduced baseball to Japan. The sport immediately caught on and just five years later a team from the University of Wisconsin played a series of games in Tokyo against Japanese teams. Japanese culture traditionally emphasizes the group over the individual; the team over the star; tradition over innovation; fitting in rather than standing out; homogeneity rather than heterogeneity.
>
> Japanese baseball naturally mirrors Japanese culture. Japanese baseball managers are mostly concerned with their team's sense of harmony. Japanese managers make decisions via conferences with coaches and key players—a sharing of authority unprecedented in the United States (and which causes the Japanese game to last much longer than the American game). Japanese managers never get fired for losing. They are given "leaves of absence" to contemplate their team's problems while an "interim" replacement "temporarily" takes over—permanently.
>
> Japanese players never hire agents and rarely negotiate for higher salaries; that would imply that one has placed himself ahead of the team. Japanese players do not display temper over "bad" calls; that would destroy the harmony of the game and show disrespect. Japanese players do not skip workouts (and Japanese teams are notorious for their dedication to physical fitness).[3]

Culture can be obvious, like the rules of the game, but it can also be subtle, like player deportment. The rules of Japanese and American baseball are almost identical, but the character of the games differs so much that American players who sign with Japanese teams find it frustrating. They destroy the harmony of their Japanese team and come away culturally battered. To be thoroughly effective, an American player would have to be resocialized into Japanese culture in general and Japanese baseball in particular—a process that would probably take more years than the player has in his athletic career. Moving from culture to culture is never easy or without problems. This holds for every area of behavior, including sport.

In addition to deportment, culture also prescribes general goals—what is good,

---

[3]Robert Obojski, *The Rise of Japanese Baseball Power* (Radnor, Pennsylvania: Chilton Book Co., 1975); Robert Whiting, "You've Gotta Have 'Wa'," *Sports Illustrated*, September 24, 1979, pp. 59–71.

right, just, and proper, and therefore what is worth striving for. Some of these culturally prescribed goals have special importance for sport—namely, competition, winning, and the "American way."

Competition and Creed

Social commentators endlessly remark on how American culture glorifies material success above all other accomplishments; how Americans must constantly compete if they wish to acquire wealth and rank; and how the trappings of money (Mercedes cars and apartments with a view) label you as "successful" and, by implication, "superior." Famous winners become heroes, idols, cult figures, and cultural reference points. They come to symbolize what everyone can achieve through competition. On an even broader scale, "without winners there wouldn't even be any goddamned civilization," or so claims Woody Hayes, the legendary former football coach of The Ohio State University.[4]

And what better place to learn about winning than on the sports field? That is a major justification for supporting and emphasizing sport, which is supposed to teach the "American way," how to work hard and compete and win.

That this idea may not be true could be less important than the fact that our culture induces us to believe it. We start internalizing these creeds at birth and usually conform to them without being consciously aware of doing so. If we would think about them, we would find that the creeds are a jumble of contradictory values for behavior and thought about a specific area of life. Paradoxically, creedal systems include prescriptions for how the contradictions should be resolved.

So ingrained do our creeds become, that to go against them seems deviant and perverse. Creeds touch our emotional rather than intellectual chords. They are faiths, beliefs, leaps of knowing. We stick by our creeds for social, not logical or scientific, reasons. Without being aware of it, we get bombarded by the creedal message from all quarters. We could not escape them even if we tried. To give just one illustration concerning competition and the American way:

> **Animallike.** A major department store sponsors a series of ads supporting sports for children. One ad focuses on a nine-year-old swimmer, who, the ad maintains, is participating in a "remarkable program [which fosters a] healthy perspective on competition." The nine-year-old's team has just swept to first place in an important meet and he personally won two gold medals. He says, "I get all animallike before a race." And when he gets all animallike "he has a voice like a foghorn," which he uses to cheer on his teammates.
>
> The ad concludes: "We believe in the basic ideal—to develop amateur athletes in the American Way. . . . We believe this helps [the kids] roar through life."

According to the implicit message of the ad, healthy competition means winning,

---

[4]Quoted in Robert Vare, *Buckeye: A Study of Coach Woody Hayes and the Ohio State Football Machine* (New York: Harper and Row, 1974), p. 7.

and if to win you have to get "all animallike," that's all right too because that's the American way—to roar through life as you roar through sport.

A former player for the University of Michigan and ex-President of the United States, Gerald Ford, writes, "We have been asked to swallow a lot of home-cooked psychology in recent years that winning isn't all that important anymore. . . . I don't buy that for a minute. It is not enough to just compete. Winning is very important. Maybe more important than ever."[5]

President Ford did not go so far as to assert that "winning isn't everything; it's the only thing!" He comes close though; and like the ad, he presents and publicizes and lends the weight of presidential authority to a creedal tenet dominant in American culture and in sport.

The cliche that winning is the only thing usually gets attributed (probably incorrectly) to the man who to this day epitomizes relentless lashing competition, Vincent Thomas Lombardi (1913–1970).

> **The Truth.** In the 1930s, Lombardi played on Fordham's famous line, the "Seven Blocks of Granite." Granite describes him physically and philosophically: hard, chiseled, unyielding. He became coach of the Green Bay Packers in 1958 and led the team to five National League Championships and two Super Bowl victories.
>
> Lombardi lived by the credo that, in his words, "second place is meaningless." One former Packer recalls him rallying the team before the season: "There's only one place here, and that's first place. . . . There's a second place bowl game and it's a hinky-dinky football game, held in a hinky-dinky town, played by hinky-dinky football players. That's all second place is: hinky-dinky."
>
> To achieve first place Lombardi autocratically drove his players by screaming, raving, and pummeling them. He said of one incident wherein he punched a player: "I guess I was trying to get him to hate me. . . . You must have that fire in them and there is nothing that stokes that fire like hate. I'm sorry, but that is the truth."[6]

You cannot deny Lombardi's record at Green Bay: ninety-nine wins, thirty-one losses, and four ties. The end doesn't necessarily justify the means, but nevertheless, first place and winning are, in big-time sports, the most public, most prized, and most glorified criteria by which athletes and coaches are judged. Second place is still hinky-dinky.

History of the Ideology of Competition

Though second place may be hinky-dinky now, American culture did not always glorify competition and winning. The Puritans thought of success as a spiritual matter determined by each individual's relation to God. Outdoing others was not part of that process.

During the eighteenth and early nineteenth centuries, "successful" described some-

---

[5]Gerald Ford and John Underwood, "In Defense of the Competitive Urge," *Sports Illustrated*, July 8, 1974, p. 16.

[6]Jerry Kramer, *Instant Replay: The Green Bay Diary of Jerry Kramer* (New York: New American Library, 1968), p. 65; Vincent Lombardi and W. C. Heinz, "A Game for Madmen," *Look*, September 5, 1967, p. 86.

one who had achieved a fair-to-middling income. Instead of great wealth, people tried for political and personal freedom, a sense of competence, and a pride in doing their jobs well. Interpersonal competition was not necessary because America seemingly had an inexhaustible supply of resources, wealth, and space. There existed enough of everything for everyone.[7]

This all changed. An early school of economic thought began emphasizing competition. The story goes that Charles Darwin puzzled over his vast accumulation of biological data for years. Then he happened to read Thomas Malthus, a classical economist who wrote on population pressures, and suddenly hit upon competition as the guiding principle of evolution, a principle he later applied to humans.

Following Darwin's lead in biology, early sociologists adapted the idea of competition to explain how societies work. These theorists are called, not surprisingly, "social Darwinists." A sociologist, Herbert Spencer, actually invented the phrase "survival of the fittest." According to him, wealth, prestige, social position, and personal satisfaction should be won through social competition, a process which would ensure that the most able people rise to the top. Another early sociologist, William Sumner, agreed: "It is therefore, the competition of life which is the societal element, and which produces societal organization."[8]

Sociologist Charles Cooley argued along the same lines but saw competition through rather rose-colored lenses. In 1899 Cooley wrote,

> The competitive process is thus conceived in its highest form, as an amicable testing and comparison of power, with a view to securing the happiness of all, by helping each to find his peculiar and appropriate work. It is like the preliminary practice of a football team to determine what place shall be assigned to each player: everyone, presumably, wishing to have that position in which he can gain the most applause by contributing most to the common success. The aims of the individual and of the whole are the same.[9]

Eventually everyone would end up ranked and rewarded in proportion to their ability and effort and not according to their inherited wealth, family connections, or luck. Merit, as measured by competitive success, would be the operative factor.

In many ways we can appreciate the appeal that such an ideology would have. It has a ring of fairness about it. A moment's reflection reveals how very harsh it is, however fair it may be. The social Darwinists were praising zero-sum competition; and therefore most people must lose the competitive struggle. The doctrine was simply too harsh to win wide acceptance. Even robber barons had a hard time embracing it.[10]

---

[7]Rex Burns, *Success in America: The Yeoman Dream and the Industrial Revolution* (Amherst, Massachusetts: University of Massachusetts Press, 1976).

[8]William Graham Sumner, *Folkways* (New York: New American Library, 1960), p. 31. Originally published in 1906 by Ginn and Company, Lexington, Massachusetts.

[9]Charles Horton Cooley, *Sociological Theory and Social Research* (1899; reprint, New York: Holt, Rinehart & Winston, 1930), p. 182.

[10]Richard M. Huber, *The American Idea of Success* (New York: McGraw-Hill Book Company, 1971).

During the latter part of the nineteenth century a series of softer creeds emerged. The "character ethic" became especially popular and by the time of the golden age of sport, it had become firmly entrenched in American culture.

Sportswriter Grantland Rice neatly summarized the essence of the character ethic in regard to sport in his poem "Alumnus Football":

Bill Jones had been the shining star upon his college team.
His tackling was ferocious and his bucking was a dream.
When husky William took the ball beneath his brawny arm
They had two extra men to ring the ambulance alarm.

Bill hit the line and ran the ends like some mad bull amuck.
The other team would shiver when they saw him start to buck.
And when some rival tackler tried to block his dashing pace,
On waking up, he'd ask, "Who drove that truck across my face?"

Bill had the speed—Bill had the weight—Bill never bucked in vain;
From goal to goal he whizzed along while fragments strewed the plain.
And there had been a standing bet, which no one tried to call,
That he could make his distance through a ten-foot granite wall.

When he wound up his college course each student's heart was sore.
They wept to think bull-throated Bill would sock the line no more
Not so with William—in his dreams he saw the Field of Fame,
Where he would buck to glory in the swirl of Life's big game.

Sweet are the dreams of college life, before our faith is nicked—
The world is but a cherry tree that's waiting to be picked;
The world is but an open road—until we find, one day,
How far away the goal posts are that called us to the play.

So, with the sheepskin tucked beneath his arm in football style,
Bill put on steam and dashed into the thickest of the pile;
With eyes ablaze he sprinted where the laureled highway led—
When Bill woke up his scalp hung loose and knots adorned his head.

He tried to run the ends of life, but with rib-crashing toss
A rent collector tackled him and threw him for a loss.
And when he switched his course again and dashed into the line
The massive Guard named Failure did a toddle on his spine.

Bill tried to punt out of the rut, but ere he turned the trick
Right Tackle Competition scuttled through and blocked the kick.
And when he tackled at Success in one long, vicious prod
The fullback Disappointment steered his features in the sod.

Bill was no quitter, so he tried a buck in higher gear,
But Left Guard Envy broke it up and stood him on his ear.
Whereat he aimed a forward pass, but in two vicious bounds
Big Center Greed slipped through a hole and rammed him out of bounds.

But one day, when across the Field of Fame the goal seemed dim,
The wise old coach, Experience, came up and spoke to him.
"Old Boy," he said, "the main point now before you win your bout
Is keep on bucking Failure till you've worn that piker out!

"And, kid, cut out this fancy stuff—go in there, low and hard;
Just keep your eye upon the ball and plug on, yard by yard,
And more than all, when you are thrown or tumbled with a crack,
Don't sit there whining—hustle up and keep on coming back;

"Keep coming back with all you've got, without an alibi,
If Competition trips you up or lands upon your eye,
Until at last above the din you hear this sentence spilled:
'We might as well let this bird through before we all get killed.'

"You'll find the road is long and rough, with soft spots far apart,
Where only those can make the grade who have the Uphill Heart.
And when they stop you with a thud or halt you with a crack,
Let Courage call the signals as you keep on coming back.

"Keep coming back, and though the world may romp across your spine,
Let every game's end find you still upon the battling line;
For when the One Great Scorer comes to mark against your name,
He writes—not that you won or lost—but how you played the Game."[11]

"But *how* you played the game"—the *how* became all important. Winning alone wasn't enough. You had to *earn* victory. You had to sacrifice and work for it. You had to attain a kind of spiritual grace through dedication and effort and then focus this grace on the challenge ahead. Victory became a triumph of character, a triumph of grace over the base and ignoble.

Adding character to the philosophy and emphasizing *how* gives competition different tone. Winning becomes the outward objective sign of the inner triumph of spirit, which is the true victory. And this becomes critical too: The effort to win can be the reward in itself, and a worthy one! In fact, losing properly is preferable to winning cheaply.

These modifications change social competition from the junglelike survival of the fittest to something more gentle. Under the doctrine thus transformed, you can win *or* lose *and* be virtuous.

The appeal of this creed, and it *is* popular, derives from its reward structure. By that we mean "you can have your cake and eat it too," as the saying goes. If you happen to be an objective victor, you can take pride in that fact and reap the concrete and social rewards that go with winning. If you are an objective loser, you still have won. To you go the rewards of having made the effort and marshaled the grace. The process of trying to win

---

[11]Reprinted by permission of G. P. Putnam's Sons from *The Sportlights of 1923* by Grantland Rice. Copyright 1924 by Grantland Rice; renewed © 1952.

can be just as valuable as the winning itself. However naive it may seem, under the competitive ethic of sport there need not be any losers.

Of course everyone recognizes that this isn't always the case. Spiritual victors seldom win college scholarships or go on to sign multimillion dollar professional contracts. That the rewards of objective victory come to overshadow those of spiritual victory surprises no one. Nor does it surprise anyone to find that competition can have some rather disturbing side effects—effects that raise the issue of just how desirable competition is. We now turn to that issue.

Controversy: Is Competition Good?

Social Darwinists liked competition, but modern sociologists usually dislike it. Reflecting this, introductory textbooks criticize competition—if they mention it at all.[12]

Current thinking holds that competition results in too many bad byproducts—such as hostility and violence between competitors—byproducts that occur despite the creedal tenet about being a good loser.[13] Apparently it's easier to say than to do. Writes a much-respected sociologist, George Homans:

> In short, the proposition that loss in competition tends to arouse anger remains true, though its proof is sometimes masked by stronger forces. . . . If both competitors accept the rules of the game and play fair according to the rules, then it is just and right that the [person] who played better should win and the loser's natural hostility will be much diminished. Even so, there is plenty of evidence that it is hard work being a good loser: it goes against the Old Adam.[14]

Sports competition causes other byproducts. A common justification for sport is that it teaches people to compete in American society—an educational benefit that stays with them long after they have completed sports competition. Some sociologists claim that if that is true, then sport teaches something that is largely irrelevant to modern life. According to one commentator: "We live in the most cooperative interdependent society the world has ever known. . . . Whether we like it or not, we are thoroughly and completely dependent upon the goodwill and cooperation of others at every moment of our lives. . . . We are indeed, 'our brothers keepers' as never before in history."[15]

If for the sake of argument you concede that competition is undesirable, would it be possible to get rid of it? Could the institution of sport, and our larger society, exist without it?

---

[12]Garrett Hardin, *Stalking the Wild Taboo* (Los Altos, California: William Kaufmann, Inc., 1973).

[13]Muzafer Sherif and others, *Intergroup Conflict and Cooperation: The Robber's Cave Experiment* (Norman, Oklahoma: The University Book Exchange, 1961); Muzafer Sherif, "Superordinate Goals in the Reduction of Intergroup Conflict," *The American Journal of Sociology*, January 1958, pp. 349–56. See also Howard L. Nixon, II, *The Small Group* (Englewood Cliffs, New Jersey: Prentice-Hall, Inc., 1979), pp. 300–306 for a discussion of the effects of cooperation and competition in a number of settings.

[14]George Homans, *Social Behavior: Its Elementary Forms* (New York: Harcourt Brace Jovanovich, Inc., 1961), pp. 131–32.

[15]Arthur W. Combs, "The Myth of Competition," in *Sport Sociology*, ed. Andrew Yiannakis and others (Dubuque, Iowa: Kendall/Hunt Publishing Company, 1976), pp. 81–92. Italics omitted.

Before trying to answer this question, we ought to recognize that no scientific evidence shows how much competition and cooperation currently exist in American society. We can only speculate and make educated guesses.

Those arguing against competition cite examples of societies that seem to do without competition in sport.[16] A preliterate tribe in New Guinea (the Gahuku) play a field game in which one team starts with one point, the other team with no points. The team with zero takes the offense and when it scores one point the contest ends in a draw. What usually gets overlooked about this sport is the fact that (according to the anthropologist who did the field research) it "invariably degenerated into something closer to hand-to-hand combat than organized competition."[17] The game goes from noncompetitive interaction straight to interpersonal violence. (Competitive sport seems preferable to that.)

The culture of the Zuni Indians prohibited interpersonal competition but encouraged backbiting gossip about one's neighbors. Whether the one follows from the other we cannot say. However, we should not pick out statistically rare events (that is, preliterate cultures without much competition) and hold them up as models for modern American life; at least not without examining them very thoroughly.[18]

We must also consider that pure cases of zero-sum competition only exist in laboratories. In real life, competition requires cooperation. Without your opponent no competition could take place. You must agree to compete. You must agree to show up on time, agree to the rules, and agree to proper deportment. You must agree to make the proper effort to win. Your competitor must be your cooperator too. As a result, alliances, organizations, and friendships form—the associational responses talked about at the beginning of the chapter. In a real sense, competition renders the world more orderly and friendly.

SOCIALIZATION INTO SPORT: FROM NAKED APE TO ATHLETE

The human infant has been called a "naked ape"—at birth a helpless ignorant animal with great potential but a long way to go before realizing it. The process of becoming human, of learning not to be a naked ape, goes under the term *socialization*. More formally, socialization is "the process through which an individual learns to be a member of society . . . [It] is the imposition of social patterns on behavior."[19]

---

[16]For example, George Ritzer, Kenneth C. W. Kammeyer, and Norman R. Yetman, *Sociology: Experiencing a Changing Society*, 2nd ed. (Boston: Allyn & Bacon, Inc., 1982), p. 488.

[17]Kenneth E. Read, *The High Valley*, copyright © 1965 by Kenneth E. Read (New York: Charles Scribner's Sons), p. 19. Reprinted with the permission of Charles Scribner's Sons.

[18]Wilbert Marcellus Leonard, II, *A Sociological Perspective of Sport* (Minneapolis, Minnesota: Burgess Publishing Co., 1980), p. 76. The classic statement on the Zuni is found in Ruth Benedict, *Patterns of Culture* (Boston: Houghton-Mifflin Company, 1934). See David Riesman, Nathan Glazer, and Reuel Denney, *The Lonely Crowd* (Garden City, New York: Anchor Books, 1950), chap. XI, for a classic comparison of Zuni to American culture.

[19]Peter and Brigitte Berger, "Becoming a Member of Society," in *Socialization and the Life Cycle*, ed. Peter J. Rose (New York: St. Martin's Press, 1979), p. 9; Barry D. McPherson, "Socialization into the Role of Sport: A Theory and Causal Model," *The Canadian Review of Sociology and Anthropology*, 13 (May 1976), 165–77.

Socialization takes place both consciously and unconsciously and affects behaviors we think of as learned (such as reading and writing), as well as behaviors we think of as natural. A noted sports sociologist discusses a simple motor task—walking—among the Yemenitic Israelites:

> In their former society in the Yemen, the Jews were the outcasts, and every Yemenite could feel free to hit a Jew . . . the Yemenitic Jew would always run in order to escape this oppression. This way of walking finally became an integrated pattern of their culture. And though the environment in Israel no longer is hostile to [them], the Yemenitic Israelites still carry this pattern with them as part of [their] culture and walk in a shy and hasty way.''[20]

The conscious aspects of socialization are mostly taken care of by the formal agents of socialization—institutions such as family, school, peer group, mass media, and perhaps other agents such as church or sport, depending on circumstances. About the relation between the individual and the institution, a respected sociologist writes: "The sociologist stands on its head the common sense idea that certain institutions arise because there are certain persons around. On the contrary, fierce warriors appear because there are armies to be sent out, pious people because there are churches to be built.''[21] This statement applies to the institution of sport as well as to the church and to the military. Athletes appear because there are games to be won, which stands on its head the idea that sport arises because athletes happen to be around. Society ''produces'' the athletes it ''needs.''

We take it as given in a society as large as the United States (about 225 million) that many more people have the physical potential to achieve success in sport than actually achieve it. Physical attributes alone do not guarantee success or even participation. Somehow people get selected in and out of sport. They learn to like it or dislike it. They learn to succeed or to fail. They are socialized to be athletes, both physically and socially. This process usually begins with children's play.

Socialization and Play: Fun and Games?

George H. Mead, one of sociology's early and major theorists, considered play essential to socialization. When children play doctor or teacher or whatever, they are learning social categories and relationships. In a way, by playing teacher, they learn what teachers do and how students and others respond.

As children grow older, they engage in contests (what Mead called ''games''). He used the analogy of a baseball game:

---

[20]Gunther Luschen, ''The Interdependence of Sport and Culture,'' in *The Cross Cultural Analysis of Sport and Games*, ed. Gunther Luschen (Champaign, Illinois: Stipes Publishing Company, 1972) p. 85. Also see: Richard A. Peterson, ''Revitalizing the Culture Concept,'' in *Annual Review of Sociology, 1979*, ed. Alex Inkeles (Palo Alto, California: Annual Reviews Inc., 1979), 5, 137–66.

[21]Excerpt from *Invitation to Sociology* by Peter L. Berger, p. 110. Copyright © 1963 by Peter L. Berger. Reprinted by permission of Doubleday & Company, Inc.

The game is then an illustration of the situation out of which the organized personality arises. Insofar as the child does take the attitude of the other and allows that attitude of the other to determine the things he is doing with reference to a common end, [the child] is becoming an organized member of society. The child is taking over the morale of the society and is becoming an essential member of it.[22]

Mead further spoke of the "generalized other," by which he meant "the attitude of the whole community." Thus, for example, in the case of such a social group as a ball team, the team is the generalized other insofar as "it enters—as an organized process or social activity—into the experience of any one of the individual members of it."[23] The import of Mead's statements is this: Through interacting with peers in loosely structured situations such as sandlot ball games, children learn to participate in rule-bound situations, to make decisions on their own, to take responsibility for others, and to organize their own activities.

Another vital result is that society is being stamped into the individual's personality or character. The team becomes a standard against which children (and adults) compare their own behavior. The team promotes the attitudes, values, norms, and behaviors—the culture—of the society. Playing games is thus much more important to growing up than the words *"playing"* and *"games"* might imply; for in the process children learn not to be naked apes, but responsible adults.

Screening of Athletic Ability

At the same time this is taking place, children are being informally sorted and identified for their potential in many areas of life. This also occurs as part of play and games. Consider a pick-up game of, say, football, among grammar school children. The group informally selects two children as team captains, probably because they're good athletes. Each captain then takes turn picking their team from the remaining kids. They naturally pick the best kids first, then the second best, then the third best, and so on until the last few kids get picked, more by default than anything else.

Kids know this picking order and what it implies about their athletic ability. It's hardly subtle. And while they cannot verbalize it in sociological terms, their feelings of satisfaction or discouragement are real feelings. And these feelings punish or reward them. No matter how innocent the game might be at the moment, in time the kids selected at the end of the picking order will begin to think of themselves as poor athletes. They come to associate participation with punishment. They soon stop wanting to play. They get selected out of sport before really starting. Just the opposite occurs to the kids picked early. They identify themselves as good athletes. They enjoy playing. It rewards them, and so they play more. They get selected in. This process gets repeated millions of times a

---

[22]George H. Mead, *Mind, Self, and Society* (Chicago: The University of Chicago Press, 1967), pp. 154, 159. Based on Mead's lectures, circa 1927.

[23]Ibid., p. 154.

year throughout the country for dozens of different sports. Probably no single game has an overwhelming effect, but the cumulative impact over the early and impressionable years of childhood does.

Informal screening becomes organized screening when taken over by adult-run bureaucracies: Little League Baseball, Pop Warner Football, Peewee Hockey, Junior Tennis. In some cases, it can become quite intense. As an illustration:

> **A Long Line.** If you're a kid with abundant talent for tennis, have parents who can afford the tuition (over a thousand dollars per month), and can somehow bring yourself to the attention of a good teaching pro, you might, if you're lucky, get admitted to a tennis school. This is a place where you live in a dorm, attend academic classes during the school day, and learn, study, practice, and breathe tennis all the rest of the time.
>
> One of the most successful of these schools is in Florida and is directed by a former paratrooper. He runs his school like the boot camps of yore. According to one account, "if a youngster doesn't heed a directive he makes the kid run on the beach and denies him water." Recalls a successful graduate about his first experiences at the school: "I couldn't believe how he was yelling at me. He wanted me to use the Continental grip. I was eight years old. I couldn't even pronounce Continental."
>
> Those who make the grade at this school have a chance to make the grade as a professional. At the very least, almost all graduates win tennis scholarships to attend college.[24]
>
> The waiting line to get in is very long.

Collecting raw talent and then following up with concentrated socialization isn't unique to sport. Special schools for the intellectually gifted, art academies, computer camps, and even the mundane going-away-to-college, compare in principle to the tennis school just described.

Apparently, as skills and training get set down earlier and earlier, the level of accomplishments will rise higher and higher, faster and faster, stronger and stronger. Gymnast Nadia Comaneci, who was largely raised in a Romanian gymnastic school, achieved her peak and her then-unheard-of perfect scores before puberty. Such prepubescent world champions no longer come as surprises.

Controversy: Playing Versus Sport

Mead would contend that children should play games on their own. Many people, both lay and professional, agree. A major league baseball manager says, "It was so different from my own youth in the late 1940's, when we chose up our game in a corner lot. . . . The only adult who ever witnessed our games was Bill, who worked at the Mobile station across the street. . . . Kids need to be babies as long as possible."[25] Reminiscing can

---

[24]Barry McDermott, "He'll Make Your Child a Champ," *Sports Illustrated*, July 9, 1980, pp. 28, 29.

[25]Billy Martin, quoted in *New York Times*, May 18, 1980, sec. S, p. 3. © 1980 by The New York Times Company. Reprinted by permission.

make childhood more golden than it really was. But even allowing for that, a sociological point lies embedded in such memories. To curtail play is to curtail a major part of the socialization process in favor of what might (but not necessarily will) degenerate into a hypercompetitive contest.

Because of the potential dangers, the physical education profession has refused to support highly competitive, adult-run sports for young children ever since the 1930s. Ironically, this refusal resulted in the very developments the profession wanted to prevent. Without professional support, a void existed and community-parent organizations quickly filled it. Little League and similar groups sprang up. The family and community elected to do what the physical education profession would not.[26]

On one side of the ledger, we must record the fact that excesses do take place in organized children's sport. "Little League elbow" is real: "I pitched that whole Little League series with an elbow that hurt so bad I could hardly stand it. . . . I can't throw a baseball from here to the street now," says a former Little League champion.[27] Injuries such as that have been repeatedly documented in medical literature. Social excesses also take place, such as learning to win at any cost, learning that cheating is bad only if you're caught, or learning that the end justifies the means and that winning is the only thing.[28] In its own way, such teaching can be just as harmful as torn elbows.

On the other side of the ledger, we must record the benefits of children's sport. Commenting on rebuilding the spirit of Cambodian children after the devastating wars in Southeast Asia, a high-ranking YMCA officer claims, "The youngsters who have lived in an environment that taught them to do whatever was necessary to survive—steal, inform on their parents, etc.—what better method of retraining is there than through learning of fair play and teamwork through sport."[29] This is a rather grandiose claim, but its essence, that sport builds character, is a widely held opinion whose roots can be traced to ancient Greece. In the United States, it prevailed during the nineteenth century; and then, as now, it was cited as a major justification for sport.[30]

The character traits that sport supposedly builds are fairness, teamwork, competition, winning, obedience, discipline, religiosity, patriotism, and physical and mental toughness.[31] One popular study, entitled "Sport: If You Want to Build Character Try Something Else," notes the psychological traits of successful athletes:

---

[26]Jack W. Berryman, "The Rise of Highly Organized Sports for Preadolescent Boys," in *Children in Sport: A Contemporary Anthology,* ed. Richard A. Magill, Michael J. Ash, and Frank L. Smoll (Champaign, Illinois: Human Kinetics Publishers, 1978), pp. 3–18. Also: Susan L. Greendorfer and John H. Lewko, "Role of Family Members in Sport Socialization of Children," *Research Quarterly,* 49 (May 1978), 146–52. Several studies have been done on this point. See for example: E. E. Snyder and E. Spreitzer, "Family Influence and Involvement in Sport," *Research Quarterly,* 47 (1976), 804–9.

[27]Quoted in James A. Michener, *Sports in America* (New York: Random House, Inc., 1976), p. 104.

[28]Leonard, *A Sociological Perspective,* pp. 91–97, discusses studies on this point. Also, Jonathan J. Bower, "The Professionalization of Organized Youth Sport: Social Psychological Impacts and Outcomes," *Annals of the Academy of Political and Social Sciences,* 45 (September 1979), 39–58.

[29]Frank C. Kiehne, "How Sports World Can Become Part of Rebuilding the Cambodian Spirit," *New York Times,* April 13, 1980, sec. S, p. 2. © 1980 by The New York Times Company. Reprinted by permission.

[30]Peter Levine, "The Promise of Sport in Antebellum America," *Journal of American Culture,* 2 (Winter 1980), 623–24.

[31]See Harry Edwards, *Sociology of Sport* (Homewood, Illinois: The Dorsey Press, 1973).

> Athletes who survive the high attrition rate associated with sports competition are characterized by . . . great need for achievement . . . [and] realistic goals. . . . [They] are highly organized, orderly, respectful of authority and dominant. . . . [They] have large capacity for trust, great psychological endurance, self control, low-resting levels of anxiety and slightly greater ability to express aggression.[32]

These character traits strike us as exemplary ones. If you described a business executive this way, or an attorney, or even a college professor, you would conclude that they possessed positive character traits, deserved high praise, and were marked for success in their chosen field. The fact that the traits describe athletes should not change that judgment. Contrary to the title of the original article, we feel that *if* sport builds character the kind of character it builds is at least not negative and is probably positive.

We said "if." We equivocate for two reasons. First, the empirical evidence is spotty and the amount of research inadequate to support a definitive conclusion. Second, an equally plausible explanation is that sport does not build character but selects it. Note the phrase "athletes who survive the high attrition." Athletes appear, you recall, because there are games to be won. From sandlot to Little League, to high school, to university and the pros—at each level more selection and more socialization into a certain character mold takes place. Successful athletes are a highly selected group.

Solutions?

Though everyone might agree that problems exist, solutions remain elusive. One noted authority says, "I think that sports programs with poor adult leadership are much more detrimental for youngsters than unstructured play. But organized sports with competent leadership, where winning is kept in perspective, are immensely valuable. Children can benefit from both structured and unstructured play in different ways, and they should have time for both."[33] Hardly disputable. If competent leadership and perspective exist, and if children have both structured and unstructured play, then they will have the best of all possible athletic worlds. But this rather rosebud view is really a goal, not a solution. It neglects the source of the problem: social structure.

Children arrive at the playing field driven by their parents, wearing expensive uniforms, ready to play before an appreciative and demanding audience, because there are games to be won. Our society wants it that way. The community, family, peer group, and broader culture, ultimately lay down what is important and how the game should be

---

[32]Reprinted from "Sport—If You Want to Build Character, Try Something Else" by Bruce Ogilvie and Thomas Tutko, p. 61 in *Psychology Today* magazine, October 1971. Copyright © 1971 Ziff Davis Publishing Co. See also Bruce C. Ogilvie, "Psychological Consistencies Within the Personality of High-Level Competitors," *Journal of the American Medical Association*, 205 (September 9, 1968), 156–62. A good study, but we need to guard against indiscriminately generalizing it to all levels of competitors. More ambiguous results are reported by Jack Schendel, "Psychological Differences Between Athletes and Nonparticipants in Athletics at Three Educational Levels," *Research Quarterly*, 36 (March 1956), 52–67.

[33]Rainer Martens, *Joy and Sadness in Children's Sport* (Champaign, Illinois: Human Kinetics Publishers, 1978), p. 138.

played, not the kids—and in a sense, not the coaches or parents either. They are as much a product of socialization and as much influenced by culture as their kids.

Assuming you feel that problems exist with organized children's sport, these considerations indicate that no solutions, at least no quick easy solutions, are currently in the offing. Making major changes in society usually requires going through a series of steps, each leading to the other. At present, the step we observe is that of "raising consciousness": defining problems, publicizing them, and organizing for action.

As with so many problems, the real solution lies in the structure of society. Once bureaucracies tie in with societal values and start receiving institutional support, the bureaucracies stay. Thus, as sociologists, we anticipate that organized children's sport will be with us for many years—until some powerful social forces change society. At present, these forces do not loom on the social horizon.

SCHOOL AND SPORT: *GEMEINSCHAFT*

We've already noted in Chapter 2 that the American educational system has always supported sport. While definitive cross-cultural data are lacking, we would nonetheless say that the United States ranks high among industrialized societies in the amount of enthusiasm, publicity, and economic importance placed on interscholastic and intercollegiate sport; so high that sport frequently overshadows education.

Sport Glorified

According to research by sociologist James Coleman, the typical high school pays more attention to athletics than to scholastics. He claims that if a Martian were to take a tour of a high school, the Martian would see, for instance, a glass case with trophies commemorating athletic (not scholastic) achievement. The Martian would observe the deference paid to students who wear sweaters with big embroidered letters of the school. And he would note how the administration encourages athletics by dismissing classes early on game day; approving special rallies to whip up school spirit; allowing a section of the school paper to specialize in athletic news; and, it is rumored, "seeing no evil" if outstanding athletes are helped along with their grades. The Martian might well conclude, as Coleman does, that "the school was essentially organized around athletic contests and the scholastic matters were of lesser importance to all involved."[34]

Coleman's data support this conclusion. When asked to rank the elements that make a person popular, students rated "being an athlete" first. Earning high grades ranked fourth, only above having a nice car and coming from the "right" family. When asked to name another boy they wished they were like, male students mentioned athletes far more

---

[34]James S. Coleman, "Athletics in High School," *Annals of the Academy of Political and Social Sciences*, 338 (November 1961), 34. Also, James S. Coleman, *The Adolescent Society* (New York: The Free Press, 1961). D. Stanley Eitzen replicated the portion of this study regarding sport and found essentially the same results. See: "Athletics in the Status System of Male Adolescents," in *Sport Sociology*, ed. Andrew Yiannakis and others, pp. 114–19. There is no reason to believe that the essentials have much changed.

often than scholars. When asked to name boys who belonged to the school's leading crowd, again, athletes received overwhelming mention. "According to all evidence," Coleman concludes, "the status of athletic achievement in the schools surveyed is exceedingly high, considerably higher than that of scholastic achievement."[35]

Controversy: Too Much Sport?

The mixing of sport with formal education has resulted in a sort of oil-and-water mixture. The two institutions never quite blend into each other. The controversy comes down to the basic issue of what school should be. At one extreme, you might contend that school should concentrate on scholastics and nothing else. Or you could broaden that a bit to include vocational training and training for citizenship. Or you could go further and add training in social relationships and physical development, including interscholastic sport. The choice between these alternatives is not easy. Frankly, given the heterogeneity of American culture and lack of centralized education, we doubt if the controversy will ever be resolved to everyone's satisfaction. The balance between sport and education will always be a precarious one.

Another general consideration is this. Recall the visitor from Mars. Had the Martian assumed, not unreasonably, that the manifest or ostensible purpose of the school is to teach scholastics, he might well wonder why scholars do not receive more prestige than athletes. Why the reversal of rewards?

In fact, to answer the Martian's question, the rewards may not really be reversed. What may be reversed is attitude and behavior. Because schools are educational institutions, some people feel, quite properly, that scholastics take precedence over sport. And when they observe sport being disproportionately rewarded, they conclude something is amiss, again, quite properly.

Obviously a discrepancy exists between what people say and what they do; between their attitudes and their behaviors. This discrepancy should not be thought of as hypocrisy, rationalization, or deceit. Ideology always has some unattainable utopian goals. In practice these must be modified. No institution devoted purely, one hundred percent, to education could exist. If it did exist, it would be a grim place—so grim as to be counterproductive to education. Scholastic goals must be incorporated into a broader social environment. Sport is a part of that environment.

The typical educational bureaucracy tends to be lifeless, especially if it must process streams of youths having little motivation and little aptitude for scholastic achievement. Athletics help counter this. Athletics fill the school with a sense of community, of unity, of common purpose, of what sociologists sometimes call *Gemeinschaft*.

For example, one social commentator recalls his high school's pep rally and the school's symbol, the bulldog. He writes,

> From a quiet beginning, the twenty minute ceremony rises in fury; as the band blares its loudest the students screech the symbolic chants. . . . Rousing orations by

---

[35]Coleman, "Athletics," p. 38.

the coach and team captains are followed by tumultuous uproar. This Bulldog, then, is the school. But in a larger sense, the Bulldog is the community. . . . People who have little else in common join together to support the school's sports activities, and thus the system. Political disputes, professional rivalries, unpopular school bonds, and neighborhood animosities melt away as the town folk gather to support their team."[36]

According to Coleman, "the importance of athletic contests in both high schools and colleges lies, at least in part, in the way contests solve a difficult problem for the institution—the problem of generating enthusiasm for and identification with the school and drawing the energies of adolescents into the school. . . . Athletic contests with other schools provide, for these otherwise lifeless institutions, the collective goals they lack."[37] And it is important to note that the greatest accolades go to those few persons who manage to combine athletic and scholarly skills—while it is good to be an athlete, it is even better to be an athlete-scholar, as Table 3.1 shows.

Table 3.1. Average Number of Choices Received by Athletes, Scholars, Athlete-Scholars, and Other Boys in Ten Illinois High Schools

	BE FRIENDS WITH AND BE LIKE	LEADING CROWD	NUMBER OF FRIENDS	TOTAL	POPULAR WITH GIRLS	NUMBER OF CASES
Athlete-scholar	9.9	12.5	7.1	29.5	4.9	(54)
Athlete	4.6	6.6	5.9	17.1	2.5	(218)
Scholar	1.9	3.1	4.4	9.4	0.5	(224)
All other boys	0.4	0.8	2.9	4.1	0.2	(3,598)

SOURCE: Reprinted with permission of Macmillan Publishing Co., Inc., from *The Adolescent Society: The Social Life of the Teenager and Its Impact on Education,* by James S. Coleman. Copyright © 1961 by The Free Press. Table 24, p. 148.

Critics sometimes question the value of Gemeinschaft to education. "What do we need Gemeinschaft for?" they ask. That isn't an easy question to answer. Schools, unlike the military, need not prepare to repulse attacks; nor do students have to pull together so each individual can survive. Critics say we should not fall into the error of believing that Gemeinschaft is necessarily good for all institutions all the time.

Of course this kind of issue cannot be resolved in any absolute sense. It is a matter of values and ideology, not scientific fact. No one denies that sport builds Gemeinschaft. Whether you favor it or not, though, is a matter of personal preference. All things being equal, most people would prefer to interact within a community rather than a lifeless bureaucracy. Assuming you favor Gemeinschaft, you might consider building it through

[36]Christopher D. Geist, "The High School Mascot as Icon," *Journal of American Culture*, Fall 1978, pp. 571–72.

[37]Coleman, "Athletics," p. 41.

more academic means. Suggestions along those lines have been made, and some—giving out scholastic letters and heaping more public recognition on scholars, for example—work tolerably well.

Our reading of the evidence leads us to conclude that, on the average, sport has not hurt education. More than likely, it has helped education. You could undoubtedly find instances where schools have undermined their scholastic goals in order to achieve athletic success, and instances of just the opposite happening. Some schools have outstanding athletic *and* outstanding academic programs, others have neither, and still others have one or the other. But for the most part, athletics provides one thing that is not otherwise easily provided in educational institutions—a sense of togetherness and, occasionally, a sense of well being.

Before leaving this section, we should point out that these conclusions apply to the *institution* of education, to the educational bureaucracy. They do not apply to individual student-athletes. How sport helps or hurts the student participant is an altogether different topic, as is the deviance that sports competition can produce within the school. We must defer these issues for now.

SUMMARY

1. Competition can be viewed as a zero-sum game that produces punishment and frustration to losers and rewards and gratification to winners. It can also lead to mutually beneficial alliances and associations.
2. Culture, in addition to specifying general rules and goals for sport activities, also imparts a unique character to sport. Even though a given sport may be played in different societies, there are usually cultural differences in how it is played.
3. The modern American sports creed has evolved through time. Initially, social Darwinism argued that competition was, or should be, the abiding principle upon which society rested. Through competition, those best suited for certain tasks would rise to the top. The harshness of social Darwinism deterred most people from adopting it. Instead, the character ethic became the dominant sports creed by the 1920s. Many people oppose the sports creed. They feel that the values of winning, obedience, competition, and so forth, are not congruent with American society. On the other hand, research suggests that many athletes have a set of character traits that should stand them in good stead in later life. Whether they developed these traits from sport, had them before they got involved in sport, or got them from some other source, isn't clear.
4. Through the process called socialization, we learn to be members of our society. In regard to sport, socialization begins with loosely structured "sandlot" games. As children grow older, they can participate in organized competition supported by the community, by the family, and later, by the school. At each level of competition those who are the best endowed, physically and socially, pass on to the next level. Whether or not sport should be organized and supervised by adults is a controversial

issue. Many sociologists argue that play is a major way to socialize children. When children get channeled into organized competition, the play is lost. The physical education profession has refrained from supporting highly competitive sports for young children. As a result, community-parent organizations have stepped in. The harm and benefits of such programs are still being debated.

5. Secondary schools, colleges, and universities have long supported athletics because it provides them with a spirit of community. Moreover, by supporting athletics, education has become more closely bound to the dominant society, a good thing for long-run survival.

6. Sports competition thus presents an interesting interplay of contradictory social processes.

4

SOCIAL CLASS
AND SOCIAL MOBILITY
Acquiring Socioeconomic Status through Sport

The Medinah Athletic Club of Chicago, photographed in 1929, was a sports setting for the elite. The conspicuously luxurious surroundings depicted in the photographs of the ballroom and swimming pool denote class exclusivity and separatism. Nowadays, of course, one can swim in an indoor pool without belonging to an exclusive club, but ostentatious surroundings for sport are still with us, despite egalitarian ideals. Photos courtesy of the Library of Congress.

Answer the following questions either yes or no.

> *Section A:* Do you, your friends, or your family frequently play polo? Race sailing yachts? Attend horse shows?
>
> *Section B:* Do you, your friends, or your family frequently play tennis? Play golf? Attend football games?
>
> *Section C:* Do you, your friends, or your family frequently go bowling? Drag race? Attend roller derby matches?

Note your answers and estimate your social class as follows:

> If you answered yes to the questions in Section A and no to the others, then you're *upper class.*
>
> If you answered yes to the questions in Section B and no to the others, then you're *middle class.*
>
> If you answered yes to the questions in Section C and no to the others, then you're *lower class.*

Of course you should not take this scale too seriously because it doesn't meet the methodological canons of constructing social scales. Still it does have a bit of validity, enough to illustrate that sports reflect social class. Not always, but often enough to warrant talking about a relation between class and sport.

We devote an entire chapter to the subject for a simple reason: Class is the backbone of society, the most fundamental of all social structures. It affects everything we think or do—everything from the kind of alcohol we like, to our belief in the existence of the devil or our preferences for different sports.[1] Not only does class determine the routine of everyday life, more than any other structure it determines the distribution of wealth, prestige, and power throughout society. Writes prominent sociologist Gerhard Lenski, "Virtually all the major theorists of social class . . . have sought to answer one basic question: *Who* gets *what* and *why?*"[2]

This chapter is about who gets what and why, how sport affects that, and how that affects sport. Put another way, the subject matter concerns inequality and sport in American life or, put still another way, the relation between social class and sport in the United States.

Before beginning, we offer the following definition of a social class: all those people within a given society or community who have approximately the same amounts of wealth, education, and occupational prestige. In practice, classes aren't as clearcut as this, but the definition should keep us roughly focused on the subject matter of this chapter.[3]

---

[1]See Leonard Broom and Philip Selznick, *Sociology: A Text With Adapted Readings*, 6th ed. (New York: Harper & Row, Publishers, Inc., 1977).

[2]Gerhard E. Lenski, *Power and Privilege: A Theory of Social Stratification* (New York: McGraw-Hill Book Company, 1966), pp. 2–3. Italics added.

[3]Compare with Julius Gould and William L. Kolb, eds., *Dictionary of the Social Sciences* (New York: The Free Press, 1964), p. 648.

If only one class existed, everyone would have the same lifestyle and the same amount of power, wealth, and prestige. Obviously the world is not that way; some groups have more power, wealth, and prestige than others. Inequality is built into society—a sad and ideologically distasteful state of affairs, perhaps, but still an empirical truth that must be taken into account.

SOCIAL STRATIFICATION OF SPORT

American sport became stratified as a result of several influences: the way wealth sorts people, the different lifestyles of different groups, the desire for class exclusivity and status (snobbery), and the internalization of class norms and values. We discuss each of these factors in turn.

Wealth and Sport: Money Counts

Figure skating ranks among the most beautiful of sports, combining coordination, grace, strength, skill, and showmanship. To Olympic champions such as Dorothy Hamill, Peggy Fleming, or Robin Cook, go lucrative ice-show contracts, TV specials, endorsements, and ego gratification.

But becoming an Olympic champion requires more than having lots of coordination and grace; it also requires having lots of money.[4] If you're an aspiring figure skater, you would have an expense account similar to the one shown in Table 4.1.

Table 4.1. Two Extremes: Costs of Figure Skating vs. Basketball

COSTS OF COMPETITIVE FIGURE SKATING FOR ONE YEAR [a]		COSTS OF COMPETITIVE BASKETBALL FOR ONE YEAR	
Coaching	$10,000	Sneakers	$ 30
Special coaching	2,600	Coaching	Self taught and
Ballet lessons	2,600		provided by the school
Ice rental	5,000	Equipment	Provided by the school
Equipment	6,000	Travel	Provided by the school
Travel		Escorts and chaperones	Provided by the school
To and from practice	5,500	Miscellaneous	20
Regional competition	500	Total assumed by family	$ 50
National competition	1,000		
International meet	2,600		
World and Olympic meets	5,400		
Expenses for escorts			
and chaperone	9,000		
Miscellaneous	260		
Less training grant	−3,300		
Total assumed by family	$ 46,900		

[a] SOURCE for figure-skating costs: *The Final Report of the President's Commission on Olympic Sports,* 1975–77, Vol. II (Washington, D.C.: U.S. Government Printing Office, 1977), pp. 87–88. (Skating figures have been adjusted for inflation.)

---

[4]See source note for Table 4.1.

Figure skating represents an extreme case of how much money a sport can require. Basketball represents the opposite extreme. However, even common everyday sports can entail substantial expenses. To illustrate: An hour on a tennis court costs anywhere from nothing on a public court, to twenty-five dollars on a private court; a tennis racket costs from twenty to two-hundred dollars; tennis shorts, shirts, dresses, and shoes cost thirty dollars and up (mostly up); a set of golf clubs sells for a hundred dollars at discount stores, up to eight-hundred dollars at top-of-the line stores; playing a round of golf costs three dollars at public links during the off hours, up to an eight-thousand-dollar initiation fee and fifteen-hundred-dollar annual dues at private clubs;[5] swimming is free at public pools and beaches but swim clubs charge in the neighborhood of fifty to a thousand dollars per year.

Money provides a good explanation for why aspirants from different class backgrounds go into different sports. Money filters them into one sport or another. Basketball (or boxing) costs little, so the children of the inner city go into it. Tennis costs considerably more, so it attracts children living in affluent suburbs. Money counts, clearly.

Conclusion?   Wealth influences who goes into what sport.

If forced to choose just one factor to explain the stratification of sport, wealth would be it. The explanation would be too narrow though.

Characteristics of Sports

Characteristics of the sports themselves might be another factor. Sports that feature teamwork, physical contact, informal training, and low technology appeal to the working class, according to one line of reasoning; while sports featuring more refined skills, less physical contact, and greater technology appeal to the upper class.

A moment's reflection and a look at Table 4.2 reveal some holes in this argument. The chart shows that most of the aforesaid characteristics do not differ very much among upper-class, middle-class, and working-class sports. Team versus individual competition and physical contact are the only characteristics differentiating the classes. But you could argue the point. Polo, about as aristocratic a sport as you can find, involves team competition, whereas auto racing involves individual competition. Both require skill and training. Rugby, an upper-class sport in upper-class British schools, is a rough-and-tumble contact sport, more so than basketball, a sport further down the class ladder.

While we could go on debating the fine points of each sport on the chart, let's not. That would be tedious and we could probably never come to complete agreement. Let's adopt another tactic; let us view the issue in terms of the lifestyle of different classes. As Pierre Bourdieu has written, "class location defines the meaning conferred on sporting activity, the profits expected from it; and not the least of these profits is the social value accruing from the pursuit of certain sports by virtue of the distinctive rarity they derive from their class distribution."[6] This statement is about lifestyles. Let us expand upon it.

---

[5]William N. Wallace, "Fun in the Sun for Less?" *New York Times*, April 19, 1981, sec. F, p. 11.

[6]Pierre Bourdieu, "Sports and Social Class," in *Social Science Information*, trans. Richard Nice (London and Beverly Hills: Sage Publications, Inc., November 1978), p. 835.

Table 4.2. Characteristics Emphasized by Certain Sports and Social Stratification

SPORT	SPEED	AGGRESSION-HITTING	TEAM COMPETITION	FINE SKILL, LONG FORMAL TRAINING	HIGH TECHNOLOGY
Upper Class Sports					
Polo	yes	?	yes	yes	no
Yachting	no	no	no	yes	yes
Equestrian	yes	no	?	yes	no
Middle–Upper Middle Class Sports					
Golf	no	no	no	yes	no
Tennis	yes	no	?	yes	no
Football	yes	yes	yes	no	no
Middle–Working Class Sports					
Basketball	yes	yes	yes	no	no
Baseball	yes	no	yes	no	no
Hockey	yes	yes	yes	no	no
Boxing	yes	yes	no	no	no
Competitive Wrestling	yes	yes	yes	no	no
Working Class Sports					
Commercial Wrestling	?	?	?	?	no
Roller Derby	yes	?	?	?	no
Auto & Motorcycle Racing	yes	no	no	yes	yes

Lifestyles and Sport: Different Worlds

Rigid time schedules bind neither the very rich nor the very poor: the former because their wealth buys them leisure and the latter because they have no jobs to go to. For other people, especially those with an upper-middle-class professional lifestyle, control over their time can be critically important. For them work does not begin at 9 A.M. and end at 5 P.M. Work time blends into recreation and family time. The briefcase full of memos and letters follows them wherever they go. Consequently the need to fit recreation into the open spots on a tight time schedule often determines their choice of recreation.[7]

A businessman playing golf makes his own arrangements. He and his partners agree as to time and place without having to worry about a preestablished, rigid schedule involving other players. "We don't like being tied down every Sunday evening" is the way a married couple, both physicians, explain why they quit a mixed-doubles tennis league.

Other considerations of lifestyle are involved. Aerobic exercises, jogging, and tennis, for instance, confer cardiovascular fitness, and middle and upper classes tend to be

---

[7]Alfred C. Clarke, "The Use of Leisure and Its Relation to Levels of Occupational Prestige," *American Sociological Review*, 21 (June 1956), 301–5.

health conscious. They are also appearance conscious, perhaps following the adage that "you can't be too rich, or too thin." (These factors help explain why 9 percent of the upper class, 45 percent of the middle class, and 52 percent of the lower class, are obese.)[8]

Conclusion?   Class related lifestyles partially determine one's preference for certain sports.

The way sport developed historically—to invoke a broader lifestyle factor—led to the use of sport as a device for attaining exclusivity and status.

Exclusivity and Status: Only the Upper Crust.   You may recall from the chapter on sport and history, that our mostly structural model includes class as one of the variables in the development of the institution of sport. The athletic clubs illustrate this.

During the 1880s many athletic clubs were far from being democratic, egalitarian organizations. Only the upper crust needed to apply.

> **"I have no aspersions to cast."**   During the 1880s the New York Athletic Club set the fashion in luxury clubhouses; the rival Manhattan Club followed suit. A newspaper of the time describes the Manhattan AC's new quarters as a "magnificent and palatial clubhouse . . . which ranks today as the finest athletic clubhouse in the world." The club had a concert hall seating fifteen hundred persons, and an opulent dining room. On the roof was an ice rink which was drained in the summer and converted into a skytop eating pavillion. The club concentrated on elite sports, as suggested by their mock-up of a racing sloop that was intended to teach yachting.
>
> Elite ACs tried to keep people out. They wanted exclusivity. They welcomed only the upper class and only some of them. The clubs charged high initiation fees and dues; they required a college degree to be put on their waiting list, and the wait could be ten years. This was in an age when less than three percent of the population had even a high school diploma.[9] Members of elite ACs frequently belonged to other "waiting-list" clubs. Sixty-four percent of the members of the University AC, and 25 percent of the members of the Manhattan and New York ACs were on other waiting lists.
>
> A member of the Manhattan AC summed up the elitist philosophy: "I have no aspersions to cast on men who work for their living with their hands, but they are not exactly desirable members for a club which wants to establish itself on the plane of social clubdom."[10]

At about the same time that the ACs were going through a period of extreme elitism, country clubs were becoming fashionable. Like the ACs, they tried for exclusivity and status. They sponsored polo, horse racing, live-pigeon shoots, boating, hounds, and

---

[8]Robert G. Burnight and Parker G. Marden, "Social Correlates of Weight in an Aging Population," *The Milbank Memorial Fund Quarterly*, 45 (1967), 75–92.

[9]U.S. Bureau of the Census, *Historical Statistics of the United States, Part 2* (Washington, D.C.: U.S. Government Printing Office, 1975), Series H, 598–601.

[10]J. Willis and R. Wettan, "Social Stratification in New York Athletic Clubs, 1865–1915," *Journal of Sport History*, 3 (Spring 1976), 54.

baseball (not yet "tainted" by the working class), but not golf. Only when the St. Andrews Club of Yonkers, New York, introduced golf and subsequently formed an association with several other clubs, did golf become linked to the country club and thence to the upper class.

The elitism of the athletic and country clubs probably did not surprise Thorstein Veblen, the now-classical social theorist who lived during those times. He considered sport an example of conspicuous consumption, an activity the upper classes engaged in as a demonstration that they could afford to waste money. He wrote,

> Those who are addicted to athletic sports, or who admire them, set up the claim that these afford the best available means of recreation and of "physical culture." And prescriptive usage gives countenance to the claim. The canons of reputable living exclude from the scheme of life of the leisure class all activity that cannot be classed as conspicuous leisure . . . At the same time purposeless physical exertion is tedious and distasteful beyond tolerance. As has been noted in another connection, recourse is in such a case had to some form of activity which shall at least afford a colourable pretence of purposes, even if the object assigned be only a make-believe of purpose.[11]

For Veblen, the real purpose of hitting little balls with sticks or racing ships with obsolete power plants (sails) was to be conspicuously wasteful. In an era when most people worked long hours with little to show for it, conspicuously wasteful activity demonstrated high status.

Over time the extreme elitism of the country club and the AC has broken down, but even today they remain largely upper-middle-class in membership and orientation; and many social scientists still hold views basically similar to Veblen's. They argue that elite sports such as sailing or polo, and, to a lesser degree, upper-middle-class sports such as golf or tennis, help distinguish members of those strata from the hoi polloi—the great mass of working folk. Sport becomes another conspicuous trapping—along with ostentatious cars, deluxe apartments, and chic clothes—that helps mark one's position on the class ladder. Laments one sociologist, "Today, despite egalitarian ideals, class separation persists. We still have exclusively upper-class neighborhoods, clubs, golf courses, resorts and spas."[12]

Conclusion?   Some sports are status symbols denoting class exclusivity.

Class Subculture: Origins.   Roller derby has been cited as the archetype of what some sociologists call a "prole" or working class sport. We analyze it as an example of such and also to illustrate class subculture.

---

[11]Thorstein Veblen, *The Theory of the Leisure Class* (1899, reprint, New York: Penguin Books, 1979), pp. 258–59. Short passages do not do justice to Veblen's iconoclastic (and mordantly humorous) tone. We urge you to read the original text.

[12]Elbert W. Stewart, *Sociology: The Human Science* (New York: McGraw-Hill Book Company, 1981), p. 182.

Roller derby consists of "teams" of skaters who whiz around a track at speeds up to thirty-five miles per hour, blocking, punching, and threatening each other with great bodily harm. (We place quotation marks around the word *team* because, while they supposedly represent different cities, team members don't necessarily come from those cities. Local skaters wear uniforms with "Chicago" stitched across the back, for example. But the same promoter who sponsors "Chicago" also sponsors the opposing team, which is supposedly from another city, but which also consists of local skaters. Note that roller derby is not a sport by our definition.)

The violence is fake, of course, and so is the competition. The scores have hardly any bearing on what the fans come for. But reality isn't important here; the illusion is. According to one analysis, "If the lid were really taken off—if all things were as they seem—players would be routinely killed, or at least severely maimed. But, to the spectators, the authenticity doesn't matter. It is a grand spectacle"[13]—sort of a Roman circus but with fake violence.

Roller derby originated in "prole" subculture.

A popular prole function has always been Saturday night at the roller rink—a place where youths could meet for the exhibition of individual prowess . . . this was the 1940 to 1950 urban prole parallel to the middle class teen phenomenon of "cruising" the main drag. Roller derby is the logical sporting extension and abstraction of these "Saturday Nights," just as stock car racing is the logical sporting extension and abstraction of Appalachian whiskey running. Each is utilizing existing artifacts of prole culture to create spectacle, while at the same time reinforcing audience fantasies.[14]

Many sports grew out of class or occupational subcultures. Yacht racing developed from the wealthy shipowners who occasionally raced their working vessels. Equestrian sports originated in a time when the horse was a common beast of burden, as a hobby of the gentry, who could afford to divert a few horses to sport. The lumberjack sports such as log rolling or tree topping, which are popular in northern rural areas, and the rodeo, which is popular even in New York City, are examples of occupational and class culture spinning off a sport. To our knowledge, no study has inventoried the number of sports that have class-occupation links, but a large number surely exist.

Conclusion.   Some sports are linked to class because they grew out of class subculture.

Identity

The concept of identity has been mentioned before, but it's worth repeating: Culture not only exists outside, in society, it also exists inside our social being. Each of us is the stuff

---

[13]George H. Lewis, "Prole Sport: The Case of Roller Derby," in *Side Saddle on the Golden Calf*, ed. George H. Lewis (Pacific Palisades, California: Goodyear Publishing Co., Inc., 1972), p. 44.

[14]Ibid., p. 45.

of our culture, a partially standardized combination of cultural material. Socialization is the process of learning culture and the end product is identity, how we answer the question, Who are you?

We are constantly interacting with others, and these interactions affect our consciousness. We come to identify, to feel, to believe, and to sense who we are—both as individuals and as members of a specific societal niche such as an ethnic or age group or, in the present case, a class.

The polo player has an upper-class self-concept; the bowler, a working-class one. Reverse the roles—put the bowler on the polo field on a Sunday afternoon and the polo player in a bowling alley on Saturday night—and neither would fit into the unfamiliar social environment. "The physical laborer with strong family ties and a love for bowling may have trouble finding common grounds with a corporate vice-president, divorced, and who fits in a tennis game between working lunches and client dinners."[15]

A much-admired movie, *Breaking Away*, deals with a conflict between identity, lifestyle, and sport. A working-class youth aspires to attend the University of Indiana. He lives in Bloomington (home of the university). His father works as a stoneworker and helped cut and chisel the stones that went into the university's buildings.

An advertisement describes the story this way: "The college kids call them 'cutters.' They were guys who didn't go to college—in a college town. Outsiders in the place they were born. . . . But now the Cutters had a chance to compete in the Little 500 Bike Race. They could prove they really counted—especially to themselves."

(The Little 500 is a real race—an event that started as a cozy, good-time fraternity affair and grew into a nationally televised fund-raising event held in a three-million-dollar stadium before twenty-seven thousand fans. It is an event that brings heaps of glory and prestige to the riders who win and to the club, usually a fraternity, which sponsors the riders.)[16]

At one point in the story, the father says, "and when the buildings went up . . . [the] damnedest thing happened. It . . . it was like the buildings were too good for us. Nobody told us that. But we just felt uncomfortable. Even now. I'd like to be able to stroll through the campus and look at the limestone, but I feel out of place."

But after his son enters the university and wins the Little 500 race, the same father is described this way: "He was riding around the campus on his bike. He took this route almost every day now. He didn't feel out of place, because, after all, his son was a student, and goddammit, he had helped build the place."[17]

Conclusion.   The links between class and sports are part of our identity, and to have a social identity is to have a place in society.

Wealth, class subculture, and identity go together as a single package, an interlock-

---

[15]Steward, *Sociology*, p. 182.

[16]Malcom Moran, "The Little 500 at Indiana Speeds into the Big Time," *New York Times*, April 26, 1981, p. 1.

[17]Quotes are taken from the novelization of the movie: Joseph Howard, based on the screenplay by Steve Tesich, *Breaking Away* (New York: Warner Books, Inc., 1979), pp. 154–91, back cover.

ing set of forces which in total produces and maintains the link between class and sport. The association has endured and will endure for a long time. This makes for an orderly (if not morally just) social world. And as class endures and as sport is linked to the rungs of the class ladder, it seems reasonable to suspect that sport would affect movement up and down the ladder. And so it does—to an extent anyway.

UPWARD MOBILITY VIA SPORT: UPWARD WITH VIGOR

For many people, the influence of sport on upward mobility justifies the institution. That leads to two issues: (1) Does sport in fact produce upward mobility, and (2) How is that related to the rest of society?

The Facts: Some Climb Up

The following illustrates one case of a dream that many aspire to.

> **Success, Duquesne Style.** Duquesne, Pennsylvania (population about 10,000 and declining) has only one main source of employment: the U.S. Steel Mill which has employed virtually everyone in the town at one time or another. Upon graduation from high school, boys expect to work in the mill *unless* they get a football scholarship to college.
>
> High school football is Duquesne's major communitywide passion; and the one major pipeline out of the mills and into the middle class. One mother speaking of her son and of the consequences of being a football star was quoted in *Geo* Magazine: "Kids in Duquesne grow up hungry, you see. They know there's no free ride in life. They either make it in football or go to work in the mill. Parents . . . encourage their sons to play football. A lot of them even keep their boys out of kindergarten an extra year so they'll be more mature."
>
> A young athlete quoted in the same article remarked, "Football's a way out. Without a football scholarship, a college is a little shaky for me. I'd probably have to go work in a mill."[18]

Moving out and up via a football scholarship[19] is "Success, Duquesne Style." It is an athletic version of the rags-to-riches story, the Horatio Alger story of a boy who, through hard work, dedication, moral rectitude, and a small bit of luck, eventually ends up rich, famous, fulfilled, and respected.[20] In the days of Horatio Alger, that meant working your way up from the bottom of a business into management or, even better, it meant becoming a wealthy entrepreneur. Today moving up almost invariably requires passing

---

[18]Story from Pat Jordan, "A Football High," *GEO* magazine, October 1980, pp. 40–64. Used by permission of The Sterling Lord Agency, Inc. Copyright © 1980 by Pat Jordan.

[19]Colleges commonly hold a player back for a year as well, a process called "red shirting." Red shirting has filtered down to high schools and from there to junior highs and grammar schools. Quite apart from the ethics and social consequences for the player, the practice costs taxpayers thousands of dollars to educate players for an extra year. See, "Fattening Them Up for Football," *Time*, March 9, 1981, p. 41.

[20]Bruce E. Coad, "The Alger Hero," in *Heroes of Popular Culture*, eds. Ray B. Browne, Marshall Fishwick, and Michael T. Marsden (Bowling Green, Ohio: Popular Press, 1972), pp. 42–51.

through the higher-education system—getting more education, and thus a better job, and thus more income. (Some athletes shortcut this process—such as boxers who virtually never attend college or baseball players who enter the minors right out of high school.)

Climbing the class ladder can make a real difference. You can go from living in poverty to living in comfort to living in luxury. And sport can help you do that. "Success, Duquesne Style" really happens, as the following research demonstrates.

- Researchers studying 1,200 tenth-grade boys attending high school in southern New York state found that 83 percent of the student-athletes aspired to complete college versus 68 percent of the nonathletes. This effect was particularly strong for boys from working-class backgrounds: Among them, 87 percent of the athletes had college aspirations compared to 65 percent of the nonathletes.[21]

- These researchers also found this same mobility effect when they studied six high schools (three public and three parochial) in Pennsylvania.[22]

- A study of 300 boys from two west-coast high schools found that boys active in sport and other service activities have stronger educational aspirations than those who are not active.[23]

- Among Michigan high-school students contacted first in 1957 and then fifteen years later, athletics increased the participants' aspiration to attend college and to achieve higher occupational and income goals.[24]

- A study of 1,000 UCLA letter winners found that wrestlers, football players, and baseball players tend to come from blue-collar backgrounds; swimmers, tennis players, and rowers, to come from white-collar backgrounds; and that the blue-collar athletes make the greater mobility gains.[25] (All things equal, blue-collar athletes will necessarily climb further than white-collar athletes because they have more room at the top of the ladder. This ought to be borne in mind.)

- Notre Dame football players typically come from lower socioeconomic backgrounds but make slightly greater mobility gains than the student body as a whole, according to a different study. Interestingly, performance on the field makes a difference to later income: "Whereas 41 percent of the first team ball players are now making $50,000 or more," says the report, "this is true of only 30 percent of the second teamers and 13 percent of the reserves."[26]

- Questionnaires sent to NCAA schools showed that 62 percent of all freshmen

[21]Walter E. Schafer and Richard A. Rehberg, "Athletic Participation, College Aspirations and College Encouragement," *Pacific Sociological Review*, 13 (Summer 1970), 182–86.

[22]Richard A. Rehberg and Walter E. Schafer, "Participation in Interscholastic Athletics and College Expectations," *American Journal of Sociology*, 73 (May 1968), 732–40.

[23]William G. Spady, "Lament for the Letterman: The Effect of Peer Structure and Extracurricular Activities on Goals and Achievements," *American Journal of Sociology*, 75 (January 1970), 680–702.

[24]Luther B. Otto and Duane F. Alwin, "Athletics, Aspirations and Attainment," *Sociology of Education*, 50 (April 1977), 102–13.

[25]John W. Loy, Jr., "The Study of Sport and Social Mobility," in *Aspects of Contemporary Sport Psychology*, ed. G.S. Kenyon (Chicago, Illinois: The Athletic Institute, 1969), pp. 112–17.

[26]Allan L. Sack and Robert Theil, "College Football and Social Mobility: A Case Study of Notre Dame Football Players," *Sociology of Education*, 52 (January, 1979), p. 63.

graduated over a five-year period but that letter-winning athletes graduated at an even higher rate than that—77 percent for football, 86 percent for baseball, 82 percent for basketball, 85 percent for track and field, and 83 percent for other sports. Even allowing for exaggeration of rates (the survey might be self-serving), the typical college athlete—who is not a star at a big sport school—does at least as well as the typical student and probably better, in terms of graduating.[27] (Critics often quote graduation rates without stating the rate for nonathletes with comparable class, ethnic, sex, intelligence, and schooling characteristics. Without the comparison rate, they can draw just about any conclusion they want.)

• The study of UCLA athletes mentioned before found that 44 percent of letter winners earned advanced degrees, ranging from 29 percent of football players to 62 percent of gymnasts.[28]

Studies such as these contradict the stereotype that the college athlete is a dumb jock who can play but can't think, a "student" who can't figure out where the classroom is let alone understand what is going on inside.

Undoubtedly some athletes fit the stereotype (so do some nonathletes). But a minority of cases should not be generalized to *all* cases. The dumb jock gets the publicity, but the average players—the wrestlers, milers, shot putters, fencers, gymnasts, swimmers, cross-country runners, and tennis players not destined for lucrative professional contracts—hardly ever get publicized. No stereotype of the "smart jock" forms around them.

The mass media has a strong effect here. Stars receive the most publicity, and they do not do as well academically as the typical student. For example, only a minority of All-American football players earn degrees (about 25 percent). The best basketball players frequently put their names up for the professional draft before graduating (as "hardship cases"), and every season brings speculations about star players "going hardship" for a multimillion-dollar contract.

The relatively poor academic performance of stars makes sense in a way. They have a realistic (though not particularly good) chance of becoming a professional player—a career in which a degree has little immediate use. As the athletic director of a Big Ten school says, "You can't wave your diploma on the 50 yard line."[29] And really, how many people can honestly say they would forego a million dollars now so they could study for another year or two and earn a baccalaureate degree? Not many. (A little later we discuss what happens after the career ends or fails.)

Conclusion.   Sport produces upward mobility.

---

[27]Fred Rothenberg, "College Athletes No Longer 'Dumb Jocks,' " *Columbus Dispatch*, December 6, 1977, sec. D, p. 1; Peter Alfano, "The Tug-of-War between Athletics and Academics," *New York Times*, March 27, 1983, sec. Y, pp. 23 and 27.

[28]Loy, "The Study of Sport," Table 5.

[29]"Single Hired to Improve Northwestern Athletics," *Columbus Citizen-Journal*, December 17, 1980, p. 16.

Even sociologists critical of sport agree with that conclusion. According to two eminent researchers, "The data . . . show *conclusively* that high school athletes, when compared to nonathletes of the same social class and IQ range, have a greater likelihood of graduating from college and making more money. *Clearing superior athletes when compared to nonathletes are and will be more upwardly mobile.*"[30]

How Sport Increases Upward Mobility

For historical reasons (recall Chapter 2), much of American sport became part of the educational system—an arrangement that evolved into a permanent link and that now produces upward mobility. Had it been otherwise—say, had sport become part of the manufacturing industry and had athletes been required to maintain their status as factory workers rather than as college students—sport would not be related to upward mobility at all.

As sociologists we emphasize the link to education. The link constitutes a social structure and as long as the link remains, some upward mobility via sport will take place over the long run. That is so because higher education has become a prerequisite to the hundreds of thousands of white-collar, technical, and professional jobs created by the expansion of the economy and the explosion of technology. Student athletes find themselves linked to a system that produces middle-class people by the thousands. With that linkage, probability alone guarantees that some athletes will make it to the middle class.

Cultural values reinforce the influence of the link between sport and education. Critics often poke fun at the Protestant ethic, and its twin, the sports creed. Nevertheless the creeds portend success in American capitalistic-bureaucratic society. The willingness to work hard, to practice, to sacrifice individual ego for the good of the team, to "endure beyond endurance"—these traits fit the attitudinal requirements for success in business and in bureaucracy. Many years ago a famous sciologist, David Reisman, stated, "What matters about the individual in today's economy is less his or her capacity to produce than to be a member of a team."[31] Recently he stated much the same thing: "The path to the boardroom leads through the locker room."[32]

And the walls of the locker room have Protestant-ethic and sports-creed slogans pasted all over them: "There's no I in TEAM," "When the going gets tough, the tough get going," "It's the last rep that counts," "No pain, no gain." Athletes couldn't avoid being exposed to these values if they tried. And once exposed, athletes might be influenced by them.[33]

The school system itself intensifies the influence of the broader culture in its support

---

[30]Stanley Eitzen and George H. Sage, *Sociology of American Sport* (Dubuque, Iowa: William C. Brown Co., Publishers, 1978), p. 221. Italics added.

[31]David Reisman, *Individualism Reconsidered and Other Essays* (Glencoe, Illinois: The Free Press, 1954), p. 261.

[32]David Reisman, quoted in John Underwood, *Sports Illustrated*, February 23, 1981, pp. 66, 67.

[33]See Eldon E. Snyder, "Athletic Dressing Room Slogans as Folklore: A Means of Socialization," *International Review of Sport Sociology*, 7 (1972), 89–102.

of athletics. It does this by sponsoring athletics as an extracurricular educational activity, by holding it up as a worthy value, and by offering extra rewards, help, and encouragement to participants. According to one study, high-school teachers encourage athletes to attend college more than they encourage nonathletes.[34] The educational system also spurs athletes along. They must maintain minimum grade-point averages and make reasonable progress toward graduation. Without the spur, who knows what the grades of some players would be, or how many would ever graduate?

The spur is even sharper at the college level where athletes receive encouragements and rewards. Some are tangible, such as scholarships and meals, and some intangible, such as tutoring, special counselling from the "brain coach," study halls, advice on the "easy" courses, and who knows how much covert help. Athletes also receive alumni favors, and perhaps the most valuable benefit of all in the long run, social contacts with influential community leaders and businessmen. Upon graduation, athletes may start with one foot in the door.

Given so much help and encouragement, student-athletes *ought* to do fairly well; and they do—as the studies just cited show.

Conclusion.   For several good sociological reasons, sport promotes upward mobility.

But now we encounter an odd situation. We cannot dispute that success, Duquesne style, happens, but neither can we dispute that it does not happen very often. Only a very small amount of upward mobility can be traced to the influence of sport.

Amount of Upward Mobility

Going from humble origins to superstar to popular culture hero, as did O.J. Simpson, happens so rarely it's not worth considering as a realistic goal. Aspiring to be an average professional player would be more realistic—but not by very much. Only about one hundred football players and sixty basketball players make the professional teams each year. In all of professional sport, only some three thousand playing slots exist. There are not many jobs for professional athletes. (This fact should not be taken out of context, though. How many jobs exist for movie stars? Concert musicians? Theoretical mathematicians?)

For a gambler, picking a freshman football player in high school and betting he will win a college scholarship, graduate from college, and get a middle-class job, would be a poor bet indeed, not just in Duquesne but throughout the nation. Only about 7 percent of the over half-million high-school football players go on to play in college, and only about half of them receive financial aid. (Of course, the percentage varies. At big-time football schools over 90 percent receive some aid).

Nor would the odds increase if the gambler picked a basketball or baseball player. Approximately 3 percent of all high-school basketball players play in college, with about

---

[34]Schafer and Rehberg, "Athletic Participation."

half getting financial assistance; while about 6 percent of high-school baseball players play in college (but the best ones usually try to turn professional right after high school).[35]

Directly or indirectly, sport helps support only a tiny fraction of the approximately seven million students attending colleges and universities.[36]

Conclusion.   Sport produces only a tiny amount of upward mobility.

Conclusions do not exist in isolation and this one should be interpreted in the context of upward mobility in general. Even though the United States isn't a caste system (which has no mobility whatsoever), the chances of moving up are not really very good. If you start at the bottom rungs of the class ladder, your chances of making it to the upper rung would be about zero percent; and the chances for climbing from the bottom to the middle rungs would be approximately one percent.[37] (Several methods for measuring mobility can be used. However, no matter how measured, the probability of moving from the bottom to the top, or to the middle, is not very high.)

Considered in this light, the tiny amount of mobility due to sport does not appear so out of line. No institution in American society produces very much upward mobility, not even education. (The overwhelming majority of college students come from middle-class or upper-class backgrounds to begin with.)

All of which now brings us to a puzzling state of affairs: Why does so much hullabaloo get kicked up over so little upward mobility? Why do so many magazines and newspapers publish so many articles like the one we quoted about "success, Duquesne style?" Why do so many movies, TV programs, and books tell and retell the sports version of the Horatio Alger story? We suspect the hullabaloo has very little to do with the amount of mobility itself; rather, it concerns something much broader.

THE EFFECT ON SOCIETY: VALIDATING DREAMS

Over seventy years ago, French social theorist Emile Durkheim wrote an intriguing sentence: "There can be no society which does not feel the need of upholding and reaffirming at regular intervals the collective sentiments and collective ideas which make its unity and its personality."[38] In this sentence Durkheim summarizes the germinal idea of a theory which helps explain the hullabaloo surrounding upward mobility via sport.

---

[35]Harold Blitz, "The Drive to Win: Careers in Professional Sports," *Occupational Outlook Quarterly*, 17 (Summer, 1973), 3–16. These figures are rather old, but there is no reason to believe that major changes have occurred in the percentages.

[36]Estimated from U.S. Bureau of the Census, *Statistical Abstracts of the United States: 1971* (Washington, D.C.: U.S. Government Printing Office, 1971), Table 151.

[37]The classic empirical study is Peter M. Blau and Otis Dudely Duncan, *The American Occupational Structure* (New York: John Wiley & Sons, Inc., 1967). All figures are from their Table 2.3, "Mobility From Fathers' Occupation to First Job for Males 25 to 64 Years Old."

[38]Emile Durkheim, *The Elementary Forms of the Religious Life*, trans. Joseph Ward Swain (1915; reprint, New York: The Free Press, 1965), p. 475.

Durkheim asked why social order prevails. Why not chaos? His answer was that everyone agrees on the fundamental beliefs, creeds, and ideologies of their culture; that a cultural consensus exists and must be maintained. He further said that to get consensus, major values must be embedded in a society's structure and from time to time brought forth and reaffirmed.

In the United States, the institution of sport represents, in almost pure form, the dominant values of American culture. A contemporary sociologist remarks about the link between society and sport:

> Culture patterns must, of course, not only be learned but continually renewed and reaffirmed. . . . It seems to be universally the case that play, and often sport accompany ceremony in such forms as dancing, feasting and other modes of expressive behavior. Recall the festivals of Colonial times and the hoopla of today's big game . . . Many have noted that highly competitive sports, whatever their cost to those who fail, are especially important in a culture emphasizing success goals.[39]

If sport mirrors society (and we argue that it does), then the same values found in the one should be found in the other. And they are. Concerning dominant societal values, a prominent monograph states:

> Most Americans say they believe in equality. . . . But most believe that some people are more competent than others and that this will always be so, no matter how much we reform society. Many also believe that competence should be rewarded by success, while incompetence should be punished by failure. . . .
>   But while most Americans accept inequality in virtually every sphere of day-to-day life, they still believe in what they often call "equal opportunity."[40]

You might not have heard the American way stated quite as baldly as that, but you've surely heard versions of it before—in sport. Incompetent players get punished; they get cut. First stringers receive more rewards than second stringers, second stringers more than third stringers. That's the way it is and must be—for the good of the team. We accept it. We only stipulate that some semblance of "equal opportunity" be maintained so that all who aspire get some "fair" chance at it.

Mobility via sport is thus a subdream of the American dream which is a subpart of a broader value system, the American way. And the athlete-hero then becomes real, live evidence that those value systems remain viable and that dreams do come true. Sport validates our society. So do sports heroes. Says a sociologist:

> To reinforce people in social roles—encourage them to play those which are highly valued—and to maintain the image of the group super self are presumably the

---

[39]Erwin O. Smigel, *Work and Leisure: A Contemporary Social Problem* (New Haven, Connecticut: College and University Press, 1963), p. 45.

[40]Christopher Jencks, *Inequality: A Reassessment of the Effect of Family and Schooling in America* (New York: Basic Books, Inc., Publishers, 1972), p. 3.

classic functions of heroes in all societies. . . . A society says, "be like that" and builds educational discipline and shrines around it.[41]

"Be like that"—like all those athletes who strove and worked and succeeded in climbing the class ladder. Be like the basketball player (whose identity isn't important for sociological purposes because a story like his gets repeated yearly) who has prodigious talent. He becomes an all-American and receives a million-dollar contract to play professionally. He leaves behind him the world of the ghetto, a world in which two of his brothers are heroin addicts, one is a pimp, another chief of the Vice Lords; and he says "I know I'm a role model for a lot of people back in the ghetto. Not too many of us get the chance to get out, to go to college."[42]

Conclusion.   The tiny amount of sports mobility validates the values of American culture.

The following photo essay by Mary Howard describes the setting for many a young athlete's struggle for recognition and upward mobility through sport—in this case, boxing.

GLEASON'S by Mary Howard

Each year thousands of young men, some looking for a little income, others for fame and fortune, and still others for something to do between jobs, apply to their State's Athletic Commissioner for a license to box professionally. A small percentage return the following year to renew their licenses. And each year some suffer serious injury in this most gruelling of contests. Those who "make it" take four to five years to develop their potential. And in another ten years, the careers of even the more successful will be at an end.

Bobby Gleason's on 30th Street and 8th Avenue is a world famous training gym in New York City, the place where most young hopefuls come to be instructed in the craft and where the stars tune-up while preparing for the main event in Madison Square Garden.

The neighborhood around Gleason's abounds with the decay of yesterday's flourishing fur businesses; a luncheonette serves greasy food on worn-grey counters; belligerent itinerants lounge around a newsstand drinking their cheap liquor from pints wrapped in paper bags; a tumble down hotel advertizes day rates; a welfare office next door to Gleason's witnesses the daily stream of the unfortunate, unforgettable underclass alternately angry and apathetic. Derelicts sleep on the

---

[41]Orrin E. Klapp, *Collective Search for Identity* (New York: Holt, Rinehart & Winston, Inc., 1969), p. 219; Susan Birrell, "Sport as Ritual: Interpretations from Durkheim to Goffman," *Social Forces*, 60 (December 1981), 354–76.

[42]Ira Berkow, "Isiah's Odyssey: Perils of a Slum to the New Life," *New York Times* Service, reprinted in *Columbus Citizen-Journal*, April 28, 1981, p. 13.

Each year thousands of young men apply to their State's Athletic Commissioner for a license to box professionally, but only a small percentage of these return the following year to renew their licenses. Photos and text by Mary Howard, Copyright © 1981 by Howard Media Productions, Inc. Reproduced with permission.

sidewalk. One notorious fellow propped against the building drinking from his paper sack, drools obscenities at anxious passers-by.

Into this setting each day come young men, themselves from the underclass making their way into the rundown warehouse-like building that is Gleason's. Peeling paint, stuffy from too many bodies and too little ventilation, gloomy because little natural light filters through a dirty front window that has been painted over up to eye-level, with the sour smell of sweaty bodies and soiled clothes, the atmosphere is intense as each man measures himself against yesterday's performance and prepares for tomorrow's improvements.

In the shadow of Madison Square Garden the "would-bes" and the "has-beens," now spectators, vicariously reliving their youth, gather each day to play out a rigorously prescribed ritual. The frenetic rhythm of the speed bag counterpointed by the steady staccato of the jump rope and dull thud of the heavy bag is punctuated at three minute intervals by the ring bell. Under the tutelage of parttime managers and trainers the fighters hone their skills for competition. The regimen consumes three hours daily and requires a carefully controlled diet.

During this long apprenticeship the fighter receives minimal pay. The inexperienced fighter participates in four-round matches which may pay $75; and $200 or so for six rounds. Those fighters who show promise go on the road traveling city to city in order to get enough fights to build experience. Many, of course, never make it this far. Sooner or later these young fighters have to find a second job in addition to boxing to support themselves.

Fighters with a future are "sold" by their parttime handlers to businessmen who hire fulltime handlers and pay expenses in return for a healthy share of each purse. At this point the fighter begins to be sought after by men who enjoy being part of the "scene" and will reciprocate by making gifts of clothes, automobiles and women. For those who don't make it this far, a free drink at their local tavern may substitute.[43]

ISSUES AND SOME ANSWERS

Occasionally an athlete comes heartbreakingly close to success, Duquesne style; then fails. This happened to a basketball player from a small midwestern town.

"Not what I had in mind."   "He [Allan] was once a star. He set a national high-school record that still stands. He had dreams of playing in the Olympics and in the NBA." He was an outstanding college player, captain of his team.

He wasn't much of a college student, though. "I never cared for school," he admits, ". . . I just wanted to play ball. I was usually ineligible by the time the end of the quarter came. I usually had to go to summer school."

Allan left college during his senior year right after the team banquet. He recalls that as he was loading his car, "someone said, 'where are you going, you got half a quarter to go?' "

"I said, 'not me. I'm going to play ball.' "

---

[43]Photographs and text by Mary Howard, copyright © 1981 by Howard Media Productions, Inc. Reproduced with permission.

A professional team drafted Allan, but cut him just before the final deadline. The following year another team gave him a try out but he was cut again. He then got a clerical job in a state agency but was not happy working there. So he returned to his hometown and went to work in the coal mines, where he works today.

He now says, "My idea of making a lot of money was not an afternoon shift with the only thing to look forward to being a two-week vacation."

"It's not what I had in mind and I know a lot of people didn't have this in mind for me. . . . My parents, my relatives and my friends . . . used to tell me I was a sure shot. They were surprised when I didn't make it. I was too. I would have liked to. But you have to face it. I didn't."[44]

Moral imperatives, "oughts," get mixed into discussions of mobility via sport and we describe Allan's case to illustrate them. As we see it, there are four basic issues.

Issue: Mobility through sport is a myth. This myth should be deflated; young people should not be encouraged to aspire to success via sport.

Clearly the premise is true. Sport produces only a tiny amount of upward mobility. But what ought to follow from that premise is not so clear. Myths—the myth of the American dream, the myth of Horatio Alger, the myth of success, Duquesne style—by their nature cruelly deceive. They contain just enough truth to inspire the young and to promote cultural consensus. Social scientists realize this, yet to say "that's the way society works" does not mean "that's the way it *ought* to be."

How should it be? What might substitute for the myth? A mythless culture would be devoid of much meaning and inspiration; hollow in many ways. Perhaps a stronger emphasis on more realistic goals would be a solution. Encourage all athletes to back up their athletic aspirations with aspirations of being good accountants, engineers, computer programmers, managers, and other such careers. Emphasize and reemphasize that "if you make it professionally great! But be prepared not to!"

Issue: Athletes receive an inferior education.

If graduation rates indicate educational quality, then the facts do not bear this out. Athletes graduate at a similar or higher rate than nonathletes, cases such as Allan's notwithstanding.

The quality or toughness of the courses, however, muddies up the issue. Athletes often load their class schedules with easy "gut" courses; and if you assume easy equals inferior, then athletes receive an inferior education. Of course, so do lots of other students. Not everyone in a gut course is a "dumb jock" looking for an easy B.

Moreover if all the facts were known, the charge might not hold up empirically. A small study of former professional football players shows that about half the sample felt

---

[44]Jack Torrey, "What Happens When the Games End," *Columbus Citizen-Journal*, March 19, 1979, pp. 15, 18. Copyright © 1979. Used with permission.

they earned a "usable" college degree.[45] A valuable piece of future research would show to what extent this finding applies to athletes and nonathletes alike.

The charge also indicts the educational system as much as it indicts sport. Gut courses appear on the curriculum because curriculum committees permit it. The academic side of the college bears the responsibility for maintaining academic standards, and ultimately academic standards must change before the problem will be corrected.

Issue: Many athletes do not have the academic skills and motivation necessary for success in college.

Allan's case shows a white-collar career lost for lack of academic motivation. But again, graduation rates do not bear this out. And again, athletes are not alone. Many students do not possess college-level skills in basic subjects. Many students lack academic motivation. Many students get recruited for their special talents: skill with a musical instrument, skill with a baton, talent for acting, dancing, or drawing. Sometimes schools want students with these talents and sometimes the talents bear only a marginal relation to what we usually think of as "hard academics."

Issue: Athletes cannot be good students because they have to spend so much time practicing, playing, and traveling.

If that is true, it's unfortunate—but it applies to many other students besides athletes. Students have responsibilities: working, rearing children, serving the community, playing in the orchestra, marching in the band, performing in plays, and, lest we forget, partying and drinking beer. In all honesty, life could be harder than being a student-athlete and we fail to see why they, out of the many diversified types of students on a campus, deserve extraspecial consideration, especially when you realize how much extra help they already get.

Our overall conclusion is a sociological one. If you want to indict social class and the relation of class to sport and sports mobility, then ultimately the systems involved in these processes must be indicted: the links between school and sport, between class and subculture, between subculture and identity, between the values of society and the values of sport. Changing any one link in the system would be a hard task. Changing the entire system would be immensely harder. It might be done.

---

[45]William Lide, "Forced Retirement Among Professional Football Players With Short Termed Careers" (unpublished Ph.D. dissertation, School of Health, Physical Education, and Recreation, The Ohio State University, 1981), Tables 18, 20.

SUMMARY

1. Social class is one of the most fundamental structures of any society. The question of class is a question of who gets what and why?

2. Over time, sport has become related to class for a number of reasons, including wealth, class lifestyles, class exclusivity and status, and the psychological mechanisms of identity.

   a. Money is one of the most important determinants of class. And money determines the sports that different classes participate in. Obviously only the rich can afford such sports as yachting or polo. Even below that level many sports require a substantial amount of money. For that reason, ice skating, golf, tennis, and many other activities are generally the sports of the upper-middle class. In contrast, lower-income groupings frequently engage in lower-cost sports.

   b. The characteristics of the sports themselves, (speed, aggression, team versus individual competition, emphasis on technology), do not make one sport upper, middle, or lower class. The history of how a sport derives from class-related subcultures and occupations explains that much better. Certain sports developed as upper-class because the upper classes monopolized them as marks of exclusivity and prestige, while other sports developed out of occupational subcultures.

   c. Lastly, through the process of internalizing values (identity), our subcultural lifestyle becomes part of our being. We come to feel "out of place" when we encounter the sports activities of a different lifestyle.

3. Upward mobility through sport has long been a part of American subcultural values. Many research studies show that sport does, in fact, promote higher educational aspirations among high-school participants, and that more college athletes graduate than do nonathletes. This does not apply to star college athletes, many of whom leave college early to go into professional sports.

4. Sport produces upward mobility mainly because so much of sport is linked to the educational system, starting as early as grammar school and continuing through the university level.

5. Sport also exemplifies American values, and, to some degree at least, athletes may pick up these values through sport participation and use them for later success.

6. Particularly at the college level, athletes have the opportunity to make influential friends and establish contacts that will help them after graduation.

7. Even though sport does in fact promote upward mobility, it affects only a small minority. This raises the question of why so much attention is directed at the issue of upward mobility. We suggest that it is because sport helps confirm the values of society, and that one of the main values of American society is the dream of upward mobility. Sport emphasizes that possibility, and the few athletes who do succeed thus "prove" that anyone can do it.

8. We suggest that there are four issues involved:

   a. Sport mobility is a myth and a myth that should be deflated.

   b. Athletes receive an inferior education.

c. Athletes do not have academic skills necessary for success in higher education.

d. Athletes cannot be good students because sport demands so much of their time.

9. Overall we suggest that most of these assertions are at best only partially true, or they mistakenly focus on athletes while forgetting that nonathlete-students face similar problems. Thus the issue is not one of athletics per se, but of the educational system.

5 BLACKS IN SPORT, PART I
A Social History

Arthur Ashe's career in professional tennis represents the progress that black Americans have made in widening their participation in American sport and society. Country club sports have remained among the toughest for blacks to enter, but more and more, blacks are beginning to make their presence felt in the areas of tennis, golf, swimming, and gymnastics. Ashe, however, is realistic in his advice to black American children who dream of a career in professional sports: He advises them to learn a trade with a greater chance of success. Photo by Doug Martin.

During the 1976 Olympic Games, a seven-year-old boy and his father watched the American boxing team win medal after medal. The little boy suddenly asked, "Dad, why do the black guys always win?" His dad said, "I don't know. I guess they're very good."[1]

That little boy noticed what millions of fans can't help but notice: There are lots of black athletes on television. Being little, he could ask what many fans might hesitate to ask for fear of being thought prejudiced, but which must have crossed their minds—has sport developed into an Afro-American domain? Not too long ago, *Time* magazine called this development the "black dominance."[2]

This chapter and the following are concerned with black dominance in sport. We explore sociological-historical forces behind Afro-American participation in sport, offer a sociological assessment of the current situation, and speculate about the future. We have organized the sociological-historical section around the lives of several Afro-American athletes—some famous, some not—selected to make certain sociological points.

Before getting into this chapter, we want to define the main concepts. We use the word *race* almost as a synonym for ethnic group: a group with a unique subculture or a distinctive set of customs, values, argot, language, and history—a group which in-marries more than out-marries. (We note that our definition differs from biological definitions which emphasize the genetic transmission of distinctive physiological traits, such as skin color or eye shape. We also note that the term *race* could be dropped from the discourse altogether, but we maintain it because it has been used for so long in sociology.)

The term *ethnic group* usually implies a group which is also a *minority*. The lack of power and socioeconomic standing makes a group a minority, not its distinctive subculture, nor its size in relation to the total population.

Unless otherwise mentioned, we will use "ethnic group," "race," and "minority" interchangeably. Each term has its own history of usage, each is well accepted in some circles of sociology, and each applies to the group we will be discussing.

EARLY HISTORY

Lost History. American blacks justifiably complain that much of their history has been lost, either by not being recorded, or by being distorted by the conscious and unconscious prejudice of the mostly white recorders. Thus the name "Tom Molineaux" (sometimes spelled Molyneux) hardly pops to most people's minds when thinking about famous black athletes. In fact, he was the most famous black athlete of his day and probably the first black sports hero in America.

There is some confusion about his identity. He may have started life as a Virginia slave, or he may have been the son or grandson of a slave named Tom Molineaux (who was a slave before the Revolutionary War). Possibly Molineaux (the one we're interested in here) had a twin brother who boxed under the same name; hence the confusion over which Tom Molineaux fought which other boxers, and when.

---

[1]Personal communication from a colleague.

[2]Cover of *Time*, May 9, 1977. Copyright 1977 Time Inc. All rights reserved. Reprinted by permission from *Time*.

Attempting to cash in on Molineaux's fame, many black boxers of his time used his name: "Young Molineaux," "Molineaux, the Mooracan Prince," "Molineaux, the Black Moor," and "The Original Molineaux." This confuses the historical record even more.

But whatever the facts of his background, a free Molineaux traveled to England in 1810 to fight Tom Cribb, the English Champion. (At the time, the English champion was considered to be world champion.)

The fight took place outdoors in a drizzling cold rain before an unruly crowd of twenty thousand spectators. Like so many fights of the period, it was filled with confusion, cheating, and biased officiating.

Molineaux knocked out Cribb in the twenty-third round, but Cribb's handlers immediately accused Molineaux of hiding lead weights in his fists. A raucous argument ensued and ended up with both sides screaming at each other amid the shouting and swaying of the crowd. While this was taking place, Cribb regained consciousness and the officials ruled that the fight should continue. In the twenty-ninth round Cribb landed a decisive blow above Molineaux's right eye. By the fortieth round, the battered and exhausted Molineaux quit. The next year the pair fought a rematch, and Cribb won handily.

Tom Molineaux retired soon thereafter, apparently to Ireland, where he died in 1818.[3]

Reconstruction and Jim Crow

Slavery obviously prevented the free participation of blacks in sport, but after the Civil War the situation changed. In those days blacks rode in most major horse races and for a time, twenty to thirty blacks comprised the elite cadre of jockeys. A black rode in the first Kentucky Derby in 1876. In 1888 Pike Barns, a black, won the running of the Futurity, and Willey Simms, another black jockey, won the Belmont Stakes and the Kentucky Derby.[4] Blacks also played organized baseball. In 1884 Moses Fleetwood Walker, an Ohio native and student at Oberlin College, became the first black to play in the major leagues (not Jackie Robinson).[5]

In college athletics, blacks played mostly for all-black schools, but both William Jackson and William Lewis played for Amherst in 1889, and Lewis later played for Harvard. Walter Camp, the "Father of American Football," named Lewis to the all-American teams of 1892 and 1893. (Soon thereafter blacks would be automatically excluded from being all-Americans.)[6]

---

[3]Information on Molineaux is difficult to find. We relied on Wells Twombly, *200 Years of Sport in America: A Pageant of a Nation at Play* (New York: McGraw-Hill Book Company, 1976). Other sources give somewhat different accounts and details. See Frank G. Menke, *Encyclopedia of Sports* (Cranbury, New Jersey: A.S. Barnes & Co., Inc., 1969), p. 242; Pierce Egan, *Boxiana: or Sketches of Ancient & Modern Pugilism*, (London: George Virtue, 1829), I, 360–71.

[4]John P. Davis, "The Negro in American Sports," in *The American Negro Reference Book*, ed. John P. Davis (Englewood Cliffs, New Jersey: Prentice-Hall, Inc. 1966), pp. 775–825.

[5]Robert Peterson, *Only the Ball Was White* (Englewood Cliffs, New Jersey: Prentice-Hall, Inc., 1970).

[6]John P. Davis, "The Negro in American Sports," p. 775.

Integration and Prejudice

For a short time American sport was somewhat integrated, but that did not last. Race prejudice ran high throughout the period after the Civil War. An 1888 news story quotes a white baseball player:

> While I myself am prejudiced against playing on a team with colored players, I still could not help pitying some of the poor black fellows that play in the International League. Fowler used to play second base with the lower part of his legs encased in wooden guards. He knew that every player that came down to second base on a steal would head in for him and would, if possible, throw the spikes into him . . . About half the pitchers try their best to hit these colored players when at bat.[7]

Despite their number and long history of participation, black fighters had difficulty getting good fights with white boxers. And the heavyweight championship remained completely closed to blacks.

"I don't defend against niggers," said world boxing champion John L. Sullivan to explain why he would not fight Peter Jackson, a black contender from the West Indies.[8] In 1892 when Sullivan lost the championship to James Corbett, a white American, Sullivan said, "The championship stays where it belongs, in America, and I remain yours truly, John L. Sullivan, *American.*"[9]

Racism

John L. Sullivan's remarks illustrate a sociological point. The person who wouldn't "defend against niggers" was the same person who sincerely prided himself on being an American; like most people of the time he saw no contradiction between the two. A racist America will produce racist Americans.

During this historical epoch American society was settling back from the aftermath of the Civil War. As the federal government pulled out of the South, institutionalized racism came out into the open again. Jim Crow—the name given to that collection of legal and customary restraints on interracial contacts—emerged. The South made no effort to hide Jim Crow; "white only" and "colored only" signs were everywhere. In other parts of the country Jim Crow took a different form but was just as real.

According to one well-received monograph on the Jim Crow movement:

> Much ingenuity and effort went into the separation of the races in their amusements, diversions, recreations, and sports. The Separate Park Law of Georgia, adopted in 1905, appears to have been the first venture of a state legislature into this field, though city ordinances and local custom were quite active in pushing the Negro out of the public parks. . . . The city of Birmingham applied the principle of having

---

[7]Quoted in Peterson, *Only the Ball*, p. 41.

[8]Harry Carpenter, *Boxing: A Pictorial History* (Chicago: Henry Regnery Company, 1975), p. 30.

[9]From *200 Years of Sports in America* by Wells Twombly, pp. 99–100. Copyright © 1974 by Wells Twombly. Used with the permission of McGraw-Hill Book Company.

separate doorways, ticket booths and seating for blacks to any room, hall, theatre, picture house, auditorium, yard, court, ball park, or other indoor or outdoor place.[10]

In a nation presumably dedicated to the principles of freedom and equality, you would think that Jim Crow would not be tolerated. Yet Americans did more than tolerate Jim Crow, they liked him. A combination of cultural beliefs and ideological tenets worked to make these two seemingly incompatible values compatible. It was as if the Orwellian tenet that "some are more equal than others" had been anticipated.

A classic sociological treatise analyzes this contradiction, pointing out how American culture must continually resolve the dilemma of worshipping equality on the one side while approving race discrimination and inequality on the other. One section of the work states,

> Two principal points will be made. . . . The first point is [that] the Creed of progress, liberty, equality, and humanitarianism is not so uninfluential on everyday life as might sometimes appear.
>
> The second point is the existence in society of huge institutional structures like the church, the school, the university, [sport] . . . It is true, as we shall find, that these institutional structures in their operation show an accommodation to local and temporary interests and prejudices. . . . As institutions, they are, however, devoted to certain broad ideals. It is in these institutions that the American Creed has its instruments: it plays upon them as on mighty organs.[11]

This statement refers to all social institutions, including sport. Sport accommodates local or temporary racism while maintaining the principle of egalitarianism. The practice contradicts the principle, but the two coexist. Which one prevails—racism or egalitarianism—depends on the tempo and dominant character or spirit of the times or, as it's called, the *Zeitgeist*.[12] The Zeitgeist changes periodically, so that periods of relative egalitarianism followed by periods of relative racism run through sport as through other American institutions. The dilemma finds temporary accommodation but as yet no permanent resolution.

EARLY TWENTIETH CENTURY

Stereotype and Segregation

During a period of intensified racism, stereotyping comes to the fore. Stereotyping is the attribution of prejorative and false characteristics to all members of a category, in this case to all blacks. Although it may seem strange at first glance, the stereotypes of the time did

---

[10]C. Vann Woodward, *The Strange Career of Jim Crow*, 3rd rev. ed. (New York: Oxford University Press, 1974), pp. 99–100.

[11]Gunnar Myrdal, *An American Dilemma: The Negro Problem and Modern Democracy* (1944; reprint, New York: Pantheon Books, Inc., 1972), I, 80.

[12]Zeitgeist, of course, is not an explanation of why times change. The reader interested in the reason for the change can consult George M. Fredrickson's *White Supremacy, A Comparative Study in American and South African History* (New York: Oxford University Press, 1981), and other works.

concede that blacks were good athletes (and good entertainers). The presence of so many blacks with undeniably outstanding talent could not go unrecognized, and anyway, black athletes hardly threatened white supremacy. As long as sport remained segregated, black athletic superiority could not be systematically demonstrated by competition with whites.

Jim Crow Rules

While segregation of sport was the rule, boxing was a major exception. Boxing has been continuously integrated since the days of Tom Molineaux, but integrated in the narrow sense of the word. Blacks had always participated in boxing but with the accompaniment of Jim Crow. The life of Jack Johnson shows much of this.

The Great White Hope. In 1905 Marvin Hart succeeded James Jeffries as heavyweight champion of the world. In 1906 Tom Burns beat Hart; and in 1908 Jack Johnson beat Burns for the title. These events wouldn't be exceptionally noteworthy but for one fact: Jack Johnson was black—the first black to win the heavyweight championship.

And when he won, a cry went up to find a "Great White Hope"—a white fighter who could regain the title "for the white race." To answer the call, Jim Jeffries—middle-aged, out of shape and with deteriorated skills—came out of retirement. Johnson easily beat him when they fought in the 1911 bout in Reno, Nevada.

Johnson's victory triggered race riots. The *New York Times* headlined: "EIGHT KILLED IN FIGHT RIOTS—CLASHES BETWEEN RACES IN MANY CITIES FOLLOW CONTEST—NEGROES THE VICTIMS." Another *Times* headline: "THREE KILLED IN UVALDIA—ARMED PARTY OF WHITES ATTACK NEGRO CAMP AND DRIVE OUT OCCUPANTS."[13]

Jack Johnson loved the high life. He loved flashy clothes and champagne, and, what incensed the white public most of all, he loved white women. He married one white woman, got divorced, and then remarried another. When a former white girlfriend revealed that she had traveled with him to Reno for the Jeffries' fight, authorities prosecuted under the Mann Act (a questionable legal tactic because the Act was meant to outlaw prostitution rings operating across state lines.) Rather than go to prison, Johnson fled abroad.

In 1915 Johnson defended his title against Jess Willard in Havana, Cuba. A famous photograph shows Johnson lying on the canvas with his hand held up, ostensibly shielding his eyes from the sun, while the referee counts him out. The reign of the first black heavyweight champion thus ended—ignominiously and amid cries of "fix!"

Johnson later returned to the United States and served a portion of his sentence before being released for good behavior. In 1946, he died in an automobile crash.

The case of Jack Johnson has chronological importance: He was the first black heavyweight champion. More important sociologically, his case makes a point we might easily overlook today, when racism is neither socially nor politically acceptable. (Even

---

[13]*New York Times*, July 5, 1910, pp. 1, 5.

members of the Klu Klux Klan deny being racist.) In the days that Jim Crow rules were in effect (and the rules were widespread, publically condoned, and virulently hateful). White America would not accept a black heavyweight champion, especially one who flaunted the "rules."

If Jack Johnson had a different personality, if he had been quiet, reserved, and happily married to a black woman, undoubtedly he would not have been so hated and attacked. But a docile personality still would not have totally blunted the racism of the period. There would have been a "Great White Hope" anyway. In a sad and tragic way, Jack Johnson never had a chance. No single person can stand up alone to the crush of an entire racist society and the concerted attacks of the racist people produced by that society.

Jack Johnson was one particularly dramatic case out of millions—an illustration of a process that was clamping down tighter and tighter on American life. This process led to the formation of exclusively black neighborhoods, exclusively black businesses, exclusively black churches, and exclusively black sport. Even though very few black clubs existed, because of lack of economic support, a small all-black tennis and golf circuit did develop with the support of the tiny affluent segment of the black community. And in basketball, then in its barnstorming period, there were all-black teams that sometimes competed against white teams.

However, the most well known and best organized black sport was baseball. All-black leagues came into existence, and during their heyday black teams might draw several thousand fans to important games. Beset by organizational and financial problems, these leagues and teams had an "off and on" existence. Yet they did nurture many black players, such as Dave Brown, John Donaldson, Andrew Rube Foster, Willie Foster, Jose Mendez, Satchel Paige, Cannonball Dick Redding, Bullet Rogan, Smokey Joe Williams, Biz Mackey, Bruce Petway, Louis Santop, Buck Leonard, Ben Taylor, Newt Allen, Bingo DeMoss, Sammy T. Hughes, John Beckwith. The list is long and contains many players who were, by common judgment, as good as any that ever played the game.

Many black teams barnstormed the country, as did a few white teams.

> For fifty years the barnstormers, both black and white, brought good baseball to isolated farm towns and small cities. Their arrival in a small town generated a holiday atmosphere . . . For a small town baseball fan, white or black, barnstorming was a glamorous trade, redolent of faraway places and the lure of the road. For the black barnstormer, it was a grueling labor mixed with the constant threat—and often reality—of insult, rebuff, and discrimination. But in Negro baseball, barnstorming was necessary for survival.[14]

ERA OF CHANGE: THE THIRTIES TO THE FIFTIES

Glimmerings of change could be seen starting in the late 1930s and especially in the 1940s—an era dominated by World War II. We can see this in the way the American public interpreted Jesse Owens's victories in the 1936 "Nazi Olympics" held in Berlin.

---

[14]Robert Peterson, *Only the Ball*, p. 157.

Owens was black, yet white Americans cheered him as *their* champion. Also at about this time, the career of another black athlete had begun climbing.

Jim Crow Weakens

The Champ. In Detroit, a friend introduced teenager Joe Louis to boxing. In 1933, after an inauspicious start (he went down twice in his first fight) Louis became the Golden Gloves champion, and Jack Blackburn became his manager.

Blackburn carefully guided Louis through a series of preliminary bouts. Then victories over Art Sykes and Primo Canera put Louis in the limelight and made him a first-rank contender. During this time, Max Schmeling, a German fighter who stood for Hitler's facism in the public mind, gave Louis his only beating. After that defeat Louis went on to seven straight victories and took the crown from James Braddock in 1937, becoming the first black heavyweight champion since Jack Johnson in 1908.

A year later Louis met Schmeling for the second time. The fight drew enormous public interest and media coverage. It was Americanism versus Facism in the boxing ring. Louis devastated Schmeling in the first two minutes of the first round and all America rejoiced—black and white.

The *New York Times* headlined: LOUIS DEFEATS SCHMELING . . . 1936 SETBACK AVENGED.

According to the *New York Times* report, "All Germany, clustered around its short wave radio sets in the early morning hours, was thunderstruck and almost unbelieving at the unexpected news that Max Schmeling had failed in his heavyweight comeback try and failed by the knockout route."[15] Louis supposedly said, "There are a lot of things wrong with this country, but nothing Hitler can fix."

Riotous celebrations took place in black sections of several cities, but no interracial violence (as happened when blacks celebrated Johnson's victory over Jeffries).

When World War II broke out three years later, Louis donated fight purses to the war cause, and joined the Army and went on tour giving exhibition bouts for servicemen. In 1949 Louis retired. Later, debts forced him to try a comeback, but he was too old. He died in 1980.

This was quite the opposite of how the white public treated Jack Johnson's reign. The second black heavyweight champion triggered no antiblack campaign; no hysterical screams for a "Great White Hope"; no prosecutions under questionable legal pretexts. The white public received Louis cordially, came to respect and then honor him.

Why the different responses to Louis and Johnson?

A small part of the difference might be Louis's more conservative personality. But we should not overestimate the effect of personality. Louis came along at the moment that Jim Crow started to loosen his grip on American culture. Most fundamentally the spirit of the times, the Zeitgeist, victimized Jack Johnson; and likewise the Zeitgeist of the late 1930s favored Louis. Johnson appeared on the scene when racism prevailed; Louis appeared when egalitarian values were starting to reemerge.

---

[15]Gene Brown and Arlearn Keylin, eds., *Sports as Reported by the New York Times* (New York: Arno Press, 1976), pp. 90, 91. Originally reported, June 23, 1938.

Jim Crow Ends?

By the late 1940s, the Zeitgeist began changing at an increasing pace. On April 15, 1947. Jackie Robinson came up to bat for the Brooklyn Dodgers and so became the first black to play in the major leagues since the nineteenth century. He didn't just suddenly arrive; a series of carefully orchestrated steps led to his appearance.

Breaking the Color Line. Branch Rickey became general manager of the Brooklyn Dodgers in 1942. With the backing of Dodger management, Rickey began quietly looking for the right player to break the color line that existed in baseball.

Meanwhile in Boston, amid a political campaign to break the color line, the Red Sox and Braves agreed to hold tryouts for black players. However, nothing came of it.

New York's famous mayor Fiorello LaGuardia added more political pressure to the situation when he appointed a committee to study discrimination in baseball. And Judge Landis, the commissioner of baseball, stated: "I don't believe in barring Negroes from baseball just because they are Negroes."[16]

In 1945, after doing his military service and starring at UCLA, Jackie Robinson joined an all-black club. When Rickey decided on Robinson and signed him to the Montreal Royals, Brooklyn's major farm club, it was the top sports story of 1946.

The next year Brooklyn called up Jackie Robinson. The statement read: "Brooklyn announces the purchase of the contract of Jack Roosevelt Robinson from Montreal. He will report immediately."[17]

Rickey also worked behind the scenes with New York's black community to dampen the publicity of Robinson's signing. The community responded with a campaign based on the slogan, "don't spoil Jackie's chances."

Rickey had to put down a player rebellion on the Dodgers, with the help of many of the Dodger stars; and Commissioner Landis quelled threats to boycott games in which Robinson appeared. As has been told many times, Robinson suffered terrible racial abuses, but, under Rickey's counselling, he never fought back. He used passive resistance.[18] Robinson led the way and the color line slowly faded.

There were still many racists around to bait Jackie Robinson and other blacks, athletes or otherwise, but the cultural supports for Jim Crow had started to give way. World War II had just been fought to "save democracy," so it hardly seemed democratic to subjugate an entire race for having the wrong skin color. When the Korean War broke out, the same point was made again.

Fifties Optimism

The Zeitgeist of the 1940s overlapped into the 1950s. The Zeitgeist of the 1950s can be described as serenely optimistic. The Supreme Court ruled against segregated schools in

---

[16]Peterson, *Only the Ball*, p. 185.

[17]Ibid, p. 190.

[18]See, for example, Roger Kahn, *The Boys of Summer* (New York: New American Library, 1971), p. 133.

1954. In 1956, civil-rights leader Martin Luther King scored a major triumph in Montgomery, Alabama, when, after a prolonged boycott, the bus lines agreed to let blacks ride in the front of the bus. In 1957 Althea Gibson, a street-wise child from New York City, became the first black to win at Wimbledon—the most prestigous tennis championship. At the victory ball she took the traditional first dance with the male champion—the white Lew Hoad.

During this period black athletes who lived and traveled with their teams made hundreds of inroads against prejudice. It's easy to forget that not too long ago blacks encountered overt racist barriers at every turn. There were restrictions on where blacks slept, restrictions on what cabs they rode in, restrictions on where they ate, and restrictions on which movie theatres they attended.

> **Little Victories.** During the barnstorming era of sport, black basketball teams traveled the country. Probably the best of these teams was the Rens, a team reputedly as good as the original Celtics. The success of the Rens, both on the court and at the box office, inspired Abe Saperstein to form the Harlem Globe Trotters, a team of black basketball players better known as comics than as athletes.
>
> In 1947, the same year Jackie Robinson broke into major-league baseball, the fledgling American Basketball League (ABL) considered a motion to accept the Rens. The motion lost that year, but the following year it passed. The League moved the Rens to Dayton, Ohio, but the team quickly folded for lack of fan support.
>
> The National Basketball Association superseded the ABL and Chuck Cooper entered the stream of events. On April 25, 1950, he became the first black player in modern professional basketball. Like other "first blacks" he shouldered a burden he never asked for. "I wouldn't necessarily call it hell," he says, "But yes, the worst part was traveling. It was all those separate hotels and restaurants and cabs."
>
> In Raleigh, North Carolina, officials said he could not play, because no interracial contest had ever been held there. He did play, but could not stay at the team hotel. Little incidents piled up. "The racism. The humiliation. The loneliness." How did Chuck Cooper tolerate it? "I wasn't happy about it, but you made the best of it," he says, "It didn't seem all that important."[19]

Progress, if slow, was being made. In general, things seemed to be going along just fine—or so it appeared.

THE SIXTIES TO THE PRESENT

The 1960s shattered that. Boycotts, once an occasional tactic, became commonplace. Marches, sit-ins, and takeovers became the new tactics of protest. Race riots became the order of the long, hot summer days. Quickly other minorities joined in the fracas:

---

[19]Information about the Rens from Bruce Newman, "Yesterday," *Sports Illustrated*, October 22, 1979, unpaginated. Information about Chuck Cooper from *New York Times*, April 27, 1980, sec. S, p. 2. © 1980 by The New York Times Company. Reprinted by permission.

Chicanos, Italians, Asians, homosexuals, and perhaps the minority with the most far-reaching implications, women. The Vietnam War crept up and soon college students learned about tear gas and how to fall into a fetal position to protect their bodys' sensitive parts from clubs and kicks.

To many observers, the 1960s seemed like the beginning of the end. On the morning of January 1, 1970, the headlines of several newspapers read, "CONGRATULATIONS: YOU HAVE SURVIVED THE SIXTIES."

Sports reflected the Zeitgeist of protest and upheaval. Black athletes became increasingly militant in their demands to end Jim Crow in sport. They protested such things as the use of certain racial terms by fans, press, and coaches; the segregation of living quarters on and off the road; the ban on Afro haircuts; and the prohibition of interracial dating. On more than one occasion at more than one school, black athletes boycotted their teams to make their point.

A move was started to boycott the 1968 Mexico City Olympics. The boycott failed in that it prevented most black athletes from participating, but it did generate publicity, and when two black American champions raised their gloved fists and bowed their heads during the playing of the Star Spangled Banner at the victory ceremony, the felt injustices of the American black athletes became known worldwide.[20]

Cassius Clay won the heavyweight boxing championship, refused induction into the Army on religious grounds, and as a consequence was stripped of his title. After waging a long legal battle to regain his license, he eventually won both the right to box and the championship. During this time, Clay had become a Black Muslim, changed his name to Muhammed Ali, and created a political stir whenever he spoke out. Ali had become a heroic figure to millions of black Americans.

Black intellectual leaders preached a quasi-Marxian ideology. They argued that the white majority exploits the black athlete; that schools, fans, and owners care only for the gain made by permitting blacks to participate in sport. One leader wrote,

> The roots of the revolt of the black athlete spring from the same seed that produced the sit-ins, the freedom rides. . . . Once the black athletes' abilities are impaired by age or by injury, only the ghetto beckons and they are doomed once again to that faceless, hopeless, ignominious existence they had supposedly forever left behind them.[21]

In short, society produced the problem; and if you're black and an athlete, you're still black; and *they* will cast you aside when it suits *them*.

The Zeitgeist of the 1960s went on until the early 1970s and then suddenly stopped. The reasons for the sudden stop remain unclear, as do the details of the Zeitgeist in which we now find ourselves. Being in it, we cannot see the whole. We do not even know if the whole has formed. However one aspect stands out, and we mention it now because it has a direct bearing on this section: Race problems have become passe, undramatic. In sociol-

---

[20]Harry Edwards, *The Revolt of the Black Athlete* (New York: The Free Press, 1970).
[21]Ibid, p. xxvii.

ogy, the decline in research papers devoted to the topic makes this apparent. It is also apparent in the media (fewer stories dwell on ethnic relations) and in government policy (fewer and smaller programs, less favorable court decisions). In a discussion of this point, one of a small group of sociologists who have devoted major portions of their careers to studying ethnic relations said, "I don't know why people are losing interest in race relations, but they are. I am, and I feel kind of guilty about it."[22]

SOCIOLOGICAL CONCLUSIONS

We have only highlighted the social history of Afro-Americans in sport, but even our brief presentation leads to some basic sociological conclusions:

- Compared to other institutions, sport has been relatively open to minorities.
- The cycles of integration and segregation of sport coincide with changes in the Zeitgeist of American society.
- Racist societies produce racist people, not the other way around.
- It follows that to get rid of racism you must get rid of the institutional patterns in which racism exists.

The last point underlies most sociological thinking on ethnic relations and we therefore emphasize it: Racism can exist without racist people. As one text says,

Even when people in a society no longer subscribe to racism, the society may still contain institutional racism, racism within the institutional structure of the society. The absence of black quarterbacks from American professional football and American Indians from corporate boards of directors are instances of institutionalized racism.[23]

The four conclusions we have just drawn from Afro-American social history form the framework or perspective for analyzing the current state of ethnic relations in sport. The next chapter addresses that topic.

SUMMARY

1. We define *race* to mean a group having a unique subculture and use the term almost as a synonym for *ethnic group* and *minority*.
2. Blacks have been participating in sport since the founding of the Republic, as illus-

---

[22]Personal communication from a colleague.

[23]Elbert W. Stewart, *Sociology: The Human Science*, 2nd ed. (New York: McGraw-Hill Book Company, 1981), p. 199.

trated by Tom Molineaux, the first black athletic hero. After the Civil War, blacks participated in several sports, notably horse racing, baseball, and boxing.

3. With the coming of Jim Crow, sport was segregated along with the rest of American society. The case of Jack Johnson illustrates the racism of that period.

4. During the late 1930s and 1940s, the Zeitgeist of Jim Crow began to change. Black athletic heroes such as Jesse Owens and Joe Louis started reappearing on the American scene. After World War II, Jackie Robinson became a symbol of the breaking of the color line. The toleration of race discrimination in a country founded on principles of equality is a dilemma American society must constantly confront. Seemingly, the Zeitgeist fluctuates between the two.

5. The 1950s Zeitgeist was one of optimism in race relations, but the coming of the 1960s changed all of that. The 1960s were a period of intense racial conflict, compounded by anti–Vietnam War sentiments and the entry of various minority groups and political factions into the fray. This affected sport: Black athletes asserted their political and social independence with boycotts of teams, demonstrations at athletic events (most notably the 1968 Olympics), and an ideology of quasi-Marxism. The current Zeitgeist is hard to analyze; we are simply too close to it.

6. The social history of Afro-American sports participation leads us to conclude that:
   a. Sport has been relatively open to minorities compared with many other American institutions.
   b. Cycles of integration and segregation coincide with changes in the broader societal Zeitgeist.
   c. Racist societies produce racist people.
   d. To get rid of racism you must get rid of racist social structure.

6

BLACKS IN SPORT, PART II

Present and Future

Spring scrimmage game at the Ohio State University, 1981. Which positions in professional and college football are over-represented by white players, and which by black players? If you guessed center, quarterback, and linebackers for white players, and running backs, wide receivers and defensive backs for black players, you're right. Stacking—the assignment of playing positions according to race—has been going on for a long ime. Stacking maintains a kind of symbolic segregation on the playing field, and prevents the subordination of whites to blacks, except under rare conditions. Stacking has harmful long-term consequences for blacks. Photo by Timothy J. Curry.

CURRENT STATE OF AFFAIRS

Why the Black Dominance in Sport?

Blacks make up 12 percent of the United States population. If American society were totally colorblind as to race, then 12 percent of the workers in every occupation would be black, from skycaps to physicians. As we all can readily observe, this is hardly the case; not among skycaps, physicians, professors, plumbers, lawyers, electricians, nor in any other work group you might be familiar with, including athletes. In sport, nearly 100 percent of heavyweight boxers are black, as are approximately 60 percent of professional basketball players, 40 percent of professional football players, and 20 percent of professional baseball players.[1]

Black athletes are very good. There hasn't been a white heavyweight champion in over a quarter of a century. Black basketball players score 12 percent more points and get 10 percent more rebounds than white players. Black running backs gain 17 percent more yards and score 100 percent more touchdowns than white running backs. The lifetime batting average of black baseball players is 7 percent higher than that of white players.[2]

The black dominance of certain sports cannot be seriously disputed. The question is, Why the dominance?

One answer would be to say genetics—that blacks inherit traits favorable to sport, such as speed, coordination, build, and perhaps favorable psychological traits as well.

The genetic or biological explanation does have appeal. It's simple, seems to cover the facts, and cannot easily be disproved. Both lay and professional people have believed it for several decades. A 1906 article published in *Century* magazine sought to show empirical evidence of racial differences in cranial capacity. It concludes,

> Having demonstrated that the negro and the Caucasian are widely different in characteristics, due to a deficiency of gray matter and connecting fibers in the negro brain, especially in the frontal lobes, a deficiency that is hereditary, . . . we are forced to conclude that it is useless to try to elevate the negro by education. . . . Let them win their reward by diligent service.[3]

Even if the data were valid—*which they are not*—this reasoning is still a subtle twisting of science into racist doctrine. That becomes evident when the argument gets reduced to the following long equation:

> Biological differences ("gray matter, connecting fibers") = social inferiority ("useless to educate") = political subjugation ("diligent service").

---

[1] "The Black Dominance," in *Time*, May 9, 1977, pp. 57–60.

[2] Gerald Scully, "Economic Discrimination in Professional Sport," *Law and Contemporary Problems*, 38 (Winter/Spring 1973), 67–84.

[3] Robert Bennet Bean, "The Negro Brain," in *The Development of Segregationist Thought*, ed. I.A. Newby (Homewood, Illinois: The Dorsey Press, 1968), p. 53. Originally published in *Century Magazine*, October, 1906, pp. 778–84.

This genetic "theory" can be dismissed as illogical because the equation makes no sense at all. One part does not follow from the preceding part. In addition, and equally damning, empirical evidence does not support the theory. Points out one textbook:

Nobody proposes genetic factors, for example, to explain why East Germany has produced so many excellent swimmers, why Canadians do well at hockey, why Japanese-Americans are disproportionately represented in judo—or, for that matter, why the British are hopeless at baseball, while white Americans are equally inept at cricket. In each case, it is easy to see cultural factors, not genetic ones, are at work.[4]

We discard genetic theory; but that does not answer the question, Why the black dominance?

Our answer rests on a broad sociological process: Athletes appear because there are games to be played and won, and when won, rewarded. This very basic process explains why *any* minority group will dominate sport under the right circumstances. As an illustration of how the process works, and how it applies to different ethnic groups, consider the case of Carribean and South American youths aspiring to play professional baseball in the United States.

How to Be Rich and Famous.   Panama is the city on the Atlantic side of the Panama Canal; and if you walk its downtown streets during World Series time, you might come to believe that Central Americans are divided into two species: those with two regular ears (about one-third of the population), and those with little transistor radios attached to the place where an ear would normally grow. You might hypothesize that the transistorites are intently interested in news of an impending revolution, earthquake, or volcanic eruption. But you'd be wrong. They're actually listening to a baseball game being played in the United States, a country they have only seen in films, but whose baseball teams they avidly follow.

You see, throughout Latin America and the Spanish-speaking Carribean, the fever for American baseball runs rampant.

Thousands upon unknown thousands of Latin American kids play in loosely organized competition, and American baseball scouts constantly beat the bushes for potential major leaguers. These aspirants can barely read, come from wretchedly poor families, and have no feasible employment opportunities. They are hungry and will sign for small bonuses: two to three thousand dollars versus the twenty thousand a top American prospect commands.

Any aspirant, Latin American or not, stands an extremely small chance of ever playing in the big league; but for a Latin American player that chance must be truly tiny. They don't know the language; they don't know American culture; they don't know the nuances of American baseball; they haven't had the same caliber of coaching, training, or medical treatment; and they're much younger than American minor leaguers. Still, they hope and are grateful for even the small bonuses they receive.[5]

Essentially what happens is that a dream of luxury is dangled in front of hungry aspirants and their alternatives are cut off. An often-cited study shows how this process

---

[4]Ian Robertson, *Sociology*, 2nd ed. (New York: Worth Publishers, Inc., 1981), p. 91.

[5]See Bill Brubaker, "Hey, Kid, Wanna be a Star?" *Sports Illustrated*, July 13, 1981, p. 72.

worked with American minorities in boxing.[6] From 1909 to 1928, Irish boxers dominated the prize ring; from 1929 to 1938, Jewish boxers dominated; and since 1937, Afro-Americans dominate. (Perhaps Hispanics, now entering the ring in disproportionately large numbers, will dominate in the future.)

The study quotes a fight manager who unknowingly describes a sociological process, "They say that too much education softens a man and that is why college graduates are not good fighters. . . . An education is an escape. . . . Once the bell rings managers want their fighters to have no escape, and a fighter with an education is a fighter who does not have to fight to live and he knows it. . . . Only for the hungry fighter is [managing a young boxer] a decent gamble."[7] The study concludes, "Professional boxers are recruited from among the youth of the lower socioeconomic levels. Their changing ethnic composition reflects the ethnic shift in the urban lower socioeconomic levels. Fighting is an important road to increased social status, and successful boxers are role-models for youth."[8]

Regarding blacks specifically, Harry Edwards writes, "Black society, as does the dominant white society, teaches its members to strive for that which is defined as the most desirable *achievable goals*. . . . In high prestige occupational positions outside of the sports realm, black role models are in all but an insignificant few."[9] Harry Edwards said, "Society *teaches*." We translate this to mean that values glorifying sport saturate black subculture. Passion for sport can be found in all strata of the black community, from children practicing on the playground and parents who encourage them, to the small black upper class.

According to a study of children's baseball in St. Louis, black families believed, by a margin of four to one over white families, that having their children play in a baseball league might be the start of a professional career.[10] (See Table 6.1 for the comparison between families of similar status.)

E. Franklin Frazier, the best-known black sociologist of the 1940s and 1950s, reports,

> Once the writer heard a Negro doctor who was prominent "socially" say that he would rather lose a patient than have his favorite baseball team lose a game. This was an extreme expression of the relative value of professional work and recreation among the black bourgeoisie. . . . They follow religiously the scores of the various teams and the achievements of all the players. For hours they listen to the radio accounts of sports and watch baseball and football games on television.[11]

---

[6]S. Kirson Weinberg and Henry Arond, "The Occupational Culture of the Boxer," *American Journal of Sociology*, 57 (1952), 460–69.

[7]Ibid., pp. 461–62.

[8]Ibid., p. 460.

[9]Harry Edwards, *Sociology of Sport* (Homewood, Illinois: The Dorsey Press, 1973), pp. 201–2; Italics in original.

[10]Melvin L. Oliver, "Race, Class and the Family's Orientation to Mobility through Sport," *Sociological Symposium*, Spring 1980, pp. 62–68.

[11]E. Franklin Frazier, *Black Bourgeoisie* (Glencoe, Illinois: The Free Press and Falcon's Wing Press, 1957), pp. 207–8.

Table 6.1. Extent to which Families See Community Baseball as "A Start in Athletic Activity That May Lead to a Career in Professional Sports" by Family Status and Race

	BLACK FAMILIES (N=145)					WHITE FAMILIES (N=34)				
	Upper White Collar	Lower White Collar	Upper Blue Collar	Lower Blue Collar	Total	Upper White Collar	Lower White Collar	Upper Blue Collar	Lower Blue Collar	Total
A very important benefit	23%	32%	37%	27%	29%	0%	0%	0%	50%	6%
An important benefit	16	48	37	47	38	4	0	0	50	9
Not an important benefit	35	10	20	22	22	33	100	50	0	36
Definitely not an important benefit	26	10	6	4	11	63	0	50	0	49
Total	100%	100%	100%	100%	100%	100%	100%	100%	100%	100%

SOURCE: Melvin L. Oliver, "Race, Class, and the Family's Orientation to Mobility Through Sport," *Sociological Symposium*, 30 (Spring 1980), p. 79. Reprinted with permission.

Black subculture, permeated with passion for sport, encourages, attracts, and pushes black youth into athletics much more than white culture does with white youth. Suppose that in the United States a situation existed in which black and white youths had exactly the same talent for sports; and that both groups had the same cultural influences and the same job opportunities. Under those circumstances whites would overwhelmingly dominate sport.

Why? Numbers. Whites outnumber blacks in the United States by about seven to one.

That is the opposite of the true situation. In the real world white youths realistically aspire to careers in business, law, medicine, construction, plumbing, carpentry, and so forth. A huge number of whites with athletic talent end up doing these jobs rather than trying to make careers in sports.

For blacks those options do not exist. Poverty, discrimination, lack of education, lack of training, and lack of cultural supports mean this: Most careers, while theoretically open to blacks, are closed to them in reality. The black community knows this, and so blacks flow into sports, just as the Irish, Italians, and Jews went into boxing during earlier times, and just as Hispanics now flow into baseball and boxing.

Notice though: Blacks do not flow into just any sport. The dominance shows selectivity. Blacks are overrepresented in baseball, basketball, and football; and underrepresented in swimming, fencing, gymnastics, skiing, skating, and cycling. With some exceptions, blacks have gone into the money sports, the sports with professional outlets. An exception is track and field, especially sprints. Track and field has no professional outlet, but world-class athletes do reap much glory (like Olympic fame which might be turned into money), and can earn a comfortable living from the under-the-table honorariums paid by promoters of large meets.

Economic and social factors explain the lack of black dominance in money sports like golf and tennis: The ghetto has few tennis clubs and country clubs. Living in a sports-dominated subculture; having dreams of success; being hungry; having the opportunity to play; not having other opportunities—these are the reasons that blacks have gone into, and dominate, the money sports. It all makes perfect sociological sense.

Contemporary Racism in Sport

Looking at the history of blacks in sport and the current black dominance, a seemingly plausible conclusion would be that sport is colorblind as to race. This belief has now seeped into every cranny of American culture. Even those who have borne the animosity of race hatred believe it. For example, a book on black athletics, published under the aegis of the International Library of Afro-American Life and History, states the following:

> In the past few years, [race] has become of relatively little importance in the world of athletics. In perhaps no other field, with the possible exception of show business, have blacks been able to assert themselves with such success, to reach the top with

such ease, as in sports. Whatever is lacking in the life of the American Negro, sport stands as an example of what it might be.[12]

Those are optimistic words. Sociologists ought to give pause. Sport could be about the only place in American society where race relations work.

However, might that assessment be unduly optimistic? We hear stories about successful black athletes like O.J. Simpson, but seldom does the media tell us anything about average black athletes, or about those who have failed, or about the marginal players who barely and briefly hang on. Nor does the media discuss abstract social patterns, like structure. Yet, as sociologists, we know that structure guides the behavior of individuals. Also, certain facts contradict the belief in colorblindness:

- The performance of an outstanding black pitcher fell off. He complained of being tired, but doctors could find nothing wrong with him. His pitching problems and complaints continued. Soon fans and media were wondering if he was malingering, making excuses for his poor pitching. Subsequently doctors found a massive blood clot in his shoulder that vindicated his complaints.[13] The question arises: If he had been a white superstar, would the issue of malingering have arisen, arisen so quickly, or been so widespread? Maybe, maybe not—we'll never know, but probably not. "We always knew we had to be better," said a black teammate.[14]

- Echoing an ideological tenet begun in the 1960s, one black basketball superstar describes how college athletics operate: "The colleges are just there to use you. If you're black and haven't a nice, rich mommy and daddy . . . then you have no choice."[15]

- In order to be on the team, Afro-American athletes must be disproportionately better than whites. A study of 248 NCAA basketball teams showed that 29 percent of the players were black, but that 66 percent of the blacks were starters.[16]

- A magazine feature story about one of the few white heavyweight boxing contenders shows that the question of race will not go away. "The question dogs him. . . . Everyone wants to know how it feels as a white man in a game played mostly by Hispanics and Blacks. 'Terrible,' he says. 'It's terrible to be labeled a *Great White Hope*.' "[17]

- Concerning the marketing of professional basketball: When basketball's popular-

[12]Edwin B. Henderson and the editors of Sport Magazine, *The Black Athlete: Emergence and Arrival*, (Cornwell Heights, Pennsylvania: The Publishers Agency, Inc., 1976), pp. 1–2.

[13]William Nack, "Now Everyone Believes Him," *Sports Illustrated*, August 18, 1980, unpaginated.

[14]Ibid.

[15]Quoted in Frank Deford, "Bounding into Prominence," *Sports Illustrated*, February 19, 1979, p. 68.

[16]Norman R. Yetman and D. Stanley Eitzen, "Black Athletes on Intercollegiate Teams: An Empirical Test of Discrimination," in *Majority and Minority: The Dynamics of Racial and Ethnic Relations*, ed. Norman R. Yetman and C. Hoy Steele (Boston: Allyn and Bacon, Inc., 1971), pp. 509–17.

[17]Michael Norman, "The Rise of Gerry Cooney," *New York Times Magazine*, August 19, 1981, p. 33. © 1981 by The New York Times Company. Reprinted by permission.

ity began sliding in the late 1970s, the preponderance of black players became an issue. Would the fans—overwhelmingly white—support a sport played largely by blacks? Many observers suspected the fans would not.[18]

- And finally, in some sports, the absence rather than the presence of black athletes draws notice. No black had competed in the Masters golf tournament before Lee Elder in 1975,[19] and not until 1980 did a black athlete, Ralph Davenport, make the American Winter Olympics team. He remarked at that time, "That's one thing that really inspired me to be so gung-ho about it. As for being the first black, you can't touch it, you can't see it, you can't feel it. But it's there."[20]

Incidents like these make you wonder if sport is as colorblind as you have been lead to believe. Isolated incidents do not make up an institutional pattern, but are these incidents isolated? Or do they reflect some kind of broad societal pattern? Most sociologists would suspect the pattern, if only because sport mirrors society and everyone knows that American society has yet to get rid of racism totally. Sports sociologists have analyzed and documented at length one of these institutional patterns: *stacking*.

Stacking

Over several weekends of television watching, anyone, sports aficionado or not, would notice how many blacks play halfback, wide receiver, and defensive back in football, and how few play center, quarterback, or middle linebacker; or in baseball, the number of blacks playing the outfield and the paucity of blacks playing the infield. It's almost as if Jim Crow signs had been hung around the athletic field: "This Position Reserved for Whites"; "This Position Reserved for Blacks." The existence of this reservation system, called "stacking," has been known for many years.

- The first study (done over ten years ago) showed that in professional football 6 percent of quarterbacks, 9 percent of guards, 52 percent of running backs, and 35 percent of flankers were black—clearly a disproportionate representation. In baseball (after rounding the numbers), zero percent of shortstops, zero percent of catchers, and 35 percent of outfielders were black. The researchers saw a spatial pattern in the data. Blacks played mostly peripheral positions while whites played mostly central positions. For instance, blacks are overrepresented in the outfield of baseball teams (peripheral positions), but not the infield (central positions). In football whites play quarterback and center (central positions), while blacks play running back, defensive back, and flanker (peripheral positions). The report concludes, "The preceding findings leave little doubt that only

[18]See for example John Papanket, "There's an Ill Wind Blowing for the NBA," *Sports Illustrated*, February 26, 1979, pp. 20–27.

[19]*New York Times*, April 13, 1983, sec. B, p. 8.

[20]*Columbus Citizen-Journal*, February 6, 1980, p. 11. This athlete, Ralph Davenport, previously won gold and bronze medals in the 1968 and 1976 Summer Olympics.

a small proportion of black athletes occupy certain positions in America's professional baseball and football organizations."[21]

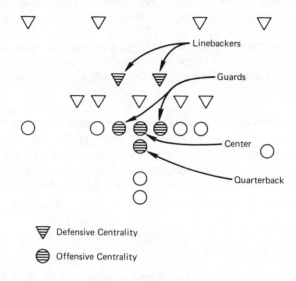

Figure 6.1. Centrality of Playing Position for Football

SOURCE: John D. Massengale, "The Prestigious College Football Coach: An Analysis of Sponsored Career Mobility," *Educational Resources Information Center*, #ED 189 080/SP 016 296, April 1980. Reprinted with permission.

• A study of NCAA schools found that "thirty-two percent of the personnel of college basketball teams were black, yet 41 percent of forwards were black, and only 26 percent of the guards were black as were 25 percent of the centers."[22]

• A statistical study of professional basketball reported, "We have observed a consistently subnormal dispersion in the number of blacks per team in the NBA. This fact does not establish the existence of racial quotas. However, if the alternative interpretation were rejected (i.e., that players of one race are superior in playing ability to those of the other race), racial quotas are the only other plausible source of subnormal dispersion we are aware of."[23]

[21]Figures computed from John W. Loy and Joseph F. MacElvogue, "Racial Segregation in American Sports," *International Review of Sport Sociology*, 5 (1970), 5–24. Also see Joseph Dougherty, "Race and Sports: A Follow-up Study," *Sport Sociology Bulletin*, 5 (Spring 1976), 1–12.

[22]D. Stanley Eitzen and Irl Tessendorf, "Racial Segregation by Position in Sports: The Special Case of Basketball," in *Psychology of Sport and Motor Behavior*, ed. Daniel M. Landers, (Pennsylvania State University, HPER Series No. 10, 1975), p. 327.

[23]Daniel R. Vining, Jr., and James F. Kerrigan, "An Application of the Lexis Ratio to the Detection of Quotas in Professional Sport: A Note," *American Economist*, 22, no. 2 (1978), 74.

Even though the studies just cited lag behind the current state of affairs, they still show a pattern, one that has remained constant over time: Afro-Americans are overrepresented in some positions and underrepresented in others. Stacking goes on. Stacking would be reprehensible on moral-ethical grounds alone, but it also has negative socioeconomic consequences, both during the black athlete's career and after he retires.

Consequences of Stacking.   Black players typically have shorter careers than whites. To illustrate, running backs have the highest injury rates in football, and because disproportionate numbers of blacks play that position, disproportionate numbers of blacks have their careers cut short by injury.

Nor do marginal black players survive as long as marginal white players. According to a study of professional basketball, 43 percent of experienced players who averaged fewer than ten points per game were black, 57 percent were white. The pattern reverses among experienced players who averaged more than nineteen points per game: 63 percent were black, 37 percent were white.[24] More so for blacks than whites, "if you aren't good, you aren't there."

The shorter careers of Afro-Americans mean they earn less during the course of their careers. Just as important over the long run, shorter careers mean fewer blacks qualify for retirement benefits (professional football requires a minimum of five playing years), a fact causing enormous resentment among black athletes.[25]

Stacking has another long-term consequence. After retirement, stacking makes it difficult for blacks to go into coaching or management. A respected sociologist writes, "One's position in the formal structure of an organization contributes to the development of role skills which are essential to career movement."[26]

Although you usually don't think of baseball teams as having formal structure, they do in the various team positions such as catcher and pitcher. Some positions require more social skill than others. Outfielders, of whom a disproportionate number are black, are isolated far away from their teammates, and do not have the opportunity for much interaction. Infielders and catchers must frequently interact with teammates, opponents, and umpires. As a whole, the infield shows leadership and spirit ("infield chatter").

Spirit, smooth social interactions, and leadership are important skills for moving up the organizational pyramid. In baseball this is the move from active player to coach or manager. Three-fourths of all baseball managers are former infielders or catchers. One-fourth played just one position: catcher.[27] Even assuming a colorblind hiring process, stacking means that relatively few blacks will get the playing background that most often leads to management and coaching—an indirect but very real consequence.

Stacking even affects the careers of the few blacks who do make it into coaching. A

---

[24]Norris R. Johnson and David P. Marple, "Racial Discrimination in Professional Basketball: An Empirical Test," *Sociological Focus*, 6 (Fall 1973), 6–18.

[25]William Lide, "Forced Retirement Among Professional Football Players with Short-Termed Careers," (unpublished Ph.D. dissertation, Department of Health and Recreation, The Ohio State University, 1981).

[26]Oscar Grusky, "The Effect of Formal Structure on Managerial Recruitment: A Study of Baseball Organization," *Sociometry*, 3 (1963), 346–47.

[27]Ibid., pp. 346–47.

survey of major college football teams shows that of the forty black coaches who responded, half worked with running backs, wide receivers, and defensive backs. No blacks coached quarterbacks and only two coached linebackers (a position entrusted with leading the defense).[28] Thus black coaches end up coaching black positions and producing black players, a few of whom will become coaches and work with blacks in stacked positions, and so on.

Stacking is so heavily documented and has been going on for so long that it cannot be a statistical quirk or the work of a few racist individuals. Stacking results from permanent, structural causes, a complicated interplay of the remnants of Jim Crow, socialization, modeling, subculture, and rational choice.

An Explanation of Stacking.   Jim Crow prescribed separation of the races, which was possible in sport so long as the color line existed. Once integration took place, however, a different kind of separation developed, stacking. Each race now played its ''own'' positions. Even though physical separation could no longer be maintained, the symbolism of it could—remnants of Jim Crow in more subtle clothes.

Jim Crow also prohibited the subordination of whites to blacks—blacks could not give orders to whites—a prohibition reinforced by negative black stereotypes. Stacking helps reinforce the prohibition. Because quarterbacks lead the offense, black quarterbacks would be giving orders to white players; black catchers would be calling pitches for white pitchers and giving white managers advice on the performance of those white pitchers. If such situations occur only when an extraordinarily qualified black appears on the scene, it could be taken as evidence that all is well in the world of sport; a kind of tokenistic display of ethnic equality. But if it happens routinely, the tenet of dominance would be seriously undermined. Stacking prevents that, both by symbolically upholding white dominance and by actually reducing the number of black athletes in leadership positions.

Another process—modeling—gets involved. Modeling is a form of hero worship—followers copying their heroes. Like play, modeling helps socialize children into certain roles and goes on routinely. According to a study of six predominantly black colleges in the South and East, 86 of 129 black athletes surveyed recalled having an athlete hero while in grammar school. In high school, over half of the 86 played the same position as their early hero. Seventy-seven of the 129 said they had an athlete hero while in high school and approximately half now (in college) played the same position as their high-school hero. Significantly, virtually all of the players who had heroes had black heroes.[29] We can surmise that the heroes played stacked positions thus inspiring their followers to play stacked positions. Stacking leads to stacking.

Individual black athletes might wish to play stacked positions for rational reasons. If coaches believe that blacks make, say, poor pitchers, then a black who insists on pitching had better be very, very good. When teachers—and coaches are a kind of teacher—think

---

[28]Oree Banks, ''How Black Coaches View Entering the Job Market at Major Colleges,'' *Journal of Physical Education and Recreation*, 50 (May 1979), 62.

[29]Sandra C. Castine and Glyn C. Roberts, ''Modeling in the Socialization Process of the Black Athlete,'' *International Review of Sport Sociology* (Warsaw: Polish Scientific Publications, 1974), pp. 59–73.

certain pupils cannot perform well, they unconsciously downgrade the performance of those pupils even though by other standards the performance is quite good. Prophecies have a way of fulfilling themselves.

The same process will work against that black pitcher. Being as good as a white pitcher will not be good enough. That black pitcher must be significantly better just to overcome the coach's (probably unconscious) tendency to downgrade his ability. Black athletes know this (although they might not describe it in the way we just did). As laypersons they would more likely think: Why buck the system? Why not just go for the positions normally filled by blacks and increase the odds of making it? Indeed, why not? Said an Afro-American who played quarterback for a major college during his junior year and switched to flanker during his senior year, "I'd have a better chance making the pros as a receiver." (As it turned out, he didn't make it anyway).[30]

In sum, stacking—assigning playing positions according to race—results from a combination of norms, values, social processes, and social structure. We can say the same thing in another way: Stacking is institutionalized racism.

FUTURE: FAILURE OF SUCCESS

Sooner or later, at some point or another, the subject of ethnic relations involves the concept of equality. Equality is not a simple concept. It includes at least two subconcepts, both tricky in their own right: equal pay for equal work and equal opportunity for equal motivation.

Consider the first subconcept, equal pay for equal work. At the *top* level of professional sport, equal pay prevails once ability gets taken into account. Black athletes earn the same salaries as comparable whites. However, blacks do not have the same range of outside opportunities as whites: endorsing products, going on the banquet circuit, getting good off-season jobs, building a network of business connections. Blacks who do manage to capitalize on their athletic fame in these ways may or may not get equal pay for equal work. Much more fundamental is the fact that most don't get the work.

The other subconcept, equal opportunity for equal motivation, cannot be empirically documented. Motivation is the methodological bugaboo. How do you define "motivation to play" let alone measure it among millions of aspirants? All we can do is point to certain facts and then make mental allowances for the motivational factor.

Consider: If you use the Jackie Robinson episode of 1947 to mark the beginning of modern sports integration, the present-day existence of stacking means that racism has lingered from 1947 until now—a period of over four decades. That is a pessimistic assertion. Other racial inequities reinforce the pessimism: the requirement that blacks have better "character," the difficulties blacks have breaking into social or club sports, the fact that marginal black players get cut sooner than whites, and the small number of black coaches. Even making a most generous allowance for the motivational factor, we would still come to a pessimistic conclusion.

---

[30]Personal communication.

On the other hand, pessimism should not overshadow the hopeful side of ethnic relations in sport. It's worth noting that sport was officially integrated before the integration of public schools, before blacks could ride in the front of the bus, and before the integration of faculty clubs in many universities. No other institution has produced so many black heroes (heroes to all races) and offered so much fame and fortune to minority aspirants.

The current state of affairs suggests both pessimism and hope, and we therefore make two predictions about the future of ethnic relations in sport:

Pessimistic prediction: Things won't be changing much, if at all.

Part of this prediction would come true simply because the easiest and most dramatic changes have already been made (the color line has been broken). The remaining changes will not be nearly as dramatic. They will mostly be small changes, such as reducing the amount of stacking a little, or increasing the proportion of black coaches by a few percentage points. These changes will not come easily and we further predict that the Zeitgeist of the 1980s will not help matters. We predict that the 1980s will be characterized by economic uncertainty, slow change, little change, or no change, and a smaller role for government. The catch phrase might be something like: "Stay the course," "Full speed ahead, slowly," "The status quo is here to stay."

This status-quo Zeitgeist means that blacks will continue to glorify sport; that black athletic heroes will still inspire black youths to follow in their footsteps; that alternative careers will remain scarce; and that the Afro-American dream will still be that "any black can be a superstar jock." Like the myth of Horatio Alger, and the myth of success, Duquesne style, the "Afro-American dream will elude all but a tiny few of those who pursue it.

We know (from Chapter 4) that, because sport and school are linked, sport produces upward mobility—*but only for a tiny fraction of the population.* Most people, regardless of race, do not have enough athletic ability. Making the situation even more dismal, evidence suggests that sports participation, which motivates high school athletes to go on to college, does not do so for blacks. (The evidence is far from complete though.)[31]

Professional sport does not offer a solution either. About ten million black male youths dream of getting one of the only three thousand jobs for players. You don't have to be a statistician to know that those are ludicrously tiny odds. According to a sociology textbook, "If young blacks were urged to aspire to a career in any other national industry that could offer only about 3,000 mostly temporary jobs, the idea would seem absurd. It is a tribute to the power of myth that it persists in the face of these facts."[32] The myth has caused a failure to expand horizons, to look beyond a glamour field to find long-term,

---

[31]See Michael Hanks, "Race, Sexual Status and Athletics in the Process of Educational Achievement," *Social Science Quarterly*, 60 (December 1969), 482–98; J. Steven Picou, "Race, Athletic Achievement, and Educational Aspiration," *The Sociological Quarterly*, 19 (Summer 1978), 429–38; Melvin L. Oliver, "Race, Class, and the Family's Orientation to Mobility through Sport," *Sociological Symposium*, 30 (Spring 1980), 62–68.

[32]Robertson, *Sociology*, p. 90.

steady, midrange success. Parodoxically, this failure means that there is still some room to maneuver. Not all options have been closed off.

Hopeful prediction: Blacks will forget about sport.

It would be naive to think the problem of race relations will end easily and quickly. If the wave of a magic wand caused all antiblack prejudices to vanish, at least a half century of improvements in education, occupation, and income would have to take place before the typical black became socioeconomically equal to the typical white.[33] The hope of the black community must therefore rest on its youths. Hopefully, they will abandon the black dream of success through sport and start aspiring to become plumbers, lawyers, clerks, accountants. Obviously more than three thousand jobs exist in those fields, and attaining a black dominance in them would do more good than athletics for the largest number of blacks. Of course, it's easy to say, be a plumber, be a lawyer, be a clerk, be an accountant—but hard for those trapped in the ghetto to attain such positions. Yet it must eventually happen or black Americans will never become just plain Americans. A black superstar athlete expresses the hope this way: "Unfortunately our most widely recognized role models are athletes and entertainers—'runnin' and 'jumpin' and 'singin' and 'dancin.' . . . We have been on the same roads—sports and entertainment—too long."[34]

We asked a black graduate student what he thought of this statement. He agreed with it. That does *not* prove anything, but what he said illustrates a more hopeful future.

I didn't play any sports in high school, no more than for recreation. I was working, I was a paper boy. I really wanted to play, but I just didn't have the time. Economics caused me to do other things. My family needed money.

One of the sports I think I could've played—I mean played and been good at—would be track because I was somewhat long winded. I think I could've run the 440 or something but I just didn't have the time.

I had a lot of friends who played football and basketball. My brother was an athlete. He received a scholarship to go to a junior college. We thought my brother would go on to college from junior college but he decided to get married and drop out of junior college.

I'm not sure why I went to college. I went to a junior college because it was close to my house: as a matter of fact it was about a couple of blocks. My ambition in life was, well, I just wanted to be something. No one in my family had graduated from college.

Like you think about the Dr. J's, Muhammed Ali's, and all these types of people, and blacks look up to those people, you know, but when you think about the situations blacks are in—sport will not pull us out of it. It'll help us financially but, you know, we need to develop our minds much more than we do. I think that sports

---

[33]For example, see Stanley Lieberson and Glenn V. Fuguitt, "Negro-White Occupational Differences in the Absence of Discrimination," *American Journal of Sociology*, 73 (September 1967), 188–200. Different studies produce different estimates but no estimate is very short.

[34]*Times*, May 9, 1977, p. 60. Copyright 1977, Time Inc. All rights reserved. Reprinted by permission from *Time*.

are good in that young black kids do have some positive role models to look up to, but blacks should try to excel academically more than they should try to excel athletically. In sports you don't develop your mind per se, you develop your body. And I think I would rather know as much as I can. I think it'll all pay off. It might take a long time. That's how I feel.[35]

SUMMARY

1. Blacks dominate many American sports because "there are games to be played and won, and when won, rewarded." We reject a genetic explanation. Such an explanation overlooks obvious cultural influences and might contain a subtle racist-ideological bias.

2. The economic incentive for blacks to enter sports is reinforced by the black subculture, which converts the successful superstar athlete into a heroic figure, and by the norms and values that emphasize the importance of sport.

3. Stacking—the assignment of playing positions according to race—has been going on for a long time. This fact has been overwhelmingly documented. Stacking has long-term consequences for blacks, all bad. We suggest that stacking is a remnant of Jim Crow. Stacking prevents the subordination of whites to blacks (except under rare conditions) and maintains a kind of symbolic segregation on the playing field.

4. The future of race relations in sport is tied to race relations in American society. The present Zeitgeist seems to be one of economic uncertainty and slow change. Extrapolating that into the future means that the current situation of blacks in America and in sports will probably remain much the same. On the other hand, it could be that black subculture will de-emphasize sport and reemphasize the notion the greatest number of Afro-Americans will benefit from midrange success in more mundane occupations.

---

[35]Ronnie Stewart, Ohio State University, as interviewed by Timothy J. Curry, 1981.

7

COACHING
AND SOCIAL ORGANIZATION
How to Win

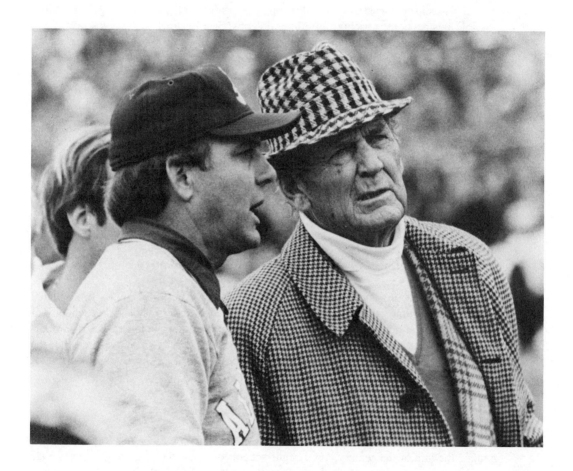

The Bear. In the final game of the 1981 football season, Alabama beat Auburn and 'Bama's coach,
William Bear Bryant, notched his 315th victory and
became the winningest football coach in collegiate
history, surpassing the fabled Amos A. Stagg. Bryant
died in 1982 and was mourned by many persons in
many walks of life. Photo by Malcolm W. Emmons.

A sports columnist describes the job of coaching at a major sports school:

> Coaching athletics is a marvelously bloodthirsty, exhilarating, gut-wrenching, re-
> warding, unstable business.
>   It is more than X's and O's. It is human relations, recruiting wars, academic
> wet-nursing, film-watching, airplane-catching and midnight oil-burning until some-
> times victory cannot be separated from defeat—and work from family.[1]

This chapter concerns that "bloodthirsty, exhilarating, gutwrenching, rewarding, unstable business" of coaching big-time athletics. The occupation involves everything from staying up late diagramming plays to charming teenage athletes to oiling legislators at cocktail parties, and much, much more. The job is complicated and broad, and we thus need a comprehensive perspective from which to view it. We use the perspective of social organization; and as it turns out, this automatically produces a little sociological discourse on how to win. Throughout the chapter we illustrate sociological points with the biographies of successful coaches, particularly Bear Bryant and John Wooden.

First, a few definitions: We take success to mean winning, and failure to mean losing; but with the stipulation that normally accepted rules and customs must be followed (otherwise we would be studying deviance).

An occupation is one's primary work. It may or may not be a profession, which is work requiring specialized theoretical knowledge that must be acquired through training, usually in college, and that gives the possessor considerable authority over clients. Everyone can coach—just find some athletes willing to take your advice (witness the thousands of adults coaching kids' leagues after work)—but not everyone has the qualifications to be a member of the coaching profession. This profession has only twenty thousand members.[2]

Throughout this chapter we will discuss coaching as a profession, with particular attention to big-time coaches: those who coach major sports at major sports schools, or who coach professional teams. Although small in number, big-time coaches disproportionately influence our culture because they control an activity that is so much in the public eye. People know what big-time coaches do, and many people copy them.

COACHING AND WINNING

Around the turn of the century, Ivy League schools dominated collegiate sport with Yale reigning supreme, especially in football. Between 1883 and 1901 Yale had nine undefeated seasons. From 1885 to 1899, Yale won forty-six straight games while outscoring

---

[1]Kaye Kessler, "You're Fired: The Defense Rests," *Columbus Citizen-Journal*, January 6, 1982, p. 11. Copyright 1982. Used with permission.

[2]George H. Sage, "An Occupational Analysis of the College Coach," in *Sport and Social Order*, eds. Donald H. Ball and John W. Loy (Menlo Park, California: Addison-Wesley Publishing Co., Inc., 1975). This is a thorough review of the literature.

their opponents by a margin of seventy to one. Amazingly, in 1888, 1891, and 1892 not a single point was scored against the team. Yale's traditional rival was, and remains, Harvard. Between 1875 and 1911, Yale won twenty-seven games, Harvard won five.[3] (A famous apocryphal story illustrates the rivalry: Just before his team went out on the field to meet Harvard, Yale coach Ted Coy told his players, "Gentlemen, in a few minutes you will play Harvard. Nothing you ever do in life will be as important."[4])

In large part, Yale's dominance can be traced to the Zeitgeist of the Robber Barons. You may recall from Chapter 2 that the Industrial Revolution had recently changed the economic foundations of American society; a change leading to new cultural values that affected sport and thence coaching.

It was to Yale that the sons of the Robber Barons went, imbuing the school with a spirit of competition, change, and winning. It was at Yale that sociologist and social Darwinist William Graham Sumner taught. "Sumner's brand of sociology reinforced several generations of Yalemen's faith in themselves as well as in their wealthy fathers," writes a social historian.[5]

It was also at Yale that Sumner's brother-in-law, Walter Camp (the "father of football") coached those enormously successful teams on a part-time basis while working full time for the New Haven Clock Company. Apparently it was a happy combination of jobs because the clock business was steady but not busy.[6] (During this period, schools commonly hired coaches on a part time or seasonal basis, a practice which continued well into the 1920s.[7])

Camp approached football like the Robber Barons approached business: he played hard and to win. He "demanded absolute obedience and dedication to the proposition that nothing superseded the importance of victory" and to the need for practice and sacrifice.[8]

"[Camp] was urging his players to struggle for victory on the gridiron [just as] Sumner was urging Yale students to struggle for wealth and power in America's market place . . . It was at Yale that the principles of Spencer [another social Darwinist] and Sumner became part of the ideology of intercollegiate football."[9]

Meanwhile, Harvard stood aloof. Harvard remained the college of choice for the old-line American aristocracy whose wealth (from shipping and agriculture) originated before the Civil War. This elite looked to Europe for models of gentility, and to the British schools for ideals about sport and competition. As we discussed in Chapter 2, the British upper classes approached collegiate sport as a form of exercise, recreation, and comrade-

---

[3]Allen L. Sack, "Yale 29—Harvard 4: The Professionalization of College Football," *Quest*, 19 (Winter 1973), 24–34.

[4]See George Plimpton, "Medora Goes to the Big Game," *Sports Illustrated*, November 16, 1981, pp. 84–98.

[5]Digby Baltzell, quoted in Sack, "Yale 29—Harvard 4," p. 30.

[6]Hartford Powel, Jr., *Walter Camp: The Father of American Football, An Authorized Biography* (1926; reprint, Freeport, New York: Books for Libraries Press, 1970).

[7]Howard J. Savage, *American College Athletics* (New York: The Carnegie Foundation for the Advancement of Teaching, 1929), pp. 166–67.

[8]Guy Lewis, quoted in Sack, "Yale 29—Harvard 4," p. 31.

[9]Sack, "Yale 29—Harvard 4," p. 30.

ship. No gentleman went all-out to win; that would not be genteel; it would ruin the purpose of the game. Harvard's much-respected president of the time, Charles Eliot, strongly supported this philosophy. In a report to the alumni he wrote, ''so called sports which require a dull and dreaded routine of hardship and suffering in preparation for a few exciting crises are not worth what they cost. They pervert even courage and self-sacrifice because these high qualities are exercised for no adequate end.''[10] Winning wasn't everything—it wasn't anything. It wasn't worth the cost.

Harvard backed a losing cause. In the end, Yale values dominated and coaches of major sports increasingly narrowed their focus down to one goal above all others—to win.

Camp had showed them how: Collect resources (players, money, and support) for a full-blown program; then organize and systematize; and then concentrate, practice, and work. And never stop short of victory.

GREAT MEN AND GREAT ORGANIZATIONS

The Bear. In the final game of the 1981 football season, Alabama beat Auburn and 'Bama's coach, William Bear Bryant, notched his 315th victory and became the winningest football coach in collegiate history, surpassing the fabled Amos A. Stagg.[11] The following year he retired with a lifetime record of 323 wins, eighty-five losses and seventeen ties. He passed away in 1983.

Bryant grew up during the Great Depression in Moro Bottom, Arkansas. As a teenager he earned his nickname when he took on a wrestling bear in a carnival. Bryant played football for Fordyce High and won a scholarship to Alabama.

After graduation he stayed at Alabama as assistant coach and then moved to Vanderbilt, also as assistant coach. He joined the Navy when World War II broke out and eventually ended up coaching football at a preflight school in North Carolina. After the war, he became head coach at Maryland but resigned when the university president overruled his decision to suspend some players for disciplinary reasons. He moved to the University of Kentucky and stayed there for eight years. Then he moved to Texas A&M, where he ran afoul of recruiting violations and mercilessly drove his players in 100-degree-plus weather. In 1958 Bryant returned to his alma mater, overhauled a floundering program, and earned the reputation of supercoach.[12]

The Wizard. In 1947, the UCLA basketball team had a record of twelve wins and thirteen loses. In 1948 John Wooden became head coach and promptly won twenty-two and lost eight—the best season in UCLA history up to that time. In all the years he was to be at UCLA, Wooden would never have a losing season and, near the end of his career, he would be called ''Wizard of Westwood'' (the community in which UCLA is located).

Wooden eventually won ten NCAA championships (a record probably never

---

[10]Quoted in Sack, ''Yale 29—Harvard 4,'' p. 31.

[11]*New York Times*, November 15, 1981, p. 27.

[12]Bryant's biography is taken from Paul W. Bryant and John Underwood, *Bear: The Hard Life and Good Times of Alabama's Coach Bryant* (Boston: Little Brown & Company, 1975); *Time Magazine*, ''Football's Supercoach,'' September 29, 1980, pp. 70–77; Clyde Bolton, *The Crimson Tide: A Story of Alabama Football* (Huntsville, Alabama: The Strode Publishers, 1979).

to be equalled in our lifetimes) but it took him sixteen years to start. In 1964 he won his first and in 1965 he won his second. He then won seven straight NCAA championships (1967 through 1973). In 1975 he won his tenth and then retired.

Despite the first sixteen years of comparative obscurity, Wooden has always been a super-success. He starred as a high-school player in Indiana. He matriculated at Purdue where he made all-American three times and College Player of the Year once. In 1960, he was elected to the Basketball Hall of Fame as a player; in 1972 he was elected as a coach. He is the only person to be in the Hall in both roles.[13]

If you measure greatness by winning, then Bryant and Wooden most assuredly qualify as great coaches. Such greatness is rare—and intriguing. For a long time scholars have asked: What makes great people great? Many long books have been written trying to answer that seemingly simple question.

Success and Charisma

At retirement, Bryant described himself as a sixty-nine-year-old man who was worn out. Whether true or not, that was definitely not the case when he was active. He seemed to have a special quality: charisma.

A former player said of him, "This must be what God looks like."[14] The governor of Alabama said he is "larger than life," and one of Bryant's assistant coaches described his staff meetings: "He just had that magic about him: if he was going to say anything you were going to be sure you didn't miss it."[15]

These statements describe charisma. Max Weber defined charisma as "a certain quality of an individual personality by virtue of which he is set apart from ordinary men and treated as endowed with . . . exceptional powers or qualities. These are not accessible to the ordinary person . . . and on the basis of them the individual concerned is treated as a leader."[16]

Undoubtedly some people have the magical quality of charisma; and it obviously helps them to succeed in any endeavor. This is especially true in coaching, which requires so much interpersonal contact: convincing athlete and parents that the coach's school is the best one to attend; getting along with the administration; courting a favorable press; and gaining help of the alumni. In situations like these, which are highly important to the coach's success, the ability to inspire followership by the sheer power of personality—charisma—is a tremendous help. Perhaps it accounts for greatness.

Perhaps it does, but it probably does not. Even putting aside the troublesome

---

[13]From John Wooden, *They Call Me Coach*, as told to Jack Tobin, copyright 1972, 1973, Key-Word Edition; used by permission of World Books, Publishers, Waco, Texas, 76796. Dwight Chapin and Jeff Prugh, *The Wizard of Westwood: Coach John Wooden and his UCLA Bruins* (New York: Warner Paperback Library, 1973).

[14]*Time*, "No. 1 and Still Counting," December 7, 1981, p. 68.

[15]*Time*, "Football's Supercoach," September 29, 1980. Copyright 1980 Time Inc. All rights reserved. Reprinted by permission from *Time*.

[16]Max Weber, *Theory of Social and Economic Organization*, trans. Talcott Parsons and A. M. Henderson (New York: The Free Press, 1965), pp. 358–59.

question of precisely what charisma *is* (a question never completely answered by Weber or by later scholars), we still have a puzzle. Did, say, Bryant succeed because he had charisma? Or did his success make him charismatic? Which came first? Which is cause and which is effect?

We submit that most of the time success is the cause and charisma is the effect. Writes a respected sociologist: "Authority [power] when it is massive and continuous, calls forth, by its mere existence, the attribution of charisma."[17] Coaches have great power. For example, they routinely make decisions affecting the careers of their players. Responding to a journalist's inquiry, Bryant once went over a list of his redshirts: "He'll never play . . . He'll never . . . He might play sometime . . . He'll play . . . Might play . . . Won't ever . . . Won't ever . . ."[18] Bryant had a list of names and was deciding, or had already decided, the athletic careers of these players.

Major sports also become major businesses, pumping millions of dollars through school and community. Under Bryant, Alabama football revenues paid for ten million dollars worth of athletic facilities. Just managing the athletic budget has become a matter of high finance.

Reporters dog coaches for quotes and interviews. Coaches regularly appear before the TV cameras, often on their own shows with wide viewing audiences. The "Bear Bryant Show" had a larger viewing audience than any TV program in its time slot.[19]

No matter what the coach's real personality—he could have all the charm of the proverbial cold fish—when the power of his position and the glamor of the media combine on a single coach, charisma results. He will become bigger than life, like Bryant and other highly successful personalities in and out of sport.

In actuality, charisma isn't so much a personality trait as it is the result of a back-and-forth social process that goes on continually: Success makes the coach charismatic, which leads to more success, which makes the coach more charismatic, which leads to more success, and so on.

While we do not doubt that individual coaches can make a difference to winning and losing, we can all too easily overestimate the influence of a single leader. At the time Bryant took over, Alabama had floundered through three losing seasons. Before that, however, Alabama won all the time. Alabama had joined the Southeastern Conference in 1933 and up to the year Bryant became head coach, had won five conference championships and one national championship, and had gone to nine bowl games. Bryant got 'Bama back on its old track, not on a brand new one.[20]

Baseball manager Casey Stengel provides another example worth pondering. His plaque in the Hall of Fame reads: "Managed New York Yankees 1949–1960. Won 10 Pennants and 7 World Series with New York Yankees. Only manager to win 5 consecutive World Series 1949–1953. Managed Brooklyn 1934–1936, Boston Braves 1938–1943, New York Mets 1962–1965."

[17]Edward Shills, "Charisma, Order, and Status," *American Sociological Review*, 30 (April 1965), 212.

[18]Rick Telander, "I Was Never Sure About Anything," *Sports Illustrated*, September 11, 1978, p. 104.

[19]*Time*, "Football's Supercoach," p. 73.

[20]See Bolton, *The Crimson Tide*, pp. 268–69.

Meaning no disparagement of Stengel's record, notice that the plaque stresses his years with the Yankees. As their manager he won 62 percent of his games, and many pennants and World Series. But when Stengel managed the Brooklyn Dodgers he won less than 50 percent and no pennants; with Boston the same.

After leaving the Yankees for the Mets, he won 30 percent of his games and again, no pennants. Stengel's charisma and leadership worked only with the Yankees—a fact suggesting that the Yankees had a great deal to do with Stengel's success.[21]

These biographical facts do not deny the existence of individual greatness; they just affirm that only rarely will a leader chance upon the scene and make a major difference. The conclusion generalizes to other coaches and sports, as documented by several statistical studies.

- In professional baseball, bringing in a new manager will not necessarily turn a losing team around. The change improves performance 60 percent of the time, but the same statistic also means that 40 percent of the time performance does not improve.[22]

- A study of college basketball teams concludes that "poor teams will probably improve their records with or without a coaching change."[23]

- New leadership might even make things worse. Whenever a new coach takes over, everything changes—personnel, rules, philosophy, and tactics—resulting in substantial disruption. According to a study of professional baseball, the more frequently teams changed managers, the further behind the leading team they were, on the average. Whether being behind caused the teams to change, or whether the change caused them to fall behind, cannot be determined from the data.[24]

- Of big-time football colleges from 1945 through 1978, only fifteen out of 176 Division 1–A or 1–AA teams have ever been ranked among the top ten more than ten times. Oklahoma leads with twenty-two. Considering the top ten teams, the chances are almost 50 percent that five out of the ten will repeat from one year to next. This means only five new teams (or coaches) can break into the top ten elite each year.[25] It follows that coaching at one of the five repeating schools greatly aids the coach's probability of success. (See Table 7.1.)

Very often greatness consists in having the foresight and ability to become head coach of a team with a long history of winning. Given the scarcity of such teams and the

---

[21]This is also true in private industry. Both Henry Ford and William Durant (founder of General Motors) failed at one time or another. See Howard E. Aldrich, *Organizations and Environments* (Englewood Cliffs, New Jersey: Prentice-Hall, Inc., 1979), p. 19.

[22]William A. Gamson and Norman A. Scotch, "Scapegoating in Baseball," *American Journal of Sociology*, 70 (July 1964), 69–72. Also see Oscar Grusky, "Managerial Succession and Organizational Effectiveness," *American Journal of Sociology*, 69 (July 1963), 21–31.

[23]D. Stanley Eitzen and Norman R. Yetman, "Managerial Change, Longevity, and Organizational Effectiveness," *Administrative Science Quarterly*, 17 (1972), 115.

[24]Nancy Theberge and John Loy, "Replacement Process in Sport Organizations: The Case of Professional Baseball," *International Review of Sport Sociology*, 11, no. 2 (1976), 73–93.

[25]Yung-Mei Tsai and Lee Sigelman, "Stratification and Mobility in Big-Time College Football: A Vacancy Chain Analysis," *Sociological Methods & Research*, 8 (May 1980), 487–97.

fierce competition for so few openings, getting the job is by no means a trivial accomplishment.

Consequences of Winning and Losing

At times, sport can be the most coldblooded of institutions. The moment you stop producing, you're out. The athlete gets cut or traded as soon as the value of his productivity falls below his cost to the team. So too with coaches. When their records fall below organizational expectations—if they don't win enough—they're fired with hardly a thank you for past devotion. When a professional football team recently fired its losing coach, the general manager said, "[He's] a good man. I'm sorry to see him leave, but it's the bottom line, wins and losses."[26] The fact that changing coaches probably will not help much, is either not known, not appreciated, or ignored.

And so losing coaches lose their jobs in a kind of ritual sacrifice, a symbolic throwing of someone to the wolves ("howling" fans, alumni, and media must be appeased). The losing coach expects and accepts the role of scapegoat. "Any time I don't do my job, they can fire me. And they ought to!" said Woody Hayes, former supercoach of Ohio State football, in a television interview.

On the other hand, because great success is so rare, a supercoach gets a stranglehold on his position. Firing him for any reason other than losing, becomes virtually impossible. The history of Woody Hayes, one of the ten most winning coaches in history, shows this.

> **Entrenchment.**   Hayes served as head coach at OSU for twenty-eight years, beginning in 1951. During his reign he amassed 205 victories and only seventy-two losses and ten ties. He won or shared thirteen Big Ten championships (six in a row during one string), and three national championships.
>
> Without question, Hayes met the goal. He won. Just as unquestionably, he created controversy. He figured in at least eight major incidents, about one every three years. In 1956 he personally advanced extra money to some players. As a result of this violation, the NCAA placed Ohio State on probation. In 1958 Hayes barred the Big 10 Skywriters (a group of visiting sports reporters), resulting in a reprimand from the university. In 1959, after losing the Rose Bowl, Hayes either punched or shoved two reporters in the postgame locker room, for which the American Coaching Association censured him. In 1961, when the university's faculty council, supported by the president of an important alumni group, voted not to allow the team to go to the Rose Bowl, the fury of the media and fans ended in campus rioting and the local newspaper published the names and addresses of the faculty members who voted against going. As a result, the alumni president left and the faculty council lost its right to decide on subsequent bowl invitations, a clear political victory for Hayes.[27] In 1971, during the closing moments of a loss to Michigan (OSU's traditional rival) Hayes ripped the yard markers, demanding a penalty be called on a Michigan player. In 1973 Hayes pushed (some say punched) a photographer at the Rose Bowl. In 1977, after Michigan made a crucial intercep-

---

[26]"Colts Appoint Kush, Let McCormack Go," *New York Times*, December 22, 1981, p. 24. © 1981 by The New York Times Company. Reprinted by permission.

[27]Robert Vare, *Buckeye: A Study of Coach Woody Hayes and the Ohio State Football Machine* (New York: Harper & Row, 1974), chap. 6.

tion near the end of the game, Hayes punched a television cameraman in the stomach, for which he drew his second Big Ten probation. In 1978 during the Gator Bowl, when a Clemson player intercepted a last-ditch pass, ending OSU's hopes, Hayes punched the Clemson player in full view of a national television audience, for which he was fired.

We leave you to judge Hayes's behavior for yourself. We want to make a sociological point: How can a winning coach survive a career filled with so many incidents?

The basic reason is simple: Winning is highly prized and winning coaches are few in number, so the winning coach can do just about whatever he wants. By winning he eliminates the one major reason for which he might be fired. And in the course of winning year after year, he accumulates so much charisma, power, adulation, and support that he becomes politically unassailable. Firing a winning coach would cause a communitywide, perhaps even statewide or nationwide controversy and trauma, a reaction few administrators dare to face.

Some Conclusions

The logic, the examples of famous coaches, and the statistical studies all lead to these conclusions:

- Great coaches do exist and the quality of their greatness can be explained sociologically.
- Charisma comes from having a powerful position such as head coach, from media hype, and from success.
- Changing leadership will not necessarily improve team performance and might even hurt it. Coaches are fired mainly as part of a scapegoating ritual.
- The successful coach becomes entrenched in his job.

These conclusions leave us up in the air. Because success cannot be attributed to a quality such as charisma, and because changing coaches will not necessarily improve win-loss records, it follows that the characteristics of individual coaches, their psychology and character traits, are not overwhelmingly important. The explanation of success requires something more. We suggest that social organization is the "something more." Sociological evidence leads us to believe that organization determines everything, and statements by successful coaches reinforce the belief. Bryant used to claim, "I don't have time to coach individuals any more. I organize; my assistants coach."[28] Another successful collegiate coach prides himself on coaching his coaches. He says, "The key thing is to be well-organized, to pay attention to details and not be sloppy and poorly disciplined."[29]

---

[28]*Time*, "Football's Supercoach," p. 71. Copyright 1980 Time Inc. All rights reserved. Reprinted by permission from *Time*.

[29]Don James, head football coach of Washington University's 1980 and 1981 Rose Bowl victories; quoted in the *Columbus Citizen-Journal*, December 26, 1981, p. 14.

Table 7.1. Thirty Top Nationally Ranked Teams Since 1945

NUMBER OF TIMES INSTITUTIONS RANKED					
22.	Oklahoma	12.	Arkansas	5	Navy
21	Notre Dame	11	L.S.U.	5	Wisconsin
20	Alabama	11	Tennessee	5	Minnesota
18	Michigan	10	Mississippi	5	Iowa
17	Ohio State	10	U.C.L.A.	4	T.C.U.
16	Texas	7	Auburn	4	Rice
13	Michigan State	7	Georgia	4	Illinois
13	U.S.C.	7	Army	4	Missouri
13	Nebraska	7	Georgia Tech	4	North Carolina
13	Penn State	5	Maryland	4	Miami

Rankings refer to the number of times a team was ranked in the top ten by the Associated Press and/or United Press International. Others receiving ranking were: (3) Houston, Syracuse, Pittsburg, Washington, Oregon State, Southern Methodist, Texas A&M, California, Stanford, Purdue; (2) Pennsylvania, Colorado, Clemson, Kansas, Arizona, Princeton, Indiana, Kentucky, Arizona State; (1) Pacific, Texas Tech, Air Force, Oregon, West Virginia, Oklahoma State, Baylor, Duke, Wyoming, St. Mary's, Utah State, and Northwestern.
SOURCE: John D. Massengale, "The Prestigious College Football Coach: An Analysis of Sponsored Career Mobility," *Educational Resources Information Center*, #ED 189 080/SP 016 296, April 1980. Reprinted with permission.

A social scientist writes, "the organization of personnel in professional football is almost a caricature of the discipline of a modern corporate military industrial society . . . the primer for coaches might be military manuals and for players *The Organization Man.*"[30]

Whether the term *organization* refers to the act of "arranging in an orderly way," as the coaches quoted above used it, or to the formal sociological concept defined below, organization provides the bedrock for coaching success.

SPORTS ORGANIZATION

Big-time sports organizations resemble typical business organizations. For instance, an athletic department has a hierarchy of authority and a complex division of labor: a director, assistants, bookkeepers, secretaries, public relations experts, administrators, coaches, trainers, student managers, and athletes. Several million dollars flow through an athletic department every year, as Table 7.2 shows.

A major sports organization easily fits the so-called goal model. It has an unambiguous fix on a major goal (winning), an easy and public way to measure the goal

[30]Michael R. Real, *Mass Mediated Culture* (Englewood Cliffs, New Jersey: Prentice Hall, Inc., 1977), p. 106.

(win-loss records), and an almost monomaniacal dedication to achieving the goal.[31] The goal model provides a way to organize complicated activities into manageable form. The model goes beyond that, though. It also implies values and ways of thinking. From goal-model organization, and the values and thinking that go along with it, come many of the beliefs and practices that coaches have to deal with: strict control over athletes, rationality, and bureaucracy.

The Coach as Bureaucratic Manager

During a game, Bear Bryant would refer to a scrap of paper on which he had written notes to himself. If you read the paper, you would not find any earthshaking secrets: "Keep an orderly bench," "Use time outs intelligently."[32] Even though Bryant had charisma and was backed by a superlative football organization, he saw to the "teeny-tiny" details, as he called them.

John Wooden also knew the importance of tiny details. "Over the years I have become convinced that every detail is important and . . . that makes for the difference between champions and near champions. . . . Little things make big things happen, and that's what I try to get across to my players."[33]

When it comes to recording details, Wooden showed great bureaucratic persistence. He wrote everything in a notebook or on three-by-five cards: "I can go back twenty-four

Table 7.2. Estimated Athletic Budgets of Ten Major Universities

The Ohio State University	$9,713,000
University of Michigan	8,000,000
University of Missouri	7,134,000
Arizona State University	6,345,000
Iowa State University	6,000,000
U.C.L.A.	5,268,000
University of Oklahoma	5,200,000
University of Arkansas	5,000,000
University of Wisconsin	4,400,000
University of Washington	4,117,000

SOURCE: Data from James E. Odenkirk, "Intercollegiate Athletics: Big Business or Sports?," *Academe*, April 1981, pp. 62–66. Reprinted with permission.

[31] Because the goals of many organizations are so ambiguous, researchers have increasingly turned to other approaches. See W. Richard Scott, *Organizations: Rational, Natural, and Open Systems* (Englewood Cliffs, New Jersey: Prentice-Hall, Inc., 1981), p. 21; Ronald G. Corwin, "Patterns of Organizational Control and Teacher Militancy," *Research in Sociology of Education and Socialization*, 2 (1981), 268–71. Big-time sports organizations, however, are distinguished by the clarity and measurability of their major goal.

[32] *Time*, "Football's Supercoach," p. 76. Copyright 1980 Time Inc. All rights reserved. Reprinted by permission from *Time*.

[33] From John Wooden, *They Call Me Coach* as Told to Jack Tobin, copyright © 1972, 1973, Key-Word edition, pp. 102–3; used by permission of Word Books, Publisher, Waco, Texas 76796.

years and tell you what we did at 3:30 P.M. on a given afternoon. . . . My assistant and I spend two hours every morning closeted away planning a practice that may not last that long. Every entry is made on a white 3 × 5 card that I carry in my pocket."[34]

Bryant and Wooden were implicitly making the same distinction that Max Weber and other scholars of organization make—the distinction between getting things done through charisma and getting things done through bureaucratic management. Wrote Weber, "Charismatic authority is thus specifically outside the realm of everyday routine. . . . It is sharply opposed both to rational, and particularly bureaucratic, authority."[35]

Too often we overlook the importance of bureaucratic management because it tends to be unglamorous and tedious and because it takes place behind the scenes. Forms have to be filled out, purchase orders mailed, telephone calls returned, courtesy visits made—teeny-tiny details, none perhaps overwhelmingly important in itself, but all together vitally important to an effective organization. Someone has to take care of these details, and usually that someone is the coach. He has to be a bureaucratic manager.

Highly successful football coach Paul Brown says, "In a big institution the coach often doesn't pay enough attention to [equipment purchases], so the people who do the selling find they can set up deals with people on the inside."[36]

When the sports program of a major school in the Rocky Mountains failed, a real estate executive and prominent alumnus pointed the finger at the coach's lack of management ability: "[He] brought on the mess, and you don't have to look any further. Our athletic program is the laughingstock of the country. He has shown no ability whatsoever to administer." A professor of management at the same school agreed: "Somebody has to be responsible."[37]

Taking the responsibility for details, planning, organizing, controlling, and leading a team involves at least as much management as coaching. Indeed the distinction between the two occupations may be one more of subject matter—coaches manage sports teams while executives manage business enterprises—than of broad differences in job requirements. A classic definition of management states that it "is getting things done through people."[38] Successful coaches are highly involved in that process too.

---

[34]From John Wooden, *They Call Me Coach* as told to Jack Tobin, copyright © 1972, 1973, Key-Word edition, pp. 104–5; used by permission of Word Books, Publisher, Waco, Texas 76796. For formal statements see Susan L. Greendorfer, "Intercollegiate Football: An Approach Towards Rationalization," *International Review of Sport Sociology*, 3, no. 12 (1977), 23–32; George H. Sage, "The Coach as Management: Organizational Leadership in American Sport," *Quest*, 19 (January 1973), 35–48.

[35]Weber, *Theory of Social*, p. 361. Also see Trevor Williams and John J. Jackson, "A Typology of Sport Organization," *Review of Sport and Leisure*, 6 (Summer 1981), 97–113.

[36]Paul Brown and Jack Clary, *PB: The Paul Brown Story*, p. 74. Copyright © 1979 by Paul Brown and Jack Clary. Reprinted with the permission of Atheneum Publishers.

[37]Douglas S. Looney, "There Ain't No More Gold in Them Thar Hills," *Sports Illustrated*, October 6, 1980, p. 36.

[38]Harold Koontz and Cyril O'Donnel, *Principles of Management: Analysis of Managerial Functions* (New York: McGraw-Hill Book Company, 1955), pp. 3, 64. This is a standard text which has gone through many editions.

Rationality

John Wooden relates an incident from his high school coaching days:

> I try to be fair and give each player the treatment he earns and deserves. . . . And it's always been my premise to give the ones who do the best in practice the vast majority of the playing time in the games.
>
> On this particular weekend during Eddie's [the fifth-string guard] junior year, we had stopped in a restaurant [after a game] . . . when I noticed Eddie . . . all alone in a corner. "What's the matter, Eddie?" I asked. "Coach," he said, "I know I can play ball if I just had a chance." I thought I'd just shut him up real quick. "All right, Eddie," I said. "I'll give you a chance. I'll start you against Fort Wayne . . . tomorrow night."
>
> To this day I've never figured out why I did that. I try never to compromise my judgment because of my affection for a boy. Decisions must be based on reason, not emotion.[39]

Notice that Wooden doubts the wisdom of his own behavior. He wants to base his decision on rational premises: Athletes who practice well should play well. Personal feelings towards an athlete have nothing to do with playing him; judgments must be rational, not emotional. His views reflect goal-model thinking.

A sociologist states a core aspect of the goal model: "Organizational rules, procedures, and regulations are derived from goals in a manner that says, 'If this is the goal, then this is the most rational procedure for achieving it.' "[40] In major sports, everyone from fans up through the president of the organization knows the goal—to win. The coach's job consists of figuring out rational means for achieving the goal. As Wooden says, "Decisions must be based on reason, not emotion."

Most of the time rational decisions produce better results than emotional ones but, paradoxically and unfortunately, coaches (like all managers) cannot always make rational decisions. The coach and the organization simply do not have that much rationality at hand; and never will. A classic analysis of administrative behavior asserts, "The capacity of the human mind for formulating and solving complex problems is very small compared with the size of the problems whose solution is required for objectively rational behavior in the real world—or even for a reasonable approximation to such objective rationality."[41] Real-world problems simply overwhelm the human's limited ability to reason. Call this "bounded rationality."

The principle of bounded rationality also applies to the organization. Says a highly regarded text, "The reasons for the limits on rationality are linked to the inability of the system as a whole [e.g., the athletic department] to provide maximum or even adequate

---

[39]From John Wooden, *They Call Me Coach* as told to Jack Tobin, copyright © 1972, 1973, Key-Word edition, pp. 57–58; used by permission of Word Books, Publisher, Waco, Texas 76796.

[40]Richard H. Hall, *Organizations: Structure and Process* (Englewood Cliffs, New Jersey: Prentice-Hall, Inc. 1972), p. 15.

[41]Herbert Simon, *Models of Man: Social and Rational* (New York: John Wiley & Sons, Inc., 1957), p. 198.

information for decision making, and the inability of the decision maker [e.g., the coach] to intellectually handle even the inadequate information that is available.''[42]

Bounded rationality puts the coach in that unpleasant position between ''the rock and the hard place.'' Strongly supported by administration, fans, and media, the athletic department hands the coach a mandate to win consistently and big, but cannot provide enough wisdom (rational capacity) to tell the coach how to do it. Failure will inevitably occur in the long run, except in the case of the few supercoaches, like Bryant and Wooden.

Control Over Athletes

The goal model rests upon certain philosophical-social beliefs about human nature. Most of the beliefs seem so natural, so commonplace and routine, that we seldom think about them; yet they guide our behavior.

> **Control.** In 1896 Walter Camp described a typical day in the life of his players. We pick up after practice: ''dinner is served at the football training table at 6:30 o'clock. At the head of the table sits the captain, with the doctor or trainer at the foot. With dinner the work of the day is not always complete. Very often there is signal practice. Perhaps there is a brief black board talk. In no case, however, are these protracted beyond the hour of 9:30, for at ten o'clock the player packs himself off to bed [in the athletes' dormitory]. The consoling evening pipe, or longed for cigarette, is of course denied him but walking along in the darkness to his room, he is hailed by half a dozen of his college mates and is repaid liberally for all the trouble and exactions of the day.''[43]
>
> Paul Brown, a modern coach famous for being highly organized, described his training camp for professional football players: ''I never left anything to the player's imagination: I laid out exactly what I expected from them, how I expected them to act on and off the field and what we expected to accomplish. . . . Our team had training rules, too, and we enforced them even though they were grown men . . .''[44]

The more things change, the more they stay the same: Brown's modern-day program rests on a philosophy very similar to Camp's. Of the many ways to organize and train an athletic team, why would you choose their way, which is the typical way, rather than some other way?

You might give any number of reasons: the need for total concentration on the sport, or the efficiency of teaching, or the avoidance of disrupting influences. While we would not dispute the validity of those reasons, a more fundamental philosophical-social reason exists. ''Behind every managerial decision or action are assumptions about human nature and human behavior. A few of these are remarkably pervasive. They are implicit in most

[42]Hall, *Organizations*, p. 266.

[43]Walter Camp and Lorin F. Deland, *Football* (Publisher unknown: 1896), pp. 82–83. Ellipses omitted.

[44]Paul Brown and Jack Clary, *PB: The Paul Brown Story*, pp. 13, 15, and 17. Copyright © 1979 by Paul Brown and Jack Clary. Reprinted with the permission of Atheneum Publishers.

of the literature of organization and in much current managerial policy and practice.''[45] This statement, made about business organization, also fits athletic organization.

Most coaches basically believe that they should do the telling and athletes should do what they're told; that athletes must be closely controlled and supervised or they will backslide and get out of line; that athletes need detailed rules enforced by punishments; and that a goal-model organization provides the best means for implementing these beliefs.[46] The literature on management calls this set of beliefs ''Theory X,'' And even though many scholars criticize Theory X as dehumanizing in its assumption that people must be closely controlled, the theory does fit many big-time sports.

We must remember that athletes competing at the big-time level have been highly selected and socialized into sport since childhood. They grew up in the climate of Theory X organizations and we suspect that they believe in Theory X as much as their coaches, who also were former athletes. A statement by a professional football player illustrates our suspicion: ''I went up to him [the coach] after the game and just said, 'thanks a lot.' It all started with him—the discipline, the conditioning. He whipped us into shape, mentally and physically, and made us believe we could win football games again.''[47]

Of course not all sports are like big-time football, a sport which easily lends itself to Theory X. At the other extreme are the ''lonely'' sports: marathon running, cross-country bicycling, cross-country skiing, and long-distance swimming. Such sports demand long, lonely hours doing roadwork, swimming laps, and lifting weights. When athletes wake up in the morning darkness for several miles of running or swimming or cycling, their coaches must trust them to really train and not just amble along. The goal may be the same as in big-time football (to win) but the most rational means for achieving it involves a different set of assumptions—''Theory Y.'' According to Theory Y, athletes can exercise self-discipline, they don't need a lot of rules and close supervision; they have self-motivation. A top track coach frequently tells his runners to ''stop and smell the roses.''[48]

Concludes an article on Theory X and Theory Y: ''In arguing for an approach which emphasizes the fit among tasks, organization, and people, we are putting to rest the question of which organizational approach is best. In its place we are raising a new question: What organizational approach is most appropriate given the task and people involved?''[49]

Not all sports, not all athletes, not all coaches, and not all organizations are alike. So no single set of managerial practices can possibly cover all situations. Coaches, like managers, must adjust accordingly. ''But probably as important as anything is

---

[45]Douglas McGregor, *The Human Side of Enterprise* (New York: McGraw-Hill Book Company, 1960), p. 33.

[46]Sage, ''The Coach as Management''; McGregor, *The Human Side of Enterprise*.

[47]''Lapham Credits Coach Gregg for Bengal's Successful Season,'' *Columbus Citizen-Journal*, December 15, 1981, p. 15.

[48]Rick Telander, ''Nobody's Bigger Than Jumbo,'' *Sports Illustrated*, March 10, 1980, p. 74.

[49]John J. Morse and Jay W. Lorch, ''Beyond Theory Y,'' in *The Editors of the Harvard Business Review On Management* (New York: Harper & Row, Publishers, Inc., 1975), p. 388. Also see William G. Ouchi, *Theory Z: How American Business Can Meet the Japanese Challenge* (Reading, Massachusetts: Addison-Wesley Publishing Co., Inc., 1981).

adaptability,'' wrote Knute Rockne of Notre Dame over fifty years ago, ''a coach must thoroughly adapt himself to surrounding conditions.''[50] During the 1960s when youths were challenging old conventions, Bryant says he didn't like long hair (he wanted to jerk it out by the roots) but ''I gave a lot and I'm glad I did because anything that is important to the kids is important.''[51] One's philosophy of human nature and the resulting organizational structures must respond to changes in the tempo of the times. Nothing ever stands still for very long.

In sport, an entire organization succeeds or fails depending on the actions of a relatively small number of key participants—perhaps two dozen football players, for instance, or half a dozen basketball players. On a moment-by-moment basis during practice and during the game, the nitty-gritty of coaching is getting those athletes to perform in a specific way designed to maximize the chance of victory. In addition to organization and management, the coach needs to achieve teamwork, spirit, cohesion, and harmony among his athletes. These can be achieved via the right social organization.

ORGANIZATION AND TEAMWORK

Time magazine once said of Bear Bryant:

> What fascinates Bryant about winning football games [is] the challenge of melding 95 very young men into a whole, making each man's vision of himself interdependent with those of his teammates. For all its excesses—and football has more than its share of faults—sport can be, at its best, a social compact of high order. ''I'm just a plowboy from Arkansas,'' Bryant insists, ''but I have learned over the years how to hold a team together. How to lift some men up, how to calm down others, until finally they've got one heartbeat, together, a team.''[52]

A coach starts with recruits, many of whom are strangers to him. They have different amounts and kinds of talents and diverse personalities, and they are young and far away from home for the first time. Most have been athletic stars all their lives and have become egocentric. A thousand complexities of these personnel must be coordinated and then overlaid with the technical complexities of the sport itself.

In big-time football, the offensive team has practically nothing directly to do with the defensive team. They are not on the field at the same time. They seldom practice together. Sometimes they hardly know each other's names. Within each team, however, a great deal of interaction must be coordinated. The movements of eleven players must be responsive to the moves of the eleven players on the opposing team. Moreover, subteams exist: backfield and line, center and quarterback, for example.

What we initially perceive as one team, turns out to be a series of teams and

---

[50]Knute K. Rockne, *Coaching* (New York: The Devin-Adair Company, 1925), p. vii.

[51]Bryant and Underwood, *Bear*, p. 15.

[52]*Time*, ''Football's Supercoach,'' p. 77. Copyright 1980 Time Inc. All rights reserved. Reprinted by permission from *Time*.

subteams when we look more closely. It is a very complicated organism, and achieving one heartbeat is a very difficult task. While much of the job remains a mysterious art—few coaches know the scientific basis for what they are doing; they just do it—some coaches do know factors which greatly increase the likelihood of putting together a team with one heartbeat. A right mix of the right sociological factors does exist.

Textbooks and monographs on coaching, and the coaches themselves, speak of teamwork in reverent tones, imparting to it an almost moral quality. John Wooden gives a typical definition of team spirit: "an eagerness to sacrifice personal interest or glory for the welfare of the team. It can also be regarded as consideration for others. The team must come first."[53]

Many social scientists use what amounts to Wooden's definition, with some variations. Over thirty years ago a highly regarded sociologist defined team spirit as "the willing, enthusiastic subordination to social organization."[54] Both the coach's definition and the sociologist's definition emphasize an emotional and ethical relinquishing of personal rewards for the greater good of the group. The words "eagerness," "sacrifice," "consideration," "enthusiastic," and "subordination," connote as much. However, the sociologist does add a key phrase: "to social organization."

We follow up on this seemingly small addition because it has large consequences. Making the distinction permits us to distinguish between *team spirit* and *teamwork*. *Teamwork* becomes the social organization of a team—the arrangement of goals, tasks, roles, rewards, and punishments in a design meant to accomplish victory. Individual sacrifices on the part of some athletes will be necessary to carry out the design—to achieve teamwork; if they sacrifice enthusiastically, we call it *team spirit*. And if team members enjoy working and playing together, we call it *team harmony*. And lastly, if players value membership—that is, strongly want to belong to the team—we call it *team cohesion*. Of these four concepts—teamwork, spirit, harmony, and cohesion—teamwork is the most fundamental.

As a special kind of social organization, teamwork has the same advantages as social organization in general:

> The parts [players] can be replaced without disturbing the integrity of the organization and new parts may be brought in to take their place in the pattern. . . . [Social organization] is exterior to the individual in the sense that it contains characteristics which are not present in its members originally, or in all members at any one time. . . . It endures . . . It exercises a dominance over its parts.[55]

Thus teamwork means control over the actions of individual athletes. Teamwork means coordination of individual abilities. And teamwork results in continuity. Substitutes can be brought in smoothly. The team outlives the playing career of any individual

---

[53]John Wooden and Bill Sharman, with Bob Seizer, *The Wooden-Sharman Method: A Guide to Winning Basketball* (New York: Macmillan, Inc., 1975), p. 119. Copyright © 1975 by Project Basketball, Inc.

[54]Robert E. L. Faris, *Social Psychology* (New York: The Ronald Press Company, 1952), p. 66. Faris uses the term "morale" rather than "team spirit."

[55]Faris, *Social Psychology*, pp. 5–6.

athlete, and in some cases, any individual coach. History and traditions develop around it.

Successful coaches consciously or unconsciously know all of this. Wooden always talks about team spirit while *teaching* teamwork. Once two social scientists observed fifteen of Wooden's practice sessions and divided his teaching behaviors into categories—giving instructions, calling for hustle, praising, scolding, and so on. Contrary to what you might expect, Wooden did nothing spectacular: 75 percent of his teaching consisted of verbal instructions about what to do and how to do it, with strong emphasis on fundamental skills; another 15 percent consisted of scolding, or scolding followed by instruction. Aside from sometimes calling for hustle (14 percent), he delivered no exhortations, no tirades nor did anything particularly dramatic. Claims Wooden, "The best teacher is repetition, day after day, throughout the season."[56]

Football coach Paul Brown illustrates the same point with his prepractice routine: "In our system everything had to be done a certain way. . . . I made sure each player was in his assigned seat in our football classroom. . . . I always talked to my players before practice, sometimes on subjects other than football, and laid out our objectives for that day and how long we expected to work . . ."[57]

Brown's and Wooden's secret, if it is one, lies hidden in the open, imprinting a clear social organization onto the interactions of their athletes.[58] Once a coach establishes good teamwork, then other positive results willl follow.

Research shows that the desire to affiliate (be part of the team) and the desire to achieve excellence are the two strongest motives athletes have for participating.[59] A professional football player remarking on a losing season provides an example: "This has been my most frustrating year. . . . It's been an unfun season, not because we're 4–10 but because of the environment here; with the continuous changes in personnel, there is just no camaraderie in the club, . . . just fragments really that no one can put together as a unit."[60]

Without organization (teamwork), team cohesion, harmony, and spirit cannot be achieved. In a disorganized state, there can be no team spirit because players really don't know what they are supposed to do and therefore have little idea of what sacrifices they are being asked to make. In a disorganized state, each player, rather than helping or rewarding a fellow player, hinders him. This means players frustrate and so punish each other, that they eventually come to dislike each other. Team harmony doesn't exist. In a

---

[56]Quoted in "What a Coach Can Teach a Teacher" by R. G. Tharp and R. Gallimore, p. 76, in *Psychology Today* magazine, January 1976. Copyright © 1976 Ziff Davis Publishing Co.

[57]Paul Brown and Jack Clary, *PB: The Paul Brown Story*, pp. 71 and 74. Copyright © 1979 by Paul Brown and Jack Clary. Reprinted with the permission of Atheneum Publishers.

[58]Authoritarianism may facilitate social organization. For certain kinds of groups and tasks, the advantages of crystal clear organization sometimes outweighs the benefits of democratic participation. Hence authoritarian coaches tend to be more successful than less authoritarian coaches. But this is only a tentative hypothesis. See Kenneth Apenman, Douglas N. Hastad, and William L. Cords, "Success of the Authoritarian Coach," *Journal of Social Psychology*, 92 (February 1974), 155–56.

[59]Wayne R. Halliwell, "Strategies for Enhancing Motivation in Sport," in *Coach, Athlete, and the Sport Psychologist*, eds. Peter Klavora and Juri V. Daniel (Toronto, Ontario: University of Toronto, School of Physical Education, 1979), pp. 187–98.

[60]Quoted in Halliwell, "Strategies," p. 194.

disorganized state, the collective goal—winning—is hard to achieve, so no one gets rewarded no matter what their individual excellence. Cohesion won't come about either.

But with good social organization (good teamwork), fragments are put together in an orderly goal-directed design, and cohesion, team spirit, and harmony come about almost as byproducts. All these elements combine to increase the chances of winning. Once the team starts winning, that makes for better team spirit, harmony, and cohesion, thus increasing teamwork even more, which then makes for more winning, . . . and so on. When things go well, they get better, and when they get better, they get even better.

As sociologists, we believe that social structure determines more human behavior than any other single factor. Social organization is a type of structure, and we have therefore linked it to coaching. From the microunit of the team to the broadest philosophical assumptions of human behavior, with bureaucracy and management in between, social organization explains what coaches do and why some succeed while others fail.

In the opening paragraph of the chapter, we mentioned that the emphasis on social organizations would automatically generate clues on how to win. That has been the case; and we conclude this chapter with a list of the top ten sociological principles for success.

CONCLUSION: TEN SOCIOLOGICAL PRINCIPLES FOR SUCCESS

The preceding discussion has mentioned principles of success, but implicitly. We herewith make them explicit and present them in the approximate order they appeared in the chapter:

- *Be smooth.* Interpersonal relations play a critical role in coaching. No one can become charismatic (in Weber's sense) through reading self-help books and taking leadership courses. However the social graces and the art of small talk can be acquired through practice, and will pay off in recruiting players.
- *Get a job with a winning organization.* Over the long run, an organization with a history of success will probably be successful again. Behind a great coach is a great organization.
- *Be a politician.* Court the support of administrators, alumni, students, and media. They can help you; or at least, they won't hurt you.
- *Be rational.* Even if rationality fails, everyone else expects you to be rational and will not give you much credit for being right intuitively or for being lucky all the time. But realize that rationality won't always work. At times playing hunches, following intuition, or relying on social instincts will work out better.
- *Be a bureaucrat.* Tiny details often make all the difference between winning and almost winning. Consequently, inside every successful coach resides a successful bureaucrat.
- *Be a manager.* A good deal of coaching consists of managing the organization. In all likelihood management based on the goal model and Theory X will work best—but adjustments to circumstances must be made.
- *Be adaptable.* Society and people change; new strategies, technology, and techniques develop. Without adaptability, you will be left behind.

- *Be daemonic*. Successful coaching at the big-time level requires an almost obsessive drive for work. If you aren't daemonic, you won't be able to hold your own against those who are daemonic. They'll just outwork you.
- *Be a fanatic for teamwork*. Make sure every player knows precisely what you expect, when, how, and why. This is teamwork. Team spirit, harmony, and cohesion will follow it.
- *Organize! organize! organize!*

SUMMARY

1. Max Weber argued that some people are endowed with charisma, a kind of charm. Charisma is sometimes used to account for great success in and out of sport. We suggest that more often than not charisma comes about because certain people have great power and are the focus of media attention. Charisma is a result, not a cause. We argue that great individuals very often are great because they have joined a great organization.
2. Statistical studies suggest that changing a team's leadership will not necessarily improve team performance. The firing of losing coaches is really a ritualized form of scapegoating.
3. Successful coaches often become deeply entrenched. The demand for victory is so intense and the supply of winning coaches so low, that those who succeed can write their own ticket.
4. In many respects, a big-time sports organization resembles a typical business. However, unlike many businesses, the goal of a sports organization is crystal clear: Win. Called a goal-model organization, this type of organization and the thinking that goes with it dominate big-time sport. Several consequences follow: The coach must be a bureaucratic manager looking after the details of his organization. The coach must use rational decision-making techniques because rationality is part of the goal model.
5. Unfortunately not enough rationality exists in any human being or any organization to always guarantee success (winning). This concept is called *bounded rationality*.
6. The goal model and goal-model thinking are based on certain assumptions of human nature: Strict control over athletes must be maintained lest they backslide and "goof off," a system of punishments and rewards must be installed, and the leaders (coaches) should give orders and athletes should follow them. This set of assumptions has been called Theory X. For sports such as marathon running or long-distance swimming, a different set of assumptions, called Theory Y, is more appropriate. This set of assumptions argues that the athlete can be trusted to have a high degree of self-motivation. Neither Theory X nor Theory Y are totally true or totally false. Different organizations, coaches, sports, and athletes require different approaches.
7. We define teamwork as the social organization of a team: the arrangement of goals, tasks, roles, rewards, and punishments in a design meant to achieve victory. Teamwork viewed in this way means that the team has a life of its own: It has a pattern

exterior to any individual, it permits the replacement of individuals, and it allows for the routinization of complex tasks. Most successful coaches stress teamwork as we define it, even if they speak of teamwork in a more spiritual sense. With good teamwork, team spirit, cohesiveness, and harmony will follow.

8. We summarized ten sociological principles of success. They are: Be smooth. Get a job with a winning organization. Be a politician. Be rational. Be a bureaucrat. Be a manager. Be adaptable. Be daemonic. Be a fanatic for teamwork. And above all: organize.

8 A CORPORATE VIEW OF SPORT

Cartels, Fights, Money, and Profanation

Before television, most people had never seen a pro football or baseball game. When TV broadcasts of sports became a reality, the nature of our society was altered. These days, Thanksgiving and New Year's Day would seem empty without football on the tube. Drawing by Alajalov; © 1949, 1977, The New Yorker Magazine, Inc.

The *New York Times* publishes photo reproductions of memorable sports stories. If you perused the volume on baseball, you would see the following headlines:

February 7, 1876: A MEETING OF MANAGERS . . . NEW RULES.

November 14, 1900: A NEW BASEBALL LEAGUE. ORGANIZATION OF EIGHT CLUBS WAS FORMED IN CHICAGO YESTERDAY.

August 30, 1903: NATIONAL BASEBALL AGREEMENT . . . PROFESSIONAL INTERESTS IN THE GAME THROUGHOUT THE COUNTRY TO BE PROTECTED.

December 23, 1915: LONG BASEBALL WAR IS SETTLED. FEDERAL LEAGUE PASSES OUT OF EXISTENCE—CONTRACT JUMPERS REINSTATED.

September 29, 1920: EIGHT WHITE SOX PLAYERS ARE INDICATED ON CHARGES OF FIXING 1919 WORLD SERIES.

October 8, 1926: BOY REGAINS HEALTH AS RUTH HITS HOMERS.

December 11, 1935: ESTIMATED YAWLEY HAS SPENT $3,500,000. HUGE SUM EXPENDED FOR RED SOX AND PLAYERS IN SEARCH OF PENNANT WINNER.

August 27, 1939: GAMES ARE TELEVISED. MAJOR LEAGUE BASEBALL MAKES ITS RADIO CAMERA DEBUT.

June 6, 1949: BAN ON MAJOR LEAGUERS WHO JUMPED TO MEXICO LIFTED BY CHANDLER. WELCOME ASSURED OF EXILES' RETURN.

March 19, 1953: BRAVES MOVE TO MILWAUKEE. MAJORS' FIRST SHIFT SINCE '03.

July 13, 1976: NEW BASEBALL CONTRACT LIMITS RESERVE SYSTEM.[1]

As these headlines indicate, professional baseball has come a long way since 1869—the year the Cincinnati Red Stockings went on tour, drew two-hundred thousand spectators, and earned each player six-hundred to fourteen-hundred dollars for the eight-month season.[2]

At that time, baseball existed in a state of disorganization. Only slowly would organization and permanence be achieved. It would be achieved because organizations, whether in sport or otherwise, tend to form stable networks. As one study says:

Interorganizational relations [networks] are everywhere in evidence. Corporations forge ties with banks, supply houses, and law firms; banks are linked to one another by clearing houses; armies establish liaisons with one another; professional societies grant or withhold support of educational enterprises; revolutionary groups form alliances, and federal agencies concur with or oppose organizations from society's several institutional sectors.[3]

---

[1]Gene Brown, ed., *New York Times Encyclopedia of Sports, Volume 2* (New York: Arno Press, Inc., 1979).
[2]Ibid., p. vii.

[3]Herman Turk, *Organizations in Modern Life: Cities and Other Large Networks* (San Francisco: Jossey-Bass, Inc., Publishers, 1977), p. 1. Italics omitted.

So too with sport; perhaps especially so.

You're probably familiar with most or all of the following: the NFL, AL, NL, AAU, NCAA, NHL, NBA, and AIAW. The world of sport is an alphabet soup of acronyms that stand for networks of organizations. In a sense, these networks are the framework of the sportsworld; they provide form, continuity, stability, and order.

This chapter delves into the subject of sports networks. Using baseball as a case study, we examine its social history, from which we derive a model that can be applied to other sports. Throughout the chapter we emphasize corporate sport, or sport as a money-making business. This emphasis swings attention to professional sports, although what we say applies to many so-called amateur sports. They make money too.

PROFESSIONAL BASEBALL: FROM DISORGANIZATION TO ORGANIZATION

The First Leagues

In 1876 owners and representatives of ten baseball teams gathered in New York and formed a league of clubs (not an association of players as had been tried before). The new organization called itself the National League and set three goals: (1) Encourage, foster and elevate the game of baseball; (2) Enact and enforce proper rules for the exhibition and conduct of the game; and (3) Make baseball playing respectable and honorable.[4] The goals stressed improving baseball's image, which is understandable since the image was one of rowdyism, violence, cheating, and corruption. Notably, the goals did not mention monetary profits.

The National League turned out to be a success, and in 1881 a rival (or outlaw) league emerged—the American Association. For ten years it competed with the National League.

While the American Association and the National League were struggling with each other, another competitor arose—the Union Association. The Union openly raided both the National League and the American Association for players. Although fifty players initially joined, most reneged amid public indignation over the Union's tactics. The Union Association soon failed.

In 1885, the first players' union appeared: the Brotherhood of Professional Baseball Players. Over the years athletes had become, and would continue to become, disgruntled. They felt that owners unfairly manipulated salaries with the "reserve system": Every athlete's contract had a clause binding him to play for whichever team owned the contract. Athletes had no say in the matter.

In response to this and other developments, the Brotherhood rebelled and organized a rival eight-city league in 1889. The Player's League lasted about a year. At the same time that it collapsed, the American Association and the National League merged.

---

[4]Allison Danzig and Joe Reichler, *The History of Baseball: Its Great Players, Teams and Managers* (Englewood Cliffs, New Jersey: Prentice-Hall, Inc., 1959), p. 46.

The Western League, not viewed as particularly important at the time, was formed in 1893. It remained a minor league until 1900, when Ban Johnson expanded the Western League into a major league, changed its name to the American League, and began challenging the National League. The resulting league war proved costly, and in 1903 the two warring leagues signed the National Agreement establishing the core of organized baseball as we now know it.

Just before World War I erupted on the continent, another outlaw league challenged organized baseball. A wealthy Chicago businessman, James Gilmore, formed the Federal League. Organized baseball's "unprecedented attendance and profits, the visual evidence of newly constructed concrete-and-steel ball parks, and the enthusiasm for the annual World Series all made baseball look like an attractive investment," writes an authoritative sports historian.[5]

Organized baseball responded by threatening to ban athletes who signed with the outlaw league: "There will be no place in organized baseball, either now or in the future, [for those who 'jump']," said a spokesman and then, in a strange twist of nonlogic, added, "There will be no blacklist."[6]

To a large extent, the challenge took place in the courts. In the most notable suit, the Federal League charged organized baseball with being an illegal monopoly. The judge who presided over the suit, Kenesaw Mountain Landis, would later play an important part in baseball history. He killed the suit by not acting on it. The struggle between the leagues went on.

The dispute was causing severe financial pains—in the one- to two-million-dollar range—to both organized baseball and the Federal League. Later that year the two leagues agreed to stop fighting. Organized baseball accepted two Federal League clubs, paid a six-hundred-thousand-dollar indemnity to Federal League owners, and agreed not to blacklist players who had played for Federal League teams. After this war, organized baseball would not face another outlaw league until the 1950s. But in the interim, baseball had to survive a series of political developments.

Even though the golden age of sport had arrived (recall Chapter 2), professional baseball remained darkly troubled. The National Agreement had not solved all problems. Innuendo, rumors, and facts of bribery, fixes, and scandals continued to beset organized baseball. And then suddenly the darkest hour came: The Black Sox scandal, or the fixing of the 1919 World Series. (See Chapter 12.)

The scandal catalyzed owners into resolving a series of long-simmering disputes: They placed baseball under the leadership of a single commissioner-czar. The post went to Judge Kenesaw Mountain Landis, the federal judge who had, by delaying action, rendered moot the suit brought by the Federal League against organized baseball. The Supreme Court greatly increased Landis's power in 1922. The Court ruled that although baseball teams traveled across state lines to compete with one another, such travel did not consti-

---

[5]Harold Seymour, *Baseball: The Golden Years* (New York: Oxford University Press, 1917), p. 200; Eugene C. Murdock, *Ban Johnson: Czar of Baseball* (Westport, Connecticut: Greenwood Press, 1982), chap. 4.

[6]Seymour, *Baseball*, p. 201.

tute interstate commerce; and so federal antitrust laws did not apply. Organized baseball was exempt. Three years later the Supreme Court conceded that the decision was a mistake, but let it stand.

By the end of the 1920s, organized baseball had put the scandals behind and had begun to spread its web into other domains.

In order to acquire new talent, major-league clubs would annually draft players from minor-league teams. The rules of the draft continually changed as various factions sought to make the procedure more equitable (to themselves). Under the rules then in effect, less financially well-off clubs had difficulty competing for the best players. St. Louis, a poor team, found itself in this situation.

Then St. Louis hired Branch Rickey, who invented the farm system. St. Louis bought financial interests in minor-league teams and could thus farm out prospective players to its own minor-league teams, and after due seasoning, the best ones could be brought up to the parent team. Said Rickey, "If we were too poor to buy [good players], we would have to raise our own."[7] (The same Rickey later went to the Brooklyn Dodgers and helped break the color line; see Chapter 5.) Strangely enough, even with Rickey's farm system St. Louis never won a pennant or attracted exceptionally large crowds during this period, although they did get out of poverty. By selling surplus players to other clubs, St. Louis became the most profitable club in organized baseball. Seeing St. Louis's profit picture and flow of talent, other clubs quickly followed suit. Eventually, major-league clubs came to control over half of all minor-league teams.[8]

The farm system did not make much economic sense. What is good for one member of an organizational network may not be good for all members. The rich teams got richer while the poor teams got poorer; the difference was in who became rich and who became poor. Under the farm system, the Yankees and Dodgers succeeded richly; others not so well.

By the late 1930s, organized baseball had settled down into a semisolid form. The czarlike commissioner kept the warring factions of owners from rekindling self-destructive fights; scandal was largely forgotten; the image of the sport as the national pastime remained pure. When World War II came, organized baseball, like the rest of the country, found itself wracked by the war effort. The manpower demands of the military emptied the teams. President Roosevelt urged Landis to keep the sport going for morale purposes, and Landis did.

After the war, another outlaw league arose—the Mexican League. A wealthy businessman tried to establish a major league in Mexico and began raiding organized baseball for athletes. Organized baseball turned to the tried-and-true tactic: blacklisting players who signed with the outlaw league. By this time, organized baseball had become so firmly established that the Mexican League had little chance for success; it quickly collapsed.

---

[7]Quoted in Robert Obojski, *Bush League: A History of Minor League Baseball* (New York: Macmillan, Inc., 1975), p. 41.

[8]Lance E. Davis, "Self-Regulation in Baseball, 1909–71," in *Government and the Sports Business*, ed. Rogert G. Noll (Washington, D.C.: The Brookings Institute, 1974), pp. 349–86.

Boom Era

The postwar era differed from what had gone before. The world was radically changed by World War II and by the wars that followed; by communism, socialism, and nationalism; by the bomb, jet airplanes, computers, and television; and by the thousands of other social and technological developments. Sport also changed.

The boom era arrived—an era of political sport, cross-continental and international leagues, and multimillions of fans sitting in front of TV sets.

Organized baseball rapidly expanded. For years baseball had consisted of eight National-League teams and eight American-League teams located in the East and Midwest. Then in 1953 the Boston Braves moved to Milwaukee; in 1958 the St. Louis Browns moved to Baltimore and became the Orioles; in 1958 the Brooklyn Dodgers moved to Los Angeles and the New York Giants to San Francisco; in 1961 the Washington D.C. Senators announced they would move to Minneapolis–St. Paul; in 1962 New York obtained a National League team (the Mets) and Houston was admitted for the first time; in 1963 the Milwaukee Braves announced they would move to Atlanta; in 1969 baseball became international when it admitted Montreal; and in 1969 the Seattle Pilots played one season and then moved to become the Milwaukee Brewers. Moves of old and new teams across the country along with the addition of new franchises eventually resulted in the current twenty-six teams of organized baseball.

Jet air travel became common during the late 1950s, making cross-country trips routine; but television had the greatest impact. Before television, most people had never seen a major-league game from beginning to end. Newsreels showed only clips and then only of important games. Television revolutionized visual communication.

During the 1950s, organized baseball had a less than organized response to television. Each owner went on his own, selling television rights in whatever way he wanted. This usually meant televising as many games as possible. Television destroyed the minor leagues. Starting in 1949—about the time television was becoming widespread—the number of minor league clubs plummeted 68 percent.[9]

Television threatened organized baseball itself. For example, the Boston Braves televised virtually all their home games from 1949 to 1952, and their stadium attendance fell 81 percent.[10] Fans would not come out to games they could watch free in their living rooms. Some kind of coherent policy was needed.

Over the years specific agreements have come and gone (and surely will continue to do so); but essentially they share a core: restrictions on the number of games each club can televise and restrictions on the geographic areas into which the telecast can be beamed. In 1961 Congress passed the Sports Broadcasting Act. The act permitted professional baseball, basketball, football, and hockey to sell broadcast rights as a cartel. (We will return to television later.)[11]

---

[9]Reported in Wilbert Marcellus Leonard II, *A Sociological Perspective of Sport* (Minneapolis, Minnesota: Burgess Publishing Co., 1980), p. 275.

[10]Ibid.

[11]Ira Horowitz, "Market Entrenchment and the Sports Broadcasting Act," *American Behavioral Scientist*, 21 (January/February 1978), 415–30.

By the end of the 1960s, organized baseball had settled into a fairly stable form—which is not to say that changes haven't taken place since them. Attacks on the reserve system, big money, and television had, and continue to have, unsettling effects. Nevertheless we now have at hand enough historical material to accomplish our first goal: construction of a model of interorganizational relations.

A MODEL OF INTERORGANIZATIONAL RELATIONS

The term *model* has many definitions. Here we use it to mean a parsimonious description-explanation. Our model derives from studying organized baseball and has four elements: sport as a business, the product it sells, the environment it exists in, and the existence of cartels.

Business

The sports industry consists of sport firms (clubs or teams) which sell a product (competition-entertainment) to consumers (fans). When revenues fall below costs, sport firms lose money and may eventually go out of business. The social history of baseball shows that failures have been common, both of individual clubs and of entire networks of clubs (leagues). The Union Association, the Player's League, the Federal League, and the Mexican League all could not turn a profit and so collapsed, as did most of the clubs in these leagues.

Perhaps it's too obvious, but we should always remember:

Factor One.   Sport is a business.

We must hastily add qualifications. Sport is not a very good business—good in the sense of behaving like a well-managed, profit-seeking enterprise. As a business, it suffers from certain irrationalities. Among them are the lack of intense profit motivation on the part of some owners, and the importance placed on loyalties among cliques of owners.[12]

Irrationalities translate into poor business practices. The farm-club system demonstrates this. In the long run, the successful, wealthy teams became more successful and more wealthy—almost in a winner-take-all fashion. "When, instead of failing, Rickey's experiment succeeded, the owners, failing to see what was profitable to one could not be profitable for all, wanted no restrictions on jumping aboard the farm-team bandwagon."[13]

In addition to loyalties and poor business practices, certain cultural values blunt the profit motive. Sport holds a special place in American culture. It has the obligation to uplift us, to provide heroes and role models, to demonstrate love of country, family, and all that comprises the best of the American way. While sport might be a business, these values remove it from the realm of the coldblooded profit seekers.

---

[12]Davis, "Self Regulation in Baseball," pp. 381–82.
[13]Ibid., p. 363.

No one denies that owners want profit, but not if profit means totally destroying all the values attached to sport. Owners get a sense of worth from being involved in a socially admired enterprise. Owners also have the enjoyment of basking in the haloes of athletic heroes. (Who would have heard the names "Comiskey," or "O'Malley," or "Steinbrenner" were they not owners of sports clubs?)[14] One owner illustrates the point: "You don't get into baseball to make money, I mean big money. You can't. But I also know you don't go in to lose money . . . It's funny, though. Hardheaded businessmen sometimes lose their perspective when they get into something like baseball. A certain—call it romance—takes over."[15]

All of which leads to:

Corollary to Factor One.   Sport is a business, but a romantic one.

Product

The United States Bureau of the Census classifies professional athletes as entertainers. That is reasonable. Among other things, sport provides entertainment; and this entertainment comes from competition—the heart of sport.[16]

Pure and unregulated competition between teams might be entertaining for a little while, but not in the long run. Under those circumstances, only one, or a few, teams would rise to the top of the competition pyramid and stay there, forever. True competition would cease to exist, and therefore sport would not have a product to sell. The business would eventually fail.

To have a product, sport requires an even spreading out of competition—all teams must have the potential of becoming champions, serious contenders, or at the very least, able to be a "spoiler" from time to time. (A spoiler is a team that prevents other ones from winning championships by beating them.)

All of which leads to:

Factor Two.   The product that sport sells is competition-entertainment.

Environment

Baseball found and exploited a plush legal environment from its very beginning. The idea of contractually binding employees to employers and thus holding down salaries, is hardly unique to sport. However, outside of sport it is illegal. States an article written by an

---

[14]Jonathan J. Brower, "Professional Sports Team Ownership: Fun, Profit and Ideology of the Power Elite," *International Review of Sport Sociology*, 12 (1977), 79–98.

[15]Eddie Einhorn of the Chicago White Sox, quoted in *New York Times*, June 21, 1981, sec. Y, p. 24. © 1981 by The New York Times Company. Reprinted by permission.

[16]Walter C. Neale, "The Peculiar Economics of Professional Sports," *The Quarterly Journal of Economics*, 78 (February 1964), 1–14; reprinted in John W. Loy, Jr., and Gerald S. Kenyon, *Sport, Culture, and Society: A Reader on the Sociology of Sport* (New York: Macmillan, Inc., 1981), pp. 211–22; James Quirk, "An Economic Analysis of Team Movements in Professional Sports," *Law and Contemporary Problems*, 38 (Winter/Spring 1973), 42–66.

attorney for an athletes' union: "Team owners lead a charmed life developing the reserve system. Not only did they control salaries and therefore maximize profits, but the system was immunized from attack by an early decision of the U.S. Supreme Court."[17]

In 1972, baseball player Curt Flood renewed the legal assault on the reserve system. Rendering a decision "which reads like a catechism of the virtues of baseball," according to a legal analysis,[18] the Supreme Court recognized that organized baseball's exemption made no legal sense, but went on to say that Congress should rectify the situation, not the Court.

Congress has hardly followed the Supreme Court's advice. Up until the 1960s, the belief that sport deserved special exemptions dominated the thinking of legislators. That thinking did not change even though fans, owners, and athletes have busily petitioned Congress for legislation favorable to their own causes. From 1960 through 1978, approximately two hundred bills on professional sport were introduced in Congress, but "as is generally the case with modern legislatures, the time and attention given to professional sports in committee deliberations and the floor debates have been translated into relatively few pieces of legislation."[19]

In addition to favorable court decisions and legislation, professional sport receives other legal favors. Tax laws and accounting procedures accepted by the Internal Revenue Service make sport a business in which profits can be made rather easily. This may account for the nonchalant attitudes some owners have toward the business aspects of sport. Complex tax-legal-accounting maneuvers permit owners to join or separate their teams from their other enterprises in ways that help the owner's overall profit picture. An owner might "lose" money on his team while increasing profits of his other holdings.[20]

Recent court decisions, along with pressures from powerful players' unions, have given athletes more freedom to bargain with owners. The details of the free-agent system vary from time to time and sport to sport. However, all systems basically permit athletes to change teams after playing on one team for a specified number of years. If an athlete switches teams, compensation rules require that a team taking a free agent compensate (with money or draft rights) the team from which the athlete came. The free-agent system has had mixed results. It made a few highly talented baseball players into multimillionaires but has had almost no effect on football players. Even football superstars can't get offers because the rules require so much compensation.[21]

All of which leads to:

Factor Three.   Sport exists in a highly favorable social, political and legal environment.

---

[17]Edward R. Garvey, "From Chattel to Employee: The Athlete's Quest for Freedom and Dignity," *The Annals of the Academy of Political and Social Science*, 445 (September 1979), 96.

[18]John P. Morris, "In Wake of the Flood," *Law and Contemporary Problems*, 38 (Winter/Spring 1973), 85.

[19]Arthur T. Johnson, "Congress and Professional Sports: 1951–1978," *The Annals of the Academy of Political and Social Science*, 445 (September 1979), 114.

[20]See Leonard, *A Sociological Perspective of Sport*, chap. 11.

[21]"Now Pro Footballers Want the Big Money," *Business Week*, February 22, 1982, pp. 122–23.

Even though sport is a romantic business, it does have to stay in business. And in order to have a product (competition-entertainment) to sell, sports organizations invariably form cartels.

Cartel

Terms such as *cartel*, *monopoly*, and *trust* have bad-sounding rings to them, connoting Robber Barons and unrestricted exploitation of consumers and workers. All that may be true, but stripped of emotional loadings, a cartel is just an agreement among organizations to regulate prices, outputs, and markets while preserving their independence in areas not covered by the cartel agreement.[22]

Under some conditions, competition among organizations naturally leads to a cartel arrangement. An important research paper says,

> [in] a clustered environment in which there is more than one system of the same kind, i.e., the objects of one organization are the same as, or relevant to, others like it . . . competitors seek to improve their own chances by hindering others . . . On the other hand, stability may require a certain coming-to-terms between competitors.[23]

Organizations seek to improve their competitive position by hindering others—ultimately driving others out—or by coming to terms with their competitors. Sport has done both.

Baseball was initially a haphazard collection of competing (hindering) teams. The teams formed into leagues (came to terms); the leagues warred against each other (drove some others out of business). On finding wars too costly and self-destructive, sometimes the leagues worked out compromises until finally the National League and the American League signed the National Agreement of 1903 and formed organized baseball. The new organization set forth rules limiting competition for player talent, split the market up into territorial franchises, established an orderly system of team play, and authorized a high commissioner to administer the organization. Once established, organized baseball endeavored to gain public confidence. Finally, in the 1950s, organized baseball easily fought off the Mexican League. Currently, organized baseball is secure. All of which leads to:

Factor Four.   Cartels dominate sport.

---

[22]Compare with Julius Gould and William L. Kolb, eds., *A Dictionary of the Social Sciences* (New York: The Free Press, 1964), p. 73; Campbell R. McConnell, *Economics: Principles, Problems, and Policies*, 6th ed. (New York: McGraw-Hill Book Company, 1975).

[23]F. E. Emory and E. L. Trist, "The Causal Texture of Organizational Environments," *Human Relations*, 18 (February 1965), 31; Howard E. Aldrich, *Organizations and Environments* (Englewood Cliffs, New Jersey: Prentice-Hall, Inc., 1979).

Oftentimes sport cartels do not behave in textbook fashion. States an economist: "In the area where partnership is needed . . . the practice in effect is basically one of each club for itself in a quasi-winner-take-all."[24]

In a perfect cartel, quasi-winner-take-all would be replaced by a complete dedication to a one-for-all-and-all-for-one philosophy. Professional baseball opted for neither. Owners agree to share revenues but not always on a fifty-fifty basis. In addition, the draft and the farm-club and free-agent systems do not work equally well for all teams.

A minority of owners can effectively block the actions of the majority. And while the commissioner has substantial power, he serves at the owners' pleasure. The two leagues occasionally go their own way, as illustrated by the designated-hitter rule, which the American Leagues uses while the National League does not.

Organized baseball is too loosely coupled to be a perfect cartel. A text on organization describes a loosely coupled system as follows: "If two elements have few variables in common, or if variables common to both are weak compared to other variables influencing the elements, then they are relatively independent of each other and thus loosely coupled."[25]

In a loosely coupled network, the actions of one segment of the network do not much affect other segments of the network. Having the designated-hitter rule in one league doesn't necessarily force the other league to adopt it.

Loosely coupled cartels benefit from size while maintaining flexibility. If one segment of the network fails, that does not bring down the entire network. However, on the negative side, if a loosely coupled system finds it must respond to a challenge as a whole, the response may be slow in coming. The segments cannot be quickly mustered and forced to take collective action. Luckily for baseball, quick responses have not been required, even in league wars. This loose coupling, we suspect, is the main reason organized baseball has been the exception to the general rule that cartels seldom survive for long.

All of which leads to:

Corollary to Factor Four.   Some sports cartels are loosely coupled.

The factors of the model are related as follows: Big-time sports are businesses (often romantic ones) selling competition-entertainment to fans. To maintain competition, sports organizations form leagues; and because the legal and sociopolitical environment favors sport, leagues become cartels (often loosely coupled). In a nutshell, that is the model.

GENERALITY OF THE MODEL: OTHER SPORTS

Since baseball is the national pastime, students of sport find it important in its own right. It is redolent of the pastorale and of Americana, of kids playing pick-up games, of leisure, and of the common person.

---

[24]David S. Davenport, "Collusive Competition in Major League Baseball: Its Theory and Institutional Development," *American Economist*, 13 (Fall 1969), 24.

[25]Aldrich, *Organizations and Environments*, p. 77.

We recognize all of that to be sure, but we studied baseball for another reason: to derive the model just set forth. We now should ask, To what extent does the model generalize?

Professional Football.   Around the turn of the century, professional football was an unorganized collection of teams, most of them short lived. Not until 1920 was the Professional Football Association formed (and later renamed the National Football League). The Association was more a name than a functioning cartel: Teams left and joined and played each other or nonleague teams almost at will. Despite periodic reorganizations, things did not go well. By 1931 the NFL had shrunk to just eight teams. Nevertheless, the NFL managed to scrape by, putting down small outlaw leagues in 1936 and 1940. World War II drew away so much manpower that the league had to modify its schedule and some teams temporarily merged.

After the war, a major outlaw league, the All-American Football Conference opened with eight franchises, four of which competed head to head with NFL teams. The ensuing bidding war for athletes and fans proved costly, and in 1949 the two leagues merged. Ten years later another outlaw league formed: The American Football League (AFL). The new league had eight teams and began drafting college players in competition with the NFL. Like the war with the All-American Football Conference, this one could not go on; it cost too much. So in 1966 the NFL merged with the AFL to form the NFL we now know. After the merger, organized football easily put down still another challenger, the World Football League, in 1974.[26] Currently a new league, which plays its games in the spring rather than the traditional fall, is competing with the NFL. The outcome of this war has not been determined.

Like baseball, professional football began moving out of a state of disorganization in halting steps. A weak league was formed and somehow managed to survive. It beat down challenges from rival leagues, and merged with the strongest rivals to eventually reach a position of preeminence. The league now shares revenues from television, splits home gates, limits franchises, and is administered by a strong commissioner. In short, the NFL developed into a cartel.

Professional Golf.   The Professional Golfers' Association (PGA) governs the sport. In the late 1960s, the PGA formed the Professional Golfers' Association Tour (PGAT).

The PGAT controls the top echelon of professional golf. To compete in a PGAT tournament, an aspiring golfer must have a tour card. To try out for a tour card, the aspirant must attend a PGAT school. To pass the school and get the card, the aspirant must satisfy what amounts to a secret set of criteria. Few do—no more than 5 percent of those attending the school.

The PGAT sanctions (approves) tournaments, agreeing to provide a representative

---

[26]*Official 1981 National Football League Record Manual* (New York: A National Football League Book, 1981), pp. 117–32; *The NFL's Official Encyclopedia of Professional Football* (New York: Macmillan, Inc., 1977).

field of golfers in exchange for prize money and television royalties. Within limits, each PGAT golfer decides which tournaments to enter.

Naturally, tournaments want star golfers, and the demand for stars exceeds the supply. So the PGAT requires golfers to compete in a minimum number of tournaments each year. This assures that at least some stars will be mixed in with lesser knowns at least some of the time. The PGAT forbids appearance fees (money guaranteed to stars regardless of their performance.)[27]

The PGAT is an interesting case because it demonstrates that the model describes both sports organizations and individuals who form cartels. Individual athletes also compete in professional sports such as bowling, racketball, and tennis. While we can never be absolutely sure without research, we strongly suspect that the basic form illustrated by the PGAT applies to those sports too.

College and University Sports.   While technically not professional, big-time college sports are businesses, and like many businesses, have found the cartel advantageous. The NCAA illustrates this. Currently the NCAA governs big-time collegiate sport, with over eight hundred member schools. It was not always so. At the time of the NCAA's founding (1906) other athletic conferences were already in existence. For example, the Southern Intercollegiate Athletic Association had been formed in 1894 and the nucleus of the Big Ten in 1895.[28] (The Southern Intercollegiate Athletic Association eventually split into what are now the Southeastern, Southern, and Atlantic Coast Conferences.)

Rather than compete with these conferences, the NCAA brought them under its umbrella by giving each conference local autonomy over rule enforcement. The NCAA did not assume enforcement powers until 1952.[29]

The NCAA does everything a cartel does. It controls competition for high-school athletes by placing limits on the number of scholarships a school can give. Once the athlete enrolls at a school, the NCAA limits the number of years athletes can compete, and penalizes them for transferring to another school. No matter what the expressed intent ("for the good of the student-athlete"), these rules and many others, prevent a few wealthy schools from stockpiling most of the good athletes.[30]

The NCAA restricts output. Only a fixed number of games can be played each year (eleven in football plus a bowl appearance); and only within a designated period of the year (the football season). The NCAA controls the number of games shown on television and the number of times a team may appear.

The NCAA shares the wealth Robin Hood style. Each conference member receives

[27]Rex L. Cottle, "Economics of the Professional Golfers' Association Tour," *Social Science Quarterly*, 62 (December 1981), 721–34.

[28]Gordon S. White, Jr., "Colleges Find Advantages in Conferences," *New York Times*, February 24, 1980, sec. S, p. 10; John D. McCallum, *Big Ten Football: Since 1895* (Radnor, Pennsylvania: Chilton Book Co., 1976), chap. 1.

[29]Robert N. Stern, "The Development of An Interorganizational Control Network: The Case of Intercollegiate Athletics," *Administrative Science Quarterly*, 24 (June 1979), 256.

[30]James V. Kock, "A Troubled Cartel: NCAA," *Law and Contemporary Problems*, 38 (Winter/Spring, 1973), 135–50; James V. Kock and Wilbert M. Leonard II, "The NCAA: A Socio-economic Analysis," *American Journal of Economics and Sociology*, 37 (July 1978), 225–39.

a share of the revenues when one of their members plays in an NCAA championship basketball tournament or postseason football game, or appears on television. For example, each Big Ten school receives about a hundred thousand dollars, no matter which school plays in the Rose Bowl.[31]

Policy on televising football games has caused dissension. When the NCAA recently signed a $282-million contract with the television networks, two universities sued on the grounds that the contract violated antitrust laws. A federal judge agreed, saying that the NCAA's policies and entire course of behavior made it a classic cartel. Years will pass before the legal issues are thrashed out in court.[32]

Back in 1906 the founders of the NCAA did not think they were setting up a cartel. Nowhere does the NCAA's statement of goals mention forming a sports monopoly. But regardless of whether or not the NCAA recognizes the fact, the fact remains: the NCAA is a business cartel.

The sheer number of sports cartels makes them seen natural, while the revered position of sport dampens criticism of them. That was not always true (see Chapter 2). And it may not be true in the future. The corporate aspects of sport create problems.

PROBLEMS: GREED AND SPECTACLE

Sport, as we have said many times, is steeped in the virtues of the American way, making it a sacred institution.

Profanation

Profanation threatens sacred institutions. In a classic treatise on religion, Emile Durkheim wrote,

> Since the idea of the sacred is always and everywhere separated from the idea of the profane . . . the mind irresistibly refuses to allow the two corresponding things to be confounded, or even to be merely put in contact with each other; for such a promiscuity, or even too direct a contiguity, would contradict too violently the dissociation of these ideas in the mind. The sacred thing is *par excellence* that which the profane should not touch, and cannot touch with impunity. To be sure, this interdiction cannot go so far as to make all communication between the two worlds impossible; for if the profane could in no way enter into relations with the sacred, this latter could be good for nothing.[33]

[31]Bob Baptist, "Ohio State to Realize No Financial Bonanza in Fiesta Bowl," *Columbus Citizen-Journal*, December 21, 1980, sec. D, p. 1.

[32]Gordon S. White, Jr., "N.C.A.A's Television Rights on Football Are Struck Down," *New York Times*, September 16, 1982, p. Y24.

[33]Emile Durkheim, *The Elementary Forms of the Religious Life*, trans. Joseph Ward Swain (New York: The Free Press, 1965), p. 55. Originally published in French, 1915.

While modern sociologists would not use the term *mind*, a human attribute, to refer to culture or social structure, Durkheim's statement does point out an important fact: What culture defines as sacred must not be desecrated by contact with the profane. Yet at the same time, the sacred and the profane must occasionally come in contact for practical reasons.

Hence a dilemma. Business is a secular or profane institution and sport a sacred one. How can sport be a business and still remain sacred? This dilemma has troubled sport ever since sport became organized. It was a problem for the ancient Greeks, you may remember—but we do not have to go back that far to understand the current situation in the United States.

Money and Greed

In 1923 football coach Alonzo Stagg pleaded,

> To co-operate with Sunday professional football games is to co-operate with the forces which are destructive of the finest elements of interscholastic and intercollegiate football. . . . If you believe in preserving interscholastic and intercollegiate football for the upbuilding of the present and future generations of clean, healthy, right-minded and patriotic citizens, you will not lend your assistance to any of the forces which are helping to destroy it.[34]

Stagg believed that professionalism corrupted the true spirit of sport. Many people still agree with that position.

Nevertheless, the forces of professionalism have prevailed. Just two years after Stagg's plea, Red Grange of Illinois dropped out of school and signed with the Chicago Bears. An agent represented Grange and he received a percentage of the gate. For his first game, Grange earned $30,000. What that would be in today's dollars boggles the mind.

When Grange arrived in Chicago to join the Bears, "there were so many promoters awaiting him with contracts in their pockets that the crowd looked like a reception committee to the Prince of Wales. There were offers to appear in movies, to write for newspaper syndicates and to do this and that. All were willing to pay Grange whatever he asked."[35]

After Grange played that first game, the *New York Times* ran the headline:

> 70,000 SEE GRANGE IN PRO DEBUT . . . HIS SHARE ABOUT $30,000 . . . CROWD IS GREATEST EVER TO ATTEND PRO GAME AND ALL SHOUT FOR THE HERO.[36]

Professional athletes like Grange have been earning lots of money for a long time. However, huge player salaries used to be the exception while nowadays they are com-

---

[34]Quoted in the *New York Times*, November 2, 1923; reproduced in Brown, *Encyclopedia*, p. 86.
[35]*New York Times*, November 23, 1925; reproduced in Brown, *Encyclopedia*, p. 87.
[36]Ibid.

monplace. Figures vary depending on source of data, sport, and year, but the average annual salaries of professional athletes are approximately: football, $90,000; baseball, $185,000; and basketball, $190,000. Of the eighty athletes with the highest earnings, yearly salaries range from a low of about $100,000 (the top woman golfer) to a high of $1.5 million (a major-league baseball player).[37]

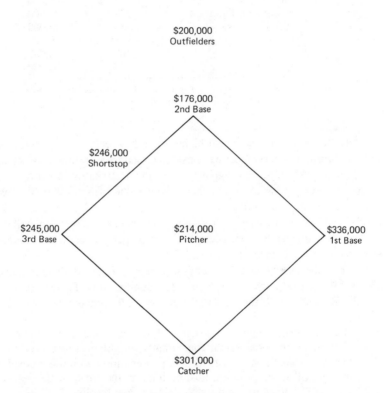

Figure 8.1.   Average Salaries of Major League Baseball Players, by Position, for 1981.

SOURCE: Data supplied by Major League Baseball Players Association. Dollar amounts are for major league players with sixty-six or more games at position specified, and for pitchers with twelve or more starts.

[37]"Now Pro Footballers," *Business Week; The World Almanac & Book of Facts*, 1982 (New York: Newspaper Enterprise Association, Inc., 1981), p. 861. Data also supplied by National Football League Management Council and Major League Baseball Players Association.

Table 8.1. Average Salaries of National Football League Players

POSITION	NUMBER OF PLAYERS	AVERAGE SALARY
Quarterbacks	85	$160,000
Running Backs	196	95,000
Defensive Linemen	213	93,000
Receivers	242	86,000
Offensive Linemen	290	85,000
Linebackers	234	85,000
Defensive Backs	241	80,000
Kickers	61	66,000
TOTAL	1,562	90,000

SOURCE: 1981 data supplied by the National Football League Management Council.

These dollar amounts seem higher than they really are. Athletes have short careers and their current salaries must be considered against a lifetime of working at much lower rates, against inflation, and against taxes. In the jargon of finance, assuming approximately a seventy-year life span, the present value of $190,000 (the average basketball salary) earned this year will be worth but a few thousand by the year 2050, unless invested wisely—which is not easy, as thousands of business investors will testify. Even so, athletes do earn much more than the average person, and rank among the upper one percent of all wage earners.

From the viewpoint of economics, salaries reflect supply and demand. Demand for highly talented athletes is high and the supply low. Hence salaries go up. Many sociologists agree with that specific point. A well-known paper states,

> But if the skills required are scarce by reason of the rarity of talent or the costliness of training, the position, if functionally important, must have an attractive power that will draw the necessary skills in competition with other positions. This means, in effect, that the position must be high on the social scale—must command great prestige, high salary, and ample leisure, and the like.[38]

This statement describes the top athletes in major sports. They have rare talent, need years of training, and perform a service which employers, fans, and American culture deem important. Consequently, top athletes command prestige, high salaries, ample leisure, and other amenities.

People inside professional sport sometimes hold this economic view. The agent of a superstar basketball player expressed it this way: "He's worth whatever anyone wants to

---

[38]Kingsley Davis and Wilbert E. Moore, "Some Principles of Stratification," in *Class, Status, and Power: Social Stratification in Comparative Perspective*, 2nd ed., eds. Reinhard Bendix and Seymour Martin Lipset (1945; reprint, New York: The Free Press, 1966), p. 49.

pay for him. That's what he's worth."[39] Or as a spokesman for the professional football players' union replied when asked by what right players were demanding a percentage of gross revenues: "Because we are the game."[40] A baseball owner says of the situation, "The moral of the story is either that athletes were grossly underpaid in the past, or they're making too much now. I'm inclined to think they're close to where they ought to be now."[41]

Regardless of how low or high athletes' (or anyone's) salaries are, it is the excessive striving for more money—greed—that profanes whatever it touches, according to American values. We therefore need to focus on greed. Has greed touched sport and so profaned it? Some critics say yes. "The widespread resentment of the star athletes among followers of sport—a resentment directed against the inflated salaries negotiated by their agents and against their willingness to become hucksters, promoters, and celebrities—indicates the persistence of a need to believe that sport represents something more than entertainment."[42]

This sentiment may lie behind the hostility fans showed toward professional football players who in 1982 went on the longest strike in sports history. After fifty-seven days the strike was settled, but there was no gush of enthusiasm among spectators. Players found themselves being booed and performing before thin crowds. The first games, after the strike ended, drew 76 percent of stadium capacity compared to the past average of 94 percent.[43] Even before the strike, a national poll showed 62 percent of fans agreeing that "athletes are paid too much money"; and 87 percent agreeing that "there is too much emphasis on money in sport" today.[44] Apparently, in the fans' minds, greed has profaned sport.

The same pole showed that when fans compared themselves now to themselves five years previously, over 80 percent had the same or more interest in spectator sports, got the same or more fun out of watching sports, had the same or more loyalty to their favorite teams, and had the same or more enthusiasm for star players. Dislike of big money has not precipitated a decline in enthusiasm among the fans. If anything, the opposite has occurred.

At first glance, such behavior and attitudes seem incongruous; but upon closer examination, it makes social psychological sense. A much admired text states a helpful principle: "Human nature abhors incongruity—dissonance—imbalance, or, as we shall loosely say . . . inconsistency."[45] Many social psychologists prefer a weaker statement of

---

[39]Gerald Eskenazi, "Athletes' Salaries," *New York Times*, August 16, 1981, p. 27. © 1981 by The New York Times Company. Reprinted by permission.

[40]"Now Pro Footballers," *Business Week*.

[41]Quoted in Ray Kennedy and Nancy Williamson, "Money in Sport: Part 1," *Sports Illustrated*, July 17, 1978, p. 52.

[42]Christopher Lasch, *The Culture of Narcissism: American Life in an Age of Diminishing Expectations* (New York: W. W. Norton & Co., Inc., 1978), p. 119. Also see Ray Kennedy and Nancy Williamson, "Money in Sport: Part 3," *Sports Illustrated*, July 31, 1978, pp. 34–50.

[43]Michael Janofsky, "Football Players Return to Field But Many Fans Remain Home," *New York Times*, November 11, 1982, pp. 14, 32.

[44]Kennedy and Williamson, "Money in Sport: Part 3."

[45]Roger Brown, *Social Psychology* (New York: The Free Press, 1965), p. 604. This is a standard textbook.

the principle: ''The wholesale assumption that people always abhor inconsistency has more recently been rejected in favor of the notion that at least some people sometimes act in such a way as to minimize inconsistencies. But on other occasions people can live with their inconsistencies quite well.''[46]

Regardless of how you prefer to state it, the principle of consistency means that people try to bring different beliefs, attitudes, facts, and behaviors into harmony or equilibrium. The stronger the belief in something, the harder they try. Because sport is a sacred institution, and because changing beliefs is a soul-wrenching experience, believers (fans) will go to great lengths to make discordant beliefs (greed permeates sport) consistent with their initial views.

Various tactics can be used. They can selectively tune-in and seek out confirming information; selectively tune-out and avoid contradictory information; reinterpret information; or not think about contradictory information.

Fans choose a combination of tactics. Almost three-fourths of the fans polled said they forget about the overemphasis on money once the game begins. About the same percentage were not interested in knowing the details of contract negotiations and player salaries, nor would they be interested in joining a fan group formed by consumer advocates.[47] Fans cannot help knowing about money in sport—the media blast them with the information. But that does not mean they wish to know. Once they do know, they try not to think about the issue, and do not want to act upon it. And perhaps many fans just live with their inconsistencies.

Despite the money pumped into sport, much of it from television, greed has not profaned sport—at least not yet. The image of the institution might be tarnished, though not too much. Fans remain loyal. The social-political-legal environment remains favorable. The virtues of sport remain intact. Sport remains sacred.

Of course, everything could change. Television, in addition to providing all that money, threatens to transform the basic nature of sport from sacred ritual into profane spectacle.

The Effects of Television

No one knows whether television caused the boom era of sport, whether interest in sport caused television to cover it, or whether the two processes fed on each other. But whichever, the resulting match has been almost perfect.

Many sports fit the requirements of television like a glove. For example, breaks in the action, and intervals between innings or quarters, provide natural spots for showing advertisements: ''The quarter's over. We'll be right back after these important commercial messages.'' Rules can be altered unobtrusively to create strategically placed breaks. Professional football put in the two-minute warning for television. Action stops just before the most exciting parts of the game, thus locking the audience into the commercial. And if

---

[46]Lawrence S. Wrightman and Kay Deaux, *Social Psychology in the 80's*, 3rd ed. (Monterey, California: Brooks/Cole Publishing Co., 1981), p. 345.

[47]Kennedy and Williamson, ''Money in Sport: Part 3.''

rules do not provide suitable breaks, officials can always call a "television timeout," as they do in college football.[48]

More importantly, sport fulfills the most basic cultural requirements for popularity among viewers and media producers. "The ideal, from the standpoint of the [television] system, is content that will capture audience members' attention, persuade them to purchase goods, and at the same time be sufficiently within the bounds of moral norms and standards of taste so that unfavorable actions by regulatory components are not provoked," say two sociologists who have long studied the media.[49]

What fits these requirements better than sport? Sport represents noncontroversial, sacred American virtues, which means that sport provokes little opposition when shown in prime time. Sport captures the audiences' attention. Leave your seat and you're likely to miss the big play. Sport is dramatic. The drama builds during the game and over the season and culminates in the World Series or the Superbowl, or the Championship. And unlike many dramas, the audience can take sides, cheering for one team over another. In a mass anonymous society such as the United States, people have few emotional attachments to their broader community. "Their" team is one of the few attachments. Fans gather in bars, clubs, and homes to watch the Big Game. They mourn when "their" team loses, and celebrate when "their" team wins. The winner of the World Series always gets a Special Day and a parade down the main street of their home city, while the losers . . . well, there's always next year.

Televising sports creates more fans. Sport finds itself in the pleasant position of having television pay for the right to broadcast it; and in the very act of broadcasting, it advertises itself for free. When the game comes on your set, the probability of watching it increases; and if you do, the probability of being converted from nonfan to fan increases. The increase in number of fans then increases demand for televised sport, which then increases the profitability of televising sport, which then makes for more sports on television, thus advertising sport some more, and that makes for more fans, . . . and the cycle starts over. One-third of the all-time most viewed television programs in history are Super Bowls and the World Series.[50] Television thus depends on sport as much as sport depends on television.

Because audiences are large, advertising on television is relatively cheap. Even on the most expensive regular sports telecast ("Monday Night Football"), the cost of a commercial works out to be less than one cent per viewing household, and that household consists of a "captive audience [males, aged 18–49, above low income] that is especially ready, willing and able to purchase the sponsors' products."[51] Accordingly, NFL television contracts have gone from $4.6 million in 1962, the year after Congress passed the Sports Broadcasting Act, to almost two billion dollars today.[52]

---

[48]See Joan M. Chandler, "TV & Sport: Wedded with a Golden Hoop," *Psychology Today*, April 1977, pp. 64–76.

[49]Melvin L. DeFleur and Sandra J. Ball-Rokeach, *Theories of Mass Communication*, 4th ed. (New York: Longman, Inc., 1981), p. 178.

[50]*The World Almanac & The Book of Facts*, p. 430.

[51]Horowitz, "Marketing Entrenchment," p. 420.

[52]*Official 1981 National Football League*, p. 124; *New York Times*, February 27, 1982, p. 1.

Sport and television have evolved into a commensal arrangement: each feeds off the other and prospers. So long as they cooperate and do not get greedy, no end to the feast is in sight.

Critics object to the influence of television on sport. They say sport depends too heavily on television revenues, thus becoming television's lackey. As evidence, they point to accommodations made to television's demands, such as changing rules and moving starting times to attract a larger audience. One sociologist wrote in 1971:

> Professional sports have attempted to enliven the game by introducing rule changes, spectacular accoutrements, and innovative publicity promotions. Concommitantly, values within professional sports have also changed, thus tending to support the entertainment value of sport rather than the idea of the intrinsic value of the game in and for itself.[53]

Furthermore, critics say, spectacle has replaced competition. "What began as an attempt to invest sport with religious significance, indeed to make it into a surrogate religion in its own right, ends with the demystification of sport, the assimilation of sport to show business."[54]

Asks *Time* magazine about the Super Bowl, "Is it really only a game?"[55] implying that it has become an entertainment spectacle as famous for its hype as for the athletic contest. The Super Bowl makes a good illustration of what critics dislike about television's influence on sport. According to one analysis of American culture:

> Although mass-mediated culture tends to profane a civilization's most sacred and powerful words and images, in the process it manages to elevate otherwise mundane events of no real consequence to the status of spectacles of powerful, quasi-sacred myth and ritual. The Super Bowl telecast conveys this feeling of larger-than-life drama. . . . Historically, the Super Bowl parallels the spectacle of the Coliseum in Rome.[56]

No matter which athletes or teams play in the Super Bowl, the event draws TV audiences of 100 million or more fans, preceded by a media blitz of parties, interviews, pregame shows, TV specials, and endless speculation on the outcome.

Might the Super Bowl really be a hollow media extravaganza put on for the sole purpose of drawing huge viewing audiences? Certainly no one can deny that a lot of media hype goes on. In response to criticism, the NFL has curtailed much of the hype. No longer, for instance, does the NFL sponsor gigantic pregame parties attended by

---

[53]R. Terry Furst, "Social Change and the Commercialization of Professional Sports," *International Review of Sport Sociology*, 8 (1971), 168.

[54]Lasch, *The Culture of Narcissism*, p. 124.

[55]*Time*, February 8, 1981, p. 82. Copyright 1981 Time Inc. All rights reserved. Reprinted by permission from *Time*.

[56]Michael R. Real, *Mass-Mediated Culture* (Englewood Cliffs, New Jersey: Prentice-Hall, Inc., 1977), pp. 96, 113.

thousands of guests, celebrities, and media personnel.[57] Perhaps the hype should be cut back.

The charge of spectacle is most easily documented for an event like the Super Bowl, but most sports telecasts are nothing like that. Most are "meat and potatoes"; they basically show the game and perhaps a half-time show. For them, the charge of spectacle is much less applicable. We should be careful not to generalize indiscriminantly from one event to all events.

Even though critics mention the danger of what *might* happen, not of what *has* happened, the danger is real and close by. We might think about it. If sport becomes purely show business, a kind of grand spectacle put on to earn more and more money, then sport will surely lose its special hold on American culture. Conversely, as long as sport remains the stronghold of traditional values, and as long as these values at least occasionally override purely economic concerns, then sport as sport—however imperfect and tainted by threats of greed and spectacle—will survive.

Organized sport currently faces the problem of balancing commercialization, money, and spectacle against traditional values—the age-old dilemma of the sacred versus the profane. Emile Durkheim, who posed this dilemma, saw no ironclad solution; neither do we. We do suspect that the dilemma will be resolved slowly in a two-steps-forward, one-step-backward fashion. As sport becomes more greedy and spectacular, the media, fans, analysts, and social critics will cry for a return to traditional values. Sport will then retreat towards the sacred. After a time, greed and spectacle will again increase, and the cry for tradition will again go out, and again sport will retreat. This process will go on for a long time and the end result will not be known for many years to come.

SUMMARY

1. This chapter concerned the corporate or business aspects of sport.
2. Professional baseball was used as a case study to develop a model applicable to most big-time sports.
3. Professional baseball evolved from a state of disorganization. The National League started in 1876 and successfully competed with several other leagues. When the American and National Leagues merged in 1903, organized baseball came into being. After a period of scandals and the trauma of the Great Depression and World War II, sport entered a boom era. Organized baseball expanded, put down a rival league, and came to grips with television and international competition.
4. From the social history of baseball we derived a model consisting of the following factors: sport is a business, but a romantic one; sport has flourished partly because of an extremely favorable legal, social, and political environment; sport sells competition-entertainment; and lastly, sports organizations and individuals form cartels to govern competition.

----

[57]*Time*, February 8, 1982, p. 82.

5. The model also applied to professional football, professional golf, and the National Collegiate Athletic Association. It was speculated that if more research were done, the model would be found to apply to other sports as well.

6. The chapter discussed two main threats to corporate sport: greed and spectacle. As a sacred institution, sport is constantly threatened with profanation. Money presents a major problem. The salaries of big-time athletes, sometimes large in the past, have become even larger, while the number of players receiving top salaries has increased as well. However, the real danger to sport is not large salaries per se, but greed.

7. The attitude of the public, as measured by a poll of fans, seems ambiguous. They believe that sport is too concerned about money, but are enthused about sport nonetheless. The principle of consistency helps explain the ambiguity.

8. It is also possible for sport to be converted from serious competition to a show-business spectacle. Television threatens to do this.

9. Television and sport have found a mutually profitable association. Sport is noncontroversial, dramatic, has fan loyalties, and creates more fans as it goes. Consequently, sport audiences are consistently large, and sports programming attracts advertising dollars.

10. The charge that big-time sport is too dependent on television dollars, and the charge that television in its ever-increasing drive to attract bigger audiences will convert sport into profane spectacle, seems exaggerated at present. However, it does remain a potential danger.

9

THE SPORTSWOMAN
Today, Yesterday, and Tomorrow

Gymnastics, with its emphasis on the physical attributes of balance and flexibility, is one area of sports in which women athletes characteristically excel. Most sports emphasize strength and speed and thus give the average male athlete a physical advantage over the average female one. Photos by Dana Worsnop.

Cause Célèbre. Sleet mixed with snow fell all during the 1967 Boston Marathon. One K. Switzer from Syracuse University lined up in the starting pack, dressed in a sweatsuit and hood to guard against the weather.

The race began. Switzer was running along with the pack when the press truck came by loaded with photographers and reporters. They noticed what the race officials had not: Switzer was a woman! Today that would cause absolutely no comment whatsoever; but in 1967 the Boston Marathon was for men only.

Years later, Switzer recounted to a journalist, "When they [the press] saw I was a girl, they went absolutely crazy. A girl in the race!"

A race official named Jock Semple suddenly ran up behind Switzer trying to tear the number off her jersey. According to Switzer: "I see this awful face, this awful, angry face, and I'm frightened. Jock is screaming at me, 'I'm going to get you out of this race!' When all of a sudden here comes [my boyfriend]—I mean, without a sound, he comes over and hits Jock a cross-body block. . . . And it was amazing. Jock went four feet into the air. The rest of the race was an agony to me. I felt drained. Emotionally drained.

"It was the first time in my life that somebody came down on me that hard just because I was a woman. I wanted to scream at them and say, 'Jock, I've been training at least ten miles a day in Syracuse, with snow up to my knees, and my eyebrows frozen over, and puking out my guts. I'm an intelligent woman, I'm studying at the university, and I'm here because I love to run. I love it with a passion. And you're not counting any of those things. You're throwing me out just because I'm a woman.' "[1]

The Switzer incident made big news; all the papers and news programs carried the story. Her case became a *cause célèbre*, a rallying point over sex discrimination in sport. She was not alone; her story was just more publicized. In one way or another and to varying degrees, what happened to Switzer happened to millions of women. This chapter concerns those millions of women and the problems they have had to confront, and still confront, in playing out the role of sportswoman. We explore why the sportswoman has been treated so shabbily; how the situation came about; what it means for women; and where it is all going.

As always, we will first explain our terminology. When we use the words *sex*, *male*, and *female*, we are referring to biological matters: chromosome structure, hormonal levels, reproductive organs, and so on. Biology determines our sex; biology makes us male or female.

Sex has sociological importance only insofar as it has social consequences, which it does in vast array. When we speak of social matters associated with sex, we use the words *women*, *men*, and *gender*. Two genders exist—masculine and feminine—and they correspond to the biological categories of male and female. The last term, *gender role*, refers to the norms, values, and behaviors that culture prescribes and proscribes for each sex.

---

[1] Joe Falls, *The Boston Marathon* (New York: Macmillan, Inc., 1977), pp. 107–10. Ellipses omitted.

THE SPORTSWOMAN: MYTH AND REALITY

Gender Roles and Stereotypes

American culture imposes gender roles on everyone, expecting, sometimes demanding that "real men" be good at quantitative and mechanical tasks; know all about cars, motorcycles, bicycles; be good at math; like action, physical vigor; have strength; and enjoy athletics and be knowledgeable about sports.

American culture also demands that "real women" like the more refined things of life such as art and literature; be passive and nonaggressive; be dependent (ask "real men" to help them when their bicycles get flat tires and their cars won't start on cold mornings); and not be too athletic or know too much about sports. No "real man" needs to read a book entitled *Football for the Fan*, or *How to Watch a Baseball Game*. The "real man" could write such books. Those are for the "real woman" who wants to learn enough about sport to please her "real man."

Because these expectations demand so much that is unsubstantial, and in many instances completely false and pejorative, gender roles are really stereotypes. By attributing certain traits to women, gender role stereotypes help justify the exclusion of women from many realms of life. If the typical woman is passive, nonanalytical, and nonvigorous, then she can't possibly succeed in law, business—or sport.

Until recently, if a woman did enter a "man's" field, then she was the one-in-a-million exception; and was considered abnormal. The stereotypes were so widespread, so imperceptible, and so insidious that those who bore the onus came to believe them—a situation called "false consciousness." Just as blacks at one time suffered the false consciousness of believing they were inferior to whites, so too have women been socialized to accept "their" place, an acceptance which automatically makes them second-class citizens.

Myths

Myths go hand in hand with stereotypes. Probably the most insidious myth about women and sport is that men have a genetic endowment which makes them athletically superior to women. We have debunked the genetic myth in several different forms (see Chapters 6 and 13). Let us debunk it once again regarding the supposed male superiority in sport.

No one disputes sex differences in athletic performance or physiological functions. Males are males and females are females because each has certain clusters of biological characteristics. As it turns out, the average man is 20 percent stronger than the average woman, has a 25-percent faster reaction time, has greater visual-spacial acuity, has greater muscle mass by about 25 percent, and has VO_2 max. values (a measure of cardiovascular capacity) anywhere from 25 to 50 percent greater than the average woman.[2]

---

[2]Ellen Gerber and others, *The American Woman in Sport* (Reading, Massachusetts: Addison-Wesley Publishing Company, Inc., 1974), part 4.

These differences give the average man an advantage in many sports. All things equal, men will have more power, speed, quickness, and strength. In Olympic events performed by both sexes such as the 100-meter run, men's performances exceed women's by 10 to 50 percent.[3]

We can adduce many reasons for this state of affairs, from the most sociological of reasons to the most biological. We reject the biological reasons.

Anatomy is not athletic destiny. Even sociobiologists do not claim that it is. The originator of this discipline says: "women match or surpass men in a few other sports, and these are among the ones furthest removed from the primitive techniques of hunting and aggression: long-distance swimming, the more acrobatic events of gymnastics, precision (but not distance) archery, and small-bore rifle shooting."[4]

The impression that anatomy is athletic destiny comes about because sport bears a male imprint. Sport developed within masculine-dominated cultures, and consequently placed a premium on the supposed male characteristics: aggressiveness, size, and quickness. The ancient Greeks, a major source of Western athletic tradition, did not even allow women to witness some athletic contests, let alone participate. (The Spartans were a major exception.) The British schools, another major source of modern-day sports, were attended only by males, who viewed sport as a way to build and preserve traditional masculinity.[5]

If the male physique is better suited to most sports, it is because males developed sports to suit their physiques. "But if women had been the historically dominant sex," a social philosopher writes, ". . . competitions emphasizing flexibility, balance, . . . timing, and small size might dominate Sunday afternoon television and offer salaries in six figures. Men could be clamoring for equal press coverage of their champions."[6]

Another part of the genetic myth concerns the supposed delicacy of the female constitution. According to this myth, women are easily injured, especially their breasts and reproductive organs. Even in swimming, long an "approved" sport, women were not allowed to train very hard. A former swimmer remembers her experiences on a high school-team during the 1940s. Once she was in the midst of swimming a mile when her coach noticed her and quickly told her to stop: "Girls shouldn't do this! You'll ruin your heart! You won't be able to have children when you grow up!"[7] Her coach, a person of good intentions but woefully misinformed, sincerely believed the myth.

Today the vast majority of informed people reject the myth completely. In a survey of 125 college athletic trainers, 97 percent said that males were as prone to injury as females, and 86 percent approved of women participating in contact sports. According to

---

[3]Ibid.

[4]Edward O. Wilson, *On Human Nature* (Cambridge, Massachusetts: Harvard University Press, 1978), pp. 126–28.

[5]An extreme example is documented in K. G. Sheard and E. G. Dunning, "The Rugby Football Club as a Type of 'Male' Preserve: Some Sociological Notes," *International Review of Sport Sociology*, 8 (1973), 5–21.

[6]Jane English, "Sex Equality in Sports," *Philosophy and Public Affairs*, 7 (Spring 1978), 276.

[7]Joan Ackermann-Blount, "Mistress of the Masters," *Sports Illustrated*, May 31, 1982, p. 36.

statistical tabulations, male and female athletes received much the same types of injuries.[8] It is not anatomy that determines destiny, but culture.

THE SPORTSWOMAN TODAY

Socialization

What are little boys made of?
Snits and snails and puppy dog tails;
That's what little boys are made of.

What are little girls made of?
Sugar and spice and everything nice;
That's what little girls are made of.

Genes determine sex, but culture determines gender. We are socialized into playing out masculine and feminine roles, and like all fundamental socialization, we can't escape it. We learn its rudiments long before becoming intellectually aware of what is happening. The most thorough review of the research done to date concludes, "We do find a consistent trend for parents to elicit more 'gross motor behavior' from their sons than from their daughters. . . . The form of the motor stimulation undoubtedly changes drastically with the age of the child, but the continuing themes appears to be that girls are treated as though they were more fragile than boys."[9]

A classic article written before gender and the sportwoman had become a major social issue, pointed out that by ages eight to eleven, children know their sex roles very well. Boys will tell you: "they have to be able to fight in case a bully comes along; they have to be athletic; they have to be able to run fast; they must be able to play rough games; they need to know how to play many games—curb-ball, baseball, basketball, football . . ."[10]

Another researcher studied 181 middle-class children aged ten to eleven. She observed the children at play, interviewed them, and had them keep diaries. According to the researcher, more boys engage in complex play-sport activities than do girls. She suggests,

It is reasonable to suspect that the following social skills will be cultivated on the playground: the ability to deal with diversity in memberships where each person is performing a special task; the ability to coordinate actions and maintain cohesive-

---

[8]Christine E. Haycock, and Joan V. Gillete, "Susceptibility of Women Athletes to Injury: Myths vs. Reality," *Journal of the American Medical Association*, 236 (July 12, 1976), 165.

[9]Eleanor Emmons Maccoby and Carol Nagy Jacklin, *The Psychology of Sex Differences* (Stanford, California: Stanford University Press, 1974), pp. 307–9.

[10]Ruth E. Hartley, "Sex-Role Pressures and the Socialization of the Male Child," in *The Forty-Nine Percent Majority: The Male Sex Role*, eds. Deborah S. David and Robert Brannon (1959; reprint, Reading, Massachusetts: Addison-Wesley Publishing Co., Inc., 1976), pp. 238–39.

ness among group members; the ability to cope with a set of impersonal rules; and the ability to work for collective as well as personal goals.

Team sports furnish the most frequent opportunity to sharpen these social skills.[11]

Not only do boys and girls participate in different kinds of games, and so presumably learn different social skills, each gender learns to move in a different manner. The physical educator Eleanor Metheny drew upon interviews with college women and found that feminine movements involve aesthetically pleasing patterns (as in gymnastics), artificial devices that enhance maneuverability and speed (as in figure skating), light instruments that are used to overcome light resistance (as in croquet and tennis). She also found that feminine movements do not involve body contact, violence, or brute force (as in wrestling and boxing, which are not considered feminine).[12] More generally, so-called feminine body movements can best be described as light, airy, flowing, and contained (small steps, limb movements held in close to the body).[13]

The situation in which the movements occur also has a bearing. Movements such as jumping or leaping are considered masculine when done on a football field. But the same movements done in a ballet theater would be considered art.

Look at cheerleading. It requires coordination, conditioning, practice, teamwork, and daring (routines such as human pyramids have been banned as too dangerous). By themselves, these would be considered "masculine" behaviors and traits, but considered in the context of cheerleading, they are "feminine."

This is because cheerleading conforms to the stereotypical tradition of women encouraging men engaged in the fray. Cheerleading also plays on another traditional stereotype: women as sex objects. A cheerleader says, "They [the rivals] had better dancers, but we always had the best-looking girls."[14] The fame of the Dallas Cowboy Cheerleaders has more to do with their sex image than their acrobatic ability.

Effects of Socialization

It follows from all of this that anyone—regardless of sex—who is socialized into the feminine repertoire of physical movements, attitudes, and behaviors would fare poorly in male-imprinted sports.

Take just one illustration: "throwing like a girl." Throwing is fundamental to many sports, including tennis, in which serving is described as "throwing the racket at the ball" because much the same movements are used.

---

[11]Janet Lever, "Sex Differences in the Complexity of Children's Play and Games," *American Sociological Review*, 43 (August 1978), 480.

[12]Eleanor Metheny, "Symbolic Forms of Movements: The Feminine Image in Sports." This article is widely reprinted; for instance: George H. Sage, ed., *Sport and American Society: Selected Readings* (Reading, Massachusetts: Addison-Wesley Publishing Co., Inc., 1974), pp. 289–301.

[13]Laurel Walum Richardson, *The Dynamics of Sex and Gender: A Sociological Perspective*, 2nd ed. (Boston: Houghton Mifflin Company, 1981), pp. 71–72.

[14]Bruce Newman, "Eight Beauties and a Beat," *Sports Illustrated*, March 16, 1981, p. 34.

Little boys go around throwing rocks at cats, pebbles into lakes, sticks at each other, and all kinds of balls during recess, pickup games, and in organized leagues. Boys learn to "throw like boys"—largely through play supplemented by instruction from their fathers, teachers, and coaches. Girls do not often have this opportunity.

In a bitingly humorous article, a woman journalist tells of her frustration at not being able to throw a baseball very well and her quest to find out why. Several professional baseball coaches told her that she had been starting her motion with the wrong foot, that she had been leading with her elbow, that her throwing arm was not parallel or slightly above her shoulder, that she faced squarely forward rather than somewhat sideways, that she didn't pivot into the throw and shift her weight, that she didn't follow through, and that she didn't correctly grasp the ball with her hand.[15] The problem of this female journalist, like that of so many women (and not a few men who missed a portion of their socialization), is not that she "threw like a girl," but that she had never been taught to throw at all.

We do not argue that the average woman can throw as hard or as far as the average man. Mass and strength make a difference, but such comparisons make no more sense than arguing that a heavyweight boxer is superior to a lightweight. What we do argue is that the average woman *and* man can learn to perform up to the limits of their physiques and motivation. We all can learn to "throw like a person."

Unfortunately, learning to throw like a person, or engaging in many other athletic activities, violates the so-called role of women. And anytime women step outside this role (or men, outside of theirs), they get "punished"—made to feel guilty, ashamed, anxious, or at minimum, uncomfortable. They encounter role conflict.

Role Conflict

A Busy Park. We frequently walk past a park which has, by our count, six baseball diamonds, sixteen tennis courts, two soccer fields, a fifty-meter public swimming pool, a one-and-a-quarter-mile jogging trail, and three play areas filled with jungle gyms, sandboxes, swings, tether balls, and slides. During summer vacation, kids swarm over the park from early in the morning to late at night, practicing and competing in dozens of sports.

Observing these activities you would immediately notice that most of the kids are boys, by a margin of over twenty to one.

The pony football league (grammar-school age) has girl cheerleaders; and for a few weeks a cheerleading clinic takes place in a corner of the park. Only girls attend. A few girls' softball teams compete in an all-girl league, as do a few soccer teams later in the Fall.

The girls' coaches—all men as far as we have seen—have an easygoing attitude. They don't scream at their players. When a player muffs a play, there is none of that "take a lap," "ten push-ups" kind of discipline. No coach shouts at a reluctant player, "will you hit somebody for a change!" When an outfielder misses an easy pop fly, the coaches don't swear or stamp their feet; "good try, good try!" the coach calls out.

---

[15]Joan Ackerman-Blount, "Up in Arms About My Arm," *Sports Illustrated*, July 16, 1979, pp. 40–49. Also see David Monagan, "The Failure of Coed Sports," *Psychology Today*, March 1983, pp. 59–63.

What's going on here? Without a doubt, gender is making a big difference. But why? Isn't this the day and age of gender equality? Of sex roles breaking down? Of the sportswoman? After all, K. Switzer and hundreds of pioneering female athletes did their thing two decades ago. Today consciousness has already been raised, the myths debunked. Or have they?

As you can see at this park, and other parks, recreation centers, schools, playgrounds, and clubs across the nation, the girl athlete does not get treated like the boy athlete.

Despite much change, our culture continues to define sport in male terms and socializes people to believe in gender-stereotypes. Even those who favor change—as female athletes, their coaches, and their parents undoubtedly do—find themselves unconsciously agreeing with selected portions of the stereotypes.

The recurrent theme in the criticism of female athletics is masculinization—the unfounded but still panicky fear that sport makes the female more male in physique, attitude, emotion, and role.

The sportslike activity of bodybuilding provides an exceptionally clear illustration of what we mean. From Charles Atlas through Arnold Schwarzenegger, male bodybuilding has moved toward an ideal of greater mass, sharper muscle definition, and symmetry.[16]

Women have recently taken up bodybuilding on a serious competitive level and now find themselves trying to answer the question, What is a feminine muscular physique? In competition, women bodybuilders refuse to hold poses that emphasize muscle mass—such as the "crab" pose in which the builder hunches over, pushes both hands together in front of the chest, grimaces, and flexes, making the major muscles of the arms, chest, shoulders, and neck pop out in one dramatic burst.[17]

One female bodybuilder talks about how people react to her: "Everyone thinks I'm a hulk, big, bulky and muscular. I'm not . . . Oh, I've gotten 'why would you want to look like a boy?' but that's OK because I don't try to look like a boy. . . . I want the femininity of a bodybuilder portrayed. If they just want muscles, they can go to a men's contest."[18] As this builder recognizes, there is a conflict between what she does in the gym and what our culture defines as feminine.

Another clear example of conflict is the shotput, an event requiring great muscle bulk and strength. In an article on a female shotputter a journalist writes, "Besides giggly displays in restaurants, people stop and gape at [her]. . . . For a female beginner in an event calling for muscle, and mass, and grunting, for God's sake, it must take a wondrous internal sureness to begin and persist and improve."[19]

Developing muscles and developing strength are two activities at odds with tradi-

---

[16]Charles Gaines and George Butler, *Pumping Iron: The Art and Sport of Body Building*, 2nd ed. (New York: Simon & Schuster, Inc., 1981).

[17]Dan Levin, "Here She is, Miss, Well, What?" *Sports Illustrated*, March 17, 1980, pp. 64–75. See also Nik Cohn and Jean-Pierre Laffont, *Women of Iron* (Wideview Books, 1981).

[18]Quoted in the *Columbus Citizen-Journal*, April 18, 1980, p. 6. Copyright © 1980. Reproduced with permission.

[19]Kenny Moore, "Making a Hole in the Sky," *Sports Illustrated*, March 26, 1979, pp. 32, 37.

tional femininity. They may be extreme examples, but nevertheless, research shows that, regardless of the sport, society punishes the female for her athleticism. Some research follows.

- A study of 268 female varsity athletes in thirteen colleges reveals that slightly over half perceive a conflict between being an athlete and being feminine; and 40 percent had personal experiences with the dilemma of athletics versus femininity.[20]

- When a sample of college women were asked, "Do you feel there is a stigma attached to women's participation in sports?" 65 percent answered yes. In other samples, skilled women athletes were asked, "Do you feel there is a stigma attached to women who participate in the sport you specialize in?" A little over half answered yes.[21]

- The results of a survey of women athletes were in almost perfect accord with cultural prescriptions about feminine physical activities: Fifty-six percent of female basketball players (a sport requiring speed, upper-body strength, and willingness to bump and hit) felt there was a stigma attached to the female player; 50 percent of female track-and-field athletes felt a stigma; 40 percent of female swimmers and divers (sports historically acceptable for women) felt a stigma; and a suprisingly high 31 percent of gymnasts (probably the most "feminine" sport of all, requiring grace, flowing movements, flexibility, and aesthetics—part of it is done to music) felt a stigma.[22]

- Another study shows that college students generally approve of females participating in figure skating (like gymnastics, a highly "artlike" sport) but not in hockey (a heavy contact sport).[23]

- Perhaps as women increasingly enter sport and as male sport comes under heavier criticism, the images will change. For instance, 120 nonathletes attending a southwestern college rated the social acceptability of female softball players as no different from female dancers.[24]

- One researcher, who found that respondents highly approved of the idea of "female athlete," speculates, "Her [the female athlete's] emergence has not as yet been accompanied by substantial instances of public criticism or disrepute, as has been the case with the male's involvement in sport. She may be as yet in the Cinderella stage of achievement and recognition."[25]

---

[20]George H. Sage and Sheryl Loudermilk, "The Female Athlete and Role Conflict," *Research Quarterly*, 50 (March 1979), 88–96.

[21]Eldon E. Snyder, Joseph E. Kivlin, and Elmer E. Spreitzer, "The Female Athlete: An Analysis of Objective and Subjective Role Conflict," in *Psychology of Sport and Motor Behavior*, ed. Daniel M. Landers (Pennsylvania State University HPER Series Number 10, 1975), pp. 165–80.

[22]Ibid.

[23]Fred Promoli, John McCabe, and Susan Shaw, "Attitudes Towards Individuals Participating in Sex Stereotyped Sports," *Arena Newsletter*, 1 (April-June 1977), 17–18.

[24]Joan L. Kingsley, Foster Lloyd Brown, and Margaret E. Seilbert, "Social Acceptance of Female Athletes by College Women," *Research Quarterly*, 48 (December 1977), 727–33.

[25]Joan Vickers, Michael Lashuk, and Terry Taerum, "Differences in Attitude Toward the Concepts 'Male,' 'Female,' 'Male Athlete,' and 'Female Athlete,' " *Research Quarterly for Exercise and Sport*, 51 (May 1980), 415.

So, even while sex barriers are crumbling, a stigma still clings to the female athlete, forcing her to confront the conflict between femininity and the feared masculinizing effect of sport. The fact that sport does not actually make for masculinity is less important than that American culture says sport does; and that masses of people believe sport does; and that they respond to the female athlete as a tomboy, or worse, a weirdo who "wants to be like a guy."

The stigma and conflict create real pressures: discomfort, defensiveness, anxiety. They must be resolved. And most women learn to handle them, if not perfectly, at least well enough to get along. Several tactics can be used, either singly or in combination.

Avoidance.   One effective way to resolve the conflict between femininity and athleticism is to avoid sport. Those women who perceive the most stigma and feel the most anxiety from the female sports role, do not become athletes in the first place. We have no statistical data showing how many women opt for this tactic, but the number must be very large.

Disregard.   The opposite tactic from avoidance is to ignore gender all together. Women have recently organized amateur hockey leagues played essentially with men's rules, and with the same enthusiasm. There are some three hundred women's hockey teams in the United States, a few sponsored by colleges. Says a referee of the play, "they skate and shoot well and they play rough."[26] Perhaps eight thousand women of all ages play the less violent but still rough and traditionally unfeminine sport of amateur soccer.[27] A few women have gone into boxing and some into semiprofessional women's football.

Complete avoidance and complete disregard represent extreme tactics. Most female athletes resolve any perceived gender-role conflict by using tactics somewhere in between.

Role Signs.   One of the most common tactics is to decorate the sports role with feminine accoutrements and cosmetics.[28] Watch a track meet for example, and you will see female athletes with their long hair tied in back with pink ribbons, wearing earrings, nail polish, and lipstick. Illustrating this, a female long-distance runner says, "I always worry about looking nice in a race. I worry about my calf muscles getting big. But mostly I worry about my hair. . . . I suppose it's because so many people have said women athletes look masculine. So a lot of us try, subconsciously maybe, to look as feminine as possible in a race. There's always lots of hair ribbons in a race."[29]

---

[26]Barry Stavro, "Women's Ice Hockey: It's Rough, Tough Stuff," *New York Times*, March 10, 1980, sec. C, p. 2. © 1980 by The New York Times Company. Reprinted by permission.

[27]For additional examples, see William H. Beezley and Joseph P. Hobbs, " 'Nice Girls Don't Sweat': Women in American Sport," *Journal of Popular Culture*, 16, No. 4 (Spring 1983), 42–53.

[28]Michael Banton, *Roles: An Intruduction to the Study of Social Relations* (New York: Basic Books, Inc., Publishers, 1965), Chap. 4, a standard work on roles.

[29]From *Women: Psychology's Puzzle*, by Joanna Bunker Rohrbaugh, Copyright © 1979 by Joanna Bunker Rohrbaugh, Basic Books, Inc., Publishers, New York.

Role Splitting.   A closely related tactic is to split the role. As the term *role* implies, the participant can be one person while ''on the screen'' and an entirely different person ''off the screen.''[30] The female athlete can be ''masculinely'' rugged and aggressive while competing, and ''femininely'' soft and compliant at other times. For example, there are two twins who play collegiate basketball. They stand six feet three inches tall, weigh 170 pounds, and major in industrial engineering and business (traditionally unfeminine majors). They take out their frustrations by donning boxing gloves and are noted for their aggressive play and physical strength on the court, but they also work hard to maintain traditional femininity when not engaged in athletics. According to one of them, ''When I'm not playing, it's time to be a lady.''[31]

Denial.   The female bodybuilder quoted earlier uses yet another tactic. She asserts that great bulk, strength, and aggression are not goals of bodybuilding. In other words, she denies that bodybuilding has to be masculine.

On ethical-moral grounds, you might argue that accommodating to a role conflict between femininity and athleticism should not be necessary. We agree. Why should sport be defined as primarily masculine? By the same token, why should homemaking be defined as primarily feminine? More generally, why should any activity bear a gender-related tag?

At one time in the history of the human species, there could have been sound reasons for assigning certain tasks to women and other tasks to men. We do not know if that was ever the case, but certainly whatever the reasons, they are obsolete in today's technological world. What we see in the gender-role conflict of the female athlete is culture lag. Changes in technology and social structure have spurted ahead of changes in norms and values defining femininity and masculinity. To understand this, we must understand how it all came about. And to understand that, we have to go back about two hundred years in history.

THE SPORTSWOMAN YESTERDAY

The Greatest. Babe Didrikson is usually considered to be the greatest woman athlete who ever lived. She once scored 106 points in a basketball game. In the 1932 Olympics she won gold medals in the eighty-meter hurdles, and the javelin, and had apparently won the high jump when judges ruled she illegally dove over the bar. Later she pitched for a touring softball team. Then she took up golf and went on to become one of the game's finest players.

She made lots of money, much of it from side bets, and freebies from sponsors, and from public appearances. She was befriended by the rich and famous. Compared to most people at the time of the Great Depression, she led a good life.[32]

---

[30]See Ralph H. Turner, ''The Role and the Person,'' *American Journal of Sociology*, 84 (July 1978), 1–23.

[31]Roger Jackson, ''USC Has Double Its Fun,'' *Sports Illustrated*, February 22, 1982, p. 34.

[32]William Oscar Johnson and Nancy P. Williamson, *''Whatta-Gal'': The Babe Didrikson Story* (Boston: Little, Brown & Company, 1975).

Had Didrikson lived during the Victorian era, all her great talent would have been for nought. The Victorian era was a time when "men were men" and "women were women." The very idea of a vigorously athletic woman simply did not exist. Didrickson would have been hard put to do more than play croquet for fun, shoot a bow, and ride a bicycle—slowly.

Even as it was, she lived "too soon." During the late 1920s and the 1930s, society had only a few slots for women athletes, no matter how talented. We don't feel sorry for Didrickson, however; only a handful of athletes (of either sex) have ever accomplished more than she. The tragedy lies in society. Since society would not fully accommodate the "greatest woman athlete of all time," how much accommodation do you think was given to the typical woman? Not much, you can be sure.

From a historical perspective, the situation came about quite naturally—which is not to say justly. As with the rise of sport, the rise of the sportswoman involves basic sociological structures and processes.

Culture and Class

During the nineteenth century, sport was a male domain. That could only be expected, for the exclusion of women from sport parallels the exclusion of women from other institutions, such as medicine, law, and business. Males dominated society.

The odd ideology that justified female exclusion developed principally from the ideology of upper-class Victorian England. It sanctified women as porcelain figurines mounted on pedestals: fragile, delicate, and beautiful, for men to admire and care for.

The odd ideology had nothing to do with the lower-class reality. Those women worked as field hands, in the coal mines, and as factory drudges—hardly the occupations suited for the porcelain woman. However, it is a sociological truism that the upper class imposes its ideology on the rest of society.

Industrialization pulled people into the factory, and men established a monopoly on the mechanical and business aspects of work. The traits necessary for success at work quickly became defined as part of the male role: facility with numbers and tools, rationality, business sense, aggressiveness, and competitiveness.

As for upper-class women, they were pulled into the house. To them fell the lot of raising children, supervising servants, being submissive, supportive, and warm. The household became their domain.[33] "The ideal of feminine perfection," writes one historian, "[was] softness and weakness, delicacy and modesty, a small waist and curving shoulders, an endearing ignorance of everything that went on beyond household and social life."[34]

In women's fashion we can see how the odd ideology worked and how it affected the sportswoman. The Victorian lady was buried from throat to ankle in yards of crinoline

---

[33]Howard Zinn, *A People's History of the United States* (New York: Harper & Row Publishers, Inc., 1980), chap. 6.

[34]Janet Dunbar, *The Early Victorian Woman: Some Aspects of Her Life (1837–57)* (London: George G. Harrap & Co., Ltd., 1953), p. 20.

dress, petticoat, stays, and corset. The ideal waist size was sixteen inches—obtainable only by trussing a whale bone corset to its tightest while the woman held her breath.

The well-dressed Victorian lady had problems getting about. She had difficulty walking down steps because her skirts obstructed her vision; and getting in and out of coaches and through small doors was no easy task. Her dress thus ensured that she would have to depend on some gallant gentleman to help her; and trussed up as she was, she could barely walk for want of breath let alone run or engage in vigorous physical activity.[35] "Sport for women, as we know it, did not play any part in the leisure hours of a girl a hundred years ago; she would have thought of an 'athletic' woman with horror."[36]

Opposition to Victorian practices did exist—but only as voices in the wilderness. A few physicians spoke out against corsets and called upon women to exercise vigorously. After spending five months observing various "Establishments for Young Ladies," the early sociologist Herbert Spencer concluded, "once, indeed, we saw one [girl] chase another round the garden; but, with this exception, nothing like vigorous exertion has been visible." He then asked rhetorically, "Why this astonishing difference? Is it that the constitution of a girl differs so entirely from that of a boy as not to need these active exercises?"[37] Obviously not.

The surname of reformer Amelia Bloomer became the name of a new and scandalous form of dress, long, voluminous pants.[38] Bloomers became a symbol of feminine freedom but were not popular among the majority of women.

Upper-class women might engage in mild physical activities. In playing tennis, social convention prohibited women from running hard after the ball, or using powerful strokes—pat-pat back and forth was the woman's game. In any event, they could hardly do much else while wearing mountains of clothes.[39]

Perhaps archery was the most popular sport for women. The archer's pose, with bow drawn, back straight, and arms forming a V, was greatly admired as an example of feminine grace. Croquet and decorous horseback riding became popular later in the century. Women also ice-skated, even in the summer (on artificial ice, naturally). According to a writer of the period, "Without denying that a little of the attractiveness of skating is due to opportunities it affords of a little quiet flirtation, it deserves support as a means of exercise and a stimulus to active locomotion."[40]

Times change. Women began entering college. Oberlin graduated a woman theology student in 1850. Women played prominent parts in the abolition movement, in the

---

[35]For one interpretation of Victorian dress, see Helene E. Roberts, "The Exquisite Slave: The Role of Clothes in the Making of the Victorian Woman," Signs, 2 (Spring 1977), 554–69.

[36]Dunbar, The Early Victorian Woman, p. 92.

[37]Herbert Spencer, Education: Intellectual, Moral, and Physical (New York: D. Appleton and Company, 1898), p. 254.

[38]Zinn, A People's History, pp. 111–112.

[39]Angela Lumpkin, Women's Tennis: A Historical Documentary of the Players and Their Game (Troy, New York: The Whitston Publishing Company, 1981).

[40]From a periodical of the time, "The Ladies' Treasury," quoted in Dunbar, The Early Victorian Woman, p. 93; Margery A. Bulger, "American Sportswomen in the 19th Century," Journal of Popular Culture, 16 (Fall 1982), 1–16.

temperance movement, in the suffrage movement, and in the labor movement. Victorian strictures began opening up an inch or two.

The bicycle became immensely popular near the end of the nineteenth century. Obviously you can't bicycle in a corset overlaid with yards and yards of petticoats and dress. One of the ablest public leaders of her time wrote,

> If women ride they must, when riding, dress more rationally than they have been wont to do. If they do this many prejudices as to what they may be allowed to wear will melt away. Reason will gain upon precedent, and ere long the comfortable, sensible, and artistic wardrobe of the rider will make the conventional style of woman's dress absurd to the eye and unendurable to the understanding.[41]

Controversy sprang up over what the bicycling costume should be. "The Bicycle skirt and blouse of tweed, with belt, rolling collar, and loose cravat, the skirt three inches from the ground; a round straw hat, and walking-shoes with gaiters . . . no person of common sense could take exception."[42] The more daring riders wore bloomers and knickerbockers.

In the twentieth century, the pace of change quickened. During World War I, national policy encouraged all women to enter industry and to work the farms.[43] The military draft exposed the physical unfitness of American youths, and the subsequent introduction of physical education into public schools affected both women and men.

The Roaring Twenties came along and flappers smoked, drank gin, danced the Charleston, and wore skimpy short skirts—just the opposite of the proper Victorian woman.

American women finally won the right to vote.

As with World War I, government policy during World War II encouraged women to join the work force. Rosie the Riveter—the oil-smudged woman in overalls who took factory jobs formerly held by men—became a civilian heroine. The military accepted women, though not out of any sense of sexual equality. A high-ranking officer testified to a Congressional appropriations committee, "we have found difficulty in getting enlisted men to perform tedious duties anywhere nearly as well as women will do it."[44] But tedium aside, the image of the woman soldier was heroic. One recruiting poster showed a picture of a uniformed woman against the backdrop of the American flag proclaiming, "This is My War Too!"

After the comparatively placid 1950s, the civil rights movement arose and later, so

---

[41]Frances E. Willard, "A Wheel Within a Wheel: How I Learned to Ride," excerpted in Stephanie L. Twin, *Out of the Bleachers: Writings on Women and Sport* (Old Westbury, New York: The Feminist Press and the McGraw-Hill Book Company, 1979), p. 109; Sidney H. Aronson, "The Sociology of the Bicycle," *Social Forces*, 30 (March 1952), 305–12.

[42]Ibid., p. 114.

[43]Penny Martelet, "The Woman's Land Army, World War I," in *Clio Was a Woman: Studies in the History of American Women*, eds. Mabel E. Deutch and Virginia C. Purdy (Washington, D.C.: Howard University Press, 1980), pp. 136–46.

[44]Quoted in Susan M. Hartman, "Women in Military Service," in Deutch and Purdy, *Clio Was a Woman*, p. 198.

did the women's movement. In the 1960 Olympics, American sprinter Wilma Rudolph won three gold medals and became a sports heroine. Ten years later, tennis emerged as the springboard for women's professional sport. When Bobby Riggs (a former tennis champion) played Billie Jean King in a $100,000 winner-take-all tournament, and was soundly beaten before a national television audience, women's sport had symbolically arrived.

In 1972 Congress passed Title IX of the Educational Amendments Act. By a stroke of the federal pen, women's sport ostensibly became equal to men's. Title IX mandates that whatever sports activities, amenities, facilities, coaching, and rewards a school offers to men, it must also offer to women, though not necessarily on a dollar-for-dollar basis.[45]

Federal guidelines for the administration of Title IX have been under continual revision and the final outcome remains unknown; but over the past decade some startling changes have occurred. Average budgets for women's collegiate sport have increased from 2 percent of the total athletic budget before Title IX to 16 to 24 percent. The number of sports offered for women about doubled. And the number of females in intercollegiate athletics increased 100 percent; in high school athletics, 500 percent.[46]

The major point is this: Developments in society ultimately determined the rise of the sportswoman.

Organizations and Sponsorship

In the late nineteenth century a few men's athletic clubs accepted women members while other clubs had separate women's branches. In 1877 the Ladies' Club of the Staten Island Cricket and Baseball Club was formed with some thirty members. It offered lawn tennis for women (not to be confused with the highly competitive game played by women today) and grew to about three hundred members in ten years.[47]

Schools sponsored physical education and sports, and when women started going to college, they participated. Mount Holyoke had women's physical education as early as 1837, Rockford College in 1849, Vassar in 1868, Smith and Wellesley in 1875. Physical education was being introduced into the curriculum "not merely to secure health, but also a graceful carriage, and well-formed bodies," stated Smith's 1875 course catalog.[48] Leadership of women's physical education resided mainly among eastern colleges, although Oberlin College of Ohio established the first women's department of physical education and eventually conferred the first full professorship on a female physical educator.[49]

Unlike the development of men's sports, which became big business dominated by professional coaches and athletic departments, women's sports came under the leadership

---

[45]Ellen W. Gerber, "The Legal Basis for the Regulation of Intercollegiate Sport," *Educational Record*, 60 (Fall 1979), 467–81.

[46]Statistics reported by Candace Lyle Hogan, "Revolutionizing School and Sports: 10 Years of Title IX," *Ms.*, May 1982, p. 26.

[47]Gerber, *The American Woman in Sport*, chap. 1.

[48]Ibid., p. 50.

[49]Mabel Lee, *Memories of a Bloomer Girl* (Washington, D.C.: American Alliance for Health, Physical Education, and Recreation, 1978).

of female physical educators. They emphasized health and downplayed competition. A well-known female physical educator wrote of her program, "Whatever the game, we encourage each girl who enters it to play her level best. . . . We don't want our girls to miss the fun of sports because they can't all be champions. A game for every girl—that is what counts, to my mind."[50]

A small amount of intercollegiate competition did take place. An early form consisted of the intramural champion of one school playing the intramural champion of another school. This gave everyone a chance to compete at the intramural level while allowing champions to test their skills against other champions. This form of competition lasted well through the 1930s, with about one out of five schools using it.[51]

A few sports organizations were geared to big-time women's competition. The AAU assumed sponsorship of women's track and field in 1922, and all women's sports in 1923, despite the opposition of female physical educators. They preferred an alternative organization which developed from a conference of female physical educators started in 1923: The Women's Division of the National Amateur Athletic Federation.[52]

For the next several decades, the Women's Division provided the leadership for most of women's sport and went by the sixteen-point creed, a statement of goals deemphasizing big-time competition. For instance, the sixteenth point was: "To discourage athletic competition which involves travel." That clearly precluded intercollegiate competition.

Most of the organizations concerned with women's athletics, except the AAU, endorsed the creed. Rather than having teams composed of the highly recruited, highly trained, and highly talented few, the emphasis was on activities such as playdays, sportdays, and telegraphic competition. The motto became "a team for every girl and every girl on a team."

Then the situation changed. A women's golf championship held annually at Ohio State University was the focal point. Female physical educators mostly opposed the tournament because it went against the philosophy of the sixteen-point creed. When Ohio State offered to give up the tournament, a consortium of women's sports groups took over its sponsorship. In 1966 the consortium revamped itself and stated: "In order to encourage the holding of intercollegiate competitive events and to assist those who are currently conducting such events, the Commission will provide the service of a sanctioning procedure."[53] The new consortium was soon sponsoring women's championships in golf, tennis, gymnastics, track and field, swimming, badminton, volleyball, and basketball. In 1972 the Association for Intercollegiate Athletics for Women (AIAW) took over. Big-time women's sport had arrived.

---

[50]Gertrude Hawley, quoted in Helen Ferris and Virginia Moore, *Girls Who Did: Stories of Real Girls and their Careers* (New York: E. P. Dutton, 1927), p. 12. Copyright © 1927 by E. P. Dutton.

[51]Gerber, *The American Woman in Sport*, chap. 1.

[52]Mary A. Daniels, "The Historical Transition of Women's Sports at the Ohio State University, 1885–1975 and Its Impact on the National Women's Intercollegiate Setting During that Period" (unpublished Ph.D. dissertation, Department of Physical Education, The Ohio State University, 1977).

[53]Quoted in Gerber, *The American Woman in Sport*, p. 84.

The major points are these: (1) Women's sport quickly came under the auspices of organizations which provided stability and order to a changing institution; and (2) during the 1950s and 1960s, women's sports came to a fork in the road, and took the side leading to big-time intercollegiate competition.

Women and the Olympics

One highly organized area in which women's competition has long been deadly serious is the Olympic Games. Reflecting the era's Zeitgeist, the early Olympics discouraged women athletes. Baron Pierre de Coubertin, founder of the modern Olympics, stated,

> Would such sports practiced by women constitute an edifying sight before crowds assembled for an Olympiad? . . . Such is not our idea of the Olympic Games in which we feel we have tried and that we must continue to try to achieve the following definition: the solemn and periodic exaltation of male athleticism with internationalism as a base, loyalty as a means, art for its setting, and female applause as reward.[54]

Coubertin believed (not atypically for his time) that women should be in the stands applauding the men who competed on the athletic field.

The 1900 Games held in Paris introduced women's tennis and golf. Only twelve women competed. (Charlotte Cooper of Great Britain became the first female gold-medal winner.[55]) Very slowly, women increased their participation. In the 1904 St. Louis Olympics, eight women participated (all from the United States); in the interim Olympics held in 1906, seven women competed. In the 1908 Olympics forth-three females competed in four sports: archery, figure skating, tennis, and sailing. The introduction of women's swimming competition was one important stepping stone. By the 1920 Olympics, half of the 136 female competitors were swimmers.[56] An organization rivaling the Olympics sponsored a Women's Olympic Games in 1922, and again in 1926. As a result, the 1928 Olympics introduced women's track and field (the center-piece events of the Games), thus firmly establishing the principle of women's participation.

A wide gap remains, however, between principle and practice. Currently the Olympics provide about three times as many events for men as for women; women make up only 20 percent of all Olympic competitors; and only about half of all countries have women on their teams.[57] Because women's medals count just as much as men's in determining who wins the Games, Soviet bloc countries have heavily recruited female

---

[54]Ibid., p. 137.

[55]Uriel Simri, *A Historical Analysis of the Role of Women in the Modern Olympic Games* (Netanya: The Wingate Institute for Physical Education and Sport, 1977).

[56]Ibid.

[57]Ibid.; U. Simri, "The State of Women's Sports: The Olympic, International, and National Scenes," in *Olympism*, eds. Jeffrey Segrave and Donald Chu (Champaign, Illinois: Human Kinetics Publishers, 1981), pp. 89–97.

athletes; a development which undoubtedly spurred many other nations to do the same.[58] Despite over eighty years of changes, women remain underrepresented in the Olympics— the most prestigious amateur athletic competition in the world. The Olympic sportswoman has come a long way, but still has miles to go.

A Model

The obvious facts of social history concern the Ws: Who, What, and When. The Why remains ambiguous, for facts are just dots on a blank sheet of paper; discerning what picture the dots form requires human interpretation, and humans interpret facts from different angles. Here we will provide a sociological explanation, or model, for the rise of the sportswoman.

The explanation, it seems to us, requires more than one variable; it requires a multivariate model. The appearance of today's sportswoman must take into account culture, false consciousness, organization, and the institutional characteristics of sport. Consider:

1. The restrictions imposed upon women during Victorian times kept them passive and physically inactive. The reality of lower-class women working in "unladylike" occupations, as field hands or miners, for example, did not matter because the upper classes handed down the odd ideology of the porcelain woman.
2. Sociologist Georg Simmel wrote in 1911, "We measure the achievements and commitments . . . of males and females in terms of specific norms and values; but these norms are not neutral, standing above the contrasts of the sexes; they have themselves a male character."[59] In other words, false consciousness prevailed. The male imposed his standards on the female, and the female accepted them.
3. Mild physical activity for women slowly became more acceptable. Most often, existing organizations could be modified to take over the support of women's sport—a fortunate situation because creating new organizations is difficult.
4. Unlike men's sport, women's sport came under the auspices of physical education. Reflecting a kind of false consciousness and the Zeitgeist of their day, female physical educators considered big-time competition anathema for the female, and endorsed the idea of noncompetitive, sex-segregated activities that did not require great physical exertion. Women did engage in intercollegiate competition and in other big-time events, most notably, the Olympics—but never on a massive scale.
5. Though women's sport started with slow and halting steps, once a certain point was reached, it simply burst forth. We suspect that women have made more rapid and dramatic gains in sport than in any other major institution of our society. This is easy to explain sociologically:

---

[58]An interesting analysis is provided by Moshe Semyonov, "Changing Roles of Women: Participation in Olympic Games," *Social Science Quarterly*, 62 (December 1981), 735–43.

[59]Quoted in Lewis A. Coser, "Georg Simmel's Neglected Contributions to the Sociology of Women," *Signs*, 2 (Summer 1977), 872.

a. As the twentieth century rolled along, the Victorian notions of the porcelain lady gave way to an acceptance of limited physical activity for women. The norms and values favoring physical activity and competition were there. The qualifiers had to be changed from "limited" to "unlimited." It is much easier to modify qualifiers than to build entirely new norms and values.

b. The same point applies to organizations. Women already had formal organizations devoted to noncompetitive physical education. When more competitive sports moved to the forefront during the 1960s, the AIAW could be formed out of preexisting organizations; and later when women's sport became more big time, the already existing NCAA took over sponsorship. Girls could join already existing Little Leagues, model their competition after already existing boy's varsity competition, use already existing facilities. Without this preexisting base of organization, the development of women's sport would have been immeasurably slower.

c. The drive to open sport to females greatly benefited from the drive to make sport more equitable for ethnic minorities, and from the Zeitgeist of protest, change, and radicalization that occurred in the late 1960s and early 1970s. Title IX greatly helped. The women's movement became one wedge among the dozens being driven to open up American society. Changes in one area of society cause spin-off changes in other areas, and those changes feed back on the original changes and spin off more changes. . . . Once the Zeitgeist gets moving, it moves at an increasingly faster rate.

d. The women's movement found widespread support among women of different social backgrounds. Older women who opted for a more conservative approach, and radical young women (many in colleges and universities) shared the common experiences of sex discrimination and the desire to eliminate it.[60]

e. Less obvious, but no less important, sport as an institution maintains the egalitarian ideal of "may the best man win" regardless of race, religion, or creed. It was a relatively short jump to "may the best person win." Helping this ideal along, sport has highly detailed rules and scoring procedures. Oftentimes, the best person may be determined unambiguously. Anyone who runs 100 meters in ten seconds, both easily measured quantities, is "fast" regardless of sex. Certain sports require judging (diving, gymnastics, figure skating), but most of the time consistent scoring takes place; or if it is inconsistent, the numbers are up there for everyone to see and judge for themselves.

What happened in the past, and how those developments worked out sociologically, determined what we see in the sports world today. But what of tommorow? What does the future hold for the sportswoman? Will things get better? Or worse? We can only guess at the answers to those questions, but educated guesses are better than blindly stumbling into tomorrow.

---

[60]Richardson, *The Dynamics*, pp. 251–57.

THE SPORTSWOMAN TOMORROW

Today the typical woman probably feels "funny" about participating in extremely vigorous physical activities requiring aggression, bulk, strength, and physical contact. She feels that way because norms, values, and structures define femininity along different lines. But that can change. Cultures are flexible.

The famous cultural anthropologist Margaret Mead studied three tribes in New Guinea. The first tribe defined both males and females as passive, warm, gentle, and equally responsible for child rearing. The second tribe defined both men and women as aggressive and violent, and neither sex cared much for children. The third tribe defined women as domineering, energetic, and responsible for supporting the household, while men were defined as gossipy, emotional, and child oriented.[61]

These instances demonstrate that culture and the human being it produces can take on a myriad of shapes and qualities. There is nothing inherent in the constitution of humans, nor in the constitution of society, that prevents a redefinition of femininity and masculinity.

We think the redefinition will happen soon in the United States and will encompass a redefinition of the role of the sportswoman. Sometime around the year 2001, women's sports will be popular enough to attract major television contracts; women's collegiate sports will be much like men's; and female athletes will not experience conflicts between the norms of sport and femininity. In accordance with this redefinition, we expect the following developments:

Acceptance.   The genetically determined characteristics of mass, height, or strength confer an indisputable advantage in some sports but not in others. This means different sports will take different paths.

Women have been shut out of certain sports, such as football, boxing, and Olympic wrestling. The stigma of "being like a boy" has been the roadblock. However as society opens up, women will increasingly enter, and be accepted in, all sports. The popularity of women's soccer, rugby, bodybuilding, power lifting, hockey, and football suggest that that will come to pass.

Sports which already have well-established women's competition, such as gymnastics, tennis, and figure skating, will remain sex segregated but will achieve parity with men as to prestige and earnings.

Certain sports, such as marathon running, long-distance swimming, and auto racing, will follow the lead set by shooting, yachting, and horseback riding. That is, women will compete directly against men without handicaps of any kind.

Professional Outlets.   As women come to play a larger role in big-time sport, professional outlets will develop. Women's tennis provides a case in point. Tennis has been a "proper" female sport since Victorian times. Before professional circuits de-

---

[61] Margaret Mead, *Sex and Temperament in Three Primitive Societies* (New York: William Morrow & Co., Inc., 1935).

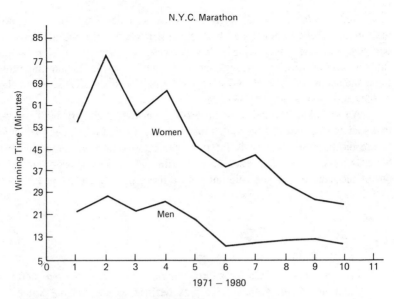

Figure 9.1. Heading toward Parity

The difference between women's and men's winning times in the marathon has decreased over the past ten years, as these data from the New York City Marathon illustrate. (To obtain actual time, add 120 minutes to the time shown on the graph).
SOURCE: New York Road Runners Clubs, 1980.

veloped, women's amateur tennis meant great prestige and not a little money. Thus it was sociologically natural for tennis to be among the first women's sports to succeed professionally.

We think other professional sports will eventually follow suit; notably basketball, and perhaps volleyball. A women's professional basketball league did exist for a few years, and so did a mixed professional volleyball league. These failed financially, but if you look at history, you can see that men's sport occasionally failed too.

Problems.   The complete acceptance of big-time athletics for women will not be entirely painless, nor always for the better. Women will come up against essentially the same problems as men have.

Recently, the NCAA replaced the AIAW as the major sponsor of women's intercollegiate sport. If women come under men's rules in regard to recruiting, financial assistance, and splitting television revenues, then women will have achieved parity and the problems that go with it: recruiting violations, illegal payments to athletes, unremitting pressures to win. Women coaches and athletes can, and will be, as deviant as men.

Other criticisms of men's sport will also apply to women's sport: overemphasis on victory at the expense of academic performance, exploitation of female athletes, coddling of athletes, and so on. Very soon now, women's sport will be fast forwarding through what men's sport went through not too long ago (and is still going through).

But we should not be overly negative. A positive side exists. The woman blessed with great athletic talent has a right to use her talent. Like the male, she has the right to compete and win—or lose. She has the right to earn prestige, to attend school on a full-ride scholarship, to represent her school and country. Outstanding athletes gain much fame and access to networks which open doors in business. These doors should be open to women too. And soon they will be.

All sociologists, and most laypeople, know that society isn't necessarily just, and that society does not change very rapidly to rectify past injustices. Yet changes do occur. While the current situation is far from perfect, women have made significant progress towards equality. We happen to live at a time when the sportswoman is starting to break out of the cage of her sex role and into a more open society—at last.

SUMMARY

1. This chapter concerned the sportswoman and society. Sex was defined as biological; gender as social. Gender role was defined as the norms, values, and behaviors prescribed and proscribed for each sex.
2. Gender-role stereotypes attribute certain characteristics to males and females. By doing so, the stereotype helps justify the relegation of women to second-class citizenship.
3. Women have usually agreed with the stereotype, a situation called false consciousness.
4. The overriding myth concerning the sportswoman is that the male anatomy is inherently better suited to sport. Male-female differences do exist but that does not prove the myth to be true. The myth arises because the physical movements, attitudes, and emotions required for success at sport were developed primarily in male-oriented cultures. Males, so to speak, developed sport to suit their own physiques.
5. Culture determines what is proper for each gender. Through socialization we become feminine and masculine. This occurs via the popular media, family, peer group, school, and private organizations. Boys are socialized to be aggressive, competitive, physical, and active in sports. Girls are socialized to be passive, domestic, not too active, to move gracefully and with containment, and to be indifferent to sport. Socialization accounts for much of the difference between men's performance and women's performance in sport.
6. The woman athlete finds herself being stigmatized because sport is supposedly unfeminine. Despite a more open society, the stigma persists.
7. Role conflicts arise. Women athletes resolve the conflicts by avoidance, disregard of the traditional masculine qualities of the sport, use of role signs, use of role splitting, denial of the masculinity of the role. The fact of stigma and the resultant necessity to resolve role conflict is morally unjustifiable.
8. Victorian women were considered porcelain figurines. Physical vigor was strictly taboo. Males dominated society.

a. As the Zeitgeist changed, it became proper for women to engage in mild physical activities. Later, more vigorous activities became acceptable, as did participation in the work force in traditionally male jobs.

b. Women's fashion clearly shows the social role women came to play; voluminous skirts, petticoats, and corsets restricted their physical activity. Dress reform, spurred by the desire for more freedom, became a social cause.

d. Already existing organizations helped by sponsoring, encouraging, and governing the rise of women's physical education. The federal government came to eventually have a major effect when Title IX mandated certain forms of sex equality in sport.

e. For most of this century, women's physical education ruled women's sport and discouraged big-time competition. Whether that was good or bad can be debated.

f. It was not until comparatively recently that women began intercollegiate competition on a major scale.

g. After a grudging start, the Olympics accepted the principle of women competitors, but even today women are statistically underrepresented in both number of competitors and number of events open to women.

10. The future bodes well for the sportswoman. We think that society will change in the following ways.

a. More and more women will participate in sports of all kinds without stigma, and role conflict will modulate and disappear.

b. The well-established women's sports will remain sex segregated but will achieve parity with men's sports as to prestige and earnings.

c. Certain sports will become mixed, and women and men will compete head to head.

d. Big-time athletics for women will be accepted. This will have both advantages and disadvantages.

10 POLITICS AND SPORTS, PART I

A Social History

In 1936 the Nazis turned the Olympics into a major political spectacle. Hitler personally led the parade of dignitaries during the opening ceremonies and stayed to cheer for the German athletes. In an infamous incident, Hitler refused to shake the hands of victorious black American athletes, whom he had previously derided as "America's Negro auxiliaries." This did not stop Jesse Owens from becoming an Olympic hero. Photos courtesy of The Ohio State University archives and the Library of Congress.

Case 1: An Olympic Dive. The late Babe Didrikson is considered one of the all-time great athletes. In the 1932 Olympics she won gold medals in the javelin and high hurdles but was denied victory in the high jump because she dived over the bar: Her head went over before the rest of her body. From later evidence it seems certain that she did, in fact, dive.

Case 2: A Better Mousetrap. A man recently invented a cam device which, by replacing or supplementing the chain, makes the bicycle significantly easier to pedal. The head coach of the United States Olympic cycling team commented on it: "The bicycle has been set for the last 40 or 50 years, with only minor changes, so this is quite a departure."[1]

According to the inventor, four American cyclists used cam-equipped bicycles in a 750-mile European road race; and all placed in the top 2 percent of 1,800 racers—by far the best overall American performance to date. One goal of the inventor is to get the cam approved for Olympic competition.

Case 3: Famous Basketball Coach, Bobby Knight, Says, "Anyone who thinks we can compete internationally without politics being involved is either a complete moron or incredibly naive." (NBC television interview, March 2, 1980.)

Are these three cases political? On the surface the first two seem not to be. Case 1 concerns enforcing a rule against an illegal high jump technique. Case 2 is a classic example of building a better mousetrap, or in the present instance, a better bicycle. But however nonpolitical these two cases appear when examined casually, when they are examined sociologically both turn out to be thoroughly immersed in politics.

We would predict that if someone did use a cam-equipped bicycle in the Olympics, a really raucous brouhaha would erupt. The press, fans, and athletes would be charging and countercharging: "It's illegal"; "It's legal"; "It's not fair"; "It is *so* fair"; "It's unsportsmanlike"; "It is *so* sportsmanlike"; and so on. And some person or organization would have to decide the issue; and that process must be political.

The case of Babe Didrikson didn't involve technology but a technique: diving over the high jump. Just why the technique was illegal then (it no longer is) did not really matter to Didrikson losing the gold medal. However arbitrary and irrational the rule might have been, some group had the right to make it and some group had the power to enforce it. As with the bicycle cam, the situation turns into an issue of governance and thus becomes an inherently political problem.

As these cases suggest, sport is thoroughly political—regardless of how it seems to be, and regardless of whether it should be.

The Dictionary of the Social Sciences, a standard reference work, defines politics as the study of conflicts, power, and policy. Of the three elements, power is studied most. Another source, a widely used sociology text, says politics is "the institutionalized system through which some individuals or groups acquire and exercise power over others. . . .

---

[1]June Watanabe, "Problems Delaying New-Type Bicycle," *Columbus Citizen-Journal*, January 13, 1980, sec. E, p. 1. Associated Press Newsfeatures.

Politics is about power—who gets it, how it is obtained, how it is used, and to what purpose it is put.''[2]

Power is the probability ''that one actor [group or individual] within a social relationship will be in a position to carry out its own will despite resistance.''[3] Sociologist Max Weber offers this definition in an essay on the political order. Viewed in this general way, politics involves more than how elections work. We see conflicts, power, and policy everywhere. The processes seep into our daily lives, into all societal institutions including sport, and become something largely taken for granted. In fact politics seem so natural that the absence of political constraints may startle people. Finding that no rules govern the size of tennis rackets, for example, surprises most people. Player may use rackets from the size of spoons to the size of brooms or larger. Only tradition and practicality prevent them from doing so.

For many years tennis had the image (probably correct) of being a fusty upper-class sport. It epitomized the old British ideal of the rich gentleman-athlete. Max Weber would have undoubtedly considered tennis a good example of governance based on traditional authority. (He defined authority as legitimate power and coercion as illegitimate power.) We unthinkingly comply with tradition because it has a semisacred aura and because everyone else has always complied with it. Encrusted so heavily with tradition, many tennis rules never needed to be written down in manuals or enforced by a governing organization. It would have been unthinkable to use a racket differing from the type that has always been used. Breaking with tennis tradition would be unsportsmanlike, gauche, and simply not done!

Not until fairly recently did racket size become an issue. We expect that explicit rules will soon be made to regulate racket size and other technological changes. As traditional authority breaks down, a new kind of power becomes necessary to insure compliance. As Weber would have said, tennis will change from tradition-based authority to what he called legal-rational authority: legitimate power controlled by formal organizations in accordance with written rules and standard procedures.

You can see this in the National Collegiate Athletic Association, in the Amateur Athletic Union, or in the local school sponsoring a kids' soccer league—organizations governing through legal-rational authority. They have the right to impose sanctions (usually disqualifications, bannings, or fines), and their power is approved by society, and accepted by the governed. The alternative would be ungoverned sport, a state in which sport could not exist as we know it.

THE NEED FOR POLITICS

Changes.   The Olympic motto is *citius, altius, fortius*: higher, faster, stronger. The motto succinctly summarizes a major goal of modern sport: to get better and better.

---

[2]Ian Robertson, *Sociology*, 2nd ed. (New York: Worth Publishers, Inc., 1981), p. 479.

[3]Max Weber, *The Theory of Social and Economic Organization*, trans. and ed. by A.M. Henderson and Talcott Parsons, p. 152. Copyright © 1947 renewed 1975 by Talcott Parsons. Used by permission of Macmillan Publishing Co., Inc.

Motivated by this goal, athletes and coaches push rules to the limit and constantly seek new technology and technique. The cases of the bicycle cam, diving over the high-jump bar, and the tennis racket illustrate this. Other cases are: Should limitations be placed on the way running tracks are constructed? Should skin suits be permitted in swim meets? Should tumbling be legal in the long jump? Should twirling the javelin be a legal throw? For every advocate of change in technology or technique, you can expect someone to oppose it. Conflicts break out. Adjudication is required. Politics become necessary.

Rewards. In addition to constant change, other forces tug at sport and cause conflicts which then require politics. Today sport provides great rewards: money, fame, and status. Quite naturally a fundamental issue is, Who gets the rewards? The athletes? The fans? The owners? It's not totally clear who ought to be the primary beneficiary; and groups and individuals constantly fight over the rewards of sport.

Consider examples of what has happened.

- One enterprising baseball fan sued the San Francisco Giants to prevent the team from raising hotdog prices by five cents. He contended that once inside the stadium fans become a captive audience, either paying whatever the Giants charged or going hungry. The court agreed and granted an injunction.
- On a larger scale, two consumer advocates formed the organization F.A.N.S. (an acronym for Fight to Advance the Nation's Sports)—an overt attempt to translate the interests of fans into explicit political rights. They dedicated the organization to "the interests of sports fans wherever such representation is needed—before the league . . . Congress and other federal bodies, state and local governments, the courts, and other appropriate forums."[4]

Fans aren't the only ones going to court to protect their rights. Athletes increasingly seek redress under the law. For instance, most professional sports in some way restrict players from freely switching teams after their original contracts expire. Fighting this economic disadvantage, players have repeatedly challenged the restrictions in court. As of yet no final resolution involving all sports has been handed down by the courts. Until that time, litigation will undoubtedly continue. The stakes are so big that the litigants are not about to quietly give up and go away.

The community also benefits from sport. The Super Bowl injects almost one hundred million dollars into the economy of the host city—little wonder that cities compete for the prize.[5] And local teams claim they generate large revenues for the communities in which they play. Apparently communities agree. To attract a team, communities will renovate stadiums or build them from scratch (often largely at the taxpayers' expense). The Rams football team simply moved from Los Angeles to Anaheim (a freeway suburb of Los Angeles) when Anaheim gave them a better deal on a renovated and enlarged stadium. The City of Los Angeles then offered seventeen million dollars to

---

[4]Quoted in Roger Rosenblatt, "Justice in the Stadium," *Harper's*, February 1978, p. 79. © 1978 by *Harper's* magazine. Reprinted by permission.

[5]*Time*, January 10, 1977, p. 28.

the Oakland Raiders to come and fill the void left by the departing Rams. The City of Oakland then initiated legal action to keep the Raiders. A private citizen went to court to enjoin Los Angeles from offering the seventeen million dollars, charging misappropriation of public funds. And the owners of the National Football League went to court to prevent the move because they felt that it violated the NFL constitution. The NFL lost but has the case on appeal.[6]

We could go on citing illustrations, but these suffice to illustrate the struggle by groups, individuals, athletes, and communities for the rewards of sport. Many groups make well-intentioned, sincere claims, from the single fan unhappy about hotdog prices up through the cities competing between themselves for a football team. And oftentimes the complexity of the issues and the intransigence of the disputants lead to messy arguments.

Some arguments concern trivial issues, others are obviously important. Most are short lived but some have gone on for a long time. Probably the longest standing dispute with the most far-reaching consequences is between the National Collegiate Athletic Association (NCAA) and the Amateur Athletic Union (AAU). We shall examine the dispute in some detail but before doing that, we ought to warn of the forthcoming deluge of organizational acronyms. To achieve some reduction in the number, we always refer to an organization by its current acronym even though the acronym may have been different in the past.

THE ISSUE OF CONTROL

The following incident took place several years ago and still provides an exceptionally clear illustration of the struggle between the NCAA and AAU.

> **The NCAA versus the AAU.** Every four years the Maccabiah Games take place in Israel and bring together the best Jewish athletes in the world. In 1969, the NCAA refused to sanction the Games, and thus prevented American college players from participating. How this all came about goes back to a welter of political quarreling.
>
> In 1934, the International Olympic Committee formed an organization called the Fédération Internationale de Basketball Amateur (FIBA) to govern international basketball competition. FIBA then awarded the American franchise to the AAU; in other words, the AAU controlled the United States' international basketball teams. This arrangement lasted for a number of years and criticisms abounded.
>
> During the 1960s, disenchantment grew to a head and several sports organizations—the National Federation of State High School Associations, the National Junior College Athletic Association, and most importantly, the NCAA—formed a rival organization called the Basketball Federation of the United States of America (BFUSA). BFUSA wanted the basketball franchise. In an unusual move,

---

[6]Reported in *Sports Illustrated*, April 25, 1983, p. 15.

FIBA approved both AAU and BFUSA but later reinstated AAU as the sole governing body.

That was how affairs stood when the 1969 Maccabiah Games took place. The AAU and NCAA (through BFUSA) were warring over the franchise for an Olympic sport and using athletes for cannon fodder.

Fearing the wrath of the NCAA, several outstanding Jewish-American basketball players declined to play in the Maccabiah Games, but not Jack Langer of Yale. He participated and afterwards played for Yale during the 1969–1970 season.

In retaliation for this breach of its policy, the NCAA demanded that Yale rule Langer ineligible. Yale refused for reasons outlined in the following statement to the NCAA: "Yale is convinced that the NCAA was wrong when it boycotted Maccabiah basketball for reasons unconnected with the purity or legitimacy of the Maccabiah Games. The first victims of the wrong were the students at other colleges who dropped off the Maccabiah team in the face of the NCAA threat. Now the NCAA would add Langer and his fellow students at Yale.

"This University has persistently condemned the NCAA practice of using students as pawns in the endless NCAA struggle with the AAU."[7]

This protest went unheeded. The NCAA placed Yale on three years probation. No Yale athlete in any sport (not just Langer or the basketball team) could participate in any NCAA postseason or championship play, nor could Yale appear on television.

The Final Report of the President's Commission on Olympic Sports says of the incident, "the NCAA's failure to approve the 1969 Maccabiah Games basketball competition was really part of a larger strategy to wrest the U.S. basketball franchise away from the AAU . . . The result desired by the NCAA ultimately occurred in 1973 when FIBA revoked the AAU's franchise and awarded it to an NCAA backed federation."[8]

You might find this incident convoluted, confusing, illogical, and the result unjust. It was definitely all of that. To gain a clearer understanding of how such an incident could come about in the first place, one must have some inkling of how the AAU, NCAA, and the Olympic Committee developed historically and how they operate.

Development of Organizations

Amateur Athletic Union.   Recall from Chapters 2 and 4 the support that athletic clubs gave to amateur sport during the latter part of the nineteenth century. Throughout that period, various groups attempted to form a governing association of clubs. None succeeded until 1888, when the New York AC organized fifteen clubs into what was later named the Amateur Athletic Union. The AAU claimed jurisdiction over twenty-three sports and threatened to bar athletes who participated in competitions which it (the AAU) did not sanction. The AAU met instant success. By the next year it had effectively consolidated control over most amateur athletics in the United States.

---

[7]*The Final Report of the President's Commission on Olympic Sports*, Volume I (Washington, D.C.: U.S. Government Printing Office, 1977), p. 60.

[8]*The Final Report of the President's Commission on Olympic Sports*, Volume II (Washington, D.C.: U.S. Government Printing Office, 1977), p. 342.

The AAU soon changed from a confederation of exclusive athletic clubs into a national organization based on geographic areas. Today the AAU is divided into regions and associations and is composed of 7,000 sports clubs and governs 330,000 athletes.[9]

National Collegiate Athletic Association.   At the same time athletic clubs were trying to form an umbrella organization, another branch of amateur sport was rapidly growing: intercollegiate competition. Football in particular had become vastly popular— and violent; much too violent for many people. In 1905 President Roosevelt sponsored a meeting which led to another meeting where thirty-eight schools agreed to form a permanent organization. This subsequently became the National Collegiate Athletic Association. Said the association's first president in 1907: "The purpose of this Association is, as set forth in its constitution, the regulation and supervision of collegiate athletics throughout the United States, in order that the athletic activities in the colleges and universities may be maintained on an ethical plane in keeping with the dignity and the high purpose of education."[10] At the time these lofty words were spoken, no one had any idea that the new NCAA would come to loggerheads with the AAU over control of the Olympic basketball team.

Currently the NCAA encompasses virtually all major sports conferences. It has over eight hundred member schools, supervises thirty sports and fifteen thousand student-athletes, and has a professional staff and a multimillion-dollar budget.

Olympic Committee.   The NCAA wasn't in existence when James Sullivan organized the United States Olympic Committee in preparation for the first modern Games (held in 1896). Sullivan played a prominent role in the New York AC and in organizing the AAU. As the only well-established national organization governing amateur sport, the AAU soon took control of the United States' Olympic team.

Disputes

When the NCAA came into existence, more and more amateur athletes were attending college; so the NCAA increasingly demanded a voice in controlling the Olympic Committee. This brought on a long and still unresolved political confrontation. To go through all the details of the dispute as it went on over the years would take books and books; fortunately, a summary will suffice for our purposes.

The original U.S. Olympic Committee functioned through 1921 without bylaws or formal rules. According to most accounts, it did a poor job. The Committee lacked clear direction and consistent policy. Athletes found serious fault with transportation facilities to the Games and living accommodations at the Games. The disorganization and shoddy

---

[9] Arnold William Flath, *A History of Relations between the National Collegiate Athletic Association and the Amateur Athletic Union of the United States (1905–1963)* (Champaign, Illinois: Stipes Publishing Co., 1964); Richard Wettan and Joe Willis, "Effect of New York's Elite Athletic Clubs on American Amateur Athletic Governance—1870–1915," *Research Quarterly*, 47 (October 1976), 499–505; "The Amateur Athletic Union of the USA" in *The Final Report*, Volume II, pp. 277–298.

[10] Quoted in Flath, *A History*, p. 24.

facilities of the 1920 Olympics caused such a furor that the Olympic Committee was reformed. In hopes of strengthening it, the Secretaries of the Army and Navy, the Young Men's Christian Association, and the NCAA joined the Committee. This temporarily patched up the situation, but by the 1928 Olympics the patches began coming off. Several organizations withdrew from the Olympic Committee, notably the NCAA, the Navy, and the YMCA. General Douglas MacArthur became Committee president and he managed to hold the organization together for the next Olympics.

In 1930, organizational changes in the Olympic Committee led to a truce between the NCAA and AAU, and the 1932 Olympics reflected a new spirit of cooperation. That quickly petered out. The 1936 Olympics caused great controversy over whether or not the United States should participate in the Nazi Olympics (discussed later in the chapter). The looming of World War II and the cancellation of the 1940 Games rendered Olympic politics moot for a time.

After the war the NCAA and the AAU agreed to a common set of goals and a smoothing of relationships—for a little while. All during the 1950s muted criticisms of the AAU accumulated, and the NCAA and AAU went back to quarreling.

In 1960, Attorney General Robert Kennedy tried to hammer out the differences once and for all. He convened a meeting of the NCAA, AAU, and several other interested organizations. Everything collapsed when the AAU refused to endorse several agreements. Next, President Kennedy called upon General MacArthur (again) to mediate the dispute. MacArthur attained another truce until after the 1964 Olympics. When the next round of NCAA-AAU quarreling broke out, the U.S. Senate, and Vice President Humphrey, appointed the "Kheel Board" to resolve the dispute. The board failed.

The Olympic Committee's handling of the 1972 Munich Games came under heavy fire because of poor organization (two American sprinters missed their heats and were disqualified; a swimmer who won a gold medal later lost it because no one had reported that he was taking a drug for asthma). After the Games, the NCAA withdrew from the Olympic Committee and endorsed a rival organization. The dispute did not have much effect on the 1976 Olympics, but afterwards the NCAA took the Olympic Committee to court over rule changes. The United States boycott of the 1980 Olympics forestalled another round of quarrels.

Dispute Structure

These developments have not taken place randomly; they have form. The pattern is this: The NCAA and AAU quarrel with each other over the right to control the Olympic team; as the Games grow near, the government prods the two organizations into setting aside their differences; they agree to a truce and the resulting Olympic team usually does fairly well. As soon as the Games end, however, the NCAA and AAU go right back to quarreling as if nothing had changed.

Making a truce for each Olympics has become the standard resolution (if you want to call it that) to the problem. It is far from satisfactory and you would think that by this time a better resolution would have been found—but none has. The reason a permanent agreement cannot be worked out presents an interesting sociological problem.

One reason could be the personalities of the people involved. We cannot rule that out with 100-percent certainty because some of the personalities have been uncompromising. However, the dispute has gone on for over half a century and follows a predictable pattern. Something more than personality must be involved. We ought to look at the structure of the situation.

The structure is this: The International Olympic Committee (IOC) delegates responsibility for each Olympic sport to an international federation (IAAF). The IAAF awards franchises for its sport to a country's national associations (called National Governing Boards, or NGBs). Different organizations can hold the franchises for different sports. The AAU holds it for track and field and the NCAA holds it for basketball. The more franchises an organization holds, the more it controls the Olympic team.[11]

Many years ago, German sociologist Georg Simmel analyzed this type of structure. He introduced the concept *tertius gaudens*, meaning a third party who controls the relationship between two other parties:

> The formations that are more essential here emerge whenever the *tertius* makes his own indirect or direct gain by turning toward one of the two conflicting parties—but not intellectually and objectively, like the arbitrator, but practically, supporting or granting. This general type has two main variants: either two parties are hostile towards one another and therefore compete for the favor of a third element; or they compete for the favor to the third element and therefore are hostile towards one another.[12]

Like many earlier sociologists, Simmel does not hold fast to a distinction between an individual person and a more abstract entity, such as an organization. If we make allowances for this, his basic arguments stand.

Rather than thinking of the NCAA-AAU dispute as involving two stubborn, shortsighted, selfish, power-hungry organizations, Simmel's analysis reminds us of the third party: the IAAF. The IAAF acts as the *tertius*, granting the franchises for which the other two organizations compete.

According to Simmel's theory, the NCAA and AAU either became hostile toward one another as a result of their competition for the tertius's favor; or they began competing for franchises because they were hostile to begin with. No matter what the process, the end result will be the same: conflict and hostility. As long as the IAAF has the power to grant franchises, the dispute between the NCAA and AAU will continue, unless one of the three fades away or is destroyed, or unless two merge together. None of that seems likely.

All parties to the present dispute have survived for many years, remain separate, and give every indication of continuing to do so for a long time. Therefore, by coldbloodedly applying Simmel's logic, we can only conclude that the NCAA-AAU dispute will con-

---

[11]Eric Danoff, "The Struggle for Control of Amateur Track and Field in the United States," *Canadian Journal of History of Sport and Physical Education*, May 1975, pp. 43–86; December 1975, pp. 1–43.

[12]Georg Simmel, *The Sociology of George Simmel*, trans. and ed. Kurt H. Wolff (New York: The Free Press, 1950), p. 154. Originally published in German in 1908.

tinue. It has no permanent resolution. Perhaps the truce made prior to each Olympics is as good a resolution as can be hoped for under these circumstances.

Admittedly it would be ideal if political conflicts could be removed from sport, but that can never realistically happen. Even if the courts, Congress, and other authorities could totally adjudicate all disputes, politics would still be necessary. Any large, important, and complicated activity must be governed. And governance is politics.

A further complication exists. While politics *in* sport is inescapable, so too (apparently) is the politics *of* sport. We haven't forgotten Case 3 from the first page; we just required time to get to it. Though you might not like Bobby Knight's phraseology about the moronic or naive, he does make a point. Politics dominate modern international sport. We consider that topic now.

THE POLITICAL USE OF SPORT

Ancient Times

Manipulating sport to gain ulterior political ends isn't a new development by any means. Its possibilities and advantages were evident long ago, as the antics of Roman emperor Nero show. Most famous for supposedly fiddling while Rome burned, Nero also gained sports infamy as a chariot racer. He believed that winning Olympic honors would enhance his reputation as emperor and so he competed in the two-hundred-eleventh Greek Olympiad.

> **Nero's Olympic Victory.**   Unfortunately Nero fell out of his chariot while the race was in progress. But the judges, ever quick thinking, immediately called time so that he might climb back aboard—which he did with considerable help from his minions. Even though for some unknown reason he did not finish the race, the judges still declared Nero the victor. He then went on to win the lute and singing events—events which he added to the Games so he could win them.
>
> Upon receiving the victory laurels, Nero freed the Greek province of Achea (site of the Olympics), remitted their taxes, and granted the judges Roman citizenship. It was rumored but never proved that he bribed the judges with 250,000 drachmas.[13]

Nero's Olympic "victories" demonstrate one way to use sport as a political tool. Though the two-hundred-eleventh Olympiad resembles a charade acted out by clowns and buffoons, it is reasonable to suppose that no one laughed. Nero could just as easily have razed Achea as freed it; and the Olympic judges knew it. The traditional conduct of sport thus gave way to naked power. (Interestingly, after Nero committed suicide, the Olympic judges struck his name from the official victory list.)

Ancient Greek ideals usually were not so blatantly trampled upon. In their pure and (probably never fully achieved) Utopian form, conceived before Nero's time, the Greek

---

[13]Ludwig Drees, *Olympia* (New York: Frederick A. Praeger, 1968), p. 55.

Olympics pitted athlete against athlete with victory demonstrating the superiority of one over the other. Even if the pure form actually existed, it could not last very long. Important public events invariably involved religion. This included the Games. Athletic victory quickly took on religious overtones. Victory came to imply the favor of the gods; and everyone wanted to bathe in the victor's godly halo. To attract the best athletes, and thereby gain the gods' favor, the Greek cities began paying athletes. Athletes occasionally chose to represent the highest bidders and a simple form of professional representative sport came into existence. It is still with us.

Modern Times

The idea of representative sport has survived for a long time. Today it is the most common way to organize sport, from a Little League team sponsored by the local pizza parlor, to an Olympic team sponsored by a multimillion dollar government contribution. Sport can even represent entire coalitions of nations—the free world versus the Communist world, for instance. Not surprisingly, sports competition between individual athletes thus becomes a political contest between the organizations athletes represent. The victories of a Cuban boxer become victories for the Cuban nation. They "prove" the superiority of the revolutionary government and society that produce such a truly outstanding athlete.

So victory comes to mean more than the accomplishments of individual athletes; it becomes a matter of national and international importance. After the unusually good American showing in the 1980 Winter Olympics, President Carter dispatched three jets to bring the entire team to the White House for congratulatory ceremonies. United Press International described the event: "Flanked by beaming Olympians wearing their red, white and blue 'USA' team jackets and cowboy hats, [President Carter said] 'This has thrilled our nation. We are all deeply grateful for your wonderful achievements. Our Olympic athletes are 'modern day American heroes.' ''[14]

In 1936, the Nazis turned the Olympics into a major political spectacle for the first time. Because the Olympics has come to epitomize political sports, we take a moment to discuss the Berlin games. In some respects it remains the most dramatic example.

Nazi Olympics: Propaganda Coup for Hitler. The International Olympic Committee (IOC) had awarded the Games to Germany in 1932 when the democratic Weimar Republic still existed.[15] Several months later, Adolf Hitler became Reich Chancellor and by July of 1933, the Nazis controlled the German government. They perceived the forthcoming Berlin Games as a propaganda bonanza, a vast showplace for glorifying Nazism. Karl Diem, a long-time German sports leader, organized the Games and introduced or magnified most of the spectacle we now see on TV.

The Opening Ceremony. The last and most distinguished of the relay runners, his identity a secret up to this time, enters the stadium bearing the torch of

---

[14]Reported in *Columbus Citizen-Journal*, February 26, 1980, p. 1.

[15]The basic source for the 1936 Games is Richard D. Mandell, *The Nazi Olympics* (New York: Macmillan, Inc., 1971).

the Eternal Olympic Flame. He runs up the stairs to the top of the stadium, lights the Olympic flame, and officially opens the Games, amid thunderous applause, flocks of freed birds, music, and maudlin descriptions of the event broadcast to listeners throughout the world.

Certainly there must be some irony in the fact that Karl Diem largely invented this ceremony with an aim to glorify athletics, Hellenism, and . . . Nazism.

During the years preceding the Games, the Nazis stepped up their racism and anti-Semitism. They officially stripped German Jews of all political rights and social privileges. They encouraged anti-Semitic propaganda and feelings. The effect on sport was that German Jews could not participate in the extensive network of sports clubs which acted as a feeder system for German athletics and therefore could not be on the German Olympic team.

In the United States substantial public and political sentiment favored a boycott of the Games as an expression of opposition to the Nazi regime and as a way to take the luster off their publicity extravaganza. An American team did participate, but not without controversy and some assurances that German Jews would be allowed to compete. And a token few did compete. Hitler was so anxious to show off Nazism that he gave in to IOC demands and ordered anti-Semitic signs removed from highly visible public places. Hitler also personally watched and openly cheered for German athletes. In an infamous incident, he refused to shake the hands of the victors when it became apparent he would have to shake hands with black American athletes, whom he had derided as "America's Negro auxiliaries." Concludes one study, "From the Nazi point of view the 1936 Olympics were value for money. They must go down as one of the biggest propaganda victories in history."[16] (See Table 10.1.)

1980 Olympics: Propaganda Coup for Moscow?   Some forty-five years later, the United States led a boycott of the Olympics. Considered very abstractly, the reasons were the same as for the attempted boycott of the Nazi Olympics: opposition to the host country's political policy, protest of their violations of human rights, and a wish to prevent that regime from propagandizing their political system through sport.

The Soviet Union's invasion of Afghanistan in January 1980, triggered the boycott. During a nationally televised speech announcing trade embargoes against Russia, President Carter threatened that the United States would boycott the forthcoming Moscow Olympics. "Although the United States would prefer not to withdraw from the Olympic Games," he said, "the Soviet Union must realize that its continued aggressive actions will endanger both the participation of athletes and the travel to Moscow by spectators who would normally wish to attend the Olympic Games." In March he said again, "They will not go."[17] In April, bowing to heavy political pressures, the U.S. Olympic Committee voted not to enter a team. Over the next few months approximately forty nations joined the boycott, including West Germany, Japan, seventeen black African countries, and

---

[16]David Childs, "The German Democratic Republic," in *Sport Under Communism*, ed. James Riordan (Montreal: McGill-Queen's University Press, 1978), p. 74.

[17]Quoted in *Time*, January 21, 1980, p. 21; and *Columbus Citizen-Journal*, March 22, 1980, p. 1.

Table 10.1. German Victories in the 1936 Olympics

EVENT	MEDALS		
Track and Field			
Men's	3 Gold	2 Silver	4 Bronze
Women's	2 Gold	2 Silver	3 Bronze
Swimming			
Men's		1 Silver	1 Bronze
Women's		2 Silver	2 Bronze
Gymnastics			
Men's	5 Gold	1 Silver	6 Bronze
Women's	1 Gold		
Wrestling		3 Silver	4 Bronze
Fencing		1 Silver	2 Bronze
Shooting	1 Gold	2 Silver	
Equestrian	6 Gold	1 Silver	
Weight Lifting	1 Gold	2 Silver	2 Bronze
Cycling	2 Gold		1 Bronze
Yachting	1 Gold	1 Silver	1 Bronze
Rowing	5 Gold	1 Silver	1 Bronze
Canoeing	2 Gold	3 Silver	2 Bronze
Boxing	2 Gold	2 Silver	1 Bronze
Pentathalon	1 Gold		
Field Handball	1 Gold		
Field Hockey		1 Silver	
Water Polo		1 Silver	
Totals	33 Gold	26 Silver	30 Bronze

SOURCES: Several sources were used to verify this medal count. The most interesting of these was *Sports Shots* by Dr. Paul Wolff (New York: William Morrow and Co., 1937), a masterly photo-essay of the 1936 Olympics. For a tally of each country's total medals (subdivided by event and sex), see *Die Olympischen Spiele von Athen bis Mexiko-Stadt* (Berlin: Sportverlag, 1969).

Great Britain. (Unlike the U.S., the British Olympic Committee sent a team to Moscow in defiance of its own government.)

In the United States only a bare majority favored the boycott and then waveringly.[18] Sport purists felt that politics should be kept out of sport. Those more pragmatically inclined said that politics inevitably mixes with sport, especially the Olympics. Both sides much lamented the plight of the athletes, but efforts to stage an alternative Olympics failed.

The Soviet government officially denounced the boycott and downplayed possible effects on the games. Nevertheless the Soviet government could not have been happy about it. They had spent three billion dollars building facilities, refurbishing Moscow, and even ordering children out of the city during the games. Many American businesses lost their financial investments in ventures such as souvenir sales, tourist packages, and

---

[18]*Newsweek* poll, January 28, 1980, p. 21.

advertising rights. NBC television was the most publicized big loser, with losses of about thirty-six million dollars. As it turned out, Soviet bloc countries won about 90 percent of all medals. Had the boycotting nations participated, the figure might have been about 75 percent (the same percentage as in the 1976 Olympics). Boycott or no, Soviet bloc countries would have "won" the Olympics.

The boycott did help publicize the Afghanistan situation, bringing it into the political consciousness of millions who otherwise might have let it pass unnoticed. Obviously it did not cause the Soviets to withdraw from Afghanistan; the fighting continued. All in all, and history may prove this wrong, the boycott pretty much failed. It generated great clamor and thunder but little in the way of concrete, permanent results.

The examples of Greek athletics, the Nazi Olympics, and the Moscow boycott all demonstrate a social reality: Sport and politics constantly mix. At the international level, you might even say that sport *is* a form of politics. Try naming a national government which has not politically capitalized, or would not politically capitalize, on sport in some way to some degree. It's very difficult to come up with a name.

SUMMARY

1. Politics is the study of power, conflict, and policy. Because sport involves constantly changing techniques, technology, and rules, political processes are necessary to govern sport.
2. Politics is also necessary to govern sport because the monetary and social rewards of sport are so great that conflicts often erupt as different parties contend for a share of the rewards.
3. In the past, traditional authority (power) played a large role in sports, but today political power is based on legal-rational authority: the power vested in organizations.
4. The AAU and NCAA have quarreled over the Olympic team for many decades. Temporary truces arbitrated by the federal government have been the most common way to resolve the dispute. Because it involves three parties (it includes the International Olympic Committee) no permanent resolution seems likely in the near future.
5. There is also a politics of sport: the use of sport for political purposes. This use goes far back in history. We still see a variation on this old theme: Victory is tantamount to victory for the political system that the athlete represents.

11 POLITICS AND SPORT, PART II

Present and Future

During the 1980 Winter Olympic Games, when the United States hockey team defeated a heavily favored team from the Soviet Union, the nation celebrated widely. President Carter dispatched three jets to bring the entire team to the White House for congratulatory ceremonies. This mixing of sports and politics has made the Olympics a battleground of competing ideologies, rather than just a friendly international sporting event. Photo by Heinz Kluetmeier for *Sports Illustrated*.

If you find mixing sport and politics repugnant, the reason probably has something to do with political ideology. Everyone has a political ideology, a set of values or beliefs which justify, explain, and interpret the political order. For instance, ideology explains why it is right, just, and proper (legitimate) to have capitalism, or socialism, or separation of church from state (or not), or separation of state from sport (or not).

According to American ideology, people should turn to government as the last resort, not the first, and therefore mixing sport with politics ought to be held to an absolute minimum. Writes one analyst, "Traditionally, Americans have always felt an anathema toward federal intrusion into what they deem a private sector, and sport was no exception."[1] This statement also describes the ideology of other nations, both eastern and western.

Ideological beliefs, are they lies or rationalizations? While we can't prove it one way or another, we seriously doubt that they are either one. States a sociologist, "The moral effort to lie deliberately is beyond most people. It is much easier to deceive oneself. It is, therefore, important to keep the concept of ideology distinct from notions of lying, deception, propaganda or legerdemain."[2] Most people believe *sincerely*.

The historical trends of the nineteenth century (see Chapter 2) hardened the material-structural parts of American society in such a way that direct government sponsorship was largely unneeded. Educational institutions and private enterprise already sponsored sport and, in general, did so successfully. The ideological tenet of keeping politics out of sport found a congenial home in the United States. The tenet also cleanly dovetailed with the sports ideology inherited from the British tradition, and with the overall American ideology of laissez faire, the belief that the least government is the best government. As sometimes happens, a supposedly unrelated event—this time, a war in Europe—helped crystallize the ideology into a larger social gestalt.

IDEOLOGY AND THE MODERN OLYMPICS: CRYSTALLIZING IDEAS

Although the average American now has only the vaguest, if any, knowledge of the Franco-Prussian War of 1870–1871, this war had one consequence everyone knows about: the modern Olympic Games.

Baron Pierre de Coubertin, a wealthy French aristocrat, felt personally humiliated by France's overwhelming defeat and set out to do something about it. He chose a rather oblique path: revitalizing the physical condition of French youth. As a spur to this goal he invented the modern Olympics.

Coubertin followed and later led the trends of his time. His idea of combining sport, military preparedness, and politics was already part of the current Zeitgeist. In Germany "Turnerism" was an established social movement emphasizing sport as a political and

---

[1]Roy Clumpner, "Federal Involvement in Sport to Promote American or Foreign Policy Objectives—1950–1973," in *Sport and International Relations*, eds. Benjamin Lowe, David B. Kanin and Andrew Strenk (Champaign, Illinois: Stipes Publishing Co., 1978), p. 440.

[2]Excerpt from *Invitation to Sociology* by Peter L. Berger, p. 112. Copyright © 1963 by Peter L. Berger. Reprinted by permission of Doubleday & Company, Inc.

military tool. To that end the Turners had organized a network of sports clubs throughout Germany, and had become an important political group. Turnerism attracted the upper class, while a similar movement and club system existed among the German working class. The Sokols had also gained political importance. They were a group resembling the Turners but dedicated to pan-Slavic political goals rather than pan-Germanic ones.[3]

The British sports system also greatly impressed Coubertin; and even though British (and American) ideology stressed separation of sport from state, the supposed military spinoff was greatly appreciated. "The battle of Waterloo," said Napoleon's conqueror, Lord Wellington, "was won on the playing fields of Eton"; by which he meant that physical vigor and moral rectitude learned from sport was related to the military performance of a nation. Making the same point, General Douglas MacArthur (1880–1964) wrote:

> Upon the fields of friendly strife
> Are sown the seeds
> That, upon other fields, on other days
> Will bear the fruits of victory.

This poem is inscribed on the wall of the West Point gym.[4]

Thus Coubertin worked within an existing prosport Zeitgeist as he organized the first modern Olympics in Athens in 1896. His original emphasis on physical vigor for war seems to have dropped out of his thinking. At the Athens Olympics he was already advocating a sports ideology similar to the one prevailing in Britain and the United States, both then and now. His ideological tenets have a remarkably modern sound.

Describing the Athens Games, Coubertin writes: "Needless to say that the various contests were held under amateur regulations. . . . It is impossible to conceive the Olympic games with money prizes."[5] So strongly did he emphasize amateurism that he set up special competitions for military fencers. He also believed that sport should be quasi-religious, pure, and morally uplifting.

Coubertin had a sense of the theatrical which heightened the quasi-religious nature of the Games. He writes of the Athens marathon: "[Greek women] offered up prayers and votive tapers in churches, that the victor might be Greek! . . . The King of Servia, who was present [at the finish] will probably not forget the sight he saw that day. A flight of white pigeons was let loose, women waved fans and handkerchiefs . . . some spectators tried to reach [the victor] and carry him in triumph . . ."[6]

These quotations from Coubertin express a particular sports ideology that is still dominant in many societies including the United States. The key tenets are:

---

[3]Andrew Strenk, "What Price Victory? The World of International Sports and Politics," *Annals*, 445 (September 1979), 128–40.

[4]William Manchester, *American Caesar: Douglas MacArthur, 1880–1964* (Boston: Little, Brown & Company, 1978), p. 12.

[5]Baron Pierre de Coubertin, "The Olympic Games of 1896," *Century Magazine*, November, 1896; reprinted in Lowe, Kanin, and Strenk, *Sport*, p. 123.

[6]Ibid., pp. 122–23.

Competition produces harmony between competitors and the organizations or nations they represent.

Sport should be quasi-sacred and spiritually uplifting.

Sport is its own reward.

Therefore sport is corrupted by professionalism and commercialism.

In the American case a special emphasis on not politicizing sports should be added.

For convenience we call this collection of ideological tenets the laissez-faire sports model; laissez faire because it stresses sport as a nonpolitical, nongovernmental institution.

Of course, not everyone advocates the laissez-faire model. Nations comprising the so-called Communist bloc advocate the opposite ideology: the best government is the most government. Government should be monolithic, total—it should do everything and be everywhere. Everything is politicized to varying degrees, including (perhaps especially) sport. This becomes the basis for what we refer to as the Soviet sports model.

Presumably Communist bloc nations trace the merging of politics and sport to the writings of Lenin and Marx. One analyst points out that Lenin said, "[young people] must have strong and healthy bodies, must have a steel will and torso to meet this challenge [the task of communism]."[7] The emphasis on physical well-being is integrated into the political foundations of the Russian nation; it is contained in the Russian constitution. Over the years the Soviet Union has assigned to sport the political tasks of demonstrating the superiority of communism, of encouraging friendly relations with neighboring socialist states, and of helping to achieve socialist unity on Soviet terms.[8]

In a similar way East Germany (German Democratic Republic or GDR) holds that "sport and politics cannot be separated any more than one can separate a gymnast from the bars or vault, a swimmer from the water, or a soccer player from the soccer field."[9] And so the GDR uses sport to propagandize the superiority of their system and as a tool for gaining diplomatic recognition (something that Western nations hesitate to give because Russia carved the GDR out of Germany after World War II).

The politicization of sport by Communist bloc nations includes using rhetoric and propaganda, but goes much deeper than that. They deliberately (and by Western standards, callously) manipulate the material-structural parts of their societies to produce athletic and hence political victory. They have taken the institution of sport and organized, structured, directed, and funded it for political purposes. For example, potential athletes are scouted, recruited, trained, supported, and, if they meet the goals of the state, feted. One instance follows.

Olga Korbut, Where Did You Come from?   The Russian gymnast Olga Korbut burst upon the international sports scene during the 1972 Olympics. She was a truly gifted athlete, a darling of television.

---

[7]Quoted in Martha M. Seeban, "Political Ideology of Sport in the People's Republic of China and the Soviet Union," in Lowe, Kanin, and Strenk, *Sport*, p. 308.

[8]James Riordan, *Sport in Soviet Society: Development of Sport and Physical Education in Russia and the USSR* (Cambridge: Cambridge University Press, 1977), chap. 11. A basic source.

[9]Quoted in Andrew Strenk, "Diplomats in Track Suits: Linkages Between Sports and Foreign Policy in the German Democratic Republic," in Lowe, Kanin, and Strenk, *Sport*, p. 352.

She is one extraordinarily successful example of what a sports system can produce. The Soviet Union has about 220,000 subsidized sports clubs, 6,000 sports schools, and twenty-four sports universities or institutes. In Russia physical educators routinely scout children for gymnastic potential at about kindergarten age. Those showing promise on tests of strength, agility, and daring receive further scrutiny. Their parents might be examined for clues as to genetic defects which might appear after the child matures.

If the girl and the parents consent, she enrolls in a gymnastics club near her home, initially going two hours per day three days per week and working up to four hours per day six days per week. At about age eleven the most promising girls are selected into sports boarding schools where they participate in the morning, go to school and practice in the afternoon, do their homework at night, and then go to sleep.[10]

While Olga Korbut dramatically exemplifies the Soviet sports system, she is not unusual except in the way television publicized her. The Soviet system nurtures thousands of potential athletes in an effort to find those few who can win worldclass competitions, particularly in sports of political importance. Consider the Olympics because they have become the *sine qua non* of political sport. The USSR entered for the first time in 1952 and promptly won seventy-two medals (gold, silver, and bronze combined), just five fewer than the United States. Because of the cold war then raging, the Soviet accomplishment frightened the Western world. And it was no fluke. Except for the 1968 Olympics, the USSR has won every Olympics since then. More recently Cuba and Romania organized their sports programs along lines similar to the Soviet model and have quickly become major sports powers even without large populations to draw upon for raw athletic talent.

Clearly the Soviet model works and works extraordinarily well. Analysts of all political persuasions agree to that. An authoritative analysis of the Soviet sports model concludes:

What is certain is that there can no longer be any belief that success is, as it was in the past, primarily a matter of the physical and moral resources of the individual participant. . . . [The Soviet sports model] has demonstrated that the highest realization of human potential can be most effectively achieved through the planned application of societal resources towards that desired goal.[11]

"Gone are the days," says another student of political-sport, "when a man could set his cigar beside the track, run a couple of laps and even set a record, then pick up his cigar again as if nothing had happened."[12]

---

[10]*New York Times*, January 27, 1980, p. E2, Riordan, *Sport in Soviet Society*, chap. 10; Craig R. Whitney, "220,000 Sports Clubs Power the Soviet Medal Machine," *New York Times*, July 20, 1980, sec. S, p. 1; Yuri Brokhin, *The Big Red Machine: The Rise and Fall of Soviet Olympic Champions*, trans. Glenn Garelik and Yuri Brokhin (New York: Random House, Inc. 1978).

[11]Riordan, *Sport in Soviet Society*, p. 395. For an earlier analysis, see: Alex Natan, *Sport and Society* (London: Bowes & Bowes Publishers, Ltd., 1958).

[12]Richard Espey, *The Politics of the Olympic Games* (Berkeley: University of California Press, 1979), p. 5.

These conclusions have a certain plausibility, and they have serious implications for many areas of life beside sport. We ought to ponder them a little more. What would have happened if bloc nations had adopted a laissez-faire sports system? had relied more on individual motivation, private support, and chance? Under those conditions would the same quantity and quality of athlete have emerged?

To answer this question two features of the Soviet model must be evaluated: (1) success in producing champion athletes; and (2) success in political goals. Using the case of Olympic basketball as a concrete point of reference, let us evaluate the two features.

Athletic Success.   Bloc countries keep their national basketball teams together continuously while the United States gathers a team every four years solely for a specific Olympics. Consequently, U.S. players have little opportunity to train together, to learn the new coach's system, and to develop teamwork. And sometimes the very best amateur players forego Olympic competition for professional play. Yet, despite these drawbacks, the United States has dominated Olympic basketball, losing the Olympic gold medal only once.

This dominance has an easy cultural explanation. Basketball is *the* American sport. American physical educator Dr. James Naismith invented it in 1891 as an indoor winter game and it quickly diffused into American culture. It's difficult to imagine an American child not being acquainted with basketball. Children and adults play countless thousands of pickup games on playgrounds and in gyms and backyards across the nation. The hoop and backboard mounted above the garage is a standard feature of the suburban tract home. Formal competition runs up from grammar school through high school, college, and professional levels. And each level provides coaching, facilities, social support, and both monetary and symbolic incentives, all largely free to the player.

When you think about it, this adds up to a laissez-faire system for producing basketball players. A long string of victories would not be possible in Olympic basketball, or in any other international sport, without a system.

This comparison also highlights two other points. First, laissez-faire works best over the long run, the Soviet model takes effect more quickly. If Communist bloc countries had adopted a laissez-faire approach, they might have eventually achieved in certain sports the same results they achieved with the Soviet model—given enough time. However, we suspect that, in the short run, government must overtly intervene and manipulate a society in order to achieve specific goals, particularly if external rewards are not present.

The second point concerns the external rewards. The laissez-faire system requires them: the lucrative income and fame of professional sports, and the prestige and glamor of many amateur ones. In the United States different laissez-faire systems produce numerous outstanding baseball and football players, and in lesser numbers, outstanding tennis and hockey players, boxers, and skaters. (Not all of these participate in international competition.)

For those sports with prestige and glamour but without many lucrative professional outlets (diving and swimming) laissez-faire works, but less well. And if a sport leads to neither prestige nor monetary rewards, then the laissez-faire model begins sputtering and sometimes fails outright.

Skiing in the United States illustrates this. Despite its popularity as recreation, U.S. skiing is not consistently up to world class standards and sometimes gets trounced in major international competitions. One ski coach gives a sociological reason: "In the U.S. skiing is a strictly personal sport. In Europe skiing not only means money, but it also determines your social standing. If you are a ski racer, you have a position for life."[13] Quite naturally, the best European athletes tend to go into skiing while the best Americans get siphoned off into baseball, football, or some other externally rewarding sport.

For the same reason—lack of monetary or social rewards—the United States has consistently done badly in "forgotten" sports such as race walking, luge, or team handball. In the forgotten sports, finding, training, and supporting athletes and coaches becomes a matter of luck and of individual motivation. Table 11.1 documents just how many Olympic sports are neglected in the U.S. educational system, where high schools serve as the major feeder system for colleges and universities, which in turn support, or have supported, the bulk of Olympic athletes. This feeding system works well for some sports, but not too well, or not at all, for Olympic competition. The table shows that most high schools and colleges do not have varsity competition in twenty-three out of the thirty Olympic sports. The appearance of fencing and gymnastics (both well-known sports) on the list is surprising. Other Olympic sports are virtually unknown in this country. How many Americans would recognize biathlon, luge, or modern pentathlon?

In the Soviet Union, finding, training, and supporting athletes and coaches is a matter of state policy and systematic search; as a result, consistent success is almost inevitable. The surprising thing isn't that the United States wins fewer medals than Soviet bloc nations, but that the United States does so well with an uncoordinated, unorganized, and unsupported system for producing Olympic athletes; success is more difficult to explain than failure.

Political Success.   From the bloc perspective, the criterion of success is not athletic victories per se. Sport *is* politics, and therefore the critical test takes place in the political arena rather than on the athletic field. How successful has sport been in achieving political goals?

We know bloc athletes have consistently won major competitions but this is just about the only hard fact we have. From it we must do a lot of speculating. Sociological theory tells us that sports victories can be used to manipulate the symbolic world of people's daily existence.

If people can be convinced that athletic victory represents victory for the system, that it proves the superiority of one political philosophy over another—that itself is the proof. The claim becomes reality. This follows from a basic sociological premise: All of us create and live in a world of symbolic truths which are indisputably real to us. As sociologist W. I. Thomas said, "Things that are defined as real are real in their conse-

---

[13]Quoted in William Oscar Johnson, "The Land of the Also-Rans," *Sports Illustrated*, January 28, 1980, p. 38. American skiers may have begun to get the support they need to win according to one more recent report (*Sports Illustrated*, April 5, 1982, pp. 9–10).

Table 11.1. United States Collegiate and High School Involvement in the Olympic Sports

Olympic Sports	VARSITY PROGRAMS IN MOST	
	Universities	High Schools
Basketball	yes	yes
Swimming	yes	yes
Track and Field	yes	yes
Wrestling	yes	yes
Women's Volleyball	no	yes
Diving	yes	no
Soccer	yes	no
Archery	no	no
Biathlon	no	no
Bobsled	no	no
Boxing	no	no
Canoeing and Kayaking	no	no
Cycling	no	no
Equestrian	no	no
Fencing	no	no
Field Hockey	no	no
Figure Skating	no	no
Gymnastics	no	no
Ice Hockey	no	no
Judo	no	no
Luge	no	no
Modern Pentathlon	no	no
Rowing	no	no
Shooting	no	no
Skiing	no	no
Speed Skating	no	no
Team Handball	no	no
Weight Lifting	no	no
Water Polo	no	no
Yachting	no	no

SOURCE: *The Final Report of the President's Commission on Olympic Sports, 1975–1977,* Volume I (Washington, D.C.: U.S. Government Printing Office, 1977), pp. 96–97.

quences,"[14] If propaganda can change these definitions or "truths," the accompanying consequences will change. Sports propaganda then becomes more than bragging and publicity, it becomes a kind of political influence, or, what amounts to the same thing, political power through sport.

In practice, deliberately creating symbolic truths—good propaganda— is difficult to do. First of all, sociologists agree that propaganda cannot contradict or change actual

---

[14]W. I. Thomas, *The Child in America: Behavior Problems and Programs* (New York: Alfred A. Knopf, Inc., 1928).

events.[15] To effectively propagandize, sport requires the right events (victories), and even then a single victory or single outstanding athlete can always be dismissed as luck. By herself Olga Korbut would not convince you of Soviet political superiority. But if you're exposed to a never-ending stream of Olga Korbuts—bombarded by hundreds of victories in all sports year in and year out—then the impact begins to accumulate. It snowballs. And when considered alongside Communist bloc accomplishments in art, military preparedness, medicine, and other areas, the snowball grows huge. It becomes a great gestalt symbolizing the goodness of the Communist bloc political system in all realms of life, not just sport.

Sociological research on political propaganda shows that no matter how large the propaganda package and no matter how much you bombard people, it usually won't change their predispositions. Over a lifetime of socialization, people build up certain predispositions that are reinforced by their social environment. People's friendship groups, work situations, families, neighbors, all reinforce their beliefs and acts. In the short run, propaganda will not change so much as catalyze and guide predispositions along lines they were already likely to follow.

The specific case of sports propaganda should work in the same way. That is, it will activate people's dormant predispositions toward believing in their political and social systems and will raise their level of consciousness. It will also draw them together in pride and purpose. Two illustrations of the last point follow:

> **Cheering for Your Side.** During the 1980 Winter Games, when the United States hockey team beat a heavily favored Russian team, the American media set aside any pretense of objective reporting. As the clock ran down, the rinkside television announcer cried, "Do you believe in miracles?" The announcer in the control booth was visibly moved and exclaimed, "I haven't seen anything like it, well, since World War II!" The media proudly trumpeted the news and pictures of the U.S. team were suddenly everywhere. Crowds greeted the triumphant Olympians waving flags and singing the National Anthem. Patriotism returned.
>
> At the Montreal Summer Games in 1976, Irish middle-distance runner Eamonn Coghlan finished fourth in the 1,500-meter race. "He may not have won," said an Irish fan who saw the race on TV, "but, by God, for four minutes he united Ireland."[16]

No matter how much their accomplishments were propagandized by media and government, neither the U.S. hockey team nor Eamonn Coghlan could change the ongoing course of their country's history. Nevertheless their accomplishments were real and the patriotic responses to them were real. Over the long run, the pen *might* be more powerful than the sword; or at least we should not dismiss the possibility out of hand.

Chairman Mao said that political power grows out of the barrel of a gun, but observe: Nations do not *always* turn to the gun. As a scholar of political-sport points out,

---

[15]Robert K. Merton, *Social Theory and Social Structure*, rev. and enlarged ed. (New York: The Free Press, 1957), chap. 16; Paul F. Lazarsfeld, Bernard Berelson, and Hazel Gaudet, *The People's Choice: How the Voter Makes Up His Mind in a Presidential Campaign*, 3rd ed. (New York and London: Columbia University Press, 1968). These are classic statements.

[16]Kenney Moore, "The Man Who United Ireland," *Sports Illustrated*, June 25, 1979, p. 66.

''The physical size, industrial capability, and military strength of the two Blocs are of such peerless magnitude that competition between the two has forced confrontation on numerous fronts around the world.''[17]

Under these circumstances both sides hesitate to use economic or military power because the consequences are so grave. They turn to less risky alternatives, and symbolically based power thus becomes an important political weapon. True, it requires great patience to obtain results, and any single result may not (in fact, probably will not) be overwhelming. But given the alternatives, and in the long run, who can say what the ultimate consequences will be?

THE THIRD WORLD: SPORTS AS A WEAPON

The Third World is underdeveloped and poor. It lacks know-how, trained work forces, financing, production capabilities, and military strength. Politically this means the Third World nations lack material power. They cannot impose military and economic pressures; they have no big stick to wave around. Without much material power, the Third World must turn to symbolic power:

> **Violence and Terror.** During the 1972 Munich Olympics, eight Palestinian terrorists invaded the section of the Olympic village housing the Israeli team. They killed two Israelis who resisted and took nine athletes and coaches hostage.
> The terrorists were seeking the release of 200 prisoners in Israeli jails. After hours of indecisive negotiations, the West German authorities helicoptered the terrorists and their captives to the airport where a jet transport was waiting. As a few terrorists walked from the helicopters to the transport, apparently reconnoitering the situation, the police opened fire. During the brief gunfight, one terrorist threw a grenade into the helicopter holding the hostages and killed them.
> Apparently the strategy was shoot the terrorists before they could react and harm the hostages. Obviously the strategy failed.

Third World nations and political groups realize that sport has vast potential for symbolic political maneuvers. The attack by the Palestinian terrorists really had nothing to do with sport. They chose the Olympics because it put them on a worldwide stage. In contrast to the many small attacks that hardly get reported by the American press, the Olympic attack totally dominated TV screens and headlines. It is still remembered as an infamous historical event. Says Richard Espey: "The Olympic Games had once again become the staging ground, this time in a barbarous fashion, for a particular political cause. The Munich massacre vividly underscored the unique simultaneity of the Olympics as actor and stage, participant and arena.''[18]

The Palestinian incident was the bloodiest but not the largest-scale political use of sport by the Third World. The grandest, most elaborate sports exposition of Third World

---

[17]Espey, *The Politics*, p. 14.
[18]Ibid., p. 158.

social and political causes was GANEFO (Games of the New Emerging Forces) held in Indonesia in 1963. Forty-eight nations participated. A few developed countries also sent teams to demonstrate support for the Third World (but not the United States). According to one author, GANEFO symbolized "the economic and political independence sought by nations recently freed from the bonds of colonial rule."[19] Some Third World leaders also viewed GANEFO as an alternative to the Olympics and as a means to promote a permanent political alliance. That never happened and subsequent developments scuttled GANEFO. Since then Third World nations have occasionally held sports festivals with that type of atmosphere, but without dramatic success in achieving political goals.

Currently the Third World uses political sports mostly to attack apartheid in South Africa. In 1948 the South African Nationalist Party formally initiated apartheid by passing a series of acts legalizing racial segregation in virtually all areas of life: where people lived, traveled, worked, played, walked, sat, talked, and much more. What had been informal *de facto* segregation became concretized into a *de jure* class system with whites (about 18 percent of the population) isolated at the top of the socioeconomic pyramid and the mass of nonwhites at the botton.[20] Apartheid applied to sport also, as the following example illustrates.

> **Papwa Sewgolum: Systemic Pathos.** Papwa Segolum was an outstanding South African golfer, a worldclass competitor who, according to apartheid, had the misfortune of being Indian and thus nonwhite. But because he was so very good, he received permission to compete in the 1963 South African Natal Open. He won, beating 113 white golfers.
>
> It rained during the awards ceremony. As a nonwhite, Sewgolum could not go into the clubhouse. He stood in the rain, says one account, while "the trophy was handed through a window in the club house where 113 white participants were being served drinks by the Indian servant." South Africa later prohibited all interracial sports.[21]

In later years, Third World countries combined with other nations to convince the IOC and the International Amateur Federation to expel South Africa. This means that South African athletes cannot compete in the most prestigious sports events in the world, events ranging from the Boston Marathon to the Olympic Games.

Protests and boycotts have not been confined to South Africa. Rhodesia was barred from the 1972 Olympics for much the same reasons. And a few days before the 1976 Olympics began, some thirty black African countries abruptly shipped their athletes home. They called the boycott because the IOC permitted New Zealand to compete in the Games even though a New Zealand rugby team had previously toured South Africa.

---

[19]Swanpo Sie, "Sports and Politics: The Case of the Asian Games and the GANEFO," in Lowe, Kanin, and Strenk, *Sport*, p. 295.

[20]In South Africa, the category of nonwhite includes blacks, Asians (mostly Indians), and "coloreds" (mixed descent or Hottentot, Bushman or East Asian). See Robert Schoen, "Towards a Theory of the Democratic Implications of Ethnic Stratification," *Social Science Quarterly*, 59 (December 1978), 468–81.

[21]Richard E. Lapchick, "Apartheid Sport: South Africa's Use of Sport in Foreign Policy," *Journal of Sport and Social Issues*, 1 (1976), 60.

Several smaller incidents have occurred. A South African team toured Great Britain in 1979, much to the distress of antiapartheid groups. Unlike some ten years earlier when violent prolonged protest erupted against a South African rugby tour, the 1979 tour was met with relatively decorous public demonstrations.[22]

More recent tours have not been so calmly received. The Springboks, a South African worldclass rugby team with only one black player, traveled to New Zealand for a game in 1981, and touched off a firestorm of protest. Antiapartheid demonstrators attacked the parliament building and littered the streets around the stadium with rocks, broken bottles, and flares. Riot police cleared the area.

The Springboks also toured the United States. One game had to be held at an unannounced site in order to thwart demonstrators. (Ironically, the chosen site was in the black ghetto of Milwaukee.) The governor of New York state barred the Springboks from playing in Albany, but a federal court overturned his order. Cold and rain kept the crowds down. However, a bomb explosion caused great damage to the offices of the American club hosting the Springbok match. The Springboks next went to Indiana for a match, and a bomb destroyed the Indiana team's clubhouse. That game was cancelled.[23]

In an interesting countermove involving another sport, South Africa persuaded several of Great Britain's top cricket players to come over and compete in a series of important matches. Evidently money was a major motivator. South African sponsors reportedly paid British athletes anywhere from $45,000 to $135,000, depending on their reputation. "They are being used as political pawns and have succumbed to greed," said one commentator.[24]

Just what overall, long-run effect these incidents will have on South Africa cannot be known at present. Some future historian will have to tell us. However, South Africa has inched toward liberalizing apartheid in sport. Their international teams now have a few black athletes and blacks occasionally compete against whites, The black American boxer, John Tate, fought the white South African, Gerrie Coetzee, for the World Boxing Association version of the heavyweight championship. The fight took place in Versfeld Stadium, Pretoria, before a racially integrated audience. For the first time nonwhites sat next to whites in the stands. Many South Africans seem to favor changes such as these.[25]

While we do not dismiss these changes, other observers do. A prominent American civil-rights leader toured South Africa and then brushed aside the integrated seating at the Tate-Coetzee fight as a mere gimmick.[26] His stance coincides with the claim that truly important progress will come about only by changing the system of sports clubs that

[22]Clive Bammon, "All's Quiet in England . . . For Now," *Sports Illustrated*, October 15, 1979, pp. 97–101.

[23]*Time*, August 3, 1981, p. 43; Neil Amdur, "South Africa and Foes Deploy," *New York Times*, April 26, 1981, p. 25; Paul Montgomery, "Albany Rain Keeps The Turnout Small for Springbok Game," *New York Times*, September 23, 1981, pp. 1, 17; *New York Times*, September 26, 1981, p. 7.

[24]R. W. Apple, Jr., "British Cricketers Defy Ban to Play in South Africa," *New York Times*, March 3, 1982, p. 3. © 1982 by The New York Times Company. Reprinted by permission.

[25]Carey Winfrey, "Fight Fans Accept Integrated Seating," *New York Times*, October 21, 1979, p. S6.

[26]Reported in *Sports Illustrated*, August 20, 1979, p. 58.

controls athletics in South Africa. All you see now, many observers say, are tiny hairline cracks in the surface of apartheid. And the target is apartheid in all social institutions of South African society, not just in sport. Boycotting nations hope to bring down an entire society.

Few people really believe that sports boycotts can destroy apartheid. Still, boycotts are valuable political weapons, especially for nations without much military or economic power. The boycotts have become propaganda symbols that help unify diverse nations in achieving a common goal and at the same time, help label South Africa a pariah among the worldwide community of nations. Over time, probably a long time, the boycotts might well cause the tiny cracks in sports apartheid to grow into major fissures in all apartheid. Meanwhile, those South African athletes who wish to engage in sport for sport's sake find themselves provocateurs in a world of many conflicts and hatreds.

CONCLUSIONS: DIFFICULT CHOICES AHEAD

At this point, it would be well to stand back a moment and ask, Where do we stand? and Where are we going? To oversimplify a bit, it seems that politics *in* sport gives rise to a much different issue than politics *of* sport. Everyone agrees that sport, as a complex social institution, requires governance, and governance is politics. Debates rage over details, yet no one wants anarchy. Hence there necessarily must be politics in sport.

The politics of sport is a different beast all together. Again to oversimplify, the United States seems to be allowing the laissez-faire sports model to slip away little by little. The model appears moribund, perhaps already dead. If the trend continues, one of two basic scenarios—imaginary descriptions of what the future might be like—seems probable. In one scenario the politicizing of sport continues to increase as time goes on; in the other scenario sport becomes less political and its original function is restored. Let's consider these two in turn.

First Scenario: Leaning Laissez Faire.   Sometime in the next century the United States completely abandons the current laissez-faire sports model and replaces it with leaning laissez faire. Under the revised system an uneasy coalition of free-market forces and governmental policies support American sport. Those sports doing well under laissez faire get left to market forces. They do not need government help and so the government pretty much leaves them alone.

However that describes only a few sports. For most sports—those of international importance but not well supported under laissez-faire—the federal government takes on the main fiscal responsibility.

The small buttresses erected in the past, such as subsidizing Olympic training camps, funding facilities for the Games, monetary grants to USOC, and State Department sports tours, serve as precedents that justify more government funding, and hence control, of most sports programs. The government also feels perfectly free to use the sports boycott whenever the political situation demands. President Carter's boycott of the Moscow Olympics in 1980 serves as the main precedent. Only the political meaning of sport matters any more; sport and politics are one and the same.

Second Scenario: Pure Laissez Faire.   By the next century American sport, rather than becoming more politicized, moves in the opposite direction, back toward the pure notion of sport as a contest between individual athletes rather than between social-political systems. This ideology grows so strong that when other nations propagandize their victories, the American news media and national leaders dismiss it as pure political claptrap. They say the propaganda only shows the emptiness of Communist bloc ideology since no meaningful social philosophy would convert sport into politics.

Ironically pure laissez-faire has become a sort of metapolitical ideology. Not politicizing sport is the accepted "political" posture towards sport; and so the government deliberately dismantles the federal buttresses erected in the past. For the same reason, the United States ignores all sports boycotts. A pure laissez-faire sports model is now the goal.

In further pursuit of this goal, the United States, and its allies succeed in depoliticizing international competitions, particularly the Olympic Games. The Games (and all international contests) are held only in neutral countries and on a permanent basis. This circumvents the politics associated with selecting a host nation and precludes the host nation from pulling off a propaganda coup.

The trappings of the Games (and other sports events) are modified. No longer can national anthems be played. Flags cannot be raised, nor uniforms worn. Nor can athletes march as a single unit because that implies a team representing a specific nation. Olympic symbols, which represent individual achievement, replace the former trappings. At the victory ceremony athletes stand dressed in one uniform—the Olympic uniform. One flag is run up—the Olympic flag. One anthem is played—the Olympic anthem. Countries are not mentioned in any Olympic publications nor listed in record books. Teams are identified only by number and names of athletes. Thus the symbolic emphasis shifts from inter*national* competition to inter*personal* competition; from dividing people into nations to uniting them under common banner.

In their suggestion of what the future might hold, scenarios serve as a form of science fiction. And like science fiction, scenarios may or may not come true. According to sociological theory, material-structural forces largely determine what the future will be like. Most people, to use an old metaphor, get swept along by the tides of history. Only very few can resist.

A society moves like a steam roller. A huge social mass must first be set in motion. Once moving, it rolls along slowly and relentlessly. This analogy suggests a widely accepted principle of forecasting: Over the short run the future will be similar to the present.

If we apply this principle to the scenarios, it means the first will come about because it more closely resembles the present situation. You could even argue that the first scenario provides a fairly accurate description of today's sports world. Basically the scenario only changes the acceptance of political sport from covert to overt and then intensifies it. Sport becomes political—explicitly, totally, and legitimately.

Pure politicization will not come about all at once, of course. It will take place in a zigzag, forward-backward fashion. Some events will politicize sport and others lessen politicization. Some people will resist politicization and others will encourage it.

Nevertheless, when viewed in broad perspective the overall trend is towards politicization. We hesitate to predict the exact moment when the first scenario will come into existence, but we expect it within our lifetimes. Indeed, it's almost here now.

SUMMARY

1. According to Western ideology, sport should be nonpolitical. In contrast, Communist-socialist countries have adopted the Soviet model which invokes total governmental control of sport.
2. The laissez-faire model works best for those sports which lead to monetary or social rewards. Other sports are neglected. The Soviet model works for most sports but is based on a much different political philosophy.
3. Propagandizing sport is probably not too effective in changing a person's political beliefs. But propaganda can be effective over the long run for those persons already predisposed to the belief in question.
4. Sport is used as a political weapon: Various countries boycott international sports events as a way to oppose the policies of other participating nations. The Third World has made heavy use of this weapon to fight South African apartheid.
5. The United States seems to be relinquishing the laissez-faire sports model in favor of a more politicized sports system: leaning laissez faire. The trend will probably continue for some time.

12

DEVIANCE AND SPORTS
Cheating, Drugs, and Gambling

TANK McNAMARA
by Jeff Millar & Bill Hinds

Hardly a laughing matter, drugs, gambling, and cheating in sports have a long history and pose difficult problems for athletes and sport officials alike. Media coverage of deviance in sport tends toward sensationalism, as the above Tank McNamara cartoon strips suggest. Copyright, 1982, Universal Press Syndicate. Reprinted with permission. All rights reserved.

Question: What do the following people have in common: Joan of Arc, Richard Nixon, Alex Karras, Bob Welch?

Answer: They're all deviants.

Joan was a female warrior who led the French armies against the British and was burned at the stake for heresy. Nixon was implicated in the Watergate scandal. Karras, a professional football player, was once suspended for gambling. And Welch, a major-league baseball player, was an alcoholic.

Saint Joan to Bob Welch—a diverse collection of human types. They lived in different historical periods and experienced different cultures. They were loved by some people, hated by others, and completely ignored by still others. To judge by these cases:

Deviance has existed across time and throughout the world.

Whether you are deviant or not depends on the time and place and who does the judging.

Certain acts of deviance might be illegal and lead to death while others hardly cause a raised eyebrow.

You can be a deviant regardless of race, religion, creed, national origin, or sex.

Deviance can exist anywhere, in the church, in government, and in sport.

An Example. A new basketball coach at a major sport school desperately wants to make his school into a big winner, but is running into problems: The other schools in the conference are improving as fast as his.

How to catch up? First, and obviously, he needs to recruit blue-chip athletes. How? Well, if you don't succeed one way, try another. This coach tries the other ways. When he wants a player who cannot meet entrance requirements, he gets an academic advisor to "make an exception." When a good player has a poor academic record, he has another student take a course for him to bring up his grade-point average. He sends a high school player to summer basketball camp on unauthorized expenses, in violation of NCAA rules. He drives himself mercilessly—endless miles of recruiting trips, late night talks, practices—and sometimes relies on drugs and alcohol to keep himself going.

Is this coach deviant? Observing his conduct most people would answer in the affirmative: Cheating, violating rules, drinking excessively and taking drugs, being obsessed with work and with winning—all are forms of deviance. People have little difficulty recognizing deviance when they encounter extreme forms of it. However, trying to define what they recognize leaves them tied in semantic knots. Small wonder.

Deviance turns out to be one of the most tangled concepts in sociology. It has many, many meanings, so many we cannot discuss them all. Rather, we ask you to accept the following definition: Deviance is behavior that goes against widely accepted norms, values, ideology, rules, and laws of an institution, and that draws mild to severe sanctions.[1]

---

[1]A lengthy discussion is presented by Jack P. Gibbs, *Norms, Deviance, and Social Control: Conceptual Matters* (New York: Elsevier North-Holland, Inc., 1981).

By this definition, the coach in the example engages in a wide variety of deviant behaviors. A natural question is, Why does he do it? A more general question, Why would anyone do it? Even more generally, Why is there deviance in sport? These questions imply two other basic questions:

What causes people to become deviant?

How is it that institutions keep producing the opportunities for people to become deviant?

Over the years, trying to answer the first question has resulted in a potpourri of theories. Any general textbook on the subject will discuss ecological theory, Lombrosian positivism, XYY chromosomes, Sheldon's body types, superego, ego strength, frustration-aggression, defense mechanisms, differential association, anomie, and others. Says a monograph on deviance, "There are as many ways of explaining misbehavior [deviance] as there are ways of misbehaving, and there are innumerable ways of misbehaving. Indeed, the task of creating theories to explain human deviance has stood as one of the most difficult challenges for all the sciences of human behavior."[2]

The cause of deviance lies well outside the scope of this book. That leaves us with the second question: the production of deviant opportunities. To quote a well-known author, "[The] aim is to discover how some social structures exert a definite pressure upon certain persons in the society to engage in non-conforming rather than conforming conduct."[3] That is our aim too. We begin with cheating, and pay special attention to the situation of big-time collegiate athletics.

CHEATING IN SPORT

Cheating—intentionally violating rules and norms for one's advantage—is the most common kind of deviance found in sport. To cite a few examples:

- Wichita State has the distinction of being the school with the most sanctions against it in the NCAA: in 1955, a reprimand for recruiting payments, in 1958, one-year probation and firing of head and assistant football coaches, for paying players from a secret slush fund; in 1963, public reprimand for improperly paying a scout; in 1968, two-year probation and firing of all football coaches except one, for multiple recruiting infractions; in 1974, one-year probation and firing of an academic administrator for forging the high-school transcripts of a basketball recruit; and in 1982, three-year probation, two years prohibition from

---

[2]Robert B. Edgerton, *Deviance: A Cross-Cultural Perspective* (Menlo Park, California: Cummings Publishing Company, 1978), p. 18.

[3]Robert K. Merton, *Social Theory and Social Structure*, rev. and enlarged ed. (New York: The Free Press, 1957), p. 132. Italics omitted. Merton's theory has been widely applied, often as a "heuristic" device (see Wilbert Marcellus Leonard, II, *A Sociological Perspective of Sport*, Minneapolis, Minnesota: Burgess Publishing Co., 1980). However, while Merton's philosophical approach applies to sports deviance, his theory does not, principally because sport is not and has not become an anomic institution.

postseason tournaments, and two years loss of one basketball scholarship, for numerous violations and slush fund payments to athletes.[4]

- During 1980, it was revealed that the University of Southern California enrolled as many as thirty-three athletes, mostly football players, who did not meet the university's entrance requirements. Prior to that, USC had been put on probation when thirty-two players received credit for a speech course they never attended. The instructor of the course resigned but no one else was penalized.[5]

- The NCAA placed the University of New Mexico basketball team on three-year probation and fined the school $36,000 when the 1980 "Lobogate" scandal broke out. The Lobo's head coach and his assistant were implicated in a transcript-forging scheme. Both lost their jobs and seven athletes lost their eligibility.[6]

- Illegal payments to "amateur" athletes appear endemic. Says one player, now a professional: "They [the recruiters] would be real sly, talking out of the corners of their mouths, thinking that [the offer] would make a difference. Ninety percent of the major schools do it." Another heavily recruited player says, "There was one school that just handed me money as soon as I walked off the plane. . . . I asked what it was for. They said it was for traveling expenses."[7]

- Cheating goes on outside of collegiate sport too, but it is mostly of a different nature. In professional sport the issues of recruiting and eligibility do not exist. The most visible cheating takes place on the playing field. In baseball the spitball has become lore (the pitcher secretly puts a drop of spit or a dab of vaseline on the ball). A professional coach estimates that half of all pitchers doctor the ball in some way.[8]

    Basketball coaches teach their athletes how to pull an opponent's shorts to impede his running, how to stand on his toes to hinder his jump, and how to fake fouls. In football, linemen deliberately hold; punters always fall down whenever an on-rushing lineman comes anywhere near them.

These instances illustrate the cheating found in sport. You would probably agree that some forms are more serious than others. Sometimes cheating actually becomes a "game" between cheater and official. Baseball umpires will occasionally search a pitcher for vaseline. One pitcher would hide little notes on his body for the umpire to find: "You're getting warmer"; "Close, but no cigar." When a player successfully fakes a foul, the TV announcer will say, "He ought to get an Academy Award for that one"; or an official will look at the player sprawled out on the floor and intone, "No! No! No!"—meaning the acting job wasn't good enough.

But other cheating is more serious; no one treats them as "games." The NCAA estimates that 14 percent of member schools engage in serious cheating, an estimate that

---

[4]*The Chronicle of Higher Education*, January 27, 1982, p. 8.

[5]*New York Times*, October 26, 1980, p. 48.

[6]*New York Times*, February 15, 1980, p. 27.

[7]Quotes from *Columbus Citizen-Journal*, February 8, 1982, p. 13.

[8]Steve Wulf, "Tricks of the Trade," *Sports Illustrated*, April 13, 1981, pp. 84–108.

strikes many observers as ludicrously low.[9] But then without good data, the true rate might be anything.

If we set aside the question of true rates of cheating (and we might as well since the necessary data do not exist), and if we also agree to overlook nonserious cheating (such as the faked foul and the spitball, which have become institutionalized parts of sport), we are still left with a residual amount of serious cheating to account for.

At present the major episodes of serious cheating occur mainly in collegiate athletics and that will be the focus. What causes this cheating? And why hasn't the NCAA been able to wipe it out? As always, our first sociological suspicions fall on the social system.

THE SYSTEM

We previously said the system produces athletes (Chapter 3): "Athletes appear because there are games to be played, and won, and when won, rewarded." So too with cheating. Cheaters appear because games have to be won, and the way you do it becomes less important than that you do it. As *Newsweek* magazine put it, "In the relentless pursuit of victory, cheating has become the name of the game."[10]

The demand for victory generates pressures felt throughout the institution, particularly if they come from the top. Here are three instances.

- A former basketball coach recalls that the university president would give the team a locker-room pep talk and after one big victory, "There was [the president] along with the athletic director, and a bunch of other administrators, dancing in the aisles."[11] Another college president estimates that athletics takes up 10 to 20 percent of his time, even though he does not give locker room talks.[12]

- In a candid autobiography, the president of Oklahoma University during the time when the Sooners were building a national powerhouse, recounts numerous incidents in which he intervened to hide irregularities from the NCAA or prevent larger infractions from being committed.[13]

- The past president of a prestigious west coast university apparently made it clear to the admissions office that they were to "look the other way" regarding athletes with deficient high-school records. Athletes comprised 25 percent of all students admitted under the school's "special access program," a program intended to help culturally deprived students.[14]

[9]D. Stanley Eitzen, "Sport and Deviance," in *Sport in Contemporary Society: An Anthology*, ed. D. Stanley Eitzen (New York: St. Martin's Press, 1979), pp. 73–87; *The Chronicle*, January 20, 1982, p. 4.

[10]*Newsweek*, September 22, 1980, p. 54.

[11]Quoted in Rick Telander, "The Descent of a Man," *Sports Illustrated*, March 8, 1982, p. 66.

[12]Malcolm Moran, "The Pressure to Produce," *New York Times*, March 22, 1982, sec. Y, p. 34.

[13]George Lynn Cross, *Presidents Can't Punt: The OU Football Tradition* (Norman, Oklahoma: University of Oklahoma Press, 1977).

[14]Jerry Kirschenbaum, "USC: The University of Special Cases," *Sports Illustrated*, October 27, 1980, p. 19.

When presidents of universities scurry around covering infractions and violating more rules, they lend an aura of legitimacy to a sub rosa activity. They implicitly tell their followers that cheating is all right, that results justify means. A coach's ideological rationalization might go like this: "Everybody, from the president on down, is putting on pressures to win. I'll be fired for losing. So, if the rules stand in my way, well, bend the rules a little. Everybody else is doing it; the president will wink at it; and we can't compete with them unless we do it too. Just don't get caught. As they say, 'They'll fire you for losing before they'll fire you for cheating.' "

The saying has validity, not because the ones who do the firing are evil people pathologically obsessed with winning, but because these people too get caught up in a system that unrelentingly demands that certain outcomes must be met: Win, or else . . .

In order to win, you must recruit blue-chip athletes, but the demand for them exceeds the supply—a situation that puts the outstanding high-school player in the driver's seat. They will be courted and cajoled by dozens of recruiters, who tell players whatever they want to hear. A well-respected Notre Dame coach recently claimed that the going rate for an outstanding basketball player was ten thousand dollars per year, for a running back, twenty-five thousand. A number of coaches concurred while others disagreed.[15]

Whether factually accurate or not, the coach illustrates the point that blue-chip athletes received blue-chip treatment, some of it contrary to NCAA rules. As a former athletic administrator notes, "You don't go to a bowl with pre-med students."[16]

The cheating that goes on is a "willing exchange of strongly desired (though legally proscribed) goods or services."[17] This means that athletes receiving under-the-table payments are hardly likely to come forth and reveal their involvement. Enforcement authorities must dig out college cheating—which they rarely do—or wait until a media expose or some other source blows the whistle on a particular school. Enforcement is passive.

Blue-chip coaches also get treated well. One recently signed a contract worth almost two million dollars. A football coach at a major sports school earns, with perquisites and emoluments, over a hundred thousand dollars per year.[18]

Winning schools also do well financially. A good illustration is the NCAA basketball tournament held at the end of each season to determine the national champion. Once the tournament had only conference champions, but now it has champions plus teams selected by a committee; forty-eight in all. Money caused the expansion. The total purse is over twenty million dollars. The first round losers get over one hundred thousand dollars while the four teams in the finals earn approximately five hundred thousand dollars each.[19] Without that "pot of gold" waiting for the victorious school at the end of the season, the drive to win would decrease and so would the pressure to cheat.

---

[15]*New York Times*, March 27, 1982, sec. L, p. 17.

[16]Quoted in Malcolm Moran, "The Pressure to Produce," *New York Times*, March 22, 1982, sec. Y, p. 34. © 1982 by The New York Times Company. Reprinted by permission.

[17]Edwin M. Schur, *Interpreting Deviance: A Sociological Introduction* (New York: Harper & Row, Publishers, Inc., 1979), p. 451.

[18]*Columbus Citizen-Journal*, March 25, 1982, p. 1.

[19]Gordon S. White, Jr., "N.C.A.A. Event Richest Ever," *New York Times*, March 17, 1983, sec. Y, p. 24.

Revenues (or more accurately, the lack of them) generate pressures in another way. Football and basketball money supports the athletic programs that do not draw enough public interest to operate in the black. So when basketball and football run a deficit, as half the schools report they do, the money must come from somewhere else, either out of the general fund, from donations, or from loans.[20] The entire school might be indirectly tied to what happens on the athletic field.

The system has yet another feature which causes numerous problems: alumni booster clubs. Boosters tend to be wealthy alumni who receive great satisfaction from helping their alma mater's sport program. Being a good booster is viewed as a community service, as good public relations, and as an opportunity to make business contacts. There is nothing wrong with these activities—if not taken to extremes.

But over the years they *have* been taken to extremes. Half of all charges brought to the NCAA's attention involve booster groups. Booster groups often "help" programs by providing "laundry money," stereos, cars, and in one case, by allegedly providing an athlete's girl friend with an abortion. As a result of continued recruiting abuses and slush-fund payments by alumni, the University of San Francisco went so far as to drop its varsity basketball program.[21]

Winning is very important to boosters. They have intense ego involvement; they exalt in victory; they live and die for their teams. Winning also has economic consequences. At one southern school, when the football team went 0–11, the booster club managed to raise $100,000; when the team went 3–8, the club raised $400,000. After two bowl appearances the club raised $1.5 million, assumed payments on a seventy-eight-unit apartment complex in the school's behalf, paid for two expansions of the stadium, and arranged a financial contract guaranteeing the coach $100,000 if he stayed until his contract expired. Winning helps booster groups boost their team.

Booster-club money translates into booster-club power. At one school, the administration fired a coach involved in a cheating-gambling scandal, and the booster group threatened to withhold all contributions—a sum totalling several hundred thousand dollars.[22] Such sums are not trivial.

Schools can hardly control their booster clubs. Club members are neither students nor faculty; the school can neither suspend nor fire them. And should the club be disestablished (kicked off campus), the school loses an economic resource and offends a substantial body of community support. Boosters are rich, upstanding community members holding high positions (lawyers, physicians, judges, politicians, businessmen). Any organization hesitates to cut off such a base of support.

Nor can the school turn to the NCAA. The NCAA can put a school on probation, declare athletes ineligible, disallow television revenues, and so forth, but the NCAA cannot do anything to a booster group. When booster group activities lead to sanctions,

[20]Mitchell H. Raiborn, *Revenues and Expenses of Intercollegiate Athletic Programs* (Shawnee Mission, Kansas: The National Collegiate Athletic Association, 1978), Tables 4.5, 4.7.

[21]Neil Amdur, "Backers Buy Success and Trouble for College Athletic Departments," *New York Times*, March 29, 1981, pp. 1, 27; *Columbus Citizen-Journal*, February 1, 1922, p. 15; Robert H. Boyle and Roger Jackson, "Bringing Down the Curtain," *Sports Illustrated*, August 9, 1982, pp. 62–79.

[22]Amdur, "Backers Buy Success," p. 27.

the school, the athletes, and sometimes the coaches, take the punishment while the perpetrators go untouched. Recently, rules limiting booster involvement in recruiting have been instituted by the NCAA. Whether these rules will solve the problems will not be known for several years.

Critics charge that cheating threatens to destroy college sport. They say that even if the ideal of the the student-athlete was never a reality, at least the idea of the ideal was upheld—but no more. They say that nowadays the magnitude of the problem, the blatant disregard for NCAA rules, and the cynicism that comes with endemic violations make big-time college sport no more than a cutthroat, no-holds-barred, dirty business. These charges make good media stories, but they should be evaluated with an eye to history and sociology: Cheating, and deviance in general, take place throughout American society and always have.

Why Things Never Seem to Change

One of the main reasons for forming the conferences and later the NCAA, was to regulate widespread cheating. You can debate to what extent the NCAA succeeded. In 1929, an influential report produced by the Carnegie Foundation concluded that

> the recruiting of American college athletes, be it active or passive, professional or non-professional, has reached the proportions of nationwide commerce. In spite of the efforts of not a few teachers and principals who have comprehended its dangers, its effect upon the character of the school boy has been profoundly deleterious. Its influence upon the nature and quality of American higher education has been no less noxious.[23]

That conclusion is as appropriate to the modern situation as it was to the situation of the 1920s. Nothing basic has changed: Recruiting still constitutes a business and the business adversely affects athlete and school. The examples with which we opened this section simply repeat old stories.

The lack of reform despite repeated calls for reform, raises one's sociological curiosity. A well-known sociologist writes,

> Deviant forms of conduct often seem to derive nourishment from the very agencies devised to inhibit them. Indeed, the agencies built by society for preventing deviance are often so poorly equipped for the task we might well ask why this is regarded as their "real" function in the first place . . . In this sense, the agencies of control often seem to define their jobs as that of keeping deviance within bounds rather than that of obliterating it altogether.[24]

---

[23]Howard J. Savage, *American College Athletics* (New York: The Carnegie Foundation for the Advancement of Teaching, 1929), p. 240; sometimes called the "Savage" or "Carnegie" Report.

[24]Kai T. Erickson, *Wayward Puritans: A Study in the Sociology of Deviance* (New York: John Wiley & Sons, Inc., 1966), pp. 14, 24; Randall Collins, *Sociological Insight: An Introduction to Non-Obvious Sociology* (New York: Oxford University Press, 1982), chap. 4.

This statement may not describe all deviance in all situations, but it certainly applies to cheating in collegiate sport. An NCAA-sponsored publication admits, "It is unrealistic to think that any amount of regulation from any source can eliminate all abuses for all time."[25]

True enough, but the matter involves more than that. No matter what its manuals and spokespersons may say, the NCAA makes little more than a token effort to stop cheating. Only 6 percent of NCAA revenues go toward enforcement activities; the NCAA enforcement staff consists of less than a dozen people supplemented by volunteers who counsel the top twenty or so high-school recruits. This staff is responsible for policing the two hundred schools that compete in big-time basketball, and the one hundred schools in big-time football. And, making matters even more difficult, the schools are scattered across the nation and deploy thousands of coaches, aides, and alumni, all of whom need to be policed too.[26]

You cannot help wondering why the NCAA makes such a puny effort to resolve such a serious problem. From a sociologocal standpoint, we can offer several reasons.

The organization has a structure that virtually precludes effective enforcement. The NCAA depends heavily on television revenues for economic survival. Fees for televising football games account for 25 percent of all NCAA revenues; championship events (including the televised basketball championships) account for 60 percent.[27]

Who produces the lion's share of television revenues? The major sports schools. It is the Notre Dame's, the Oklahoma's, the Alabama's, that year after year top the national rankings and draw the biggest TV viewing audiences. Place these schools on probation and the NCAA cuts off a major source of money from itself. Of course, other schools will take their place on TV, but will they draw the same audiences? Maybe, maybe not. Major sports schools are major because fans everywhere know them, and follow them.

Just as important, the NCAA maintains a philosophy of government by the governed—which works out to mean that representatives from member schools sit on important policy-making committees. Ideologically it's difficult to fault democracy, but democracy also means that the "inmates govern the prison." Will schools involved in bending the rules strongly support a policy of cleaning house? Not unless they can get an absolute, ironclad guarantee that no one can secretly cheat. No such guarantees are possible.[28]

The sociological paradox here is that a system can allow cheating even while all members detest it. The vast majority of NCAA policy makers undoubtedly are honorable, but human. They respond to structural influences without being aware of it; or if aware,

---

[25]Jack Falla, *NCAA: The Voice of College Sport* (Shawnee Mission, Kansas: The National Collegiate Athletic Association, 1981), p. 148.

[26]Falla, *The NCAA*, chap. 7; Gordon S. White, Jr., "As Rules Violations Increase, the Enforcement Staff Grows," *New York Times*, March 23, 1982, p. 27; *The Final Report of the President's Commission on Olympic Sports*, Volume II (Washington, D.C.: U.S. Government Printing Office, 1977) chap. B-8.

[27]*Final Report*, p. 349.

[28]And when the NCAA does place a powerful university on its sanction list, it may face an angry reaction. See *Sports Illustrated*, May 10, 1982, p. 38, for the reaction from the University of Southern California when it was placed on probation in 1982.

they are not able to do too much about it. The system just grinds on. The common rule violations reported and sanctioned by the NCAA (see Chart 12.1) are just the tip of a large iceberg.

Chart 12.1.   Summary of the Most Common NCAA Rule Violations in Sports, 1978–1981

More than Twenty Times

- Improper transportation or entertainment of prospective athletes or their families.
- Improper recruiting inducements to prospective athletes, including cash payments, use of automobiles, free clothing, housing, or promises of such benefits.
- Extra benefits to enrolled athletes, such as cash payments, special bank loans, use of automobiles, meals, and clothing.

Ten to Twenty Times

- Improper financial aid, including payment of personal costs for athletes.
- Failure to give athletes adequate notice that their scholarships will not be renewed.
- Financial aid in excess of amount permitted.
- Unearned academic credits to athletes.
- Intentional serious violations by athletic administrators, or denial of allegations later found to be true.
- Improper recruiting contacts.
- Improper workouts with team members by prospective athletes.

Four to Ten Times

- Failure to prevent improper recruiting activities by outside athletic representatives (boosters).
- Out-of-season practices.
- Athletes permitted to play for more years than they were eligible.

One to Three Times

- Monetary compensation to students for participating in college sports.
- Rules violated with knowledge of college president.
- Improper contacting of news media by coaches; excessive number of games played in one season.
- Athletes ineligible because of low grade-point average.
- Excessive number of scholarships awarded.
- Excessive number of coaches.
- Failure to cooperate with enforcement procedures.

SOURCE: *Chronicle of Higher Education*, January 20, 1982, p. 4. Reprinted with permission.

DRUG ABUSE

Strung Out.   A player nominated for all-American and drafted by a professional team became one of the best players in professional football—for a while. A knee injury prematurely ended his career, but his real problem was drugs.

He sustained the career-ending injury after being strung out on cocaine for three days. In addition, he said, "I was so high on Dexedrine my knee didn't hurt when it got busted up." The night before he went into surgery for his knee, he stayed up smoking marijuana. Later traded to another club, he said, "I took a lot of Dexedrine to speed me up. I also took a lot of Percodan and Darvon as painkillers, and I smoked some pot before the games."

All things considered, life turned out well for him. He left professional football, got a job as a part-time assistant coach, and got off drugs. "I'm off drugs completely now—maybe a beer now and then, but that's all."[29]

A sports adage goes, "It's not how you play the game, but who your druggist is." Adages both exaggerate reality and contain a bit of truth. This player is an exaggerated extreme—a tragic, idiosyncratic case. The bit of truth is less dramatic but no less important: Drug use is widespread in the sports world.

Drugs Used in Sport

In itself widespread drug use would not be cause for alarm. Some drugs are medicines and all to the good. Some drugs are morally and legally acceptable. Some drugs come in foods and beverages. In fact, we can't imagine a world in which drugs are not widely used. Accordingly, we find it useful to classify drugs by the purpose they supposedly serve for athletes:

Recreational: Meant to be fun and pleasurable.
Restorative: Meant to restore the body to some desired state.
Additive: Meant to stimulate the athlete beyond normal capabilities.

This simple classification, even though it breaks down at times, will suit most of our purposes.

Recreational Drugs.   Cocaine, marijuana, alcohol, and heroin are drugs used for pleasure. One sociologist writes, "The majority of the members of our society use psychoactive drugs (which include alcohol and cigarettes), even though they know drug use involves long-term dangers, because drugs make you feel better."[30] Or as other sociologists write, "humans use drugs because they like the effect that the drugs produce."[31] Unfortunately, no one knows why only some people find drugs pleasurable and addictive.

Restorative Drugs.   Muscle relaxants and anti-inflammatories are examples of restorative drugs. Restorative drugs are frequently medicines and seldom cause a hue and cry, though they occasionally cause mild controversies. For example, applying the drug

---

[29]Story adapted from *New York Times*, August 31, 1980, sec. Y, p. 23. All quotes are from this article, ellipses omitted. © 1980 by The New York Times Company. Reprinted by permission.

[30]Jack D. Douglas, "Existential Sociology," *Existential Sociology*, eds. Jack D. Douglas and John M. Johnson (Cambridge, Great Britain: Cambridge University Press, 1977), pp. 30–31.

[31]Simon Dinitz, Russell R. Dynes, and Alfred C. Clarke, *Deviance: Studies in Definition, Management, and Treatment*, 2nd ed. (New York: Oxford University Press, 1975), p. 197.

DMSO to a swollen muscle or joint supposedly reduces inflammation. Despite medical research questioning its effectiveness, athletes continue bathing their afflicted body parts in DMSO.[32]

Additive Drugs.   Anabolic steroids (for building muscle mass and strength), caffeine, amphetamines, cocaine (for increasing alertness, wakefulness, and quickness), and barbiturates (opposite of amphetamines) are additive drugs. Additives may be common and legal, such as coffee (caffeine) and coke (again, caffeine). Other additives are strictly prohibited.

Most of the controversy over drug abuse concerns prohibited additives. Anabolic steroids are a good illustration. Research shows that steroids do in fact increase strength. They also have severe side effects: damage to liver, kidney, and reproductive organs.[33]

The side effects have not stopped many high-level competitors, though. For years steroids have been commonly taken by athletes in events requiring great strength and mass, such as weight lifting, discus, shotput, and football line play. A physician-athlete who competed in the 1968 Olympics claims that almost every American competitor in weight events used them.[34] Steroid use seems to be spreading from world-level competition on down. A survey shows that during 1971, 15 percent of Arizona State athletes admitted to using steroids; by 1977 the figure had increased to 20 percent.[35]

Traces of steroids remain in the body for a time and at important meets testing has become routine. Not too long ago, an American discus thrower set a world record only to have it disallowed when tests revealed he had been using steroids.[36] To get around the tests, athletes stop using the drug several months before a meet. (Apparently the discus thrower made a mistake in not stopping earlier).

So long as the best athletes in the world use steroids, and tests cannot trace steroids used several months in the past, we anticipate that this drug, or drugs with similar effects, will remain highly popular.

Amphetamines have a different effect: Users claim to feel more alert, less fatigued, and to have quicker reaction time. Amphetamines also produce rage and fearlessness. Studies mostly substantiate these claims.[37] Athletes take amphetamines routinely. Data gathered by a physician working for a professional football team shows that two-thirds of the players occasionally or regularly took them.[38] According to several other star athletes,

---

[32]J. D. Reed, "A Miracle! Or Is it a Mirage?" *Sports Illustrated*, April 20, 1981, pp. 71–75; Barry Tarshis, *DMSO The True Story of a Remarkable Pain Killing Drug* (New York: William Morrow & Co., Inc., 1981).

[33]Michael M. Stone and Harry Lipner, "The Use of Anabolic Steroids in Athletics," *Journal of Drug Issues*, Summer 1980, pp. 351–60.

[34]Jack Scott, "It's Not How You Play the Game, But What Pill You Take," in *Sports and Society*, eds. Robert Lipsyte and Gene Brown (New York: Arnold Press, 1980), p. 182.

[35]Jack V. Toohey, "Non-Medical Drug Use Among Intercollegiate Athletes At Five American Universities," *Bulletin on Narcotics*, 30 (July–September 1978), 63.

[36]*Time*, July 27, 1981, p. 61.

[37]G. Rank Cooter, "Amphetamine Use, Physical Activity and Sport," *Journal of Drug Issues*, Summer 1980, pp. 323–30.

[38]*Science*, 203 (February, 1979), 626.

amphetamine use is common in many sports.[39] Because additives enhance performance, it is hardly surprising to find athletes gobbling them by the dozen.

Blood doping does not involve what we mean by the word *drug* (a drug is any chemical that alters the functioning of the body or mind). We mention it here because the media discusses it as if it were an additive. Long-distance runners, cross-country skiers, and other stamina athletes have tried it. The procedure requires the help of medically trained personnel and goes like this: A few weeks before an important event, 450 to 1200 ml of blood are taken from the athlete and stored. The athlete then continues training and the natural processes of the body replenish the lost blood. Just before the event, the stored blood is transfused back into the athlete, thus increasing the capacity of the blood to carry oxygen and thus increasing stamina. Although blood doping rests on a logical theory, empirical research has not always shown that it works.[40]

With so many drugs around and more being invented all the time; some legal, and others illegal; some helpful medicines, others debilitating narcotics; and with more ways to abuse drugs than there are drugs, the drug problem is thoroughly confusing. Understanding drug use is one of the most difficult problems ever encountered by the social sciences. But difficulty notwithstanding, we should not be too pessimistic. We do know that cultural and structural features of both society and the sportsworld encourage drug use and drug abuse. The first clues for how to handle the drug problem will be found there.

Drugs in Society: History

All drugs used to be legal, but the Harrison Act of 1914 criminalized narcotics (and for a while, the Volstead Act criminalized sale of alcohol). The acts meant that drug users and abusers, who had always been labeled "disreputable" and "perverted," also became labeled "criminal." This state of affairs lasted for several decades.

In the 1950s the situation began changing. Tranquilizers—"peace in a pill"— became popular among the middle class. In the 1960s marijuana became popular, first as the symbol of the new left and then as the new "in thing" among the middle class. By the early 1970s, 11 percent of the adult population had tried marijuana.[41] Hallucinogenic drugs (such as LSD), barbiturates, and amphetamines also became popular. The best of people now popped pills and smoked a little—in addition to drinking alcohol and puffing cigarettes.[42]

With so many drugs in society, you would expect to find drugs in sport. And you do. In a manner of speaking, you cannot escape from drugs. They are everywhere: in high schools and colleges; inner city and suburb; seen on billboards and television; stocked by

---

[39]Jerry Kirschenbaum, "Uppers in Baseball," *Sports Illustrated*, July 21, 1980, p. 11. Also see *Science*, February 1, 1979; and Cooter, "Amphetamine Use."

[40]Melvin H. Williams, "Blood Doping in Sports," *Journal of Drug Issues*, Summer 1980, pp. 331–40.

[41]J. Victor Baldridge, *Sociology: A Critical Approach to Power, Conflict, and Change*, 2nd ed. (New York: John Wiley & Sons, Inc., 1980), p. 168.

[42]For a good discussion of this point, see Edwin M. Shur, *The Politics of Deviance: Stigma Contests and the Uses of Power* (Englewood Cliffs, New Jersey: Prentice-Hall, Inc., 1980).

supermarkets and government-run liquor stores; available from your doctor or your pusher.

Drug Subculture in Sport

Claims a major-league player, "A drug culture exists in baseball."[43] Undoubtedly he is correct. Humans are social creatures, and when athletes are thrown together in the same situation they interact. They form groups and these groups develop values, ideology, norms, and structure. In short, subculture develops.[44]

The subculture of sport is filled with medical and drug-related paraphernalia, knowledge and behaviors. Cultural artifacts of the athlete's daily routine include whirlpool baths, saunas, steam rooms, therapy devices, and the trainer's table piled with bandages, tapes, salves, needles, ointments, and pills. Drugs—medicinal, additive, and recreational—are just another part of the athlete's workaday world: "They're no big deal."

With drugs everywhere—back home, back at the dorm, and in the trainer's room—drug use becomes routine and like all routine subcultural activities, an ideology arises to justify it. Consider the following rationalization: "Big-time sport is all about winning, and if winning requires needles, salves, and pills . . . why not? Why should I be allowed to drink coffee but not take amphetamines? To use hot pads but not DMSO? To relax with a beer but not a barbiturate? Everyone else uses them, why shouldn't I?"

As a professional football player said to a team physician, "Doc, I'm not about to go out there one-on-one against a guy who is grunting and drooling and coming at me with big, dilated pupils unless I'm in the same condition."[45]

This ideology is logical. It recognizes that rules governing drugs are inconsistent and arbitrary. It accepts the value placed on victory, and states an ethic for how to achieve it: "You do what's necessary." The fact that sometimes you have to do what is illegal, or against rules, or against normative practices, does not really matter; "You do what's necessary."

Naturally you must learn how to do what's necessary, including how to enjoy drugs. Anyone who drinks or smokes can tell fond stories of how awful alcohol tasted the first time they tried it, or how sick they got midway through the first cigarette. Enjoying alcohol and nicotine takes practice. So too with virtually all drugs.

A well-known research report describes how marijuana smokers learn the socially acceptable techniques of smoking, how to recognize its effects, the jargon to describe the effects, and the proper responses to the effects. Only after learning, says the article, "was

---

[43] Andre Thornton, quoted in the *Columbus Citizen-Journal*, September 4, 1980, p. 13.

[44] For general sociological statements on deviant subcultures, see Edward Sagarin, *Deviants and Deviance: An Introduction to the Study of Disvalued People and Behavior* (New York: Holt, Rinehart & Winston, 1975), p. 120; Edwin H. Sutherland and Donald R. Cressey, *Principles of Criminology*, 7th ed. (Philadelphia: J. B. Lippincott Company, 1966), chap. 4. Sutherland made the classic statements about the theory of differential association.

[45] Reprinted from "Profootball Fumbles the Drug Scandal" by Arnold J. Mandell, p. 39 in *Psychology Today* magazine, June 1975. Copyright © 1975 Ziff Davis Publishing Co.

it possible for a conception of the drug as object which could be used for pleasure to emerge. Without such a conception marijuana was considered meaningless and did not continue.''[46]

Regarding heroin and morphine, subjects in another study ''indicated that they had to learn to perceive opiates as euphoric, in the face of nausea and other distress, with the help of encouragement and 'instruction' by a friend. The taste for heroin or morphine is an acquired one; to us a frivolous analogy, it is like a taste for olives or oysters.''[47]

We do not acquire our tastes, either for oysters or for drugs, without subcultural supports. Other people help us learn. Usually they are our friends. A former alcoholic and major-league pitcher says, ''I started drinking when I was 16. We were going to a football game and somebody had a bottle of Mogen David blackberry wine. They handed it to me and I said to myself, 'Here goes my turn.' I continued to drink until I was 23.''[48]

Essentially the same episode happens to thousands and thousands of people all the time. It fits a pattern discovered by research: ''A large percentage of alcoholics have had experiences in an all-male society where drinking is a symbol of manliness and group integration, and these experiences appear to have affected their drinking patterns.''[49]

Historically, male sport has cultivated the image of the athlete as macho. Among professional baseball players, beer flows freely and management has no objections, provided drinking does not interfere with performance. ''As long as I could pitch a little, nobody cared that I was getting drunk,'' says another big-league player.[50]

Getting drunk helps, among other things, in handling life on the road. Traveling may be glamorous but it also consists of long, tedious hours in cramped airplanes, eating microwave meals, riding in buses, and sleeping in strange hotel rooms. After the tensions of the game, going back to that can hardly be appealing. What to do? How about a little extra help to relax, to have a good time? How about a drink? How about a sleeping pill? How about a puff?

If our culture and subculture tell us, ''Drugs are ok,'' ''Use drugs,'' we will do what we are told. All our lives we have been socialized to conform. It so happens that athletes find themselves in a more intense drug subculture than most people. And in accord with predictable social behavior, some athletes resist subcultural pressures, most fall in the middle, and a few become extremes.

For extreme abusers, the problem may lie within them. Something psychogenic may be going on. But for the typical drug-using athlete, the problem is outside—in the norms, values, ideology, and structures of American culture and the subculture of sport. The

---

[46]Howard S. Becker, ''Becoming a Marijuana User,'' *American Journal of Sociology*, 59 (November, 1953), 235–43.

[47]Lester Grinspoon and Peter Hedblom, *The Speed Culture*, (Cambridge, Massachusetts: Harvard Univ. Press, 1975), pp. 177–78.

[48]George Vecsey, ''Bob Welch: Young, Talented and An Alcoholic,'' *New York Times*, April 20, 1980, sec. S, p. 1. © 1980 by The New York Times Company. Reprinted by permission.

[49]Reported in Marshall B. Clinard and Robert F. Meier, *Sociology of Deviant Behavior*, 5th ed. (New York: Holt, Reinhart & Winston, 1979), p. 359.

[50]Quoted in George Vecsey, ''Relief Is On Way For Players Who Drink,'' *New York Times*, April 21, 1980, sec. C, p. 9. © 1980 by The New York Times Company. Reprinted by permission.

typical user is not a deviant in a "normal" subculture but a conformist in a "deviant" one.

What makes drugs deviant is prohibition by governing bodies, as well as the confused morality regarding getting pleasure from chemicals. As moral issues slowly get resolved, drug use will become less and less deviant. We do not anticipate going back to the days before the Harrison Act when all drugs were legal, but we do anticipate that the moral taint will eventually fade from recreational drugs. Restoratives are already mostly noncontroversial, and so acceptance of recreational drugs will leave only additive drugs as a problem. We expect that problem to continue.

We doubt if additives will be accepted by the ruling bodies of sport in our lifetimes. The notion that sport should reflect the pure effort of body and mind is built into our value system. As testing becomes more sophisticated and practicable, additives will become more and more difficult to get away with. However, the final outcome will be determined by the race between the development of tests and the development of undetectable additives. We hesitate to predict how that technological race will come out.

GAMBLING AND BRIBERY

Baseball.   The most famous incident of sports gambling and bribery is the Black Sox Scandal of 1920.

> **Say It Ain't So, Joe.**   In 1919 the Cincinnati Reds upset the Chicago White Sox (soon to be called "Black Sox") to win the World Series. A year later rumors of a fix started circulating.
> According to a *New York Times* story of September 29, 1920, this is what happened: "Seven star players of the Chicago White Sox and one former player were indicted late this afternoon charged with complicity in a conspiracy with gamblers to 'fix' the 1919 series. The indictments were based on evidence obtained for the Cook County Grand Jury by Charles A. Comiskey, owner of the White Sox, and after confessions by two of the players told how the world championship was thrown to Cincinnati, and how they had received money or were 'double-crossed' by the gamblers."[51]
> An enduring sports myth formed around the Black Sox scandal. As "Shoeless" Joe Jackson, one of the accused players, came out of the Grand Jury hearing, a little boy rushed up to him and tearfully pleaded, "Say it ain't so, Joe. Say it ain't so."

Even though the accused players were found innocent in a court of law, the Commissioner of Baseball, Judge Kenesaw Mountain Landis (recall Chapter 8) summarily banned them for life. Landis perceived the scandal as an outbreak of a lingering disease, gambling. He vowed to wipe it out.

Throughout his tenure, Landis continued to ban suspected players. Just after the Black Sox scandal, he imposed a lifetime ban on a player who allegedly associated with gamblers; and then another player for the same reason, also for life; and then two players

---

[51]*New York Times*, September 29, 1920; reproduced in Gene Brown, ed., *Encyclopedia of Sports*, (New York: Arno Press, 1979), II: 25.

for supposedly being involved in gambling. In 1926 two baseball giants, Tris Speaker and Ty Cobb, suddenly resigned from their teams under suspicious circumstances. Landis then said they had been permitted to resign because of gambling accusations. During the same period, Landis fought with several owners and players over owning and betting on horses. In 1943, he banned the owner of the Philadelphia Phillies for betting on his own team.

Football.   Later, after World War II, professional football followed the Landis approach to controlling gambling. Four gamblers unsuccessfully tried to fix the NFL's championship game of 1946 by offering bribes to two players. Neither player accepted the offer but when the gamblers were convicted in court, the commissioner of the NFL suspended the players indefinitely for actions detrimental to the National Football League and to professional football. The suspension effectively ended their careers.

During the early 1960s, several players from various NFL teams established questionable relations with gambling interests. Two star players, one from the Lions and the other from the Packers, consorted with known gamblers and occasionally laid down bets (but never against their own teams). The commissioner banned them indefinitely, fined five other involved players $2,000, and fined one of the clubs $2,000 for not taking appropriate action. The two players were reinstated eleven months later.

College Basketball.   Gambling influences have also reached into college sports. Since World War II, fixing scandals have repeatedly broken out in basketball, causing much furor and anguish.

> **Surprise.**   In 1945 New York police who were staking out the home of a suspected criminal spied two young men about to enter the premises. The police confronted them and, surprisingly, discovered they were basketball players from Brooklyn College. The players later revealed they had been given $1,000 to split among five other players for dumping an upcoming game against Akron.
>
> Subsequently the gambler and his associate were convicted of conspiring to cheat and defraud, and were sentenced to a year in jail and a $500 fine. No legal charges were brought against the players, though Brooklyn College did expel them (or more accurately, expelled four; it was discovered that the fifth player had never bothered to enroll).[52]

In the late 1940s another basketball fix scandal came out. Gamblers asked a player at George Washington University to shave points. The player went to the police and the gamblers were caught and sentenced to two-and-a-half years in jail.

In 1950, a CCNY player reported that his teammates were taking bribes. Investigators traced out a long thread of scandal. It eventually turned out that from 1947 to 1950, thirty-two players in schools across the country had been involved in fixing eighty-six games. Fourteen gamblers were convicted.[53]

---

[52]George Gipe, *The Great American Sports Book* (Garden City, New York: Doubleday & Company, Inc., 1978, p. 27).

[53]Gipe, *The Great*, pp. 27–28. Also see Charles Rosen, *Scandals of '51: How the Gamblers Almost Killed College Basketball* (New York: Holt, Rinehart & Winston, 1978); Stanley Cohen, *The Game They Played* (New York: Farrar, Straus & Giroux, 1977).

Ten years later, attempts to bribe players at Seton Hall University and the University of Connecticut resulted in the arrests of two gamblers. One part of the investigation led to another and over the next two years the scandal touched St. Joseph's, La Salle, the University of North Carolina, the University of Tennessee, Mississippi State, North Carolina State, St. John's, NYU, Bradley, Dayton, University of Iowa, Bowling Green, University of Detroit, and University of Oregon. When it was over, at least fifty players from twenty-seven schools had been implicated.[54]

In 1981, four gamblers and one basketball player from Boston College were involved in a point-shaving scheme and convicted of conspiring to engage in racketeering and sports bribery. The guilty player made sports and legal history of a sort: He became the first and only college basketball athlete ever convicted in a fixing scheme. He received a ten-year prison sentence. The judge who sentenced him said, "A substantial term of incarceration imposed on this defendant will be recalled in the future by another college athlete who may be tempted to compromise his performance." Commented one coach, "A murderer will get that kind of sentence."[55]

These basketball scandals have become part of the lore of sport; and journalists and sports scholars still discuss them. Nevertheless the amount of discussion seems out of proportion to the size of the problem. For instance, since 1970 fewer than a dozen persons have been convicted under the federal sports bribery statute, a law passed in the aftermath of the 1950s basketball scandals. According to a survey done for the Federal Commission on Gambling, college athletic directors, football coaches, and basketball coaches say that very few gambling-related incidents occur among their athletes. The research concludes, "Gambling and bribery do not constitute a major problem for college athletics at present. Very few gambling or corruption incidents have occurred in the past decade and most respondents do not view the current gambling situation as a serious one for athletic programs."[56]

The same may be said about professional team sports. Organized baseball has not had a serious gambling scandal since the 1940s; football since the 1960s. And, as far as we know, fixing has not been a problem in professional basketball, golf, tennis, or hockey.

With some exceptions noted later, gambling is not a major problem in sport. You might reasonably ask, Why not? Considering the money involved, and the seeming ease of fixing athletes, you would expect gambling corruption to be the norm rather than the exception. Why hasn't gambling taken a permanent foothold in sport? Why aren't there more fixes? more scams? more people corrupted?

When looking closely, you can see several features of sport which make it relatively immune to gambling influences.

---

[54]Cohen, *The Game* pp. 226–38.

[55]*New York Times*, November 24, 1981, p. 25; Quotes are from J. Kirschenbaum, "Setting Examples," *Sports Illustrated*, February 15, 1982, p. 9.

[56]Kathleen M. Joyce, "Sports Betting and College Athletics," *Commission on The Review of the National Policy Toward Gambling*, Appendix I (Washington, D.C.: U.S. Government Printing Office, 1976), p. 312.

Gambling as Recreation

More people bet on professional football than any other team sport, followed by college football and basketball.[57] The typical sports bettor can be described as a white male, between the ages of eighteen and forty-four, with some college education, earning a middle-class income, a person who gambles primarily for social rewards.[58]

One study shows how this works. A group of bettors would customarily gather in a tavern before a game. Though they did most of their betting with bookies, they also occasionally wagered among themselves. Their expertise in picking teams, knowing the fine points of betting, placing large bets; their generosity (buying drinks), and showing a masculine image all combined to give the successful bettor high status within the group. Status was the major reward, not money.[59]

These people hardly fit the stereotype of malevolent gangsters threatening to break your legs with a lead pipe; nor are they likely to be involved in fixing. Successfully fixing a major sports event requires professional expertise, money, and the willingness to go to jail if caught. The typical sports bettor has no interest in any of that.

Thus statistics on the number of people who gamble on team sports (perhaps one out of ten adult males), can give a false impression.[60] Hordes of people are not trying to get in on a fix, let alone mastermind one.

Gambling as Business

Fixing runs afoul of another problem. Those professionals who handle bets, the bookmakers, have as much to lose from corruption as those who place the bets. Bookies engage in the business of handling bets for a percentage of the wager (called the "juice" or "vigorish"). They collect their juice no matter who wins.

Bookmakers seldom gamble. They are businessmen; and like all businessmen, they want to minimize risk while maximizing gain. This occurs when they transfer money from the winning party to the losing party, minus their percentage. Weighing the potential gain against the risks, the typical bookie, like the typical bettor, has little inclination to fix a game.[61]

Criminologists say that sure, quick (and perhaps harsh) punishments deter crime.[62] We have no way of knowing about surety—that is, how often someone fixes an event and does not get punished—but we know severe punishments have always followed the slightest hint of gambling scandal. Lifetime bans, jail sentences, fines, and expulsions have been routinely dealt out and without much regard for judicial procedures.

---

[57]Joyce, "Sports Betting and College Athletics," pp. 301–350.

[58]*Final Report of the Commission on the Review of the National Policy Toward Gambling*, Charles H. Morin (Chair), (Washington, D.C.: U.S. Government Printing Office, 1976), p. 175.

[59]R. Terry Furst, "Some Factors and Observations on the Upsurge in Gambling on Spectator Team Sports," in *Images of Crime: Offenders and Victims*, eds. Terence P. Thornberry and Edward Sagarin (New York: Holt, Rinehart & Winston, 1974), pp. 47–56.

[60]Reported in Joyce, "Sports Betting and College Athletics," pp. 301–350.

[61]See, *Final Report*, pp. 173–76.

[62]Harold G. Grasmick and George J. Bryjak, "The Relevant Effect of Perceived Severity of Punishment," *Social Forces*, 59 (December 1980), 474–91.

This places professional athletes in a position to lose a great deal. They earn upward from a $100,000 salary, get liberal fringe benefits, have chances for lucrative endorsements and opportunities for good second careers. With that much to lose, why take a bribe of a few thousand dollars?

And money aside, they will be stigmatized. Will teammates ever completely trust them again? Will coaches want them on their teams? Will sponsors pay them to endorse their products? Perhaps not for a long time, perhaps never. One of the football players suspended for laying bets in the 1960s incident lost $50,000 worth of advertising endorsements as a result; and over twenty years later, he lost an opportunity to be a TV commentator for college football games because the NCAA felt his reputation would dirty the image of the sport.[63]

Some sports are difficult to fix for mechanical reasons. To fix a team sport requires bribing several athletes. The more players involved, the more likely that the secret will leak out. Even if the secret does not leak out, the fixed athletes must be good enough actors to fool knowledgeable observers: the other players, the coaches, the press, and the fans. Such acting talent is uncommon. And if they do fool the observers, the athletes make themselves look bad. Too many flubs and mistakes and they will be out of a job. Furthermore no matter what the fixed athletes do, their "best" effort may still fail. Balls take funny bounces, athletes unaware of the fix make heroic plays. In the 1981 basketball incidents, bribed players succeeded in only two of five games.

Sports bribery, by and large, is not as common as one might believe. This is because the typical bettor and the typical bookmaker have little reason to fix a game; the professional athlete already earns a high salary and liberal fringe benefits; punishments are severe; and several mechanical features of team sports make games difficult to successfully fix. Not all sports are team sports, of course, and some sports attract a great deal of wagering and may be relatively easy to fix. The prime examples are horse racing and boxing.

Horse Racing.   Horse racing has always been troubled by bribery. A sports historian describes nineteenth-century racing: "Corruption in racing was chronic; trickery and deceit were inseparable from the conduct of the sport. . . . As for the jockeys! Interfering with other horses was common, and so were other flagrant abuses: pulling a horse up short of the finish line; getting off to a slow start; riding erratically . . ."[64]

Recently an eight-year investigation revealed some fifty races had been fixed by jockeys at Aqueduct Race Track, Belmont Park, and Sarasota Race Track during the mid-1970s.[65] The principal gambler claimed he had fixed 500 races in thirty-nine states.[66] Because of lack of legal evidence, no criminal indictments of jockeys resulted.

Without good statistics, we cannot know how much the situation has improved over

[63]Jerry Kirschenbaum, "The NCAA Squeezes the Tube," *Sports Illustrated*, April 26, 1982, p. 12.

[64]From *Sportsmen and Games* by John Dizikes, pp. 133–134. Copyright © 1981 by John Dizikes. Reprinted by permission of Houghton Mifflin Company.

[65]*New York Times*, March 3, 1982, p. 1; April 3, 1982, sec. Y, p. 14.

[66]Bill Surface, "Racing's Big Scandal," *Sports Illustrated*, November 6, 1978, pp. 26–31.

the years, if any. Considering the thousands of races that go on all over the country, all we can say is that if fixing is common, it is being well covered up.

Boxing.   Like horse racing, boxing matches are relatively easy to fix. A fighter can fake a knockout because only he knows how hard a punch lands—but some skill is required. We recall the controversy over Muhammed Ali's knockout of Sonny Liston in their second fight. One reporter described Ali's punch as "innocuous" and "grazing." When Liston went down, the referee could hardly believe it.[67]

Many, many fixes have taken place in boxing, but new economic circumstances and changes in organization have fairly well done away with the simple out-and-out fix. Much more money can be made from scams: crooked financing, shady legal deals, falsified records, and organizational cheating.

No single authority governs boxing and the two organizations that supposedly do (the World Boxing Association and the World Boxing Council) continually fight each other. Both organizations have less than outstanding leadership, and both have close ties with a handful of promoters who control most of the world's best fighters. Those promoters, in turn, are notorious for lying, cheating, and stealing.[68]

In one recent episode, ABC television cosponsored a boxing tournament with one of these promoters. ABC televised several matches from the aircraft carrier *Lexington*. But when it came out that falsified rankings had been given to certain boxers—one who hadn't fought in over a year suddenly appeared as the number three contender—ABC cancelled. In another episode, a promoter set up a boxing organization on paper and then embezzled $21.3 million from the Wells Fargo Bank.

The old-fashioned fix involving thousands of dollars pales in comparison to the multimillion dollar corruption now possible. We suspect that this form of deviance will become increasingly popular in the future.

Gambling in Society

Gambling is a multibillion dollar industry composed of legal gambling (parimutuel betting, casino games in Nevada and Atlantic City, church-sponsored bingo nights, state lotteries); and illegal gambling (numbers rackets, football spot cards, office World Series pools). It has been estimated that both legal and illegal gambling generate profits larger than the combined profits of the hundred largest manufacturers in the United States.[69]

The difference between buying a football card from a local bookie and buying stocks from a Wall Street broker lies in cultural definitions of worthiness. American culture defines one act as disreputable and illegal, the other as an investment and praiseworthy.

---

[67]Harry Carpenter, *Boxing: A Pictorial History* (Chicago: Henry Regnery Company, 1975), p. 132.

[68]One of them once told a reporter some factual information and the next day, said exactly the opposite. When the reporter brought up this discrepancy, the promoter said, in all seriousness, "Yesterday I was lying, today I'm telling the truth." Quoted in *The New York Times*, September 6, 1981, p. 22. © 1981 by The New York Times Company. Reprinted by permission.

[69]Reported in Paul B. Horton and Gerald R. Leslie, *The Sociology of Social Problems*, 5th ed., (Englewood Cliffs, New Jersey: Prentice-Hall, Inc., 1974), p. 547.

Both are gambles. At some point, says a text, "gambling becomes truly indistinguishable from the normal involvement with elements of chance that is a part of living itself."[70]

As long as society condones (or does not strongly resist) gambling, and as long as billions of dollars continue to be wagered on sports events by millions of average, middle-class, "respectable" people, fixes will occasionally take place. The sheer volume of dollars, gamblers, and opportunities guarantees it. And so long as the problem does not get out of hand—and sport has managed to control it fairly well—the current situation will not radically change.

SUMMARY

1. Deviance covers a wide variety of behaviors. The chapter emphasizes how society and the institution of sport produce opportunities and pressures for individuals to become deviant.
2. Cheating goes on routinely in sport but not all cheating is "serious." Currently, the most serious cheating concerns recruiting violations. It has been a problem for many years. Big-time intercollegiate sport is organized in such a way to produce enormous pressures leading to cheating:
   a. Victory is highly rewarded.
   b. High-level administrators sometimes condone bending the rules.
   c. Ideology easily rationalizes cheating.
   d. The high demand for blue-chip athletes leads to offering illegal inducements.
   e. No one involved in cheating is likely to blow the whistle on anyone else.
   f. Financial pressures to produce winners are great.
   g. Booster clubs are hard to control.
   h. The NCAA does little.
3. The system of intercollegiate sport has not been successful in combatting cheating. The NCAA is controlled by member schools, many of which have and are involved in cheating. The NCAA obtains much of its revenues from the performances of these schools on television.
4. Drugs are widely used in both society and sport. Of the three types of drugs (recreational, restorative, and additive), additives cause the most controversy. Most additive drugs have been banned from sport; nevertheless athletes routinely use them. Sport supports a drug subculture:
   a. Medicines and drugs are routine parts of the athlete's life.
   b. An ideology supports drug use.
   c. Socialization into drugs takes place conveniently in the sports world.
   d. The macho lifestyle and the loneliness of the road contribute to drug use.
5. Sporadically sport has been beset by attempts to fix outcomes. In baseball the Black

---

[70]Ibid., p. 545.

Sox Scandal was the most famous incident; in football during the 1960s several cases came to light; and in college sport, basketball-fixing scandals have broken out about once a decade since World War II. Nevertheless, the incidence of fixing is probably not very high, for several reasons:

  a. The typical sports bettor gambles for social rather than economic reasons, and comes from a nondeviant background.
  b. Bookmakers stand to gain little from fixing games.
  c. Punishments (bannings, fines, expulsions) have been meted out on even the slightest suspicions of gambling involvement.
  d. Professional athletes have much to lose and relatively little to gain from taking a bribe.
  e. Team sports are difficult to fix on mechanical grounds.

6. Horse races and boxing matches have probably been the sports most often fixed. They are individual sports and, as a result, fewer people need to be bribed. However, the boxing fix may be obsolete. Much more money can be made by organizational scamming.

7. Sport will always be troubled by gambling so long as gambling goes on in society; and there is no indication that gambling is on the decline. However, the amount of sports bribery and related incidents will remain relatively low.

13

VIOLENCE AND SPORT
Old, Honorable, and Legitimate

Arthur Sheppard's painting of a wrestling match, circa 1825, captures some of the intensity of violent combat, and reminds us that violence in sport is not a recent development. The roaring of the crowd adds to the atmosphere of violence. Courtesy of the Library of Congress.

A Game of Basketball. During a game between two major college teams, one team's center accidentally tripped. A player from the other team offered his hand to help pull the center up; as he came up, the helping player jerked him forward and kneed him in the groin. The center collapsed to the floor in pain. As he lay there, another opposing player stomped on his head and body. A wild melee of teams and fans then erupted.

When officials restored order, the injured player was taken to the hospital with lacerations and bruises about the face. He did recover, fortunately; and the league later took disciplinary action against the offending players.[1]

Did the attack just described repulse you? We suspect most people would be repulsed—the incident was one of the most flagrant and coldblooded of recent times. Were you also, in some sense of the word, "interested" in it? Again, we suspect most people would be—violence is news. The press prominently mentioned this incident and showed film clips of what happened on television.

Being both interested and repulsed by violence seems to be a characteristic of the times. The United States has been described as a consumer society and we consume violence in huge quantities. One Saturday morning the Woody Woodpecker Cartoon Show depicted "ten general beatings, three fist fights (or kicks), nineteen assaults with instruments or objects; one strangling; six assaults with moving objects or vehicles; six falls or collisions; nine disasters, explosions or cave-ins; and seven [other acts of violence, including various forms of cooking live animals]."[2]

"Monday Night Football" ranks among the most successful TV programs ever produced for prime-time viewing, and we all know that football is a violent game. But the issue has subtle nuances. "The Wednesday Night Fights" showed violence par excellence, and "Roller Derby" demonstrated violence par absurd; yet both lost their television ratings. Televised hockey failed outright.

The most popular and enduring television shows are often comedies. "I Love Lucy" has been on the air for over two decades. Of course much of what Lucy does may be violent, such as banging into people, dropping pots on toes, and scaring Rickey, Fred, and Ethel half to death. Sometimes it's difficult to know whether to laugh or cry. "I went to a fight the other night," comedian Rodney Dangerfield said, "and a hockey game broke out."[3]

As the issue of violence grows in society, so the issue echoes in sport. Sportswriters and sports fans now cry out that injuries are excessive, that they're unnecessary and brutal. Sport, critics charge, is degenerating into mayhem and something must be done before it is too late.

Throughout this chapter "violence" will mean an act deliberately intended to cause mental or physical pain to another person. This definition excludes accidents, because they happen without deliberate intent on anybody's part. For example, when two members

---

[1]For a description of this game and its aftermath, see William F. Reed, "An Ugly Affair in Minneapolis," *Sports Illustrated*, February 7, 1972, p. 18.

[2]Timothy Curry and Alfred Clarke, *Introducing Visual Sociology* (Dubuque, Iowa: Kendall/Hunt Publishing Company, 1978), p. 31.

[3]As quoted in *Sports Illustrated*, September 18, 1978, p. 102.

of the ten-woman expedition scaling Mount Annapurna, fell to their deaths, that was accidental—tragic, heroic, sad—but not violent. Some sports are just downright dangerous: One out of four racers who have competed in the Indianapolis 500 have eventually died in a race-car crash.[4]

EXPLANATIONS FOR VIOLENCE IN SPORT

Biological Explanation: Savage Genes?

By far the largest number of sociologists advocate social explanations for violence. But we need to discuss biological explanations because they have become popular in some circles of the scientific community.

Konrad Lorenz, who won a Nobel prize for his work in ethology, argues that even though centuries and centuries of cultural development separate modern humans from their primordial ancestors, an instinctual urge towards aggression remains part of human biological makeup. These urges accumulate until they reach a critical level, and then erupt into violence. Once discharged, tensions vanish until the next accumulation reaches the critical level, then discharges, and so on.

We cannot escape our genetically inspired urge to be aggressive, argues Lorenz. Biology traps us. However, we can take corrective action. The aggressive discharge can be channeled into socially acceptable paths. We can have "constructive" aggressions, or if not constructive, at least not destructive. Sport is one socially approved channel for the gush of aggressive behavior. Lorenz claims that sport originated in "highly ritualized but still serious hostile fighting," and is a "specifically human form of nonhostile combat."[5] This is called the *drive-discharge theory*.

On the surface drive-discharge seems like a reasonable explanation for violence in general and sports violence in particular. Unfortunately, it doesn't fare too well when examined closely. One well-known study examined a sample of twenty preliterate societies, drawing information from various ethnographic writings and noting whether the society engaged in combative sports. Ten of the societies were warlike and the other ten peaceful. If drive-discharge theory is correct, then warlike societies should not have much in the way of combative sports. War, being so massively aggressive, ought to discharge accumulated aggressions and render combative sports unnecessary. The study found that eight of the ten warlike societies engaged in combative sports but only two of the ten peaceful societies did so. Contrary to drive-discharge theory, war and combative sports went together more often than not.[6]

---

[4]Arlene Blum, "Triumph and Tragedy on Annapurna," *National Geographic*, 155 (March, 1979), 295–311; *Time*, May 31, 1982, p. 71.

[5]Konrad Lonrenz, *On Aggression*, trans. Marjorie Kerr Wilson (New York: Harcourt Brace Jovanovich, Inc., 1963), p. 271. Also see Philip Goodhart and Christopher Chataway, *War Without Weapons* (London: W. H. Allen, 1968), chap. 6.

[6]Richard G. Sipes, "War, Sports and Aggression: An Empirical Test of Two Rival Theories," *American Anthropologist*, 75 (January 1973), 64–80. Also see Don Atyeo, *Blood and Guts: Violence in Sports* (New York: Paddington Press, 1979), chap. 8.

Other evidence outside the realm of sport also contradicts drive-discharge theory. For developed nations, violent crime rates increase after major wars; one aggressive behavior does not discharge the other.[7]

Even biologically oriented disciplines criticize drive-discharge theory. For example, a leading sociobiologist advocates a theory involving the interplay between people's genetic endowment and what they learn from their culture. He calls this the "cultural pattern model": culture can control and modify genetically determined aggression. As rational human beings, we determine how and when to conduct violence. In other words, culture overlays a genetic foundation.[8]

Both drive-discharge theory and the cultural-pattern model assume that genes transmit aggressive impulses but that culture can render the aggression safe. A few sociologists might agree with this general argument, but not many.[9] There is no proof that the accumulated aggressions come from biological sources. Friends, family, or work—social sources—could just as well cause the tensions. At the very broadest level we believe that violence comes from a violent society and not from violent genes. So to understand why there is violence in sport we must first understand society.

Cultural Explanation: Savage Society?

Chapter 2 (history) showed how violent many early American sports were (for example, eye-gouging and shooting contests). Now we need to make a point explicitly: In some instances, violence *is* sport. (We have already discussed how almost any physical activity can be transformed into a formal sport. That also applies to violence.) Boxing, an old sport, and KO karate, a new one, document this point.[10]

Boxing.   Boxing is legitimate rational violence raised to a formal sport. It used to be much more violent. Ancient Greek and Roman fighters wrapped their fists with rawhide strips, and sometimes added metal spikes and lead weights. Legend has it that in a career spanning more than twenty years, Theagenes of Thasos won 1,400 championships and in the process killed more than 800 opponents. He also participated in the *pancratium*, a contest featuring slugging, kicking, hair pulling, eye gouging, finger breaking, strangling, and no time limit. Contestants fought until one would not or could not continue.

Modern boxing, however, did not start until the eighteenth century in Great Britain and the United States. By today's standards, the contests were primitive. Fighters used bare knuckles and could throw the opponent to the ground and fall on his chest (to knock out his wind). The round ended when one contestant went down. After a brief rest, if a

---

[7]Dane Archer and Rosemary Gartner, "Violent Acts and Violent Times: A Comparative Approach to Postwar Homicide Rates," *American Sociological Review*, 41 (December 1976), 937–62.

[8]Edward O. Wilson, *On Human Nature* (Cambridge: Harvard University Press, 1978).

[9]See, for example, Pierre L. Van den Berghe, "Bringing Beasts Back In: Toward a Biosocial Theory of Aggression," *American Sociological Review*, 39 (December 1974), 777–88.

[10]See John V. Gromback, *The Saga of the Fist: The 9,000 Year Story of Boxing in Texts and Pictures* (South Brunswick and New York: A. J. Barnes, 1977); Harry Carpenter, *Boxing: A Pictorial History* (Chicago: Henry Regnery Company, 1975).

boxer could not walk to the scratch line in the middle of the ring, he lost the bout because "he wasn't up to scratch."

All during this period rules continually changed, but they still made for long bloody bouts. In 1860, Heenan, of the United States, and Sayers, the British champion, fought a classic battle. Sayers went down twenty-five times but still managed to pound Heenan's eyes until Heenan could not see. After two hours and twenty minutes police broke up the fight, the crowd stormed the ring in protest, and the referee declared a draw. This fight has historical importance because it became the focal point for public outrage over boxing. It was condemned in the House of Parliament.

Trying to make boxing less bloody and more acceptable to the public, the London Amateur Athletics Club sponsored the so-called Queensberry rules, which, when finally adopted near the end of the nineteenth century, produced the sport we know today. Another organization, the London Sport Club, also supported boxing and tried to enforce standardized rules, primarily to facilitate betting. This club also conducted many legal suits to establish the principle that if one boxer accidentally kills another in the ring, it is not homicide.

KO Karate.   KO karate (full-contact karate) is a more recent sport. It further illustrates that sometimes violence *is* sport. As originally practiced in the Far East, karate was an art. Masters judged students by how well they performed preplanned, highly stylized movements resembling a dance *(kata)*. Formal competition as known in Western sport did not exist.

After World War II, as karate gradually became popular in the United States, Western sportlike elements were added. Sparring became accepted and was organized into structured competition. The rules still limited contact—punches and kicks had to be pulled and too much contact resulted in disqualification. The next step followed naturally. Rules changed to permit full contact with kicks and punches (with gloves); and rounds were introduced with referees, judges, and point scoring. All this required organization, and bureaucracies to govern KO karate were formed. The art of symbolic violence as expressed in the *kata* was now a full-fledged sport.

Other Combative Sports.   In contrast to boxing and KO karate, other combative sports had the opposite cultural history: limited or symbolic violence replaced outright physical violence. College wrestling exemplifies this. College wrestling bars dangerous techniques such as twisting joints beyond certain angles, striking with the fist, and choking. Rather than to deliberately hurt the opponent, the goal is to pin the opponent or to earn more points by taking him down, escaping, or holding him in a disadvantageous position. This does not mean that wrestling isn't physically taxing or without injury; but it does mean that an opponent can be vanquished without maiming or killing.

There are examples besides wrestling. Fencing used to be deadly but now the rules and equipment make it safe. Hits only symbolize kills. Target shooting—pistol, rifle, skeet, and trap—is another example, as is archery.

The fact that sometimes violence *is* sport, leads to this conclusion: For such sports the only way you could get rid of the violence would be to get rid of the sport; or what is effectively the same, to transform that sport so radically as to make it unrecognizable. (Boxing without punching would not be boxing.) Neither outcome is likely, although we suspect that some people do want to outlaw boxing but cannot find widespread support. One prestigious group, physicians, did call for a ban on boxing in light of recent evidence showing that fighters suffer from large amounts of brain damage.[11] Symbolic violence as sport (such as shooting and fencing) are not issues at all.

You may well object to violence as sport. Yet American society as a whole approves it. In this approval, American society is not unique. Violence exists in all known societies, especially industrial ones. The truly nonviolent society is a myth. No one knows why this is so, but it is.[12]

Perhaps in the case of the United States it has something to do with the frontier experience.[13] The frontier period only recently ended and will not be soon forgotten. Television, motion pictures, and literature tell and retell the heroic tales of "How the West Was Won."

The culture of the frontier extolled individual ruggedness—the belief that people, essentially on their own, bear the ultimate responsibility for overcoming adversity. Given the harshness and barrenness of the frontier, living in accordance with this value might have been necessary, calling forth ingenuity, courage, resourcefulness, and hard work.

The frontier had an ugly side too—gun fights, range wars, outlawry, and vigilantism; race prejudice and religious intolerance; genocide of Indians, mass slaughter of wild animals, and wholesale degradation of the land. Many, perhaps most, of these positive and negative cultural elements form a part of our current culture in one form or another.

This cultural heritage provides a very basic and very broad explanation for violence in American sport. It is a backdrop against which the action takes place. But the action itself, sports violence, needs close examination. Not all violence is the same. Some violence is mayhem and some violence is not.

Aggro.   Modern sport sanctions only a specific kind of violence—violence with form, pattern, rules, and most important, limits. This kind of violence is called "aggro" and can be found in many cultures, both modern and preliterate, and in many contexts.[14] Here is an example.

   Mayhem versus Aggro.   The Yanomamo are a small group of Indians, ten thousand or so, living in the jungle near the Brazilian-Venezuelan border. Their life is organized around warfare between villages, interspersed with short periods

---

[11]John Noble Wilford, "Physicians Journal Calls for Ban on Boxing," *New York Times*, January 14, 1983, p. 1.

[12]Examples purportedly to the contrary (the Pueblo Indians, the Eskimo, the Kung) notwithstanding. Close scrutiny has shown that these groups are far from nonviolent. See, Robin Fox, *Encounter With Anthropology* (New York: Harcourt Brace Jovanovich, Inc., 1973), chap. 7.

[13]Richard Maxwell Brown, "Historical Patterns of Violence in America"; Joe B. Franz, "The Frontier Tradition: An Invitation to Violence"; Richard Maxwell Brown, "The American Vigilante Tradition," in *Violence in America*, eds. Hugh Davis Graham and Ted Robert Gurr (New York: Bantam Books, Inc., 1969).

[14]Peter Marsh, *Aggro: The Illusion of Violence* (London: J. M. Dent & Sons, Ltd., 1978). See also Peter Marsh, Elizabeth Roser, and Rom Hare, *The Rules of Disorder* (London: Rutledge and Kegan Paul, 1978).

of peace. During peacetime, males from separate villages often gather for a feast.

After eating, arguments usually break out with each side accusing the other of gluttony and theft. As verbal exchanges grow heated, warriors brandish their weapons preluding the "chest-pounding duel."

In this contest, a man from each village steps forth. One bares his chest and stands in a braced position. The other looks him over carefully, winds up his fist much like a baseball pitcher, and then punches him on the chest with full force.

An anthropologist who saw several matches, said that when a man went down, the victor would dance around his victim in little circles, waving his hands in the air, exulting and taunting.

Unfortunately for the victor, he could not quit. If he tried to leave, the crowd would roughly push him back in the circle to await his turn at taking blows. If he gave a number of blows, he was then obligated to receive the same number of blows from a fresh fighter, or lose the match.[15]

Even though the blows cause serious damage (fighters cough up blood for days afterward), contestants fight under well-established customs: They take turns, hit only certain parts of the body, and victory comes not by killing an opponent but from making him give up. All participants abide by these customs and will enforce them even against members of their own village.

In a similar way, modern sport is not a "war of all against all" on a playing field. This is so because most of the time sports violence has rituals, unwritten rules, form, and limits. Most sports violence is aggro. You have probably watched a hockey game on TV and seen something like this:

Cooler Heads. The game is going smoothly when suddenly two players begin pushing and shoving. They throw punches, hitting each other on the helmet and shoulder pads. Teammates quickly grab and restrain them. Players along the sidelines charge onto the ice. Referees come up blowing their whistles, trying to restore order. When it's over, the announcer says, "Cooler heads have prevailed." Order is restored. The game continues.

We submit that none of the cooler heads restored order. The fight was already orderly; it was ritualized. It was, in short, aggro. A study of hockey fights documents the rituals. The dropping of gloves, for example, serves as a challenge. So long as gloves are not dropped, the challenge can be refused and the challenged party can skate away without dishonor. But once the gloves come off, skating away symbolizes that the offender is a cheap-shot artist and afraid to face his opponent in a fair fight. Few challenges get refused.

The fight itself has unwritten rules of fairness, and limits to viciousness. Why not use the stick—an excellent weapon? Why not kick your opponent in the groin with your skates rather than try to punch him on the face and risk breaking your hand on his helmet? Why allow your teammates to break up the fight in the first place? It is because once the aggressiveness and dominance of each player has been reestablished and honor restored,

---

[15]Napoleon A. Chagnon, *Yanomamo: The Fierce People*, 2nd ed. (New York: Holt, Rinehart & Winston, 1977), pp. 113–22.

the purpose of the violence disappears.[16] By ritualizing violence, it becomes an instrumental and useful tool.

The rational usefulness of aggro has received other scientific documentation. A study of college hockey finds that aggressive players (as measured by penalties assessed against them for fighting, elbowing, high sticking, and the like), score more goals and have more assists than less aggressive players.[17]

This result would not surprise sports observers and participants. They have long maintained that violence is instrumental. Concerning football, one sports writer says, "None of the rule changes have eliminated *fear* as the basic ingredient of pass defense."[18]

Violence may be instrumental even in such genteel a game as tennis. One champion, who deliberately tries to hit his opponents at the net, says, "Most of the opponents, they just get a little scared and they back up and they don't come that close to the net, so you can get better angles for passing shots."[19]

Aggro in sports thus goes beyond any naive desire to display machismo. While that might be part of it, we emphasize instrumentality. Certain kinds of violence help produce certain kinds of outcomes, either directly or indirectly. Or more generally, we conclude: Ritualized violence is rewarding. That is why so much is found in sport.

THE EFFECTS OF SOCIALIZATION

Learning Aggression

Because it is rewarding, somewhere along the way large doses of aggression and the willingness to hurt, and be hurt, get injected into players. People must be socialized into being athletes—a process involving both selection of those with potential and the teaching of techniques, attitudes, and motivation. Learning how to use violence is as much a part of the socialization process as anything else.

A former college football player explains the importance of learning to hit: "For five straight days all the linebackers did was head-on tackling. At the end of the first day there were a couple of broken bones, a broken nose, and a brain concussion. . . . But when this contact stopped, things had been completely rearranged. . . . I was easily granted superiority [by teammates].[20]

Says a professional player: "I had to work very hard to be aggressive. I used to have

---

[16]Kenneth Colburn, Jr., reported in *Psychology Today*, February 1981, p. 16.

[17]John F. McCarthy and Bryan R. Kelly, "Aggressive Performance and Its Effect on Performance Over Time in Ice-Hockey Athletes: An Archival Study," *International Journal of Sport Psychology*, 9 (1978), 90–96.

[18]Phil Patton, "Connecting With Wide Receivers," *New York Times Magazine*, November 25, 1979, p. 88. © 1979 by The New York Times Company. Reprinted by permission.

[19]Ivan Lendl, quoted in Judy Klemesrud, "Ivan Lendl: The Battle to be Number One in Tennis," *New York Times Magazine*, May 16, 1982, p. 87.

[20]Gary Shaw, *Meat on the Hoof: The Hidden World of Texas Football* (New York: St. Martin's Press, Inc., 1972), pp. 46, 70.

to start making up stuff like, 'This guy raped my mother' to get physical enough to really hit him.''[21]

Violence isn't confined to heavy contact sports. Take basketball, technically a noncontact sport; as everyone knows, however, the norms allow more contact than the written rules. Aggressiveness therefore becomes a valuable asset and is overtly taught. A basketball coach talking about a drill designed to instill aggressiveness, says, ''You put two players alongside the foul line, roll a ball down the middle; when it reaches the foul line, the players dive for it.'' When asked by a reporter whether anybody was ever hurt doing this, the coach replied, ''Only stitches, but once I had my regular center going against a little walk-on guard. This clumsy walk-on kid rumbled over and fell right on top of my center, separating his shoulder. I was so mad.''[22]

Cases like these take place not because athletes and coaches are brutes (though the system might brutalize them), but because society demands victory and legitimizes aggro. To put the matter another way, it happens because there are games to be played and to be won; and when won, rewarded.

It's worth emphasizing that although aggro has limits it does result in real pain and often in very serious injury. Learning to cope with pain and injury are part of the socialization process too. As one observer notes, ''The ability to take punishment is as important as the ability of players to dish it out.''[23]

Injury: A Little Pain Never Hurt Anybody

Of course, violence does not cause all sports injuries, but we can't determine the exact proportion because the necessary statistics have not been collected. Were it possible, we would distinguish between injuries caused by deliberate intent (violence) and injuries caused by accidents. However, even without being able to make this distinction, it is still necessary to discuss the social treatment of injuries. Without injuries, violence would not be the issue that it is.

Research shows that between 1977 and 1981, forty-one high-school football players suffered paralyzing injuries; that upwards of a dozen football deaths occur every year; and that every year all football players receive injuries considered serious enough to be recorded, but that most injuries will be deemed too minor to bother with.[24]

Yet, in the face of the threat and fact of injury, athletes (and their coaches) show a remarkable stoicism. Speaking of football players, a journalist writes,

There are linemen who will play with an injury that might send other humans into shock. . . . One broke a little finger in his hand in a game. . . . ''The bone was

---

[21]Quoted in John Underwood, ''Punishment is a Crime,'' *Sports Illustrated*, August 21, 1978, pp. 32, 34.

[22]Quotes from Kay Kessler, *Columbus Citizen-Journal*, March 8, 1979, p. 21. Copyright © 1979. Reproduced with permission.

[23]William Barry Furlong, ''Football Violence,'' *New York Times Magazine*, November 30, 1980, p. 39. © 1980 by The New York Times Company. Reprinted by permission.

[24]*New York Times* March 22, 1982, sec. Y, p. 32; Harry Edwards and Van Rackages, ''The Dynamics of Violence in American Sport: Some Promising Structural Considerations,'' *Journal of Sport and Social Issues*, 1 (Summer 1977), 3–31; Metropolitan Life Insurance Company, *Statistical Bulletin*, 46 (September 1964), 1–3.

sticking out so they pushed it back into place, taped it next to his finger, and he missed just two plays,'' remembers [the assistant coach]. ''It took 18 stitches to close the split alone, so it wasn't no hangnail.''[25]

Table 13.1.   Football Fatalities, 1970–1978

Type of Football	Approximate Number of Participants in 1978	NUMBER OF DEATHS								
		1970	1971	1973	1973	1974	1975	1976	1977	1978
Sandlot	1,000,000	3	2	3	2	0	1	3	1	0
Pro and semipro	1,500	0	0	1	0	0	0	0	0	0
High school	1,000,000	23	15	16	7	10	13	15	8	9
College	40,000	3	3	2	0	1	1	0	1	0

SOURCE: Reprinted with permission from the Metropolitan Life Insurance Co., *Statistical Bulletin*, July/September 1979, p. 2.

A television reporter once asked a female motorcyclist about being hurt. She replied that she had suffered ''some minor injuries—torn muscles, a few broken bones—that sort of thing, but only one serious injury, a crushed spine.'' Setting aside very serious injuries such as crushed spines, these responses demonstrate a casual attitude. To most people, tearing muscles or snapping bones or splitting fingers open, are major events, not something to shrug off as a minor annoyance.

Sometimes this ability to shrug off injury is explained by arguing that athletes do not feel pain to the same extent as nonathletes. That is not true. Laboratory evidence shows athletes and nonathletes do not differ in their sensitivity to pain. The critical difference is that athletes, especially those in heavy contact sports, are more willing to endure the pain they do feel—much more so than nonathletes and athletes in noncontact sports.[26] This agrees with what sociologists would predict.[27] Athletes have neurological receptors that perceive pain just like everyone else; but they have learned to cope with pain and blood in ways that nonathletes have not.

The noted sociologist Talcott Parsons said that most people play out sick roles.[28] When they are injured (or sick) they expect to be excused from certain obligations. They stay home rather than go to work; or if they go, they ''take it easy because they're not up to par.'' They expect others to excuse them because they aren't feeling well—and usually they get excused as long as they do not carry it too far and malinger.

---

[25]Furlong, ''Football Violence,'' pp. 126–27. © 1980 by The New York Times Company. Reprinted by permission.

[26]E. Dean Ryan, ''Perceptual Characteristics of Vigorous People,'' in *New Perspectives on Man in Action*, eds. Roscoe C. Brown, Jr., and Bryant J. Cratty (Englewood Cliffs, New Jersey: Prentice-Hall, Inc., 1969), pp. 88–101.

[27]See for example Mark Zborowski, ''Cultural Components in Response to Pain,'' *Journal of Social Issues*, 8 (1953), 16–31.

[28]Talcott Parsons, *The Social System* (Glencoe, Illinois: The Free Press, 1951).

The sick role makes good sense in most situations, but not in sport. We noted that injuries, some minor, some major, afflict every athlete who participates in contact sports. (In noncontact sports the ability to tolerate pain can also be critically important.) To keep the team at full strength, the injured must play. Not only that, a star who plays with an injury may contribute more to victory than a noninjured substitute. The running wounded can be valuable commodities.

As a result, injury in sport becomes endowed with a unique symbolic meaning. A former college football player says the team physician knew that the coach "didn't like guys who wouldn't get out and play when hurt," and so he patched them up and sent them out to practice as quickly as possible.[29] The usefulness of playing when hurt runs throughout sport and makes injury and the overcoming of pain a "red badge of courage."

In addition to defining injury and pain as something to overcome, the sports value system normalizes them. Through long exposure, what was once traumatic becomes routine. In a hospital emergency room, where ripped and bloodied persons gather, physicians seem unflappable and even cold because they have normalized mangled bodies. They deal with them all the time. In a similar way, athletes and coaches see injuries every day. And they normalize them. "Between college and the pro's I've had four or five concussions now, and I suppose *I'm getting used to them*," writes a former all-pro football player.[30]

Normalizing injury and endowing it with special meaning does not make it any less serious. Even small injuries can cause much misery in later life. Spinal arthritis resulting from "minor" traumas suffered during one's playing days, trick knees, and bad backs, are all very real. Nevertheless, as sociologists we emphasize the social interpretation of pain and physical injury. What seems to be serious and terrible to outsiders, may be routine, acceptable, and honorific to insiders.

Culture, social process, and symbolic meanings have been discussed as causes of sports violence. Rules and equipment were hardly mentioned. That may appear to be a major omission since many critics claim that rules and equipment must be changed lest sport degenerate into a modern day *pancratium*. The claim is hardly new.

SOLUTIONS; THE MORE THINGS CHANGE . . .

Rule Changes and Equipment Modification

Around the turn of the century, the violence, injuries, and deaths associated with football caused a national outcry. To give one illustration: At that time rules permitted the "flying wedge," a "murderous formation that placed the ball carrier in the crook of a V-shaped mass. Defenders dropped to the turf before it as if a stampede of buffalo had trampled them."[31]

---

[29]Shaw, *Meat on the Hoof*, p. 125.

[30]Jerry Kramer, *Instant Replay: The Green Bay Diary of Jerry Kramer*, ed. by Dick Schaap (New York: New American Library, 1968), p. 65. Italics added.

[31]Wells Twombly, *200 Years of Sport in America: A Pageant of a Nation at Play* (New York: McGraw-Hill Book Company, 1976), p. 60.

In 1905 President Theodore Roosevelt spearheaded a drive to clean up college football; and out of that drive eventually grew the organization that governs intercollegiate sport: the NCAA. The flying wedge was banned, and over the years hundreds of rule changes have been made. Today, the NCAA outlaws crackback blocking and makes mandatory the wearing of mouthpieces, hip pads, thigh pads, and better helmets. (Ironically, improved helmets may give too much protection. The wearer feels safe in ramming opponents with his head, or "spearing.")[32]

Though rule changes ease the problem, they can not cure it. Three-quarters of a century after President Roosevelt ordered it cleaned out, violence remains a part of sport. Judging from one government study, about 1.06 million serious sports injuries occur every year; football accounts for about one-third of them. And while football fatalities have decreased (the rate used to be about twice the current rate), the incidence of quadraplegia has about doubled.[33] Notably, defensive halfbacks sustain over half of all quadraplegic injuries, probably because their position calls upon them to do the most head-on tackling. Obviously rule changes have not eliminated basic causes.

Violence persists in even relatively nonviolent sports. The July 10, 1961, issue of *Sports Illustrated* carried an article entitled "Baseball's Secret Weapon: Terror," which claimed that pitchers throw at batters, despite official denials.[34] Nineteen years later, in the July 14, 1980, issue of the same magazine, the article "They're Up in Arms Over Beanballs" gave further evidence that pitchers try to intimidate batters by throwing at them. This is despite stringent rules giving umpires more authority to expel pitchers who deliberately throw at batters.[35] The more things change, the more they seem to stay the same.

Without doubt, rule changes and improved equipment can make for a safer game. The mandating of helmets for batters has prevented many serious injuries and may have saved a life. (In the history of modern baseball "only" one player has ever been killed by a beanball.) Such changes should therefore be encouraged, yet the social history of violence in sport forces us to conclude that those kinds of changes treat symptoms rather than causes. The disease will surely reappear, though perhaps in a different form. This will happen for three sociological reasons: (1) American culture condones violence; (2) in some cases, violence *is* sport; and (3) violence is rewarding. Very little can be done about the first two reasons. Changing culture and radically changing certain sports will take a long, drawn-out campaign, the success of which is by no means guaranteed.

More immediate relief will result from treating the third reason. If violence is rewarding, then make it unrewarding. Rather than make more rules against pitchers who intentionally throw at batters, change the reward structure. If the batter is hit, let him advance to third base, or even score an automatic run. This would be so costly that no one, neither pitcher nor manager, would want the batter hit. If one point were subtracted from the offender's team every time the opposing quarterback had to leave the game for injury

---

[32]Reported in *Chronicle of Higher Education*, April 16, 1979, p. 7.

[33]Joseph S. Torg and others, "The National Football Head and Neck Injury Registry: Report and Conclusions, 1978," *Journal of the American Medical Association*, 241 (April 6, 1979), 1477–79.

[34]Roger Kahn, "Baseball's Secret Weapon: Terror," *Sports Illustrated*, July 10, 1961, p. 26.

[35]Steve Wulf, "They're Up In Arms Over Beanballs," *Sports Illustrated*, July 14, 1980, p. 31.

caused by a tackle, defenders would be extremely careful about touching the quarterback.

Such rule changes have many pros and cons, and we could go on drawing out little scenarios about them. Obviously, though, radical changes in reward structures have little hope of coming to pass in the near future. History shows that sport has a long record of violence, and we cannot see any signs that sport is about to cleanse violence from its own house. Right now another institution—the law—is causing the most change in regard to violence.

Law: Long Arm, Deep Pocket

The law says that athletes must accept the normal risks associated with their sports, but that such acceptance does not give license for athletes to attack each other.

During a softball game, a baserunner tried to prevent a double play by running five feet out of his way to crash into the second baseman. When suit was brought, the court ruled that the second baseman did not have to accept that risk. The baserunner could be sued. In another instance, a soccer goalie was deliberately kicked while in the penalty area (where rules prohibit contact with the goalie). According to one legal analysis, "Liability in tort will result when a player's 'conduct is such that it is either deliberate, willful or with a reckless disregard for the safety of the other player so as to cause injury to that player.' "[36] Athletes need not accept the risk of being wantonly maimed. Legal constraints do exist.

In a recent incident, a professional hockey player won an $850,000 judgment against another team. The award was for pain, suffering, and punitive damages—his nose was broken by another player. Interestingly, because the hockey club's insurance policy has a limit of $500,000, the offending player may be personally liable for the remaining $350,000 of the total award.[37]

The most infamous case involved a professional basketball player (Kermit Washington) who hit another player (Rudy Tomjanovich) in the face when he (Tomjanovich) attempted to break up a fight. The blow separated many of Tomjanovich's face bones from his skull. Tomjanovich sued Kermit Washington's team rather than Washington personally, on the legal principle that one should sue the "deepest pocket." He won a judgment of over three million dollars.

Not only do the club owners have the deepest pockets, they also ultimately control professional sports. They are the ones who sanction rule changes, hire officials, and fire violent players. As a sociological rule of thumb, when the cost of something must be borne by the power-wielding group, something meaningful will change.

The costs of violence might be increased by using another legal avenue, criminal law. Battery is a crime. In many cases of violence occurring in a sports contest, there should be little difficulty in proving battery. The only legal requirement is proof of intent to injure and of some harmful consequence to the victim. Customarily prosecutors have

---

[36]C. J. Rains, "Sports Violence: A Matter of Societal Concern," *Notre Dame Lawyer*, 55 (June 1980), 796–813.

[37]George Vecsey, "The Price of Violence in Hockey," *New York Times*, August 25, 1982, sec. Y, p. 25.

not brought criminal charges because American society has traditionally relied on the governing bodies of sport to resolve their own problems.[38] However, if sport fails to do so, as it may be failing now, we suspect more and more criminal charges will be brought. And when that happens, the threat of fines and jail, and the stigma of being officially branded a criminal, will make violence too costly, both economically and socially, to be tolerated.

Violence between athletes and the possible remedies for it, do not exhaust the issue of violence in sport. The issue is big and complex. Another major part of the whole problem area is fan violence, specifically, the effect of watching violence and the reasons a collection of fans sometimes turns violent.

VIOLENCE AND THE FAN: AROUSING GAMES AND AROUSED MOBS

The crowd and crowd violence have intrigued both the lay public and professional social scientists for a long time. Consider the following several points raised in an editorial from a local newspaper.

Since 1946, about 350 boxers have died of injuries received in the fight—mostly massive blood clots on the brain . . .

Although boxers don't go into the ring intending to kill one another, as Roman gladiators did in the arena, people pay to see them try to batter each other insensible.

Death or permanent brain damage often is the only winner.

No one forces men to become boxers. They're just trying to earn an honest living.

But why, sports fans, does the crowd roar when the boxer goes down—weak, bleeding, blinded, nearly unconscious?

An ancient Roman would feel at home at a modern ringside.[39]

Catharsis Theory

Going back even farther than Roman times, Aristotle thought that the "roar" of the crowd, the excitement and arousal produced by watching an aggressive event, produced a beneficial effect: catharsis (a draining of accumulated hostilities, which left the viewer feeling better and less hostile). The idea of catharsis thus has a long and venerable history; and many have endorsed it, or some variant of it. Nevertheless, modern research suggests the idea, however venerable, is incorrect.

For instance, researchers administered a psychological hostility test to male spectators attending an Army-Navy football game. The spectators turned out to be more hostile after watching the game than before (regardless of which team they rooted for). The same

---

[38]*Ibid.* Also see William Hechter, "The Criminal Law and Violence in Sports," *Criminal Law Quarterly*, 19 (September 1977), 425–53.

[39]*Columbus Citizen-Journal*, July 16, 1980, p. 16. Copyright © 1980. Reproduced with permission.

researchers also tested samples of fans before and after a gymnastics meet (a nonaggressive sport) and found their level of hostility did not change. According to the same psychological test, both male and female spectators became hostile after watching a hockey game (an aggressive sport) but not after watching a swimming meet (a nonaggressive sport). Other studies performed in laboratories support results such as these. When shown films of violence (such as a boxing match), a symbol of violence (such as a gun), or play violence (cartoons), children and adults become more aggressive, not less.[40]

Overall, we conclude that watching aggression increases the watcher's aggressive feelings. Catharsis does not take place—at least not in regard to watching sports aggression.

Perception and Aggression

An older and now classic study of a Princeton-Dartmouth football game formally documents the fact that not everyone sees the same thing. The game caused a public uproar because of numerous fouls and dirty play. Two social psychologists subsequently showed a film of the game to Princeton and Dartmouth students and asked the students to rate the seriousness of each rule infraction they saw. Both groups saw almost the same number of infractions. However, according to the researchers,

> When Dartmouth students looked at the movies of the game they saw . . . their own team make only about half the infractions that Princeton students saw them make. The ratio of "flagrant" to "mild" infractions was about one to one when Dartmouth students judged the Dartmouth team, and about one "flagrant" to two "mild" when Dartmouth students judged infractions made by the Princeton team.[41]

The teams are physically out there on the field but the game isn't played out there. Rather, it is played in the countless social relations and perceptions that go on between individuals and their neighbors, between individuals and their predispositions, and between individuals and the social structure in which they live. Through the give and take of these relations people build a social consensus about what they perceive and this consensus becomes "truth." When simple events happen slowly, the consensus may come about unambiguously. But events like football, hockey, or most sports events for that matter, take place much too fast and are much too complicated for unambiguous consensus to form. Consequently everyone doesn't always see the same game even though they see the same event.

Because people fail to see what others see, misunderstandings arise. That alone could set the stage for hostilities, but as we already know, "viewing aggression tends to

[40]Robert Arms, Gordon W. Russell, and Mark L. Sandilands, "Effects on the Hostility of Spectators of Viewing Aggressive Sports," *Social Psychology Quarterly*, 42 (1979), 279. Also J. H. Goldstein and R. L. Arms, "Effects of Observing Athletic Contests on Hostility," *Sociometry*, 34 (1971), 83–90; A. Bandura, *Aggression: A Social Learning Analysis* (Englewood Cliffs, New Jersey: Prentice-Hall, Inc., 1977).

[41]Albert H. Hastorf and Hadley Cantril, "They Saw a Game: A Case Study," *Journal of Abnormal and Social Psychology*, 49 (January 1954), 129–34.

stimulate further aggression provided the acts observed are interpreted as being aggressive.''[42] That too is likely to happen at a sports event. For example, research on soccer "riots" shows that player violence frequently triggers violence among fans. Violence begets violence, and lack of consensus aggravates an already tense situation.

Other factors get involved, too. When you go to a game, you find yourself in the midst of other people; you are pushed, bumped, hemmed-in, and moved along with the crowd. In other words, the collective—the crowd, the group—affects your behavior.

The Sports Crowd

Most people particularly abhor crowd violence, an abhorrence magnified beyond the actual amount of any property damage, bodily injury, or deaths. Crowd violence, however mild, somehow shocks the conscience, perhaps because it represents a degeneration into chaos, a crumbling of the social structure and seems to make our lives unpredictable, unordered, and incomprehensible.

From the very beginning of the discipline, sociologists studying crowd behavior have been influenced by the image of the crowd as "great beast." They have abhorred it. Consequently they have mainly examined two issues: the crowd's seeming penchant for antisocial, destructive, and violent behavior; and the crowd's seeming homogeneity, the tendency of the people in a crowd to behave *en masse* as a single mindless entity.

In sport, the etymology of the word *fan* reinforces the negative connotations about the crowd. The word can be traced either to *fanatic* or to *fancy* (as in *fancier* or *aficionado*). The first derivation is cited more often than the second.

The word *fan* also misleadingly suggests homogeneity: It indiscriminately lumps all fans into a single category. One study claims that about half the people who describe themselves as "loyal fans" never attend a game.[43] Given the expense, time, and wear and tear involved, that seems reasonable, especially since they can usually follow their teams on radio or television. But whatever the reason for their nonattendance, about half the fans can be disregarded in a study of collective violence because they are simply not present.

Those who are present are not homogeneous, nor do they behave in lock step. If you simply look around at a sports crowd you can verify that. For instance, most fans stand and cheer when their team scores, but a few don't. Most fans watch the playing field intensely, but some lollygag. Some fans are young, some are aged, most are in between; some are male, some are female, some are black, some are not, and so on.

The same point applies to psychological states. Some fans are happy, some are angry; some are interested in the game, some are bored. Of the thousands of people in attendance, the overwhelming number are psychologically unwilling to participate in collective violence. Like most societies, American society socializes people to believe

---

[42]Alan G. Ingham and Michael D. Smith, "Social Implications of the Interaction Between Spectators and Athletes," in *Exercise and Sport Science Reviews*, ed. Jack H. Wilmore (New York: Academic Press, Inc., 1974), II: 214.

[43]Ray Kennedy, "More Victories Equals More Fans Equals More Profit," *Sports Illustrated*, April 28, 1980, pp. 34–45.

that the mob should not rule; and only a few people join the mob, and then only sometimes.

However, if out of a stadium filled with 80,000 fans, eight run onto the playing field wildly swinging beer bottles, a "riot" has happened. Statistically (and fortunately), this will not happen very often. We do not know precisely how often because no systematic data exist, but the proportion would not be very large considering that schools, professional leagues, businesses, and other organizations sponsor thousands of sports events every week and the vast, vast majority take place without any problems whatsoever.

The typical sports crowd is actually prosocial and influenced by constraints imposed by the broader society. Only rarely does it turn nasty and dangerous. If the crowd is a great beast, it is usually a tame one.

Structural Strains.   British "soccer hooliganism," gang fights between groups of fans, illustrates much of what we have just said. It also suggests the importance of relating broader societal conditions to collective behavior. Hooliganism has become so endemic that authorities now force rival gangs to sit at opposite ends of the field (in the "ends" or "terraces") separated by chain-link fences. In some stadiums, policemen with guard dogs patrol a no man's land alongside the fences.

For the soccer hooligan, the soccer stadium is a battlefield, not a sports field. The hooligan is neither a soccer fanatic nor a soccer fancier. What happens on the playing field simply cues the impending gang fight, as the following passage from a long-term study indicates.

> **A Game of Soccer.**   Ritualized chanting from each end goes on continually: "You're going to get your f—— head kicked in."
> The chanting serves to put down the rival gang without physical violence. Sometimes confrontations occur anyway. Several have been filmed for research purposes. When social scientists analyze the films, they see an orderly process going on. In one episode, for example, a gang of hooligans catch up with a single victim. The victim falls to the ground, the hooligans surround him, flailing at him with fists and boots. In the distance, a policeman comes running up. The hooligans see him and flee. So does the victim! He gets up, all rather casually considering he was just beaten and stomped, brushes off his coat, and trots away.
> In fact, the films reveal that the hooligans had never really beaten and stomped him with the ferocity you expected. Blows were stopped a bit short; kicks hit the ground just before impact on the body. Sensitive body parts were not attacked. The victim could have been beaten to a bloody, fleshy pulp—but he was not.[44]

What on superficial observation looks like vicious, chaotic, unconstrained violence, on close observation turns out to be stylized, ritualized, circumscribed, and limited. It is aggro; that ritualized limited violence we discussed earlier. (Aggro, we repeat, is dangerous even if ritualized.) Those who study the terraces say that aggro occurs because gangs serve a tribal function:

---

[44]Marsh, *Aggro*, pp. 15–16, 24, 27.

On the football terraces, fans have discovered just one way of being tribal. . . . It's the close bonding within the immediate sub-units which provide for the possibility of real social identity and restraint. . . . [Fans] can fight because their fights can be limited and kept within safe boundaries through immediate and meaningful social conventions and constraints.''[45]

Largely denied a sense of affiliation in the workaday world of lower-class factory jobs and indifferent families, and realizing the improbability of ever making much economic advancement, these youths find that through the gang they can attain the tribal solidarity that is not possible in the broader society.

This perspective—which places many causes of collective violence in the structure of society—is a good one for British soccer hooliganism, and also helps explain some fan violence in the United States. For example, in 1962 an incident of racial violence (still talked about) occurred in Washington, D.C. after a championship football game between a private white school and a public, predominantly black school. That "race riot" left over five hundred people injured.

As sport is a microcosm of society, conditions of American society should help explain what happened inside that stadium. Just as soccer hooliganism reflects British social class, violence between black and white fans reflects American race relations. Before the fans came to this game, they knew who was going to be there. Race already divided them into loose groups hostile to each other. Like the terraces, the football stadium was a place where these hostilities could be unleashed. The strains and conflicts found in society can go a long way toward explaining seemingly irrational spontaneous behavior.

Existing structure also helps explain other kinds of fan violence—violence that on the surface seems *totally* chaotic. After Pittsburgh won the 1971 World Series, approximately one hundred thousand fans jammed into the downtown area to celebrate, attracted by a team parade. For some reason, the mood of the crowd grew ugly. The police ordered the crowd to disperse. The crowd ignored the order. The mood grew uglier. What followed, according to the *New York Times*:

> The rioting erupted from what began as a boisterous but nonviolent victory celebration. . . . But the nonviolent celebration soon exploded. There was widespread bottle-throwing and stoning, and the police ordered the downtown areas sealed off.
> Cars were overturned and burned, bonfires set and telephone booths ripped apart and scattered in the streets. There was nude dancing and heavy drinking in the streets as well, and the police reported a dozen rapes. . . . Dogs were brought in, and where the jeering demonstrators refused to move, policemen used billy clubs liberally.[46]

---

[45]From Peter Marsh, *Aggro: The Illusion of Violence* (London: J. M. Dent & Sons, Ltd., 1978), pp. 150–51. Reprinted by permission of A D Peters & Co Ltd.

[46]*New York Times*, October 18, 1971, p. 50. © 1971 by The New York Times Company. Reprinted by permission. For a study of how a crowd gathers, see Clark McPhail and David C. Miller, "The Assembling Process: A Theoretical and Empirical Examination," *American Sociological Review*, 38 (December 1973), 721–35.

(Somewhat ironically, right below this story, was the headline, "COMPOSITE SCORE OF SERIES GAMES.")

Such media descriptions emphasize the dramatic: violence, mayhem, and spontaneity. That emphasis is only partially correct and is grossly misleading. Judging from past evidence, we strongly suspect that only a few fans out of the hundred thousand or so in the downtown area actually engaged in physical violence—punching, throwing bottles and the like. A great number probably engaged in verbal abuse such as swearing and booing, but most fans were probably not involved at all. And a few probably tried to quell the violence.

Riots like this one used to be interpreted as *social contagion:* People excite other people and a mutual and circular stimulation quickly spreads throughout, like a raging disease. Most social scientists do not believe in social contagion (at least in its simple form). When observed carefully, even the most tumultuous crowd fails to show any signs that contagion suddenly spreads among people, causing them to lose self-control and plunge into mayhem. Empirically, social contagion simply does not happen.

Another popular explanation has a bit more merit: *convergence* or *riffraff theory.* Groups of violence-prone people (the riffraff) converge on a particular place and then engage in violence. Soccer hooliganism is an example. Gangs meet on the terraces for the purpose of aggro. The riffraff, the hooligans, are to blame. Get rid of them and you get rid of the problem.

The riffraff theory has major shortcomings. For one, it does not say much. It does not say why the riffraff engage in violence in the first place. It simply points an accusing finger at the participants without getting at causes. And just as critically, the theory isn't always true. Often times violent people are not riffraff at all; the most respectable people get involved.[47]

If we grant that the typical sports crowd is not homogeneous and is not a great beast, that social contagion does not occur and that not all violent people are riffraff, do we need anything more than strains in the social structure to explain the crowd's occasionally violent behavior? Obviously, yes, for common observation reveals that the behavior of a crowd of fans differs from the behavior of an individual fan.

Emergent Norms.   Many social scientists now advocate *emergent-norm theory.* To illustrate:

> **Tearing Down the Goal Posts.**   For several years a team of sociologists studied a major intersectional football rivalry. We present one incident from the study: tearing down the goal post. After a home-team victory, a portion of the crowd comes pouring onto the field with great enthusiasm but very little idea of what they are supposed to do once there. They just mill around congratulating and slapping hands with each other. However, a group of about a dozen students

---

[47]See for example Stanley Milgram, *The Individual In a Social World: Essays and Experiments* (Reading, Massachusetts: Addison-Wesley Publishing Co., Inc., 1977), part 3; Michael D. Smith, "Sport and Collective Violence," in *Sport and Social Order: Contributions to the Sociology of Sport*, ed. Donald W. Ball and John W. Loy (Reading, Massachusetts: Addison-Wesley Publishing Co., Inc., 1975), pp. 277–330.

run directly to the goal post and begin pushing and shoving it. Two climb it and bend the cross bar down with their weight. Seeing this, other crowd members join in the pushing and shoving. They begin chanting something that sounds like "heave-ho." The chant helps coordinate them. All the while the police stand by, not quite sure how to respond. On the one hand, the crowd is wantonly destroying property; yet on the other, it is all in good fun. The police decide to do nothing. The goal post comes down.

The students who led the charge pick up the post and parade down the campus with their trophy. As they do, other spectators, mostly students, join in. They reach the main thoroughfare near the campus. The street is a typical college avenue, lined with small shops (clothing, records, books) and many bars. Here the parade encounters other knots of fans milling about, drinking beer. The police, decked out in riot helmets with plastic face shields, are also on patrol. Up the street goes the little parade with the goal post until it comes to a sporting goods store. The group props the goal post against the wall and a student manages to shinny up the posts. The remainder think this is humerous and point their fingers into the air—"We're number one!"

The police again find themselves in a dilemma: Should they uphold the law and arrest the students for causing a public disturbance, or should they let it go as part of the traditional celebration? They decide to let it go and join the laughter.

The police eventually arrest about two dozen fans, mostly for jaywalking against explicit orders not to, or for throwing beer cans and bottles (empty) at passing cars. The police determinedly keep the thoroughfare open to traffic although only a rather intrepid motorist would drive down it. By and large, serious violence does not occur and the carousing peters out at about 4 A.M.; celebrants just get tired and drunk and go home.[48]

This incident illustrates the workings of emergent-norm theory. First of all, the theory holds that much of what the crowd does gets determined before the crowd collects. Routinely and traditionally the victory celebration includes tearing down the goal posts; culture approves and calls for this ceremony. The police know it and that knowledge deters them from intervening.

Emergent-norm theory also emphasizes the importance of individuals who suggest new behaviors (norms) to the crowd. The crowd then follows (or does not follow) these suggestions. Oftentimes, not quashing new norms leads to their acceptance. The police stood by and thus gave *de facto* approval to the emerging norms about tearing down the posts.

The same situation occurred once the crowd propped up the posts in front of the store. By standing by and joining in the laughter, the police again approved the raucous behavior of a few individuals; and so norms emerged condoning that behavior. The opposite occurred when fans started jaywalking and bottle throwing. The police moved forcefully to counter such behaviors, making arrests in some cases. Thus, norms approving of jaywalking did not emerge, nor did norms about bottle throwing.

The incident we have been analyzing was largely routine. But there have been

---

[48]For a published report of one aspect of these studies, see A. Aveni, "The Not-So-Lonely Crowd: Friendship Groups in Collective Behavior," *Sociometry*, 40 (March 1977), 96–99. Others on the observational team include Timothy J. Curry and E. L. Quarantelli.

incidents in which the crowds become truly vicious. A Brazilian mob consisting of players and fans once killed a soccer official who made a controversial call against the home team. In the absence of good observational data, we can only speculate that only a very small group of fans started screaming and pushing at the official. Others in the crowd, also aroused and hostile, saw this and took it as a cue approving such behavior. The police did not intervene (perhaps because they weren't there). Other crowd members hesitated to help the official, because of fear and because they thought others approved. As the pushing escalated it triggered more norms approving more violent behavior. At some point the confrontation became extremely violent, and the official was killed. Even though it takes an individual person to punch, shove, and kick, in a manner of speaking the official was really killed by a set of emergent norms.

The emergent-norms explanation does not say why norms of *violence*, rather than other kinds, emerge nor does the explanation say how the norms emerge or who will accept them. Still, despite these shortcomings, emergent-norm theory does push the explanation of collective violence toward greater rationality. It does away with mystical notions of social contagion and also with the tendency to blame other people (riffraff) for all the troubles. Many sociologists believe that emergent-norm theory holds promise.

SUMMARY

1. Most sociologists prefer social explanations for violence in sport. Biological explanations are unable to explain the considerable role society has in determining the quality and quantity of violence in sports.
2. Historically, American culture supported many kinds of violence. So it's not surprising to find violence in sport.
3. Some violence has been converted into sport by overlaying the activity with rules, formal organization, and competition. For these types of sports—such as boxing and KO karate—we should expect high levels of violence because violence *is* the sport. For others—such as wrestling or fencing—the violence has been transformed into symbolic acts.
4. Violence is often instrumental and rewarding. The ritualization of violence (aggro) helps to prevent sport from becoming a totally bloody and chaotic affair, yet allows for the selective application of violence to pursue limited goals.
5. Potential athletes are selected for a variety of traits. Aggression is one of these traits. Socialization into the subculture of many sports involves redefining what injury and pain mean: Athletes come to accept injury and pain as part of the competitive process. To overcome them, and to play when hurt, is highly honored.
6. Changes in certain rules and equipment may help reduce the number of injuries in sport. But by themselves they are woefully insufficient because they do not eliminate the rewards produced by violence.
7. The violence in sport encourages litigation. Where there's injury there is the possibil-

ity of compensation. Litigation may eliminate some types of sport violence, particularly in professional sports.

8. Violence in sports affects the sports fan. Perceiving aggression heightens aggression. Existing strains in the structure of society, such as the strains between races and social classes, can erupt into violent confrontations at sports events. Emergent-norm theory holds the most promise as the explanation of how the usually benign crowd can commit violent acts.

INDEX